AN INTRODUCTION TO
THE NEW TESTAMENT MANUSCRIPTS
AND THEIR TEXTS

D1592452

This is the first major English-language introduction to the earliest manuscripts of the New Testament to appear for over forty years. An essential handbook for scholars and students, it provides a thorough grounding in the study and editing of the New Testament text combined with an emphasis on dramatic current developments in the field. Covering ancient sources in Greek, Syriac, Latin and Coptic, it

- describes the manuscripts and other ancient textual evidence, and the tools needed to study them
- deals with textual criticism and textual editing, describing modern approaches and techniques, with guidance on the use of editions
- introduces the witnesses and textual study of each of the main sections of the New Testament, discussing typical variants and their significance.

A companion website with full-colour images provides generous amounts of illustrative material, bringing the subject alive for the reader.

D. C. PARKER is Edward Cadbury Professor of Theology in the Department of Theology and Religion and a Director of the Institute for Textual Scholarship and Electronic Editing, University of Birmingham. His publications include *The Living Text of the Gospels* (1997) and *Codex Bezae: an Early Christian Manuscript and its Text* (1992).

AN INTRODUCTION TO THE NEW TESTAMENT MANUSCRIPTS AND THEIR TEXTS

D. C. PARKER

University of Birmingham

CAMBRIDGE
UNIVERSITY PRESS

BS
1904.5
P37
2008

CAMBRIDGE UNIVERSITY PRESS
Cambridge, New York, Melbourne, Madrid, Cape Town, Singapore, São Paulo, Delhi

Cambridge University Press
The Edinburgh Building, Cambridge CB2 8RU, UK

Published in the United States of America by Cambridge University Press, New York

www.cambridge.org
Information on this title: www.cambridge.org/9780521719896

© D. C. Parker 2008

This publication is in copyright. Subject to statutory exception
and to the provisions of relevant collective licensing agreements,
no reproduction of any part may take place without
the written permission of Cambridge University Press.

First published 2008
Reprinted 2009

Printed in the United Kingdom at the University Press, Cambridge

A catalogue record for this publication is available from the British Library

Library of Congress Cataloguing in Publication Data

Parker, D. C. (David C.)
An introduction to the New Testament manuscripts and their texts / D. C. Parker.
p. cm.
Includes bibliographical references and index.
ISBN 978-0-521-89553-8 (hardback) – ISBN 978-0-521-71989-6 (paperback)
1. Bible. N.T.–Manuscripts. I. Title.
BS1904.5.P37 2008
225.4–dc22
2008013706

ISBN 978-0-521-89553-8 hardback
ISBN 978-0-521-71989-6 paperback

Cambridge University Press has no responsibility for the persistence or
accuracy of URLs for external or third-party internet websites referred to in this
publication, and does not guarantee that any content on such websites is,
accurate or appropriate. Information regarding prices, travel timetables and other
factual information given in this work are correct at the time of first printing but
Cambridge University Press does not guarantee the accuracy of such
information thereafter.

JKM Library
1100 East 55th Street
Chicago, IL 60615

Contents

Plates

The plates accompanying this work are placed separately on a website. This has the advantage that high-quality colour digital images can be made available to the user without the book becoming too expensive. Moreover, the traditional series of largely black-and-white plates is far less successful in revealing either the character or the detail of a manuscript to the reader. The plates may all be viewed at www.cambridge.org/parker.

A ☛ is placed in the text where a plate is provided. I have confined the plates largely to the sections where I describe the development of text formats, namely chapters 1, 5 and 6. The following are the images:

Chapter 1.1

1. Cologny, Biblioteca Bodmeriana II (Gregory–Aland P66), page 41
2. Florence, Biblioteca Laurenziana, PSI 2.124 (Gregory–Aland 0171), recto
3. London, British Library, Add. 43725, Codex Sinaiticus (Gregory–Aland 01), Quire 79, Folios 1v and 2r
4. Vercelli, Bibliotheca Capitolare, s.n., Codex Vercellensis, Folios 181r and 196v
5. Florence, Biblioteca Laurenziana Plut. I, Syr. 56, Folio 158v–159r
6. Basel, University Library, AN III.12 (Gregory–Aland 07), Folio 102v
7. St Petersburg, Russian National Library, Gr. 219 (Gregory–Aland 461)
8. Paris, Bibliothèque Nationale, Lat. 9380, Codex Theodulphianus, Prologue to the Gospels
9. London, British Library Burney 18 (Gregory–Aland 480), Folio 66r
10. Erasmus' first printed Greek New Testament, 1516, Epistles, page 109

Chapter *1.3*

Chapter *2.4*

Chapter *4.7*

Chapter *5.1*

Chapter *5.3*

Chapter *6.1*

Chapter 6.3

Chapter 7.2

Links to URLs

I have taken the opportunity to use the website for the images to put in the links to the URLs mentioned in the text. These may be accessed at www.cambridge.org/9780521719896, and each one should take the reader straight to the site.

Acknowledgements

An introductory text of this kind, drawing as it does on several centuries of detailed research, is in itself an acknowledgement of debt to generations of scholars. It especially reflects the contribution of contemporaries, whose writings have inspired and whose papers and conversation have stimulated me. Some readers may recognise the influence of such discussion from time to time in what follows.

In particular, what I have written has no doubt been substantially moulded by the twenty years in which I have worked with colleagues in editing the International Greek New Testament Project. We began work on the Gospel of John in 1987, and in that time I have spent many hours, days and weeks in the company of others working on this project. For half of that time (since 1997), we have been working in increasingly close partnership with the Institut für neutestamentliche Textforschung, Münster. The challenges of a major project and the expertise of many colleagues leave their traces everywhere.

More recently I have benefited in my own institution from congenial and expanding text-critical surroundings. The Centre for the Editing of Texts in Religion was established in 2000. Its range was expanded in 2005 with the formation of the Institute for Textual Scholarship and Electronic Editing. Both staff and students have broadened my horizons and challenged my thinking, as has the execution of our current projects.

A number of these colleagues read this book in draft and offered encouragement, corrections and improvements. The staff of Cambridge University Press have, as ever, been helpful in many ways.

At one stage I even considered dedicating this book to all New Testament textual critics, living and departed. However, I was reminded of a promise made in the days when we read picture books together, that when I wrote one myself I would dedicate it to my children. So this book is for Louise, James, John and Alison.

Abbreviations

This list contains abbreviations, and short titles of works cited in more than one chapter. If a work is cited more than once only within a few pages, the short title is casily understood and is not listed here.

K. Aland, *Die alten Übersetzungen*	K. Aland (ed.), *Die alten Übersetzungen des Neuen Testaments, die Kirchenväterzitate und Lektionare. Der gegenwärtige Stand ihre Erforschung und ihre Bedeutung für die griechische Textgeschichte* (ANTF 5), Berlin, 1972
K. Aland, *Repertorium*	K. Aland, *Repertorium der griechischen christlichen Papyri*, vol. 1: *Biblische Papyri. Altes Testament, Neues Testament, Varia, Apokryphen* (Patristische Texte and Studien 18), Berlin and New York, 1976
Aland and Aland, *The Text of the New Testament*	K. Aland and B. Aland, *The Text of the New Testament. An Introduction to the Critical Editions and to the Theory and Practice of Modern Textual Criticism*, tr. E. F. Rhodes, 2nd edn, Grand Rapids and Leiden, 1989 (1st edn, 1987)
Aland and Juckel, *NT in syrischer Überlieferung 1*	B. Aland and A. Juckel, *Das Neue Testament in syrischer Überlieferung, 1. Die Großen Katholischen Briefe* (ANTF 7), Berlin and New York, 1986
Aland and Juckel, *NT in syrischer Überlieferung 2*	B. Aland and A. Juckel, *Das Neue Testament in syrischer Überlieferung, 2. Die Paulinischen Briefe*, vol. 1: *Römer- und 1.Korintherbrief* (ANTF 14), Berlin and New York, 1991; vol. 11: *2.Korintherbrief, Galaterbrief, Epheserbrief, Philipperbrief und Kolosserbrief* (ANTF 23), Berlin and New York, 1995; vol. 111: *1./2.Thessalonicherbrief, Timotheusbrief, Titusbrief, Philemonbrief und*

	Hebräerbrief (ANTF 32), Berlin and New York, 2002
Amphoux and Elliott, *New Testament Text*	C.-B. Amphoux and J. K. Elliott (eds.), *The New Testament Text in Early Christianity. Proceedings of the Lille colloquium, July 2000* (Histoire du texte biblique 6), Lausanne, 2003
Anderson, *Family 1 in Matthew*	A. Anderson, *The Textual Tradition of the Gospels. Family 1 in Matthew* (NTTS 32), Leiden and Boston, 2004
ANRW	*Aufstieg und Niedergang der römischen Welt*
ANTF	Arbeiten zur neutestamentliche Textforschung, Berlin (and New York)
Baarda Festschrift	W. L. Petersen, J. S. Vos and H. J. de Jonge (eds.), *Sayings of Jesus: Canonical and Non-canonical. Essays in Honour of Tjitze Baarda* (NovTSuppl 89), Leiden, 1997
Beginnings of Christianity	F. J. Foakes Jackson and K. Lake (eds.), *The Beginnings of Christianity, Part 1. The Acts of the Apostles,* 5 vols., London, 1922–39
BETL	Bibliotheca Ephemeridum Theologicarum Lovaniensium, Leuven
Biblia Coptica	K. Schüssler, *Biblia Coptica. Die koptischen Bibeltexte,* Wiesbaden, 1995–
Birdsall, *Collected Papers*	J. N. Birdsall, *Collected Papers in Greek and Georgian Textual Criticism* (TS 3.4), Piscataway, 2006
Birdsall and Thomson, *Biblical and Patristic Studies*	J. N. Birdsall and R. W. Thomson (eds.), *Biblical and Patristic Studies in Memory of Robert Pierce Casey,* Freiburg, 1963
Blanchard, *Les débuts du codex*	A. Blanchard (ed.), *Les débuts du codex* (Bibliologia 9), Turnhout, 1989
Brock, 'Syriac Euthalian Material'	S. P. Brock, 'The Syriac Euthalian Material and the Philoxenian Version of the New Testament', *ZNW* 70 (1979), 120–30
CBL	Collectanea Biblica Latina
CBNTS	Coniectanea Biblica New Testament Series
Childers and Parker, *Transmission and Reception*	J. W. Childers and D. C. Parker (eds.), *Transmission and Reception: New Testament Text-critical and Exegetical Studies* (TS 4), Piscataway, 2006

CLA	E. A. Lowe, *Codices Latini Antiquiores. A Palaeographical Guide to Latin Manuscripts Prior to the Ninth Century*, 11 vols. + Supplement, Oxford, 1934–71 + Index, Osnabrück, 1982
Clemons, *Index of Syriac Manuscripts*	J. T. Clemons, *An Index of Syriac Manuscripts Containing the Epistles and the Apocalypse* (SD 33), Salt Lake City, 1968
Colwell, 'Method in Locating a Newly-discovered Manuscript'	E. C. Colwell, 'Method in Locating a Newly-discovered Manuscript', *TU* 73 (1959), 757–77, reprinted in Colwell, *Studies in Methodology*, 26–44
Colwell, 'Origin of Texttypes'	E. C. Colwell, 'The Origin of Texttypes of New Testament Manuscripts', in A. P. Wikgren (ed.), *Early Christian Origins*, Chicago, 1961, 128–38, reprinted as 'Method in Establishing the Nature of Text-types of New Testament Manuscripts', in Colwell, *Studies in Methodology*, 45–55
Colwell, *Studies in Methodology*	E. C. Colwell, *Studies in Methodology in Textual Criticism of the New Testament* (NTTS 9), Leiden, 1969
CPG	*Corpus Christianorum Clavis Patrum Graecorum qua optimae quaeque Scriptorum Patrum Graecorum recensiones a primaevis saeculis usque ad octavum commode recluduntur*, vol. I: *Patres Antenicaeni*, ed. M. Geerard, Turnhout, 1983; vol. II: *Ab Athanasio ad Chrysostomum*, ed. M. Geerard, 1974; vol. III: *A Cyrillo Alexandrino ad Iohannem Damascenum*, ed. M. Geerard, (1979); vol. IIIA: *Addenda*, ed. J. Noret, 2003; vol. IV: *Concilia. Catenae*, ed. M. Geerard, 1980; vol. V: *Indices, Initia, Concordantiae*, ed. M. Geerard, and F. Glorie, 1987; *Supplementum*, ed. M. Geerard and J. Noret, with the assistance of F. Glorie and J. Desmet, 2003
CPL	E. Dekkers, *Clavis Patrum Latinorum qua in Corpus Christianorum edendum optimas quasque scriptorum recensiones a Tertulliano ad Bedam* (*Corpus Christianorum Series Latina*), 3rd edn, rev. A. Gaar, Steenbruge, 1995
CSCO	Corpus Scriptorum Christianorum Orientalium

de Hamel, *The Book*   C. de Hamel, *The Book. A History of the Bible*,
                          London and New York, 2001
dela Cruz,   R. dela Cruz, 'Allegory, Mimesis and the Text:
  'Allegory, Mimesis   Theological Moulding of Lukan Parables in
  and the Text'   Codex Bezae Cantabrigiensis', unpublished PhD
                          thesis, University of Birmingham, 2004
Devreesse,   R. Devreesse, *Introduction à l'étude des manu-*
  Introduction   *scrits grecs*, Paris, 1954
Duplacy, *Études*   J. Delobel (ed.), *Jean Duplacy. Études de critique
                          textuelle du Nouveau Testament* (BETL 78),
                          Leuven, 1987
ECM   *Editio critica maior*, Stuttgart, 1997–. Where
                          there is a specific reference, it is to *Novum
                          Testamentum Graecum. Editio critica maior*, ed.
                          Institut für Neutestamentliche Textforschung,
                          vol. IV: *Die Katholischen Briefe*, ed. B. Aland,
                          K. Aland†, G. Mink, H. Strutwolf and
                          K. Wachtel, Stuttgart, 1997–2005
Ehrman, *Orthodox*   B. D. Ehrman, *The Orthodox Corruption of
  Corruption   Scripture. The Effect of Early Christological
                          Controversies on the Text of the New Testament*,
                          New York and Oxford, 1993
Ehrman, *Studies*   B. D. Ehrman, *Studies in the Textual Criticism
                          of the New Testament* (NTTS 33), Leiden and
                          Boston, 2006
Ehrman and Holmes,   B. D. Ehrman and M. W. Holmes, *The Text of
  Contemporary   the New Testament in Contemporary Research.
  Research   Essays on the Status Quaestionis. A Volume in
                          Honor of Bruce M. Metzger* (SD 46), Grand
                          Rapids, 1995
Elliott, *Bibliography*   J. K. Elliott, *A Bibliography of Greek New
                          Testament Manuscripts* (SNTSMS 109), 2nd
                          edn, Cambridge, 2000
Elliott, 'Manuscripts   J. K. Elliott, 'Manuscripts of the Book of
  Collated by   Revelation Collated by H. C. Hoskier', *JTS* 40
  H. C. Hoskier'   (1989), 100–11
Elliott, *Studies*   J. K. Elliott (ed.), *Studies in New Testament
                          Language and Text. Essays in Honour of George
                          D. Kilpatrick on the Occasion of his Sixty-fifth
                          Birthday*, Leiden, 1976, 137–43

Elliott, *A Survey of Manuscripts*	J. K. Elliott, *A Survey of Manuscripts Used in Editions of the Greek New Testament* (NovT-Suppl 57), Leiden, New York, Copenhagen and Cologne, 1987
Elliott and Parker, *Papyri*	W. J. Elliott and D. C. Parker (eds.), *The New Testament in Greek IV. The Gospel According to St John, Edited by the American and British Committees of the International Greek New Testament Project*, vol. 1: *The Papyri* (NTTS 20), Leiden, New York and Cologne, 1995
Epp, *Collected Essays*	E. J. Epp, *Perspectives on New Testament Textual Criticism. Collected Essays, 1962–2004* (NovT-Suppl 116), Leiden and Boston, 2005
Epp and Fee, *Metzger Festschrift*	E. J. Epp and G. D. Fee (eds.), *New Testament Textual Criticism. Its Significance for Exegesis. Essays in Honour of Bruce M. Metzger*, Oxford, 1981
Epp and Fee, *Studies*	E. J. Epp and G. D. Fee, *Studies in the Theory and Method of New Testament Textual Criticism*, (SD 45), Grand Rapids, 1993
ETL	*Ephemerides Theologicae Lovanenses*
Fee, *Papyrus Bodmer II (P66)*	G. D. Fee, *Papyrus Bodmer II (P66): Its Textual Relationships and Scribal Characteristics* (SD 34), Salt Lake City, 1968
Festschrift Delobel	A. Denaux (ed.), *New Testament Textual Criticism and Exegesis. Festschrift J. Delobel* (BETL 161), Leuven, 2002
Fischer, *Beiträge*	B. Fischer, *Beiträge zur Geschichte der lateinischen Bibeltexte* (GLB 12), Freiburg, 1986
Fischer, 'Das Neue Testament in lateinischer Sprache'	B. Fischer, 'Das Neue Testament in lateinischer Sprache'. Der gegenwärtige Stand seiner Erforschung und seine Bedeutung für die griechische Textgeschichte', in K. Aland, *Die alten Übersetzungen*, 1–92
Frede, *Altlateinische Paulus-Handschriften*	H. J. Frede, *Altlateinische Paulus-Handschriften* (GLB 4), Freiburg, 1964
G.–A.	Gregory–Aland number
Gamble, *Books and Readers*	H. Y. Gamble, *Books and Readers in the Early Church. A History of Early Christian Texts*, New Haven and London, 1995

Gamillscheg, Harlfinger and Hunger, _Repertorium_	E. Gamillscheg, D. Harlfinger and H. Hunger, _Repertorium der griechischen Kopisten 800–1600_, _1. Handschriften aus Bibliotheken Großbritanniens_, 3 vols., Vienna, 1981; _2. Handschriften aus Bibliotheken Frankreichs und Nachträge zu den Bibliotheken Großbritanniens_, 3 vols., Vienna, 1989; (with P. Eleuteri) _3. Handschriften aus Bibliotheken Roms mit dem Vatikan_, 3 vols., Vienna, 1997
Gardthausen, _Palaeographie_ (1979)	V. Gardthausen, _Griechische Palaeographie: Das Buchwesen im Altertum und im byzantinischen Mittelalter_, 2nd edn, 2 vols., Leipzig, 1911–13 (facsimile reprint Leipzig, 1978). Reference is also made to the first edition, Leipzig, 1879
Gibson, _Bible in the Latin West_	M. T. Gibson, _The Bible in the Latin West_ (The Medieval Book 1), Notre Dame and London, 1993
GLB	Aus der Geschichte der lateinischen Bibel, Freiburg
Gregory, _Textkritik_	C. R. Gregory, _Textkritik des Neuen Testaments_, 3 vols., Leipzig, 1900–9
Gryson, _Altlateinische Handschriften_	R. Gryson, _Altlateinische Handschriften, manuscrits vieux latins. Répertoire descriptif_, vol. 1: _Mss 1–275_ (_Vetus Latina_ 1/2 A), Freiburg, 1999; vol. 11: _Mss 300–485_ (_Vetus Latina_ 1/2 B), Freiburg, 2004
Gryson, _Philologia Sacra_	R. Gryson (ed.), _Philologia Sacra. Biblische und patristische Studien für Hermann J. Frede und Walter Thiele zu ihrem siebzigsten Geburtstag_ (GLB 24), Freiburg, 1993
Gryson, _Répertoire général_	R. Gryson, _Répertoire général des auteurs ecclésiastiques latins de l'antiquité et du haut moyen âge. 5e édition mise à jour du Verzeichnis der Sigel für Kirchenschriftsteller commencé par Bonifatius Fischer continué par Hermann Josef Frede_, 2 vols. (_Vetus Latina_ 1/1⁵), Freiburg, 2007
Harlfinger, _Griechische Kodikologie_	D. Harlfinger (ed.), _Griechische Kodikologie und Textüberlieferung_, Darmstadt, 1980
Horner, _Northern Dialect_	G. W. Horner, _The Coptic Version of the New Testament in the Northern Dialect otherwise called Memphitic and Bohairic_, 4 vols., Oxford, 1898–1905; repr. Osnabrück, 1969

Horner, *Northern Dialect*, vol. IV	Previous entry, vol. IV: *The Catholic Epistles and the Acts of the Apostles Edited from MS. Oriental 424; The Apocalypse Edited from MS. Curzon 128 in the Care of the British Museum*, Oxford, 1905 (repr. Osnabrück, 1969)
Horner, *Southern Dialect*	G. W. Horner, *The Coptic Version of the New Testament in the Southern Dialect otherwise called Sahidic and Thebaic*, 7 vols., Oxford, 1911–24; repr. Osnabrück, 1969
Horton, *The Earliest Gospels*	C. Horton (ed.), *The Earliest Gospels. The Origins and Transmission of the Earliest Christian Gospels – the Contribution of the Chester Beatty Gospel Codex P45* (JSNTSS 258), London and New York, 2004
HTR	*Harvard Theological Review*
ICSBS	Institute of Classical Studies Bulletin Supplement
IGNTP	International Greek New Testament Project
IGNTP *Luke*	*The New Testament in Greek. The Gospel According to St Luke, edited by the American and British Committees of the International Greek New Testament Project*, 2 vols., Oxford, 1984–7
JBL	*Journal of Biblical Literature*
Jongkind, *Codex Sinaiticus*	D. Jongkind, *Scribal Habits of Codex Sinaiticus* (TS 3.5), 2007
JSNT	*Journal for the Study of the New Testament*
JSNTSS	Journal for the Study of the New Testament Supplement Series
JTS	*Journal of Theological Studies*
Kannengiesser	C. Kannengiesser, *Handbook of Patristic Exegesis. The Bible in Ancient Christianity*, 2 vols., Leiden and Boston, 2004
Kenyon, *Greek Bible*	F. G. Kenyon, *The Text of the Greek Bible*, rev. A. W. Adams, London, 1958; rev. edn 1975
Kenyon, *Greek Papyri*	F. G. Kenyon, *The Palaeography of Greek Papyri*, Oxford, 1899
Kenyon, *Our Bible and the Ancient Manuscripts*	F. G. Kenyon, *Our Bible and the Ancient Manuscripts*, 4th edn, London, 1939

Kiraz, *Comparative Edition of the Syriac Gospels*	G. A. Kiraz, *Comparative Edition of the Syriac Gospels Aligning the Sinaiticus, Curetonianus, Peshitta and Harklean Versions*, 4 vols., Piscataway, 2004
Kraus and Nicklas, *New Testament Manuscripts*	T. J. Kraus and T. Nicklas (eds.), *New Testament Manuscripts. Their Texts and their World* (Texts & Editions for New Testament Study 2), Leiden, 2006
Lake, *Codex 1*	K. Lake, *Codex 1 of the Gospels and its Allies* (TS 1.7/3), Cambridge, 1902
Lake and New, *Six Collations*	K. Lake and S. New, *Six Collations of New Testament Manuscripts* (Harvard Theological Studies 17), Cambridge, Mass., 1932
Liste	K. Aland with M. Welte, B. Köster and K. Junack, *Kurzgefasste Liste der griechischen Handschriften des Neuen Testaments* (ANTF 1), 2nd edn, Berlin and New York, 1994
Martini, *Codice B alla luce del papiro Bodmer XIV*	C. M. Martini, *Il problema della recensionalità del codice B alla luce del papiro Bodmer XIV* (Analecta Biblica 26), Rome, 1966
McGurk, *Latin Gospel Books*	P. McGurk, *Latin Gospel Books from AD 400 to AD 800*, Paris, Brussels, Antwerp and Amsterdam, 1961
McKendrick and O'Sullivan	S. McKendrick and O. A. O'Sullivan (eds.), *The Bible as Book. The Transmission of the Greek Text*, London and New Castle, Del., 2003
Metzger, *Canon of the New Testament*	B. M. Metzger, *The Canon of the New Testament. Its Origin, Development, and Significance*, Oxford, 1987
Metzger, *Early Versions*	B. M. Metzger, *The Early Versions of the New Testament. Their Origin, Transmission, and Limitations*, Oxford, 1977
Metzger, *New Testament Studies*	B. M. Metzger, *New Testament Studies Philological, Versional, and Patristic* (NTTS 10), Leiden, 1980
Metzger and Ehrman	B. M. Metzger and B. D. Ehrman, *The Text of the New Testament. Its Transmission, Corruption, and Restoration*, 4th edn, New York and Oxford, 2005

Migne, *PG*	J. P. Migne (ed.), *Patrologia Graeca*, 162 vols., Paris, 1857–66, cited by volume and column
Milne and Skeat, *Scribes and Correctors*	H. J. M. Milne and T. C. Skeat, *Scribes and Correctors of the Codex Sinaiticus, including Contributions by Douglas Cockerell*, London, 1938
Mullen, Crisp and Parker, *John*	R. L. Mullen with S. Crisp and D. C. Parker (eds.), *The Byzantine Text Project: The Gospel According to John in the Byzantine Tradition*, Stuttgart, 2007
Münster *Bericht*	*Bericht der Hermann Kunst Stiftung der Förderung der neutestamentlichen Textforschung*, Münster
Myshrall, 'Codex Sinaiticus'	A. C. Myshrall, 'Codex Sinaiticus, its Correctors, and the Caesarean Text of the Gospels', unpublished PhD thesis, University of Birmingham, 2005
Nestle–Aland	B. Aland and K. Aland, J. Karavidopoulos, C. M. Martini and B. M. Metzger (eds.), *Novum Testamentum Graece*, 27th edn, 8th (revised) impression, Stuttgart, 2001
NovT	*Novum Testamentum*
NovTSuppl	Supplements to Novum Testamentum
NTA	Neutestamentliche Abhandlungen
NT auf Papyrus I	W. Grunewald (ed.) with K. Junack, *Das Neue Testament auf Papyrus, I. Die Katholischen Briefe*, (ANTF 6), Berlin and New York, 1986
NT auf Papyrus II	K. Junack, E. Güting, U. Nimtz and K. Witte, *Das Neue Testament auf Papyrus, II. Die Paulinischen Briefe*, 2 vols. (ANTF 12, 22), Berlin and New York, 1989–94
NTS	*New Testament Studies*
NTTS	New Testament Tools and Studies
P. (or Pap.)	Papyrus (usually of a papyrus collection, e.g. P. Michigan refers to an inventory number in the Michigan papyri
Paléographie grecque et byzantine	Colloques internationaux du Centre National de la recherche scientifique N° 559, *La paléographie grecque et byzantine, Paris, 21–25 octobre 1974*, Paris, 1977
Parker, *Codex Bezae*	D. C. Parker, *Codex Bezae. An Early Christian Manuscript and its Text*, Cambridge, 1992

Parker, *Living Text*	D. C. Parker, *The Living Text of the Gospels*, Cambridge, 1997
Parker, 'The Majuscule Manuscripts'	D. C. Parker, 'The Majuscule Manuscripts of the New Testament', in Ehrman and Holmes, *Contemporary Research*, 22–42
Parker and Birdsall, 'Codex Zacynthius'	D. C. Parker and J. N. Birdsall, 'The Date of Codex Zacynthius (Ξ): a New Proposal', *JTS* 55 (2004), 117–31
Parvis and Wikgren, *New Testament Manuscript Studies*	M. M. Parvis and A. P. Wikgren, *New Testament Manuscript Studies. The Materials and the Making of a Critical Apparatus*, Chicago, 1950
Pasquali, *Storia della tradizione*	G. Pasquali, *Storia della tradizione e critica del testo*, 2nd edn, Florence, 1952
PBA	*Proceedings of the British Academy*
Petersen, 'Textual Traditions Examined'	W. L. Petersen, 'Textual Traditions Examined: What the Text of the Apostolic Fathers Tells Us about the Text of the New Testament in the Second Century', in A. F. Gregory and C. M. Tuckett (eds.), *The Reception of the New Testament in the Apostolic Fathers*, Oxford, 2005, 29–46
P. Oxy.	Oxyrhynchus Papyrus
PS	I. Ortiz de Urbina, *Patrologia Syriaca*, Rome, 1958
Pusey and Gwilliam, *Tetraeuangelium*	P. E. Pusey and G. H. Gwilliam (eds.), *Tetraeuangelium sanctum juxta simplicem Syrorum versionem*, Oxford, 1901
Quasten, *Patrology*	J. Quasten, *Patrology*, vol. I: *The Beginnings of Patristic Literature*, Utrecht, 1950; vol. II: *The Ante-Nicene Literature after Irenaeus*, Utrecht, 1953; vol. III: *The Golden Age of Greek Patristic Literature*, Utrecht, 1960; vol. IV: A. di Berardino (ed.), *The Golden Age of Latin Patristic Literature from the Council of Nicaea to the Council of Chalcedon*, Westminster, 1986; A. Di Berardino (ed.), *Patrology: The Eastern Fathers from the Council of Chalcedon (451) to John of Damascus*, tr. A. Wolford, Cambridge, 2006
RB	*Revue Biblique*

Schmid, *Andreas von Kaisareia. Einleitung*	J. Schmid, *Studien zur Geschichte des griechischen Apokalypse-Textes*, vol. 1: *Der Apokalypse-Kommentar des Andreas von Kaisareia. Einleitung*, Munich, 1956
Schmid, 'Genealogy by Chance!'	U. B. Schmid, 'Genealogy by Chance! On the Significance of Accidental Variation (Parallelisms)', in *Studies in Stemmatology*, II.127–43 (see below)
Schmid, *Marcion und sein Apostolos*	U. Schmid, *Marcion und sein Apostolos. Rekonstruktion und historische Einordnung der Marcionitischen Paulusbriefausgabe* (ANTF 25), Berlin and New York, 1995
Schmid, Elliott and Parker, *Majuscules*	U. B. Schmid, with W. J. Elliott and D. C. Parker (eds.), *The New Testament in Greek IV. The Gospel According to St John, Edited by the American and British Committees of the International Greek New Testament Project*, vol. II: *The Majuscules* (New Testament Tools, Studies and Documents 37), Leiden and Boston, 2007
Scrivener, *Augiensis*	F. H. A. Scrivener, *An Exact Transcript of the Codex Augiensis … to Which Is Added a Full Collation of Fifty Manuscripts*, Cambridge and London, 1859
Scrivener, *Plain Introduction*	F. H. A. Scrivener, *A Plain Introduction to the Criticism of the New Testament for the Use of Biblical Students*, 4th edn, rev. E. Miller, 2 vols., London, New York and Cambridge, 1894
SD	Studies and Documents
Skeat, *Collected Biblical Writings*	J. K. Elliott (ed.), *The Collected Biblical Writings of T. C. Skeat* (NovTSuppl 113), Leiden and Boston, 2004
SL	Sonderlesart
SNTSMS	Society for New Testament Studies Monograph Series
Souter[1]	A. Souter (ed.), *Novum Testamentum Graece. Textui a retractatoribus anglis adhibito brevem adnotationem criticam subiecit*, Oxford, 1910
Souter[2]	A. Souter (ed.), *Novum Testamentum Graece* etc., 2nd edn, Oxford, 1947

Stegmüller, *Repertorium*	F. Stegmüller, *Repertorium biblicum medii aevi*, 7 vols., Madrid, 1940–61, completed by V. Reinhardt, 4 vols., Madrid, 1978–80
Streeter, *The Four Gospels*	B. H. Streeter, *The Four Gospels. A Study of Origins Treating of the Manuscript Tradition, Sources, Authorship, & Dates*, London, 1924
Studies in Stemmatology II	P. van Reenen, A. den Hollander and M. van Mulken (eds.), *Studies in Stemmatology*, vol. II: *Kinds of Variants*, Amsterdam, 2004; online version at http://site.ebrary.com/pub/benjamins/Doc?isbn=1588115356
Swanson, *Greek Manuscripts*	R. J. Swanson, *New Testament Greek Manuscripts. Variant Readings Arranged in Horizontal Lines against Codex Vaticanus*, Sheffield and Pasadena, 1995–
Swete, *Introduction*	H. B. Swete, *An Introduction to the Old Testament in Greek*, rev. R. R. Ottley, Cambridge, 1914
Taylor, *Studies in the Early Text*	D. G. K. Taylor (ed.), *Studies in the Early Text of the Gospels and Acts*, (TS 3.1), Birmingham, 1999
Textus Receptus, Oxford, 1873	*Η Καινη Διαθηκη. Novum Testamentum, accedunt parallela S. Scripturae loca, Vetus capitulorum notatio, Canones Eusebii*, Oxford, 1873
Thompson, *Introduction*	E. M. Thompson, *An Introduction to Greek and Latin Palaeography*, Oxford, 1912
Tischendorf, *Editio octava*	C. Tischendorf, *Novum Testamentum Graece … Editio octava critica maior*, 3 vols., Leipzig, 1872–84 (vol. III, *Prolegomena*, by C. R. Gregory)
Tregelles, *Account of the Printed Text*	S. P. Tregelles, *An Account of the Printed Text of the Greek New Testament; with Remarks on its Revision upon Critical Principles*, London, 1854
TS	Teststelle (see 1.3.8)
TS	Texts and Studies (first number indicates whether it is first, second or third series)
TU	Texte und Untersuchungen
Turner, *GMAW*	E. G. Turner, *Greek Manuscripts of the Ancient World*, Oxford, 1971. There is a second enlarged edn, ed. P. Parsons (ICSBS 46), London, 1987
Turner, *Typology*	E. G. Turner, *The Typology of the Early Codex*, Pennsylvania, 1977

Turyn, *Great Britain*	A. Turyn, *Dated Greek Manuscripts of the Thirteenth and Fourteenth Centuries in the Libraries of Great Britain*, (Dumbarton Oaks Studies 17), Washington, 1980
van Haelst, *Catalogue*	J. van Haelst, *Catalogue des papyrus littéraires juifs et chrétiens*, Paris, 1976
VC	*Vigiliae Christianae*
Vetus Latina	*Vetus Latina. Die Reste der altlateinischen Bibel nach Petrus Sabatier neu gesammelt und herausgegeben von der Erzabtei Beuron*, Freiburg, 1949–
von Soden	H. von Soden, *Die Schriften des Neuen Testaments in ihrer ältesten erreichbarren Textgestalt hergestellt auf grund ihrer Textgeschichte*, 4 vols., Göttingen, 1902–13
Vööbus, *Early Versions*	A. Vööbus, *Early Versions of the New Testament. Manuscript Studies* (Papers of the Estonian Theological Society in Exile 6), Stockholm, 1954
Wachtel, 'Kinds of Variants'	K. Wachtel, 'Kinds of Variants in the Manuscript Tradition of the Greek New Testament', in *Studies in Stemmatology* II, 87–98
Wachtel and Parker, 'The Joint IGNTP/ INTF Gospel of John'	K. Wachtel and D. C. Parker, 'The Joint IGNTP/INTF Editio Critica Maior of the Gospel of John: Its Goals and their Significance for New Testament Scholarship' (paper presented at SNTS, Halle, 2005), available at www.itsee.bham.ac.uk/online/2005_SNTS_Wachtel Parker.pdf
Wachtel, Spencer and Howe, 'The Greek Vorlage of the Syra Harclensis'	K. Wachtel, M. Spencer and C. J. Howe, 'The Greek Vorlage of the Syra Harclensis: a Comparative Study on Method in Exploring Textual Genealogy', *TC: A Journal of Biblical Textual Criticism* 7, 2002: http://rosetta.reltech.org/TC/vol07/vol07.html
Wachtel, Spencer and Howe, 'Representing Multiple Pathways'	K. Wachtel, M. Spencer and C. J. Howe, 'Representing Multiple Pathways of Textual Flow in the Greek Manuscripts of the Letter of James Using Reduced Median Networks', *Computers and the Humanities* 38 (2004), 1–14

Weber, *Biblia Sacra*	R. Weber with B. Fischer, I. Gribomont, H. F. D. Sparks and W. Thiele, (eds.), *Biblia Sacra iuxta vulgatam versionem*, 5th edn prepared by R. Gryson, Stuttgart, 2007
Weren and Koch, *Recent Developments*	W. Weren and D.-A. Koch (eds.), *Recent Developments, in Textual Criticism. New Testament, Other Early Christian and Jewish Literature*, Assen, 2003
Westcott and Hort	B. F. Westcott and F. J. A. Hort (eds.), *The New Testament in the Original Greek*, 2 vols., London, 1881
White, *Actuum Apostolorum*	J. White, *Actuum Apostolorum et epistolarum tam catholicarum quam paulinarum, versio Syriaca Philoxeniana* etc., 2 vols., Oxford, 1803
Wordsworth and White	J. Wordsworth and H. J. White, *Nouum Testamentum Domini Nostri Iesu Christi Latine secundum editionem Sancti Hieronymi*, 3 vols., Oxford, 1889–1954 (for full details, see 3.3.2)
WUNT	Wissenschaftliche Untersuchungen zum Neuen Testament
ZNW	*Zeitschrift für die neutestamentliche Wissenschaft*
Zuntz, *Ancestry*	G. Zuntz, *The Ancestry of the Harklean New Testament*, London, n.d. [1945]
Zuntz, *Opuscula Selecta*	G. Zuntz, *Opuscula Selecta. Classica, Hellenistica, Christiana*, Manchester, 1972
Zuntz, *Text of the Epistles*	G. Zuntz, *The Text of the Epistles. A Disquisition upon the Corpus Paulinum* (The Schweich Lectures of the British Academy 1946) London, 1953; reprinted Eugene, Oregon, 2007

Introduction

Textual criticism and editing of the New Testament have changed dramatically in the last quarter of a century. It is rather more than thirty years since I began my first researches in the field, and during this period of time I have had to learn new approaches in most of the things which I do. There are four main causes for this. Foremost among them is the introduction of the computer. In the last fifteen years the techniques of collecting manuscript evidence, analysing it, and making a critical edition have all undergone their greatest transformation. Secondly, the study of manuscripts has undergone significant changes. It has become plainer than ever before that the examination of manuscripts and of the variant readings which they contain is more than a means to recover a lost original text – it has also a part to play in the study of the development of Christian thought and in the history of exegesis. Thirdly, the publication of new manuscript discoveries continues to challenge traditional views of textual history and of the copying of texts. Fourthly, a number of research tools have been published which place far larger and better resources at the scholar's disposal than were ever available before. Nor does there seem to be any likelihood of the pace of change slackening in the near future. The advent of digital imaging heralds a new era, in which scholars and students everywhere will be able to view pictures of any page in any manuscript.

With these developments there are signs of a greater variety of scholarship in the field of textual studies. There is and always will be the need for the traditional textual critic, strong on philology and attentive to detail; and anyone working in the field will be wise to nurture these virtues. But there are now also researchers with speed and fluency in electronic media who are bringing new ideas and new skills to the discipline. So long as textual criticism was perceived (largely from outside) solely as the task of restoring an original text, it was always going to be practised only by a few specialists, since there are pragmatic and commercial reasons why very few editions of the Greek New Testament are made in any generation. Now that it is rightly seen as so much more than this, there are opportunities for many more researchers.

Textual criticism has been rather unsuccessful at publicising these changes. The first ports of call, the natural books to go on a student reading list, tend to present 'business as usual', describing things very much as they have been for several generations but are no longer. This book offers an account of textual criticism today. I have tried to write a book with as original a shape and as fresh a content as possible. I am more interested in explaining the questions than in providing the answers, with the result that I have regularly become distracted into various exciting forays. The consequence is that this book contains some original research as well as summaries of the state of affairs.

I hope to communicate the excitement of research in this field, the achievements of past and modern scholarship, the beauty and fascination of manuscripts, the intellectual challenges of textual criticism, the opportunities for research, and the significance of what we are doing for colleagues working in other fields of New Testament study, history and theology, as well as for the criticism of other texts.

Some definitions:

1. 'Document'

The word 'document' is sometimes used to describe what in this book is called a 'text'. Properly speaking, a document refers to an artefact. Documents such as charters or autograph letters easily give their own definition to the texts which they contain. In this book, 'document' means a manuscript. The following quotation underpins not only this definition, but the entire concept of the book:

> The first step towards obtaining a sure foundation is a consistent application of the principle that KNOWLEDGE OF DOCUMENTS SHOULD PRECEDE FINAL JUDGEMENT UPON READINGS.

The source of this (the part in capitals is often quoted) is one of modern textual criticism's key texts, Westcott and Hort's introduction to *The New Testament in the Original Greek* (p. 31). The meaning of the quotation is this: before deciding which of one or more different wordings is likely to be the source of the others, the scholar should know about the character and nature of the documents which contain the different wordings. They go on to write that 'If we compare successively the readings of two documents in all their variations, we have ample materials for ascertaining the leading merits and defects of each' (p. 32).

This book follows not only the implication of Hort's famous dictum but also the example of many predecessors by beginning with an introduction to the study of the manuscripts of the New Testament, in particular those in Greek and the oldest languages into which it was translated. The focus will be on two ways of studying a document: as a physical item, of a particular size, format, age, and so forth, and as what will be called a 'tradent' of the text or texts which it contains. The former belongs to the discipline of palaeography, the latter to textual criticism. It is possible to be a palaeographer and to study the documents almost to the virtual exclusion of the texts they contain. The results of such research will be valuable to the textual scholar. But to concentrate on the text without studying the documents will produce a far less satisfactory result, as will become apparent. This distinction between the documentary and the textual may seem surprising, since it seems obvious that the only purpose of a book is to be a copy of a particular text. In fact, at all levels of interest and knowledge, there are books whose main significance lies not in their textual but in their physical characteristics. The Lindisfarne Gospels, for example, is a ninth-century Latin manuscript in the British Library which for many people has a significance independent of its contents. They may appreciate it as a superb representative of Northumbrian art even though they know no Latin and nothing of the contents. The same is true of the Book of Kells: visitors queue in the library of Trinity College Dublin to see this manuscript alone, although there are in the same place other copies of the same texts which are textually much more significant. In fact, some of the most admired pages of both of these manuscripts contain no text at all. These remarkable examples demonstrate vividly how compelling the physical characteristics of a document may be. To the palaeographer every manuscript has its attractions. The textual scholar should feel the same.

The use of the word 'document' in this book illustrates the differences between the world of manuscript transmission and the world of the printed book. If we go to buy a book, the shop will contain a number of identical copies of the text, and we will know that whichever we choose, it will contain exactly the same text. By contrast, the documents with which we are dealing are all unique items, both physically and in the wording of the text. Even on the rare occasions when we can identify copies by the same scribe, the modern eye will be struck as much by the differences between them as by the similarities. These differences may be immediately obvious in the layout of the text on the page, or in the details of the presentation. A more careful study of the text will reveal places where this manuscript contains sequences of wording not found elsewhere. In fact, it will contain variant readings. Whether any text exists in an identical form in two documents I could not know without reading every copy of every text until I found one. But (except if it were very short) I do not believe that I would find any.

Westcott and Hort. For the Lindisfarne Gospels, see, e.g., J. Backhouse, *The Lindisfarne Gospels*, Oxford, 1981; for the Book of Kells, P. Brown, *The Book of Kells*, London, 1980.

2. 'Variant reading'

A working definition of a variant reading is that it is 'a place where the wording exists in more than one form'. This is a statement about the text. The statement that 'each manuscript contains a unique form of the text' is a description of the same phenomenon. But this wording draws our attention to the fact that variant readings occur as a part of the text as it is contained in a single manuscript, much of which will be in common with that found in other documents. If we consider the concept of a variant reading from this point of view, a variant reading should be defined as 'the entire text as it is present in a particular copy'. This primary definition must be borne in mind as a principle when the term is being used normally. Because two copies of a text will have wording in common between them, in practice a variant reading describes the places where the common text ceases, and each has its own form. 'Variant reading' is in fact a simple tool for breaking down the differences between two or more copies into manageable units.

An example taken at random: John 7.40 is found as follows in two of the oldest copies:

ἐκ τοῦ ὄχλου οὖν ἀκούσαντες αὐτοῦ τῶν λόγων ἔλεγον ἀληθῶς οὗτός ἐστιν ὁ προφήτης (Codex Sinaiticus, fourth century)

ἐκ τοῦ ὄχλου οὖν ἀκούσαντες τῶν λόγων τούτων ἔλεγον ὅτι οὗτός ἐστιν ἀληθῶς ὁ προφήτης (Codex Vaticanus, fourth century)

We could express the differences as a single variation. But for practical purposes it is easier to treat them as three variations:

(1) either αὐτοῦ τῶν λόγων or τῶν λόγων τούτων (which could in fact be treated as two variants, the one being the presence or absence of αὐτοῦ and the other the presence or absence of τούτων)
(2) the presence or absence of ὅτι
(3) either ἀληθῶς οὗτός ἐστιν or οὗτος ἐστιν ἀληθῶς

Stating the differences like this breaks them into simple units, and avoids stating the pieces of wording where the two copies agree (ἐκ τοῦ ὄχλου οὖν ἀκούσαντες, ἔλεγον and ὁ προφήτης). It also makes it easier to express the differences between more copies. The Nestle–Aland critical apparatus records that there are three possible openings to this verse:

Ἐκ τοῦ ὄχλου οὖν

or

Πολλοὶ ἐκ τοῦ ὄχλου

or

Πολλοὶ οὖν ἐκ τοῦ ὄχλου

It was convenient to the editors of this edition to present the evidence in this way. But this presentation, with three variant forms of these words, is not the only possible way of describing the variation. It would also be possible to define it as two variants: the presence or absence of πολλοί and the presence (in a choice of locations) or absence of οὖν. How differences between documents are presented is the choice of the editor. The differences certainly exist, but there is more than one way of describing them. The only definition of a variant reading which is not pragmatic is that which defines it as the entire text. So I repeat: a variant reading is to be defined as 'the entire text as it is present in a particular copy'.

3. 'The New Testament'

While the previous paragraphs have tried to provide a rather careful definition of some terms, they have not been so precise in the use of the word 'text' with regard to the New Testament. It is common to speak about 'The Bible' and even 'The New Testament' as though one was speaking about a single text by a single author. But the New Testament is not a single text by a single author. Nor is it the apparent alternative, a collection of texts each with its own author. It is in fact a hybrid, being a collection which may be subdivided in various ways. One could see it as composed of three collections of texts:

Four Gospels
Seven Catholic letters and fourteen letters attributed to St Paul
Two single texts (the Acts of the Apostles and the Revelation to John).

Or one could divide it by traditional authorship:

St John: one Gospel, three epistles and Revelation
Luke: one Gospel and the Acts of the Apostles
Mark: one Gospel
and so on.

As it happens, traces of both of these understandings may be found in the manuscripts. The important thing to note is that the sets of texts may be described in various ways. Each of the texts included in the Greek and western canon of twenty-seven books is (and I am trying to pick my words carefully) a separate literary creation. Each of them therefore once existed as a separate document, and some of them survive in separate documents. But most of them were made into collections, notably the Gospels and two sets of epistles, one of them including Acts. These collections were sometimes brought together in larger compilations, most commonly comprising Acts and the two sets of epistles, sometimes with the Gospels as well, and occasionally (rarely) even Revelation.

For too long have broad generalisations been made about these texts and sets of texts under the heading 'the textual criticism of the New Testament'. There is no longer such a thing, unless as a useful definition of a field of research, as opposed to the textual criticism of Homer or Shakespeare. It is true that some aspects of the study of these twenty-seven books are very similar. But so would textual criticism of the New Testament have similarities of approach to the textual criticism of any early Christian writer, such as Origen or Augustine, as well as differences from it. Nothing more than the broadest of generalisations can be applied to all of these twenty-seven texts together. For the following reasons, a textual criticism of the entire New Testament cannot be practised, and must be replaced with a separate treatment of the different texts and sets of texts:

(1) The first reason is their differences in literary character, which had a strong influence on the way in which each text and collection was copied. For example, it is inevitable that the Gospels should be especially liable to confusion between each other, but this confusion is greater between the Synoptic Gospels, while John, which is less similar to the other three than they are to each other, is less affected. The unique content and narrative of the Acts of the Apostles is partially responsible for the fact that the textual situation is also unique.

(2) These different texts had different uses within early Christianity, which influenced the way in which they were copied. The absence of Revelation from the Byzantine lectionary is one reason why there are far fewer surviving copies, but the fact that it so often circulated with a commentary attached locates many of the copies within the textual tradition of the several commentaries.

(3) A complete New Testament as a single document containing all the books was always a rarity in the ancient world (see 1.8). The vast majority of manuscripts contain only one of the four sections. In practice, it is therefore rather misleading even to speak of them as manuscripts of the Greek New Testament. They are better described as Gospel manuscripts, or manuscripts of Paul's letters, or whatever larger combination they might contain.

(4) Since behind the three collections and Revelation lie various previous forms of collections and single texts, one has to be careful even in making general statements about all members of any of the smaller collections.

As a result of these differences in literary character, function within Christianity, and history of copying, I consider the phrase 'The Textual Criticism of the New Testament' to be a misleading one. This work therefore adopts a different approach. Having described the manuscripts and other materials for research in Part I and after an introduction to textual criticism in Part II, Part III will be in four sections, each of them devoted to a section of the New Testament. Revelation will be taken first, because it provides the easiest approach to textual criticism, and its history is most fully understood. This will be followed by the Pauline letters, Acts and the Catholic letters, and finally the four Gospels.

Having read this argument, the reader may be surprised that I continue to refer to the New Testament. I reply that to avoid it would be to overstate my case. I freely admit that to describe the documents as 'documents of the New Testament' is to overlook the real differences in content between them and that to describe the texts as 'New Testament texts' is to ignore the fact that while they *became* New Testament texts, they were not so in the beginning. At the same time, it would be pedantic to avoid 'the New Testament' entirely, perhaps with a phrase such as 'the writings later known as', or 'what was to become the New Testament', or 'manuscripts of some or all of the New Testament'. Sometimes I refer to the text of the New Testament simply for the sake of convenience.

The inclusion of both *manuscripts* and *texts* in the title is important. If one were to restrict the study of the documents to the texts which they contain, it would be possible to limit their use to the practice of textual criticism, that is to the study of variant readings and their placing in a chronology by which one, therefore to be adjudged the oldest, accounted for the formation of the others. But documents consist of more than the texts they contain, and their layout, their design and the material of which they are made, their ink and script, their marginalia and the ornamentation, paintings and bindings with which they may have been adorned all provide evidence about cultural as well as religious history and even cast light on economic, social and political matters. The study of scripts has reached the point where the date of most manuscripts and the place of writing of many may be fairly accurately determined, while the growing discipline of book history finds new kinds of evidence and new research questions in the physical characteristics of the volume. The texts they carry are also much more than potential sources of the oldest form of text. Each, in its textual uniqueness, is a witness to a particular form of the text that existed, was read, recited, remembered and compared with other texts, at certain times and in certain places. The variant readings which are not the oldest are not therefore without interest. They provide information about subsequent interpretations of the text and understandings of Christian faith and practice, including the fact that the oldest form had been modified. The title is intended to reflect this wider value of the manuscripts for historical study.

At this point I would like to avow my intention to make no further reference to a number of documents or theories which, although they are sometimes used in text-critical arguments, I do not accept as reasonable. These are: first, the Secret Gospel of Mark, which I have never believed to be genuine; second, the Gospel of Barnabas as anything other than a late-medieval text dependent on other medieval texts of interest to students of Christian–Islamic dialogue; third, the claim that there are any New Testament manuscripts among the Dead Sea Scrolls; fourth, all extravagant claims that any New Testament manuscripts known to us were written in the first century.

This book sets out to introduce the reader to the habits and practice of New Testament textual research. I have not always selected what I believe to be the most important topics or the best theories, but I have tried to introduce material which explores the major contemporary questions. Some of what I have written is about current projects in which I am involved, both because they happen to be some of the major current undertakings of New Testament textual scholarship and because by describing them from the inside I hope I can better introduce the reader to the ways of study and thinking that belong with the discipline.

I see no point in repeating things which have been much better expressed by someone else. On those occasions I simply refer the reader to that authority. As a result, this book will be of little use to anyone who hopes that it will tell them all they need to know: a bluffer's guide to New Testament textual criticism. This book is an introduction, and it attempts to imitate the skilled host in performing introductions between its readers and its topics, and then leaving them together.

I have often provided references to literature which I hope will be an Ariadne's thread for readers to find their own way through the subjects I cover. I certainly have not set out to be comprehensive, but I hope that the bibliography I have selected is such that the reader will never be more than one or two further bibliographies away from most of the materials. Where I have included a reference to collected papers or works with several authors, such as conference papers and Festschriften, the reader is invited to scan the other contributions which are not mentioned in search of further enlightenment.

My grounds for including topics are various: some are present because I have been asked about them at one time or another, some because I have needed to explain them to students, others because they are things I wanted to find out for myself. Sometimes I have described a contentious issue in some depth, not necessarily for its own sake but because it illustrates the way that textual critics argue or the development of ideas.

I have generally tried to discuss theoretical topics in the context of a specific problem, and to use an argument or a point of view to illustrate ways of studying manuscripts and texts. I have also taken representative topics in another way. For example, the only chapter in Part III to contain a history of research is the chapter on Revelation. That is because the story of the research upon this text is a microcosm of the whole, and can easily be told in some detail. In the same way, I do not have a chapter on the historical development of textual criticism. Instead, aspects of that history are told in the context of theoretical and practical problems (for example, in the history of the Christian book and the description of different kinds of edition).

More attention is paid in this book to Greek manuscripts than to those in any other language. This seems reasonable when one is writing about texts first written in Greek. After Greek, it is Latin manuscripts which receive the most attention, for several reasons. One is that they have been more thoroughly studied than those of the other translations of the New Testament. Another is that they are particularly significant to a northern European as the vehicle for the transmission of the biblical text into western cultures. A third rather less satisfactory reason is that my own studies have principally been in these areas.

A word about the structure of the book is necessary. I find footnotes unsatisfactory, because they interrupt the argument and distract the reader. Instead, I have followed the layout which I adopted in *Codex Bezae* of pausing at certain points to provide bibliographical and subsidiary information on the preceding paragraphs. These passages are set in a smaller font.

PART I

The documents

CHAPTER I

The study of the manuscripts

I.I THE CHRISTIAN BOOK

I.I.I The codex

Those writings which in time came to comprise the New Testament are almost without exception preserved in the manuscript form called the codex, the kind of book which is normative in western culture. In its simplest format, a codex is made by taking a pile of sheets of writing material, folding them in half, and then (starting at the top of the first sheet) writing the text on them. The whole pile is then stitched together through the centre fold. This is a single-quire codex. A more sophisticated version consists of making a number of such piles, four sheets (eight folios, sixteen pages) being the norm at most periods; each quire is folded separately, written on and laid aside. Each quire is bound with thread through its own centre fold, the whole set being finally bound together with cords through the threads holding the individual quires. This is a multiple-quire codex and is the form in normal use for anything larger than a pamphlet. Although books are often bound today using strong glues holding single sheets at the spine, there was no alternative in the ancient world to stitching them.

The transition from the roll form to the codex was a momentous change in ancient Mediterranean culture. Greek and Roman civilisation made copies of texts on papyrus rolls, which consisted of sheets of the material (a plant almost exclusively grown and processed in Egypt) glued together to make a long strip, on which the text was written in columns. Unlike the scrolls that are used by heralds in movies and are rolled out from top to bottom (possibly also the unconventional format adopted by Julius Caesar for his dispatches to the Roman Senate), the roll was held horizontally, the unopened parts being held on a stick in each hand. The early Christians would have been familiar with both the papyrus and the parchment or leather roll. It was in this format that the Hebrew Scriptures and the Greek Septuagint were preserved. The narrative in Luke's Gospel of Jesus preaching in the synagogue at Capernaum records that when he was given the book of the prophet Isaiah, Jesus 'unrolling the book found the place where it was written' (ἀναπτύξας τὸ βιβλίον εὗρεν τὸν τόπον οὗ ἦν γεγραμμένον, Lk. 4.17). The verb ἀναπτύσσω is used of the unrolling of a roll, and three verses later the use of the opposite, πτύσσω, describes Jesus rolling it up again.

For other examples of ἀναπτύσσω/πτύσσω, see 4 Kgdms. 19.14: καὶ ἔλαβεν Ἐζεκίας τὰ βιβλία . . . καὶ ἀνέπτυξεν αὐτὰ Ἐζεκίας ἐναντίον Κυρίου; H.B. Swete (ed.), *The Old Testament in Greek According to the Septuagint*, vol. I, Cambridge, 1909; Irenaeus 1.10.3: ὅσα τε κεῖται ἐν ταῖς γραφαῖς, ἀναπτύσσειν. Other words in Thompson, *Introduction*, p. 49. Compare R. S. Bagnall, 'Jesus Reads a Book', *JTS* 51 (2000), 577–88, with a contrary view in Elliott's introduction to Skeat, *Collected Biblical Writings*, XXV. For papyrus, see N. Lewis, *Papyrus in Classical Antiquity*, Oxford, 1974 (updates: *Papyri in Classical Antiquity. A Supplement* (Pap. Brux. 22), Brussels, 1989); *Chronique d'Égypte* 67 (1992), 308–18; E.G. Turner, *Greek Papyri, an Introduction*, Oxford, 1968 (paperback, 1980).

We have no copies of early Christian writings older than the middle of the second century, so we cannot at present know at what stage the codex replaced the roll, or even whether the codex was used for some or all of these writings from the beginning. The evidence of the forty or so manuscripts surviving from the second and third centuries is that by about 150 it was normative for Christians to copy the writings which later became the New Testament into the papyrus codex format. It is only comparatively recently that the information has become available which makes it possible to develop detailed hypotheses with regard to the transition from the roll to the codex. A hundred years ago scholars could only observe the fact that the codex had taken over from the roll by the end of the fourth century. Today the study of newly found literary texts written on papyrus before the fourth century has illuminated some aspects of the developments which went before.

It is important to note that there were two developments, not necessarily dependent upon each other, which took place in the period between the first and fourth centuries. The first was the adoption of the codex and the subsequent decline in the popularity of the roll – with certain important exceptions, most notably the copying of the Hebrew Scriptures. The second was the transition from papyrus to parchment as the preferred material on which to copy. The relationship between these two phenomena is not fully explained, partly perhaps because they are not always studied together. Older scholarship (by which I mean scholarship before about 1950) was more alert to the latter, while the interest in recent decades among New Testament scholars has been on the development of the codex. It is clear enough that the shift to the codex came before the shift to parchment, so it is better discussed first.

For the history of papyrus discovery, see I. Gallo, *Greek and Latin Papyrology* (Classical Handbook 1), London, 1986, 17–35. For an early assessment of the contribution of Christianity to the popularisation of the codex, see Thompson, *Introduction*, 52f. For a discussion of the transition from papyrus to parchment see Kenyon, *Greek Papyri*, 112–25. For the following section, see C.H. Roberts and T.C. Skeat, *The Birth of the Codex*, London, 1983, which is a revision of Roberts, 'The Codex', *PBA* 40 (1954), 169–204; J. van Haelst, 'Les origines du codex', Blanchard, *Les débuts du codex*, 13–35; Turner, *Typology*, 35–42.

This topic may be divided into two separate matters: the origin of the codex form, and the reasons for its adoption. The first may be introduced by the question whether early Christians invented the codex, or whether their contribution was to popularise an existing medium. The discussion here centres on the evidence of the Roman epigrammatist Martial (born between AD 38 and 41, died between 101 and 104). The material has been discussed in detail in all the writings on the topic, and only the broadest outline is necessary here. The second epigram of the first book runs (in my own translation):

> Since you want my booklets with you
> Round the house and on the road,
> Buy these compact parchment tablets:
> Leave the book box with the rolls;
> Hold this in a single hand!
> So you know where you can find them
> I will tell you: seek Secundus
> freedman of the Luccan savant
> Behind the gate of Peace's Temple
> And the marketplace of Pallas.

Martial's text (D.M. Shackleton Bailey (ed., after W. Heraeus), *M. Valerii Martialis Epigrammata*, Stuttgart, 1990, 1.2 (p. 15)) is as follows:

> Qui tecum cupis esse meos ubicumque libellos
> et comites longae quaeris habere uiae,
> hos eme, quos artat brevibus membrana tabellis:
> scrinia da magnis, me manus una capit.
> Ne tamen ignores ubi sim uenalis et erres
> urbe uagus tota, me duce certus eris:
> libertum docti Lucensis quaere Secundum
> limina post Pacis Palladiumque forum.

No variants are recorded in this edition. The text is identical to that given and discussed by Roberts and Skeat.

The attractions set out by Martial are that the codex can easily be taken anywhere, that it does not need a box to be kept in (being within the box of its own covers) and that it can be held in one hand (unlike a roll, whose two ends are held in the two hands). The question is whether Martial's venture was the source of the Christian idea. The answer is that we cannot know, both because we do not know which came first and because we know nothing of the impact of Martial's initiative. What we can say is that this poem is written a good fifty years before the oldest surviving Christian book (a codex) was copied and that the early Christians were not the only ones to make codices, even if they were the people who used them most.

Whether it was Martial or Christians who were the first to make codices, was there a source, an inspiration for their technology? A candidate for this role is the parchment notebook which by the first century had developed out of the wooden tablet. This notebook appears to have been a Roman invention. The parchment in question may well have been of inferior quality to papyrus, so that it was used for rough drafts, documents and copies where appearance was a secondary consideration. Did early Christians adopt this notebook and use it for their writings? It was suggested by Roberts that Mark did precisely this, taking down Peter's reminiscences (as patristic testimony such as that of Papias describes him as doing), and producing his Gospel in the codex form. Roberts and Skeat turn away from this view, presenting the alternative hypothesis that the origin lies in the Jewish custom of using papyrus notebooks to record the oral law. Tentatively locating this development in Antioch, they suggest that 'It is possible ... that papyrus tablets were used to record the Oral Law as pronounced by Jesus, and that these tablets might have developed into a primitive form of codex' (p. 59).

An alternative approach is held by van Haelst, who rejects the second hypothesis on the grounds that there is no evidence that such papyrus notebooks existed, either in the first century or at any other time. Instead, he considers the origin of the codex to be 'pagan and Roman'. He points out that Luke's 'history of Christian origins' was divided into two parts (λόγοι) for copying on two rolls. It was probably 'at Rome ... that at the end of the first or beginning of the second century [Christians] adopted for practical reasons the already existing codex to copy their Scriptures, which they received on papyrus rolls' (p. 35). Van Haelst also argues that it is a mistake to overemphasise the contrast between Christian use of codices and pagan use of rolls, by providing lists of pagan codices of the second century: one Latin (on parchment) and seventeen Greek (three on parchment and fourteen on papyrus). The early date given to the single Latin item (Papyrus Oxyrhynchus 30, an otherwise unknown work given the name *De Bellis Macedonicis*) makes it especially important: 100 is the date given by some scholars, while others prefer to be more cautious, placing it in the second century. Where Van Haelst has less to say is on the need of his hypothesis to account for a transition from parchment to papyrus codex. Here the detailed survey by E. G. Turner provides another approach. Turner challenges the traditional view that parchment came first, arguing for the priority of papyrus on the grounds of format. He concludes judiciously 'I am not here trying to argue at all costs to assert the priority of papyrus over parchment in the development of the codex, but I am arguing that the automatic assumption of the contrary needs a new justification' (*Typology*, p. 40).

This brief summary has set out the main lines of enquiry: the emergence of two formats (codex and roll) and two materials (papyrus and parchment). This debate, which might appear only technical, is of much wider significance because of the light it casts on a question which should be considered by every student of the New Testament: why did early Christians prefer the codex to the roll? This is a very important question, because implicit within the answer to it are observations about the role and status of the writings in the earliest Christian communities.

Here, since no early Christian writer thought the matter worth discussing, we are in even more speculative territory, since we are seeking motive. The main explanations are:

(1) Cost: it has been suggested that a codex may have been 25 per cent cheaper than a roll to produce.
(2) Convenience of consultation: it is possible to switch between two locations in a codex far more quickly than in a roll, where rolling and unrolling are needed.
(3) Convenience of carriage: this explanation assumes that the early Christian missionaries travelling from place to place found codices easier to transport, because they were smaller and in a safer shape, since the capsule (the 'book box' of my translation of Martial) in which a roll would have needed to be kept in order to protect it would, with the larger bulk of a roll to contain the same text, have been much less convenient.
(4) The adoption of a codex for an important early Christian text led to its being used for other texts: this may have been a Gospel (Roberts and Skeat) or the letters of Paul (Gamble).

Gamble, *Books and Readers*, 49–66; G.N. Stanton, 'Early Christian Preference for the Codex', in Horton, *The Earliest Gospels*, 40–9.

The problem with the first two explanations is that it is hard to see why these circumstances would have applied more to early Christians than to others. But it is true so far as (1) is concerned that, as has already been noted, parchment codices were used for cheap and unadorned copies of Latin texts. Perhaps the papyrus codex was a step up from this level of production. The real significance of the second explanation is as a *consequence* rather than a reason: it will be seen later that the codex form had some practical results for the way Christians studied and used their texts. It may be that (3) and (4) belong rather closely together, since the first reference in Christian literature to a codex is found in a deutero-Pauline letter: in 2 Timothy 4.13 the writer asks Timothy to 'bring the cloak that I left with Carpus at Troas, also the books and above all the parchments'.

τὸν φαιλόνην ὃν ἀπέλιπον ἐν Τρῳάδι παρὰ Κάρπῳ ἐρχόμενος φέρε, καὶ τὰ βιβλία μάλιστα τὰς μεμβράνας. Note the textual forms which add either δέ or καί after μάλιστα.

This word μεμβράναι is a transliteration into Greek of the Latin word *membranae*, whose singular form is used by Martial in the epigram quoted above. Referring to the skin of animals or plants, it is used also of skin prepared for writing, that is, of parchment. The use of a loan word seems to indicate that there was no Greek equivalent (the word περγαμηνός is first attested somewhat later).

Martial's reference to the convenience of the codex for the traveller may be a hint in favour of the third explanation, and even a hint of a connection between the Christians' codex and Martial's. But the reasons behind the adoption of the codex by a particular group may not be the same as the reasons for the codex's invention.

It is sometimes suggested that the Gospel of Luke is the longest text one could have reasonably written on a single roll. It is probably more precise to say that Luke and Acts together are too long to be contained on a single roll. Together they consist of 185 pages of the Nestle–Aland (Luke 97 pages, Acts 89). Paul's letters, including Hebrews, are a very similar length – 179 pages. If one excludes the Pastorals (for reasons which will be given below in 8.3) the length is 136 pages, or nearly half as long again as Luke. That is to say that according to Gamble's computations (see 8.3), Luke's Gospel would require a roll 1,200 cm in length.

The obvious source of evidence to corroborate these figures is the surviving ancient rolls. But we encounter two difficulties: the fragmentary nature of most finds, and uncertainty regarding the extent to which, having been found in Egypt, they reflect only Egyptian practice. The longest papyrus rolls to have been found in Egypt are:

P. Oxy. LXIII 4394, produced in Alexandria, 545 cm
P. Mich. XIII 659, over 517 cm

By contrast, papyrus rolls recovered from Petra are a lot longer (suggesting that one is right to expect regional variation). The longest is P. Petra I.2. Written in Gaza, it is 850 cm. One might surmise that rolls produced in Palestine were longer. But even this is only 8.5 m, considerably short of the length required for Luke, let alone Paul's letters according to Gamble's model. (Updated bibliography on the Petra papyri at www.bu.edu/acor/scroll-1.htm.) T.C. Skeat, 'The Length of the Standard Papyrus Roll and the Cost-advantage of the Codex', *Zeitschrift für Papyrologie und Epigraphik* 45 (1982), 169–76, reprinted in *Collected Biblical Writings*, 65–70; Skeat's other short writings on this topic, all useful, are included in this volume.

The question of the maximum possible length of a roll sounds very like the question 'How long is a piece of string?' There are in fact two questions to be distinguished. The first is with regard to the longest reasonable length of the roll itself. The second is as to the amount of text which could be contained within a roll, which is also affected by the size of writing used, the width of the columns, and the proportion of written area to margins.

The question of the adoption of the codex according to Gamble's theory thus comes down to the date of the first collection of Paul's letters. This is a matter to be discussed in due course. For the moment, it is sufficient to note that it is at a point before the oldest extant copies were made. It has to be noted also that Gamble's theory presupposes that the first Pauline collection had to be in a single volume, and therefore necessarily a codex. It might also have been a set of rolls. If we accept his premise, then the peripatetic nature of Paul's activity, the fact that the first Christian reference to codices comes in a letter attributed to him, and the practical requirements of a collected copy provide an attractive group of ideas explaining the causes of the phenomenon that early Christianity adopted the codex and that in time this adoption led to its popularisation.

Although the codex format was overwhelmingly predominant in Christianity, the roll never entirely went out of use. Parchment rolls of liturgies survive from throughout the Byzantine period. Examples include one from the twelfth century and a thirteenth-century copy of the Liturgy of St Basil. For the New Testament writings, however, the triumph of the codex was complete throughout the Christian world, so that almost all New Testament manuscripts, whatever language they are written in, are codices.

Gardthausen, *Palaeographie* (1979), 58–60 for these and other examples of liturgical rolls. The number of copies of the New Testament writings not written in codices is very small. The *Liste* (see 1.3.2) records that the following are on rolls: P12 (a late third-century fragment of Hebrews); P13 (third to fourth century, also Hebrews); P18 (similar date, Revelation); P22 (third century, Gospel of John). The manuscript catalogued as 0212, in fact a harmony rather than a New Testament manuscript (see 10.7), is also part of a roll. The category of roll can cover two different kinds of document: the original writing on the inside of the scroll, and secondary writing on the back (which would have been left blank by the original scribe). Such a secondary writing is known as an opisthograph.

These first pages have plunged into the middle of study, by addressing what has been one of the most important topics in recent study of the documents. It will be appreciated that it is not only of interest to the student of the book but also a matter which sheds light on a number of topics of general interest to every New Testament scholar and historian: the study of the character and distinctiveness of the oldest Christian writings vis-à-vis Jewish and pagan books; the emergence of a distinctive Christian identity in the second century; and the practical problems surrounding the formation of a four-Gospel and a Pauline collection of writings. It has thus been appropriate to set the scene with this study. Moreover, this approach demonstrates the importance of the principle that one should start with the documents and then study the text.

The importance of the format of a text is now well known. Perhaps the most famous study is Stanley Morison's *Politics and Script*. From the influence of Alexander's campaigns on Greek script to the design of new fonts in the railway age, Morison stimulates reflection on the ways in which document format and design represent both the political aims of their patrons and the creativity of the artist. This is as true of the New Testament documents as of any other writings. In order to appreciate just how important this is, with regard to the status and nature of the text contained in the document, and therefore of how it was understood and reproduced, the next section will provide a sightseeing tour of some representative manuscripts of the Christian tradition.

S. Morison, *Politics and Script. Aspects of Authority and Freedom in the Development of Graeco-Latin Script from the Sixth Century BC to the Twentieth Century AD*, The Lyell Lectures 1957, edited and completed by N. Barker, Oxford, 1972. An edition was made for Sandpiper Books in 2000.

1.1.2 *The development of the Christian book*

Rather than give an abstract account of the way in which the Christian book was to develop, I have chosen to illustrate it with images and descriptions of manuscripts.

It is normal for a book such as this to contain sections on ancient and medieval book production – how papyrus was made, what sorts of animal skins were available and how they were turned into parchment; the whole business of preparing the sheets, mixing the ink(s), ruling up the page, and so on. I do not intend to do this. For one thing, the handbooks of palaeography have already done it far better than I could do; for another, since we are dealing with books in various languages over fifteen centuries, I would have to provide many separate sections. Many of the statements, for example, which one finds in New Testament handbooks about parchment preparation are generalisations about alkaline preparations using lime which ignore the fact that other methods were also used (see R. Reed, *Ancient Skins, Parchments and Leathers* (Studies in Archaeological Science), London and New York, 1972, 96).

A number of books are well worth recommending for discussion and images. I select M.P. Brown (ed.), *In the Beginning. Bibles before the Year 1000*, Washington DC, 2006 (the catalogue of the exhibition of the same name which ran from 21 October 2006 to 7 January 2007, celebrating the centenary of the acquisition of the Freer manuscripts), and de Hamel, *The Book*. Another work with many images and a fresh approach is A. Berthier and A. Zali, with L. Héricher, A. Vernay-Nouri and G. Voitel, *Livres de Parole. Torah, Bible, Coran*, Paris, 2005 (published on the occasion of an exhibition of the same name in Paris, 2005–6).

What then, to begin at the beginning, did an early Christian codex look like? Apart from the brilliance of the technological innovation, it was very simple. The example chosen is a rare specimen of a complete page of a papyrus copy. It illustrates the codex in about the year 200.

1.1.2.1 An ancient papyrus manuscript

☞ (1)

The page consists of a single block of text in nineteen lines, neatly justified on the left margin and with straight lines. There is no running title, and the only clue to the place in the book is the page number in the top outer corner of the page (**NA**, i.e. 41). There are reasonably generous margins, and although the script is not elegant and is rather inconsistent in the way the letters are written, it impresses one as a businesslike piece of work. The format, 14.2 cm wide by 16.2 high, is typical for a Christian papyrus of a New Testament text. Looking at the text in more detail, there are no paragraphs and no spaces between words, or even between clauses, and the words are broken between lines without anything like our modern hyphen. What may be observed is punctuation by the placing of medial points (dots halfway up the height of the letters) dividing units of sense (there is an example in the middle of line 4). This punctuation is meagre by modern standards. The presence of a number of corrections indicates a high degree of care with the text, some shown by the scribe, some by later correctors. The correction visible on this page is in lines 4–6, and is a complicated one (see 6.1.1). Another distinctive feature is the use of *nomina sacra* ('sacred names'). This is the writing of various commonly occurring nouns in an abbreviated form with a line over them (usually a form with the last letter, thus indicating the case of the word). These include θεός, ἰησοῦς, κύριος, χριστός, πνεῦμα and ἄνθρωπος. The two examples on the page shown are both of the word ἄνθρωπος (lines 5, 16).

Overall, the book has an efficient and no-nonsense appearance. There is a strong attention to the text, and a workmanlike attitude to the copying, with a style of hand which is perfectly legible but rather quickly written, so that there tends to be a noticeable variation in the reproduction of some letters (note, for example, the differences between the alphas in line 4, both in the angling of the bow and the looping of the oblique stroke). The copying of a text involves the balancing of several factors, principally the speed of execution against the need for clarity (which requires consistency as well as a good basic technique). The extent to which the text is known to the scribe and the anticipated reader is also an important factor. Here, the use of *nomina sacra* indicates that familiarity with the general contents of the text is assumed.

This codex is interesting also because we have some information on its later history. It seems to have become part of the library of a Pachomian monastery, along with other texts and documents. It was subsequently preserved as an archive. It was discovered in the late 1940s.

For information on the introduction of running titles and page numbers into Greek New Testament manuscripts, see Parker, *Codex Bezae*, 13–22. For layout, see Turner, *Typology*, 13–32. For a discussion of the script of this manuscript and a plate, see Turner, *GMAW*, 108f. For word division in Greek manuscripts, see W. Crönert, *Memoria graeca Herculanensis cum titulorum Aegypti papyrorum codicum denique testimoniis comparatam proposuit*, Leipzig, 1903, 10–19. For punctuation, correction and other symbols, see Turner, *GMAW*, 9–16 and 17–19.

For a very recent study of certain features of early Christian manuscripts, notably the *nomina sacra*, the staurogram and the preference for the codex, see L. W. Hurtado, *The Earliest Christian Artifacts: Manuscripts and Christian Origins*, Grand Rapids and Cambridge, 2006.

The *nomina sacra* have been studied in considerable detail. Rather than repeat material from elsewhere, I shall provide a brief history of research. The starting point is Ludwig Traube's *Nomina Sacra: Versuch einer Geschichte der christlichen Kürzung* (Quellen und Untersuchungen zur lateinischen Philologie des Mittelalters 2; Munich, 1907). The data available to Traube was updated from the subsequent papyrus finds by A. H. R. E. Paap, *Nomina Sacra in the Greek Papyri of the First Five Centuries AD. The Sources and Some Deductions* (Papyrologica Lugduno-Batava 8), Leiden, 1959. A further survey is offered by J. O'Callaghan, *'Nomina Sacra' in papyris graecis saeculari III neotestamentariis* (Analecta Biblica 46), Rome, 1970. Now that most of the material has been collected, recent debate has focused on questions of origin and purpose: S. Brown, 'Concerning the Origin of the Nomina Sacra', *Studia Papyrologica* 9 (1970), 7–19; C. H. Roberts, *Manuscript, Society and Belief in Early Christian Egypt* (The Schweich Lectures of the British Academy, 1977), London, 1979.

A supplement on the *nomina sacra*: Scrivener, *Plain Introduction*, 1.251 notes of a twelfth-century copy of the Gospels (Gregory–Aland 64, now in the Schøyen Collection, see www.nb.no/baser/schoyen/4/4.1/412.html 230) that 'over each proper name of a person stands a little waved stroke', a phenomenon which he also noted in Gregory–Aland 679). This habit is fairly widespread and has been noted in a number of minuscules in the course of making transcriptions of John 18 for the International Greek New Testament Project (the stroke is not necessarily waved).

For the evidence linking this papyrus and others acquired by the Bodmer Foundation with papers relating to the monastery now in the Chester Beatty Library, Dublin, see J. M. Robinson, *The Pachomian Monastic Library at the Chester Beatty Library and the Bibliothèque Bodmer* (The Institute for Antiquity and Christianity Occasional Papers 19), Claremont, 1980; also his Introduction in W. Brashear, W.-P. Funk, J.M. Robinson and R. Smith (eds.), *The Chester Beatty Codex Ac. 1390. Mathematical School Exercises in Greek and John 10:7–13:38 in Subachmimic* (Chester Beatty Monographs 13), Leuven and Paris, 1990, 3–32.

1.1.2.2 A typical fourth-century codex

Two hundred and fifty years later the typical Greek codex looks very different. It is written on parchment, it contains at least two columns instead of one, and it has more features to help the reader. The selection of an image to illustrate this is rather difficult, because there are very few fourth-century manuscripts of which a complete page has survived. A typical fragment of a fourth-century codex looks like this:

☛ (2)

There is just enough left to establish that the text is written in two columns. Beyond these details, much is uncertain. Study is complicated by the fact that the manuscript is in more than one location (by no means a unique state of affairs), one folio being in Berlin and the other in Florence.

For the difficulties in reconstructing the text in such a document, see J.N. Birdsall, 'A Fresh Examination of the Fragments of the Gospel of St Luke in MS 0171 and an Attempted Reconstruction with Special Reference to the Recto', in Gryson, *Philologia Sacra*, 1.212–27, reprinted in Birdsall, *Collected Papers*, 125–38.

1.1.2.3 A fourth-century Bible

☛ (3)

I here present a double page of Codex Sinaiticus. The monumental character of this opening, whose eight narrow columns demand that the eye see a roll, in a very large format (the open page is a remarkable 76 cm across), the elegance of the rather large and well-formed letters, and the generous layout with plenty of empty parchment, which itself is of very fine quality, form a most striking contrast not only with P66 but in fact with most other Christian manuscripts of its day. But if one looks in a little more detail at the text, some things have not changed so much in a hundred and fifty years. There is a similar amount of punctuation, and the same abbreviations of the *nomina sacra* are present. Additional is the use of a horizontal stroke to indicate a nu at line ends. As in P66, there are frequent corrections, some made at the time of production and some later. There are no page numbers, but the quires are numbered (these numbers are called quire signatures), to help the binder to get them in the right order and there are running titles indicating the name of the book (since P66 probably contained only John, there was no need for a running title). One feature is new, the provision of a sophisticated division of the text into numbered paragraphs, with a second number which provides a cross-reference to parallel passages in other Gospels. These numbers (the Eusebian Apparatus, see 10.3.1) are written in red on the left of the column. With regard to script, the manuscript is not only one of the earliest examples of biblical majuscule (a form of script most commonly used in copying biblical manuscripts), it is also one of the best. Written with each letter within a notional square and with careful rules governing the thickness of strokes at different angles, consistency is highly regarded and achieved with such success that the three scribes responsible for the manuscript managed to match their hands very well. This is a very beautiful as well as a very easily read script.

The balance between cost and speed in the production is certainly tipped towards the former. The contrast with P66 is clear from the scaled outline of the respective sizes of the two volumes when opened (see below).

The largest New Testament papyrus to be found in the list in Turner's *Typology* is P74, the Bodmer manuscript of Acts and the Catholic epistles. It measures 19 × 31 cm. But P66 is more typical.

Codex Sinaiticus manuscript is a product of the Constantinian Church, asserting that its Scriptures are of the same status as the great texts of antiquity and that it can present them as they deserve. In one respect this

Figure 1. Comparative size of P66 and 01

manuscript is not as obviously convenient: the long lines in a single column of P66 make for quite easy reading, whereas the very short line lengths of Codex Sinaiticus, with a word broken across the line more often than not, requires more of the reader. It is also noticeable that, if convenience of carriage was a factor in early Christianity's adoption of the codex, it is no longer a concern here. Codex Sinaiticus was designed to stay in one place.

For bibliography, see 1.8.1.

1.1.2.4 A fourth-century Latin Gospel book
The fourth century is the first period from which manuscripts of translations of the New Testament survive. The example I have selected is among the very oldest manuscripts containing an Old Latin version of the text, Codex Vercellensis.

☞ (4)

The two-column layout is very similar to the majority of Greek manuscripts, while the brevity of line is reminiscent of Codex Sinaiticus. The general construction of the book is the same – gatherings are made out of four sheets of parchment, the text is written on a grid made out of a framework of points and lines, and there are running titles. There is very little punctuation, and abbreviation is restricted to *nomina sacra* (imitating the Greek pattern) and superline for final *n* or *m*. New sections are marked by a line intruding slightly into the left-hand margin (this phenomenon is called *ekthesis*). In addition to a general influence of Greek on Latin manuscript production, one wonders whether Latin copies set out to imitate their Greek originals.

   In one other respect the appearance of this manuscript is a guide to its cultural significance. It was used for the taking of oaths in the medieval period, and the countless placings of hands on its open pages have virtually destroyed much of it.

CLA IV.467 (see 1.4.2); McGurk, *Latin Gospel Books*, 108. There are three printed transcriptions of the manuscript, published in 1748 (see 6.1.3.1), 1894 and 1914. John is available in an electronic transcription at www.iohannes.com.

1.1.2.5 A sixth-century Syriac manuscript
By the sixth century the copying of manuscripts in a number of versions was well established.

☞ (5)

This manuscript in Syriac, containing the Peshitta version (see 1.5) has some similarities to Greek models: there is the two-column format, and the

Eusebian Apparatus (in a more sophisticated form, with the parallel paragraph numbers for the other Gospels written in the bottom margin), all of this being written in red ink. The numbers do not hang in the right margin, but are indented. Blank space at the end of a line is filled with little circles (column 1, line 12). Punctuation is by spaces, with four points in a lozenge formation indicating the end of a section. This manuscript anticipates Greek manuscripts in one feature: a lengthy colophon states that the copy was made in the Monastery of St John of Zagba (Mesopotamia) by one Rabbula, 'in the month of Shebat of the fourth indiction, at the full moon, in the year eighteen hundred and ninety-seven of Alexander' (i.e. AD 586).

G. Carlo Cecchelli, G. Furlani and M. Salmi (eds.), *Facsimile Edition of the Miniatures of the Syriac Manuscript (Plut. 1, 56) in the Medicaean-Laurentian Library*, Olten and Lausanne, 1959. Extracts from it are available at http://sor.cua.edu/Bible/RabbulaMs.html.

.

1.1.2.6 The Greek Gospels in the eighth century
A further step, this time down to the eighth century. Scribes have been copying the Greek New Testament for well over half a millennium, and there are time-honoured ways of doing it.
☞ (6)
The biblical majuscule script has developed and then been abandoned. The example given here again shows some similarities with what had gone before. We may see the *nomina sacra* (e.g. line 4). There is the use of *ekthesis*, and the Eusebian Apparatus is present (but in the more sophisticated form found in the Syriac manuscript just described). But there are also some changes. The script is more complicated and with a greater variation in letter size. There is more structure to the text, with two sizes of initial letter for a new section (the very large one near the bottom, and two smaller ones above); indications of church lections (a *tau* with an *epsilon* above it (= τέλος) at the end of line 14 and *alpha-rho* (= ἀρχή) in line 19), with the lection's title in the top margin. There is more punctuation, and of a number of kinds (points at different levels above the line, and a mark like a modern comma); there are breathings and some accents. These are all signs of a text that has been read and studied with great attention over a long period of time. There are also signs that the text is so well known that the scribe can rely on the reader to understand things which are not spelt out. On this page one may note the contraction of *omicron* and *upsilon* at the end of line 1, the abbreviation of καί at the end of line 9. In size this book is very typical of its era, with a page height of 23 cm and breadth of 16.5 cm.

1.1.2.7 The oldest dated minuscule Greek Gospel manuscript

Although majuscule scripts would continue to be used for another three hundred years, the ninth century saw a change in book production which in its way was as momentous as anything since the popularisation of the codex.

☛ (7)

This example is the oldest dated New Testament manuscript to be written in minuscule. The term minuscule, as contrasted with the preceding majuscule, is all one needs to know its character. It is a very compact hand, governed in its purest forms by strict rules concerning the forms of letters in sequence, so that a single letter has more than one form, depending on the letters coming before and after it (these rules ignore breaks between words). The result of this change in script was a change in format, so that this manuscript has a page size of 16.7 cm × 10.7. This is a similar height to the papyrus with which this survey began, but not so square a page. On the other hand, it has a quantity of pages – 344 – which would be unsuitable for a manuscript written on papyrus. Written in a single column, the manuscript has soft and rough breathings, accents, some punctuation, *ekthesis*, as well as the Eusebian Apparatus and chapter titles in the margin. The last of these and the Gospel titles are in majuscule, and the retention of majuscule for such material is a common feature of minuscule manuscripts. The information about the date, which also gives the scribe's name, is found in the colophon. It is dated 7 May 6343 (AD 835), and it was copied by Nicolaus. We happen to know about this scribe. Although the manuscript was not written there, it is a product of the famous Studite Monastery in Constantinople, where the minuscule hand was developed in the course of the ninth century. We even have a biography of Nicolaus, which describes him as being as swift in the hands as Asahel was in the feet (see 2 Sam. 2.18).

Textual elements on the page which are not part of the text being copied (running titles, section numbers, etc.) are sometimes described as 'paratextual elements' or 'paratext'. The German 'Auszeichnungsschrift' is a word describing the writing of parts of the text (for example, the first line, or initial letters) as well as paratext in a different script from the usual script in which the majority of the text is written. This use of a different script is intended to define the hierarchy of the text.

A. Diller, 'A Companion to the Uspenski Gospels', *Byzantinische Zeitschrift* 49 (1956), 332–5; T.W. Allen, 'The Origin of the Greek Minuscule Hand', *Journal of Hellenic Studies* 40 (1920), 1–12; E.E. Granstrem, 'Zur byzantinischen Minuskel', in Harlfinger, *Griechische Kodikologie*, 76–119. Nicolaus' life is available in Migne, *PG* 105, 863–926. The mid-ninth-century life of Theodore the Studite, Abbot from 799, records that he followed the advice of Paul (2 Thess. 3.8) ἐργάζεσθαι καὶ αὐτὸς ἤθελε πάντοτε τὰς χεῖρας ταῖς δέλτοις κινῶν, καὶ τὸν ἴδιον κόπον τοῖς ἐργοχείροις συνεισφέρων τῶν μαθητῶν. Ἐξ ὧν καί τινα τῶν βιβλίων ἔτι μένουσι παρ' ἡμῖν τῆς αὐτοχείρου γραφῆς κάλλιστα ὄντα πονήματα (*PG* 99, 152).

1.1.2.8 A Carolingian Latin codex
A revolution in Latin scripts also occurred in the ninth century, with the
development of Carolingian minuscule. This was one part of a cultural
renaissance which led to several revisions of the Bible. Within the very
distinctive type of hand known as Carolingian minuscule, many subtle
regional customs have been identified. The example shown here is not a
normal Carolingian manuscript, but an example of the combination of
scholarship and fine craftsmanship which typifies the best productions of
the age.

☛ (8)
Produced for Theodulph, Bishop of Orleans before 798, this is a codex
that combines artistic beauty – splendour, indeed – with scholarly purposes. For Theodulph, like the better known Alcuin, sought to restore the
text of the Bible. This carefully produced copy of the entire Vulgate Bible
contains many variants, noted in the margin. For example, at F196,
column 2, line 28, the text reads *salis*; the marginal note is *at solis at salutis*.
Sometimes dots are placed over letters that should be omitted. Occasionally, several lines of text have been erased and rewritten. The text is
laid out in the sense divisions (*per cola et commata*) of the Vulgate Bible.

The manuscript is the work of one scribe and contains both purple and
plain leaves. The purple is sometimes almost violet, sometimes a deep
plum. The first three leaves are purple, and the writing is in gold: uncial,
of wonderful precision and beauty, very small. The leaves containing
the Psalms are purple, the writing silver with some gold. The pages
of prefatory matter to the Gospels and the Gospels themselves are
also purple, the writing silver or gold according to the method found in
the Psalms. The final leaves are again purple. As for the undyed leaves, the
running titles and the incipits of books are in gold. Red is used in these
leaves in the same way as gold in the purple pages. The parchment is fine
and white, often with very little difference in colour between the hair and
flesh sides.

One goes away wondering at the combination of craftsmanship and
scholarly care, of imagination and perseverance, and rejoicing at the
beauty of these pages of golden uncial. Yet among the other half-dozen
copies of Theodulph's recension there is another manuscript (in the
Cathedral Treasury at le Puy) which is regarded as even more splendid.

B. Fischer, 'Bibeltext und Bibelreform unter Karl dem Großen', in W. Braunfels (ed.), *Karl der Große,
Lebenswerk und Nachleben*, Band II: *Das geistige Leben*, ed. B. Bischoff, Düsseldorf, 1965, 156–216,
reprinted in *Lateinische Bibelhandschriften im frühen Mittelalter* (GLB II), 1985, 101–202, 135ff.;
CLA v.576 (see 1.4.2); Gibson, *Bible in the Latin West*, 32.

1.1.2.9 The development of Greek minuscule

The subsequent evolution of Greek minuscule is marked by various developments, most notably the introduction of various majuscule letter forms, so that pure minuscule went out of use. In subsequent centuries, one may observe the tendency to introduce what are known as ligatures, in which groups of letters are written together or even represented by a symbol.

☛ (9)

The example taken (Gregory–Aland number 480) is by no means as full of abbreviations as some, but illustrates the work of an expert scribe of the period. Both ligatures and abbreviations are present. The manuscript was written in 1366 in Constantinople.

For bibliography on the monastery scriptorium and the scribe (Ioasaph, a renowned copyist), see Turyn, *Great Britain*, 131–4 and plates 89–90.

Another important development in the Byzantine era was the introduction of paper, which in time was to prove a cheaper writing material than parchment. The oldest Greek New Testament manuscript written on paper dates to the ninth century (0290, one of the New Finds of 1975 at the Monastery of St Catherine, Mount Sinai), but it was only from the twelfth century that it began to be used at all frequently. According to the Alands, there are about 1,300 paper manuscripts of the New Testament in Greek (2 majuscules, 698 minuscules and 587 lectionaries). Paper is also found mixed with parchment leaves, some manuscripts having a parchment outer sheet of each gathering, the inner ones being paper. Sometimes a parchment manuscript of which some leaves came to be lost was supplemented, paper being used for the replacement leaves.

J. Irigoin, 'Les premiers manuscrits grecs écrits sur papier et la problème du bombycin', *Scriptorium* 4 (1950), 194–204; 'Papiers orientaux et papiers occidentaux', *Paléographie grecque et byzantine*, 45–54; Aland and Aland, *The Text of the New Testament*, 77.

The degree of abbreviation in manuscripts produced in the fifteenth and sixteenth centuries had a considerable effect on the printing of books in Greek. The first printed Bible was in Latin, and one reason why it took some time for Greek printing to catch up may be the fact that the Greek scripts which people knew contained very many different shapes – individual letters, groups of two or more letters, and symbols indicating a cluster of letters. It was thus not until the second decade of the sixteenth century, two generations after Gutenberg, that the first editions of the New Testament in Greek were printed.

☛ (10)

1.1.2.10 The first published Greek New Testament

The use of printing was a more important change than the adoption of
paper, a more important change than the introduction of minuscule,
more important than the move from papyrus to parchment. It was
arguably even more significant than the adoption of the codex, since it
changed more radically the process for making documents. Whereas a
manuscript is made by a copyist writing the words out onto the page in
ink, this part of the process was mechanised. The human act of putting
the letters together in sequence was done by the compositor setting the
lead font. Of course, the human element was not taken out, and the result
was that a mistake of any kind was made in as many documents as were
printed rather than in a single one. However, the advantages of printing
were so obvious that the subsequent period saw the transference of
thousands of texts from handwritten to printed document. The copying
of manuscripts did not die out, and in fact strict laws governing the use of
the printing press in Greek lands under Ottoman rule meant that
manuscripts continued to be made down to the nineteenth century.
Indeed, manuscripts are still made by professional and amateur scribes.
But these copies are textually of no interest to the New Testament
scholar, since they are made either from printed editions or from known
manuscripts.

See 6.1.1 for discussion and plates of some sixteenth-century editions.

This series of examples has offered a brief introduction to the world of the
Christian book, especially of the Greek book. Even in so short a survey, it
has been difficult to avoid assuming information which has not yet been
provided. So at this point I turn to the most basic issues, by listing and
describing the resources available for the study of the documents. In
preparation, the next section will offer a brief introduction to the discipline of palaeography.

1.2 AN INTRODUCTION TO PALAEOGRAPHY

The word 'palaeography' is quite recent, Murray's *New English Dictionary*
citing no occurrence either of it or of any cognate noun or adjective
before the beginning of the nineteenth century. The word in Latin is only
a century older, having been coined by the father of the discipline in its
application to Greek writing, the French scholar Bernard de Montfaucon
(1655–1741) in his *Palaeographia Graeca sive de ortu et progressu litterarum
graecarum*, published in 1708. Montfaucon was a Maurist at the Abbey of

St-Germain-des-Prés in Paris, and his work achieved for the study of Greek manuscripts what the older Jean Mabillon (1632–1707) of the same abbey had done for Latin in *De Re Diplomatica* (1681). These two texts provided a method for studying manuscripts, which remains of lasting value even where their interpretation of the evidence has been revised. A piece of advice from Mabillon helps towards a definition of palaeography: 'non ex sola scriptura, neque ex uno characterismo sed ex omnibus simul ... pronuntiandum': 'a judgement should not be made only on the basis of script, nor of any one characteristic, but from all together'. Everything,

> the material, its nature and preparation
> the pricking and ruling to take the writing
> the make-up of the quires, whether hair or flesh is on the outside and the matching of hair and flesh inside
> the *mise-en-page* (that is, the layout of columns and other writing in proportion to the blank material)
> the general character of the hand, followed by a detailed study of the individual letter forms

contributes to the study, comparison and dating of manuscripts. There are also other historical resources for localising (that is, determining whereabouts it was copied) and dating a manuscript, such as notes in the book and ancient library catalogues.

The detailed study of a hand requires analysis in several different ways. What it does *not* consist of is the observation of the shape of certain letters and an immediate conclusion that there is an affinity with other hands producing the same shapes. The way in which the letters are formed has to be observed. A particular letter may look similar in two manuscripts, but a more detailed examination will show that the sequence of strokes which make up the letter differs. This is the study of the *ductus*. The angle of writing should also be studied, that is, the consequence of the pen's being cut in a certain way and then held in a certain way.

The primary goal of palaeography is always a very simple one, although it has succeeded so well that it is now easily overlooked. It is reading a document accurately, that is, being able to identify the letter forms and relate them to modern equivalents and to the sounds they represent. Another goal is the understanding of method in the dating and local-isation of a manuscript. The starting point in this process is manuscripts which have a fixed date. Even better are dated manuscripts whose place of copying is known. These are fixed points between which other manuscripts lacking such details may be placed. After that the date of composition of a work provides a point after which every manuscript of that work must have been copied. The purpose at this stage is not to make a fixed chronology, but to observe the differences between manuscripts and to place the hands and other production methods in a sequence. Other evidence is the presence of corrections (particularly ones of some length) or replacement leaves in a manuscript and the use of more than one script by a copyist. In the end, one has available an overall sequence of the development of hands, and their relationship to one another. The degree to which a precise date can then be given to a particular manuscript will vary enormously. One has in the first place to recognise that an individual scribe might have had a working life of half a century, writing in the same style throughout. That gives a dating of twenty-five years before or after, so that a dating to 200 means any time between 175 and 225. Sometimes special factors make a more precise dating possible. But generally, one must allow for a fifty-year period.

Here one must comment upon a tendency to move the dates of New Testament manuscripts (especially Greek ones) earlier. Some writers claim that the standard datings are the result of religious scepticism on the part of palaeographers and try to argue for earlier dates for certain manuscripts. As a rule, the views of palaeographers and papyrologists who have studied hundreds or even thousands of manuscripts (the dates of the vast majority of which cannot be of any religious significance) are to be taken more seriously than claims prompted by apologetic.

What has been written here applies principally to Greek and Latin manuscripts. The palaeography of manuscripts in other languages in which the New Testament was transmitted in ancient times has generally been less well studied. It is understandable that western European scholars, who were taught Greek and Latin from their earliest years and had the materials (especially for Latin research) all around them, should have studied the manuscripts of writers from whom so much of their culture was derived. Scholars in eastern lands did not have a chance of matching their resources, and it remains true that the conditions for manuscript study are not easy in all areas where there is a rich heritage of Christian manuscripts. Moreover, the development of Greek and Latin hands is more straightforward to study, since many different types are easily recognisable. That is not always true of manuscripts of texts in other languages. But the same principles apply to the study of all manuscripts.

In recent decades it has become common to make the separate discipline of codicology out of the study of the material and make-up of the pages, restricting palaeography to the study of the script. Whether this is a necessary or an advisable distinction is uncertain. Mabillon's dictum indicates that it may be wiser to keep a single term for all. Even more recently the history of the book has emerged as an independent area of research, baldly defined by the homepage of the journal *Book History* as 'the history of the creation, dissemination, and reception of script and print', and by the Penn State Center for the History of the Book in more detail:

book culture [is] the apparatus that exists in any advanced society for the production and dissemination of the written or printed word. Historians of the book, often using archival sources, investigate such topics as the profession of authorship, the history of printing and publishing, the growth of libraries, the development of book distribution, and the history of literacy. They study books as aesthetic objects, technological products, and cultural signifiers.

That this, applied to the study of manuscripts, is a different field of study from palaeography seems evident. That it is different from the study of the text is also evident. The history of the book as applied to the manuscripts and printed books with which I am dealing will involve certainly the topics which have been covered in this chapter, as well as many matters to be studied in what follows. Palaeography is widely conceived to be the process of dating and localising manuscripts. Their subsequent history is then viewed as a matter for the historian of the book. However, it will be observed that the palaeographer is extremely interested in the further history of the manuscripts, because of the evidence available from it for the study of yet more manuscripts, with regard to influence and development. The work of the best palaeographers (and for examples I take Nigel Wilson for Byzantine manuscripts and Julian Brown for insular manuscripts) includes codicology and includes book history as well as a knowledge of the texts. There is not yet a discipline of book history within the world of New Testament manuscript studies.

There is one piece of terminology common in other branches of manuscript study that is rarely found apropos the New Testament. This is the use of the word 'bibliography' to describe all kinds of study of the documents. This general term has various subdivisions: *enumerative* bibliography is the listing of the relevant materials; *analytical* bibliography is the examination of the materials, leading to *descriptive* bibliography (which speaks for itself) and *historical* bibliography, in which the development of the documents is studied. The whole leads then to *textual* bibliography which, while bearing all the foregoing in mind, is the same as textual criticism. 'Bibliography' thus covers the study of the text as well as the study of the document and is a term with a great deal to commend it.

If the categories of bibliography are applied by the reader in the next chapter, this will become evident.

For a description of palaeography, see J. Brown, 'Latin Palaeography since Traube', *Transactions of the Cambridge Bibliographical Society* 3 (1963), 361–81; reprinted in A. Gruys and J. P. Gumbert (eds.) *Codicologia*, vol. I, Leiden, 1976, 58–74; reprinted again in J. Bately, M. P. Brown and J. Roberts (eds.), *A Palaeographer's View. The Selected Writings of Julian Brown*, London, 1993, 17–37; and the definition 'What Is Palaeography?' in 'Aspects of Palaeography', in *A Palaeographer's View*, 47–86, pp. 47–51. For a more restricted view, D.C. Parker, 'The Magdalen Papyrus of Matthew. Was Matthew Written before 50 CE?', *The Expository Times* 107 (1995), 40–3. The two definitions of book history are taken from http://muse.jhu.edu/journals/book_history/ and www.pabook.libraries.psu.edu/histofbook/index.html. For an example of Wilson's work, see N.G. Wilson, *Scholars of Byzantium*, rev. edn, London, 1996, e.g. chapter 10, 'Greek in Italy and Sicily' (pp. 209–17). For definitions of bibliography, see D.C. Greetham, *Textual Scholarship. An Introduction*, New York and London, 1994 [1992], 5ff. A rare example of a New Testament scholar who used the term regularly is J.N. Birdsall (whose first degree was in English literature).

In addition to the method of dating of hands described above, there are a number of other possible guides to dating a manuscript. These include

(1) artistic features, such as patterned bands above the beginning of a text, coronae at the end, portraits of evangelists and other miniatures
(2) patterns of pricking and ruling and other aspects of parchment preparation
(3) method of book construction and the character of the binding

Unfortunately, like most other New Testament textual scholars, I have not given much time to the contribution of art history to the understanding of groupings of Greek New Testament manuscripts. It is highly probable that the combination of this area of study with the comparison of texts would clarify many difficulties. Unfortunately, we still tend to strip the text out of manuscripts and neglect their real-life setting. R.S. Nelson, *The Iconography of Preface and Miniature in the Byzantine Gospel Book*, New York, 1980, is a good place to start to remedy this defect. An example of what can be done is E.C. Colwell and H.R. Willoughby, *The Four Gospels of Karahissar*, 2 vols. (vol. I, *History and Text*, by Colwell and vol. II, *The Cycle of Text Illustrations*, by Willoughby), Chicago, 1936. Among the many writings of K. Weitzmann, one may mention *Late Antique and Early Christian Book Illumination*, New York, 1977 and 'The Narrative and Liturgical Gospel Illustrations', chapter 9 of Parvis and Wikgren, *New Testament Manuscript Studies*, 151–74.

There is no shortage of research and interest when we come to western illuminated manuscripts. A work which leads into a wide range of topics and bibliography is J.J.G. Alexander, *Medieval Illuminators and their Methods of Work*, New Haven and London, 1992. Many large libraries have pamphlets and booklets on their most striking manuscripts.

1.3 GREEK MANUSCRIPTS

1.3.1 Classifying Greek New Testament manuscripts

Anyone who has ever tried to arrange books on a shelf will know how difficult it rapidly becomes, since no system will cover every title, whether it be by author (multiple authors? use of two *noms de plumes* by the same writer?), title (which part do you include? what about series?), subject (how do you decide?) or date of publication (what if none is given?). The classification of Greek New Testament manuscripts has been going on for several centuries, and the involvement of many scholars over this period has led, inevitably, to inconsistency and occasional confusion. The system now in place is a classification into four categories. These are

(1) Documents written on papyrus. These are called *papyri*.
(2) Documents written in majuscule script. All but two of such documents are written on parchment (two are on paper; for one of them, see 1.1.2.9). These are called *majuscules*.
(3) Documents written on parchment and/or paper in minuscule script. These are called *minuscules*.
(4) Documents in which the text is found in the sequence of the readings of the Church's year. These are called *lectionaries*. Most of the documents in the other three categories are called, in contrast, *continuous-text* manuscripts.

There are therefore three criteria of classification: one is by writing material (papyrus as opposed to parchment and paper), two are by script (majuscule or minuscule), and one is by content (lectionary as opposed to continuous-text). A little more may be said about each. Papyri include the oldest extant copies and comprise all but a couple of the copies made before the fourth century. The most recent are of the sixth to seventh century. All documents in this category are written on papyrus. They are not all continuous-text manuscripts. When a papyrus is so fragmentary that only a part of a single folio survives, it is not always possible to be certain whether it was originally a continuous-text copy or not. Some seem to have been lectionaries, others to have contained selected passages in the order of the text.

The majuscule manuscripts are all in a form of script which in appearance is similar to what we know as capital letters. The majority of majuscule manuscripts date from the fourth to the ninth centuries.

Although minuscule scripts were introduced in the ninth century (see 1.1.2.7), it took several centuries for them to become entirely dominant, so that there are examples of majuscule as late as the eleventh.

Both majuscule and minuscule groups contain commentary manuscripts, in which the biblical text is accompanied by a commentary. This may be in one of a number of formats, with the biblical text standing either as a block on each page surrounded by commentary text, or as a short block followed by the commentary on the passage.

Lectionary manuscripts may be written in either majuscule or minuscule, the transition being at the same period as with the continuous-text manuscripts. All the manuscripts in this class are written on parchment and/or paper.

Where there are as many manuscripts as there are of the New Testament, it is particularly important to have a clear and accepted system of indicating each one. Unfortunately, the history of research has led to a number of anomalies and false starts. A few milestones explain the situation that we have today.

The first system to be used in the first critical apparatus, which was in Robert Stephanus' edition of 1550, consisted of a Greek numeral indicating each of the sixteen witnesses used. ☛ (11) A key provided a simple way for the reader to recognise which manuscript was meant (see also 6.1.2).

In 1707 the great edition of John Mill used a rather less convenient system, in which a manuscript was often indicated with an abbreviation indicating the library in which it was housed. ☛ (12) This came to be applied permanently to some especially well-known manuscripts, which are called either after their library, such as Codex Vaticanus, or in some other way, such as its alleged origin (Codex Alexandrinus), a place with which it is closely associated (Codex Sinaiticus), or a figure connected with it (Codex Bezae).

A new method was introduced by the German scholar J.J. Wettstein in his 1751–2 edition, in which majuscule manuscripts were indicated with a roman capital letter, and minuscules by an arabic number. ☛ (13) Each sequence began again with each of the main sections of the New Testament, the manuscripts which contained them all remaining constant throughout, while those with two or more parts also kept the same number.

This system worked for the minuscules, since new discoveries could be added to the sequence indefinitely. It ceased to work for the majuscules as soon as the letter Z had been reached. Even with the use of a letter for more than one manuscript, only thirty-four were listed by this system

(J and W were not used because they are not in the Latin alphabet, although W was pressed into service in the early twentieth century for a new and important manuscript). The sequence was then extended by the use of upper-case Greek letters not found in the Latin alphabet, such as gamma and delta. This added another ten. Then in the middle of the nineteenth century Tischendorf began to use some letters of the Hebrew alphabet. It was C.R. Gregory who recognised that, with an increasing flow of new discoveries, a new system was needed. His *Die griechischen Handschriften des Neuen Testamentes* (Leipzig, 1908) gave every majuscule manuscript an arabic numeral preceded by a zero (perhaps an upper-case O standing for 'oncial', the French for uncial?), which like the numeration of minuscules can be extended indefinitely. He also abolished the use of a separate numbering system for minuscules of each part of the New Testament, replacing it with a single sequence, retaining Tischendorf's first number for manuscripts containing more than one part. This was wholly satisfactory. But traces of the older systems were retained for majuscule manuscripts, namely some of the letters. The Hebrew letter ℵ is frequently used for Codex Sinaiticus, which is numbered 01. Greek letters are also sometimes used for manuscripts 036–045, while some roman letters are used twice. D is used for both 05, a manuscript containing the Gospels and Acts, and for 06, which contains Paul's letters. As a result it is fairly common to find the better-known Codex Bezae (05) cited by commentators and writers on the Pauline corpus, when they should be referring to Codex Claromontanus (06).

This confusion of names, letters and numbers has gone on for too long, and although names are justifiable when discussing important manuscripts, the letters are an anachronistic confusion. In recent years some people have produced a hybrid reference, referring to manuscripts as B03 or D05. This runs the risk of suggesting that manuscripts with a letter are more important whereas it is often no more than an indication of the point in the development of research at which it was listed. This work will use only a full name or a number, referring to a letter only occasionally to provide orientation.

In spite of the advantages of the number, it looks as though the letter will continue to be used in hand editions for the reason that a single letter is more compact than a two- or three-digit number, thus making typesetting easier and compressing the apparatus.

The classification of papyri is of more recent date, and is correspondingly simpler. Each is indicated by P, either in black letter (𝔓) or (as is increasingly common today) in plain roman upper-case. Apart from some problems of allocation, this part of the system has worked well. The same is true of lectionaries, which are indicated by the letter l, traditionally given as a lower-case italic letter, but more recently and more conveniently shown in upright upper-case.

We thus have a system by which the one-hundred-and-eighth entry in each section would be as follows:

Papyrus:	P108 (or 𝔓108)
Majuscule:	0108
Minuscule:	0108
Lectionary:	L108 (or *l*108)

A hundred years ago, a new system was developed by von Soden. This method is based not on the Tischendorfian/Gregorian concept of manuscript type, but on the contents and textual grouping of each manuscript. The result is not simple, and has not been adopted by other scholars, except that some of his symbols for groups of Byzantine manuscripts are in common use. In spite of being overcomplicated, it did have a number of benefits, for example in indicating whether a manuscript contains a commentary, and even which commentary it is.

The result of the foregoing is that there are three systems – Tischendorf's, von Soden's and Gregory's. The last is used by all scholars today, usually in the form in which it is found in the *Liste* (which I am about to describe), that is, without the presence of any Hebrew letter symbols for manuscripts, except for the use of ℵ to indicate Codex Sinaiticus. In order to convert the numbers used by older editions and reference works, it is necessary to use one of the following concordances: B. Kraft, *Die Zeichen für die wichtigeren Handschriften des griechischen Neuen Testaments*, 3rd edn, Freiburg im Breisgau, 1955 (1st edn, 1926), contains concordances permitting the conversion of von Soden's to the Tischendorf and Gregory numbers, and Tischendorf to von Soden and Gregory numbers; F. Krüger, *Schlüssel zu von Sodens 'Die Schriften des Neuen Testaments in ihrer ältesten Gereichbaren Textgestalt hergestellt'*, Göttingen 1902–1913: Gegenüberstellung der in von Sodens Apparat vorkommenden Sigla und der entsprechenden in Gregory's Liste, Göttingen, 1927, deals with the manuscripts cited in von Soden's apparatus, providing a list of lacunae, some comments on specific sigla, and four conversion tables to Gregory numbers by part of the New Testament (Matthew and Mark, Luke and John, Praxapostolos and Apocalypse). There are also tables at the back of the *Liste*: the first converts Tischendorf numbers to Gregory, the second von Soden to Gregory and the third Gregory to von Soden. An account of the history of the Gregory system is given by Elliott, *Bibliography*, 5–9.

H.C. Hoskier's numberings of the manuscripts of Revelation partially depart from other systems; tables reconciling them are provided by Elliott, 'Manuscripts Collated by H.C. Hoskier'.

1.3.2 The Liste

The document usually called the *Liste* (German for 'catalogue') is the most basic source of information about the Greek manuscripts. Its full title is *Kurzgefasste Liste der griechischen Handschriften des Neuen*

Testaments ('Summary Catalogue of Greek Manuscripts of the New Testament'). It was first published in 1963 and brought together a long series of updates to Gregory's catalogue. A second edition of 1994 is now supplemented by regular updates on the editors' website.

K. Aland, *Kurzgefasste Liste der griechischen Handschriften des Neuen Testaments* (ANTF 1), Berlin, 1963; K. Aland with M. Welte, B. Köster and K. Junack, *Kurzgefasste Liste der griechischen Handschriften des Neuen Testaments* (ANTF 1), 2nd edn, Berlin, 1994; updates are given at www.uni-muenster.de/NTTextforschung/ (previously they were provided in the Münster *Bericht* series). For details on the updates to Gregory, see Elliott, *Bibliography*, 5–9.

The *Liste* provides a brief summary of information for each manuscript which gives it a unique profile, and is the starting point for various kinds of research. The extent of information varies somewhat, but the following random example provides the basic pattern:

973   e   XII   Pg   306   1   24   19 × 13   Athos, Dochiariu, 51

This expands to provide the following information. The manuscript has the Gregory–Aland number 973; it contains the Gospels; it was written in the twelfth century; the material on which it is written is parchment; there are 306 leaves (folios), written in one column with twenty-four lines to the page. The size of the codex is 19 cm high by 13 cm wide, and it is to be found on Mount Athos, in the library of the Dochiariu monastery, in which it is numbered 51. Where a manuscript is lacunose (that is, where parts are missing), a dagger is placed after the statement of the contents. There is cross-referencing between entries which are in some way physically linked. This includes palimpsests where both the original and subsequent texts are of the Greek New Testament; renumberings, where, for example, a manuscript was wrongly classified as a lectionary and has now been recognised to be a continuous-text copy; and occasions where a manuscript had been broken up and had received two numbers before the two parts were identified as belonging to one copy. In these two last instances, square brackets are placed around the number no longer in use.

The library names are usually abbreviated but are fairly obvious to decipher. 'Bibl.' means Bibliothèque, Bibliotheca, or something similar depending on the language; 'Libr.' means library; anything like 'Nat. Bibl.' means National Library. In any case, all library names are given in full in the 'Bibliotheksverzeichnis' (see below). There are various abbreviations for class marks, which are often a number within a collection of manuscripts in the library: 'Gr.' means Greek; 'Suppl.' means supplementary, 'Add.' means additional.

The information is placed in other forms at the end of the book. In addition to the concordances with the Tischendorf and von Soden numbering systems, there is a list of all the manuscripts by library, collection and classmark ('Bibliotheksverzeichnis', 'Library index', pp. 429–507). The list proceeds by alphabetical order of place, with libraries placed in alphabetical order within the place and the class-mark in its appropriate place. Thus 973 is found under Athos, Dochiariu, after 49. There is also a summary list by country of all places where there is a manuscript to be found ('Aufbewahrungsorte', 'Storage Locations', pp. 431–4).

There are one or two things to bear in mind: the Vatican Library is found under V (not R for Rome as in the first edition), and the Escorial under E and not M for Madrid. German names are used (the only possible puzzles for the English-speaker are Venedig (Venice), Wien (Vienna) and Zypern (Cyprus). The collections on Mediterranean islands are listed under various heads: Sicilian libraries are found under the town name in the Bibliotheksverzeichnis and under Italy in the Aufbewahrungsorte. By the same principle, the only collection in Malta (Msida) is found under Msida in the Bibliotheksverzeichnis and under Malta in the Aufbewahrungsorte. Collections on Greek islands are given under the island in the Bibliotheksverzeichnis and under Greece in the Aufbewahrungsorte. Collections in Cyprus are found under Cyprus in both lists.

Square brackets around an entry in the Aufbewahrungsorte indicate that the collection either no longer exists or no longer contains any Greek New Testament manuscripts.

It is also worth remembering that the Gregory–Aland number is a convenient system among New Testament scholars for referring to the manuscripts that interest them. It is not likely to mean anything outside their guild, and any correspondence with a library should always use a manuscript's current 'real number', that is its library class-mark.

The *Liste* provides full information on the contents of papyri, but not of majuscules or minuscules. This information may be found (for all manuscripts cited in it, which includes all majuscules) in Appendix 1 of the Nestle–Aland[27], 'Codices Graeci et Latini'.

There are some numbers with special conditions attached to them. 0152 is a portal to a different category altogether: talismans. These are pieces of material with a few words (in these examples, of the New Testament) on them intended to protect the wearer from evil. 0153 is similarly a heading for the category of ostraca, where a piece of New Testament text is written on pottery. These types were catalogued by von Dobschütz in his update to Gregory's list, using black letter T and O, but have not been maintained. The talismans are listed as far as τ^9, the ostraca as far as $\mathfrak{O}^{25}$.

It is possible to use the *Liste* to collect different kinds of information. For example, one could find all those written in the thirteenth century, or with a page height in excess of 35 cm, or containing the Gospels and Revelation. Unfortunately, one still has to do so by hand, but the time is not far distant when a web-based *Liste* will allow quicker and more refined searches.

What criteria does a manuscript have to fulfil in order to be included?

(1) In the first place it should be written in the Koine Greek of the first century. A translation into a later form of Greek does not count. So 2449, a seventeenth-century copy of Revelation (Athens, National Historical Museum 71, fols. 1–29) and 2450, containing text and a commentary on a few passages of Matthew and written in the following century (Athens, National Historical Museum 112) have both been bracketed out because they are in Modern Greek (the language as spoken from 1453 onwards).

(2) It should consist of more than excerpts. 2090, which had been listed as a Pauline manuscript, in fact consists of excerpts with commentary from six chapters of the letters. Again, it has been bracketed out. There are exceptions, though. P99 is a Graeco-Latin glossary of Paul's letters, but has been included, perhaps because of its date and significance.

(3) In theory at least, it should be a copy of a manuscript and not of a printed edition. A note is supplied where a manuscript has turned out to be in this category (e.g. 296 has the note 'aus Druck abgeschrieben?' ('copied from a printed edition?'); 1802 has the note 'Einfluß eines Drucks?' ('Influenced by a printed edition?'). Of course such a manuscript has no textual value, since it provides no independent evidence (this will be the case with regard to all texts, unless the printed edition from which such a manuscript is copied (a) is lost and (b) made use of a manuscript or manuscripts which have also been lost).

(4) A commentary manuscript must not be a copy of a commentary by, for example, John Chrysostom or Origen – to include all commentaries by all commentators would add many thousands of manuscripts. Where a Chrysostom manuscript has crept in and the fact observed, the entry is bracketed and a note added (e.g. 882, 'Chrysostomos-Homilien zu J' ('Chrysostom's Homilies on John'). At least in theory, those manuscripts are included which contain a commentary which is a *catena* of earlier exegetical comments. In fact the boundaries are blurred, since commentators always tend to draw, sometimes heavily, on the views of their predecessors. Thus manuscripts containing parts of Cyril of Alexandria's Commentary on John are included. The study of such manuscripts is discussed separately (1.3.12).

Once these parameters have been established, there remains plenty of room for uncertainty. It has sometimes been pointed out that some of the papyri may not really belong in the *Liste* because they were never complete texts. As a general rule, it is worth stating that those manuscripts which should be included are those which may be stemmatologically compared to other manuscripts which are undoubtedly to be included or, in the case of fragmentary documents, could credibly be so compared were they more extensive (for stemmatological comparison see 5.1.2 and 5.1.5). Copies which do not comply with these criteria are documents which contain parts of the New Testament texts, but are not strictly speaking *copies of* the New Testament. These include service books with the Lord's Prayer or canticles, patristic texts containing citations, Gospel harmonies, talismans, and so on. But the decision whether or not to include a copy must rest finally on an assessment of the document itself and not on rigid criteria. For example, there are both papyrus and parchment manuscripts of John's Gospel with *hermeneiai* (sentences used in divination). These might seem to be an example of a category which should be excluded on the grounds that they were not intended to be used as reading copies of the Gospel. I was surprised when I studied the matter to find that they do contain textually valuable data and yield useful results when they are compared with other manuscripts.

For general discussions of papyri which should or should not be included, and how not to overlook textually significant material that has been excluded, see 3.4.1. For the *Liste* in this regard, see S.E. Porter, 'Textual Criticism in the Light of Diverse Textual Evidence for the Greek New Testament: an Expanded Proposal', in Kraus and Nicklas, *New Testament Manuscripts*, 305–37.

The case for including these witnesses is strong. Similarly, we should not exclude a document on the grounds that it is a child's writing exercise. If the child had made an accurate copy of a page of an ancient manuscript, how happy we should be!

There is a further matter to be mentioned, and it again concerns content. Not all the manuscripts included in the *Liste* consist only of some or all of the New Testament texts. There are examples in every category. Some copies of the New Testament also contain the Septuagint (see 1.8). P72 contains not only 1 and 2 Peter and Jude, but also various other texts (see 9.1), and its compilation and character have been the subject of a number of detailed discussions. Among the majuscules, 01 also contains the *Letter of Barnabas* and the *Shepherd of Hermas*. Commentary manuscripts evidently include non-biblical text. A menologion may contain many different texts (see 1.3.13). Other copies may include added texts (see 7.3 for examples), material written on blank pages, and of course extensive aids for users such as Eusebius' Letter to Carpianus

(10.3.1) or the Euthalian Apparatus (8.7). The *Liste* will not provide such evidence, and it is up to the user to be alert and not be too dependent on this single source in studying a manuscript.

The compilers of the *Liste* have more to think about than the decision whether to include a document in the first place. Once it has been added a manuscript may be removed to a new location by being lost, stolen, given away, bought or loaned. The example of the entries 1807, 1808 and 2337 is instructive. They read (in translation):

1807	e†	XII	Pg	194	1	25	21 × 16	(formerly: Trebizond, Sumela 51)
1808	e	XIII	Pg	213	1	26	19.5 × 14.5	Istanbul, Mus. Hagia Sophia 11664
2337	e	?	Pg	?	?	?	20.4 × 15	(formerly: Trabizond, Mirjamana, unnumbered)

Thus, we have two entries for lost manuscripts: 1807 from the Sumela Monastery (about which we at least have some information, although it is now lost) and 2337. All we know about 2337 is that it is (or was) a parchment manuscript of the Gospels, which was at one time in the Mirjamana Monastery and in size lies between the other two, and close to both. 1808 is a manuscript whose location and date is known. What about 2337? Is it a manuscript in its own right? Is it now in Istanbul? Or is it no more than a transitory sighting of a manuscript from the Sumela, perhaps removed from the monastery when it closed in 1923? Will it be found? Has it in fact already been found in another library, in the United States or elsewhere, and given a new number (possibly its third)?

As the example of 2337 indicates, a manuscript does not have to be of a known location, or even to be still in existence, to be included. Various notes in the *Liste* also provide sad reminders of tragedies of modern history. 2039, a twelfth-century manuscript of Revelation in Dresden has against it the word 'burnt'. The note 'destroyed, fire' against some manuscripts from Turin (e.g. 611, 613) reports the disastrous fire of 1904 in the National Library. Some whole collections are lost or partially difficult to identify. An example of the former is the group of majuscule manuscripts of Kubbet el Chazne, Damascus, 0144–0147 and 0154–0159, which have not been seen since the First World War. The manuscripts formerly in the Metropolitan Library, Berat, Albania, are apparently now in the National Archive in Tirana, but no class-mark is known. Nor does the world stand still. One leaf of 022 is listed as being in the collection of A. Spinola (Lerma/Alessandra, Italy), but was sold in 2003 and its current whereabouts is uncertain. The sale of P75 (see 10.4.3) to the Vatican Library by the Fondation Bodmer in 2006 is the most significant transfer of recent times.

Some entries do no more than record information from a bookseller's or an auctioneer's catalogue. For example, 681 and 682: 'last knowledge: London, Sotheby's'. Others have been lost sight of, such as 701: 'formerly: London, White, s.n.' (*sine numero*, unnumbered), with the footnote 'Lost according to a letter from J.-M. Olivier'. The information provided means that if such manuscripts come to scholarly notice again they can be identified.

There are not a few examples of manuscript entries needing to be removed from the *Liste*. There are various reasons. Sometimes two or more separate entries are found to refer to a single manuscript which through accident has been divided and is now in several locations.

Forgery is another occasional problem. 2735 and 2427 turn out to be forgeries by the same hand. But generally it is more likely that forged illuminations will be added to a genuine page of text, the latter being harder to represent convincingly.

A compelling case for 2427 (containing Mark) having been copied from a nineteenth-century printed text was made by S. Carlson in a presentation at the Society of Biblical Literature, Washington DC, 2006.

How are manuscripts added to the *Liste*? To specialists in New Testament, for whom their texts and documents are of prime interest, it seems obvious that all new finds are communicated to the editors and swiftly given a Gregory–Aland number. It is not so simple. A certain amount depends upon the type of manuscript. New papyrus publications are likely to be quickly noticed by the editors of the *Liste*, who are indeed likely to be contacted by the editors of the papyrus in advance of publication. All New Testament papyri published by the Oxyrhynchus editors contain a Gregory–Aland number already allocated. The same situation may apply to majuscules discovered and published in a similar way. With regard to pieces of majuscule found, for example, as bindings, and to single leaves or sheets, to new acquisitions or identifications, and in fact to all majuscules, minuscules and lectionaries there is no regular process by which they may be added to the *Liste*. Librarians are dealing with a vast variety of texts and documents, and only a large research library is likely to have specialist staff who know of the existence of the *Liste* and its value. The growth of lists of Greek New Testament manuscripts shows that finds are more likely to be added as a result of scholarly endeavour. Such lists began with editors collecting the materials for their editions. They did this by going to libraries and looking at manuscripts, or asking someone to do it for them. The place of libraries in the numberings of the *Liste* almost gives one a travel diary of former researchers. Minuscules 5–43 are mostly in Paris, 127–181 mostly in the Vatican, 182–200 all in Florence, 205–217 mostly Venice, 260–307 nearly all in Paris. Most of the minuscules down to about 750 are in European libraries. Then we have a short journey further afield to Athens (757–811), before returning briefly to Europe. Next come the big Greek collections in large blocks: Athos (922–1140, 1391–1409, 1433–1520, 1532–1681, 1717–1756); Sinai (1145–1256); Jerusalem (1312–1355). 2131–2182 are all items in Russian collections. And so on. Each such block represents a piece of work in a city or a region or a library. The notes of the precise date of examination provided by Gregory allow one to be even more precise (for example, he saw the Venetian manuscripts in early 1886, 24–7 February, 1–2, 4–6 March

1886 (28 February was a Sunday; where was he on the 3rd (Ash Wednesday was a week later)?). See Gregory, *Textkritik*, 167–9. The addition of manuscripts to the *Liste* still depends largely on such visits. For a collection of Tischendorf's writings casting light on his travels, see C. Böttrich (ed.), *Tischendorf-Lesebuch. Bibelforschung in Reiseabenteuern*, Leipzig, 1999.

Although it might seem unlikely that anyone would find a previously unknown manuscript, this is not the case: anyone who works for any length of time in the field should expect to provide some additions to the *Liste*. Dr Michael Welte of the Münster Institut, for many years the keeper of the *Liste*, reports that he usually found a previously unlisted manuscript on his annual holiday in Greece just by enquiring at local monasteries and churches. A glance at the update of minuscule manuscripts on the web reveals that their knowledge is dependent upon a network of scholarly contacts: 2857–9 are three manuscripts in Moscow which have come to light; 2860 was acquired by the Scriptorium; 2861–2 had been listed in an extension to the Duke University Library catalogue and were communicated to the editors by myself after a visit in 2000. 2863–5 were seen by me and Bruce Morrill when we were in Boston for the Society of Biblical Literature meeting in 1999. They had been known there for a good many years, but had not come to the attention of any New Testament textual critics. 2866 is in the private Schøyen Collection, with whose staff the Institut enjoys close communication. 2867 consists of some leaves previously included under 303 but in fact part of another manuscript. 2868 was found by me listed in a handwritten catalogue in a visit to Bucharest in 2001. 2869–77 are from a previously untapped collection of manuscripts in the Vatopedi Monastery, Mount Athos. Most remarkably, a visit to Corpus Christi College, Oxford by Mr Andrew Brown led to the discovery of a composite Gospel manuscript which has been in the college since the sixteenth century. It is extraordinary that it had not been noticed by the many New Testament scholars, Tischendorf and Gregory included, who have visited Oxford in search of manuscripts.

It is 2879 (Oxford, Corpus Christi College, MS 30), comprising (a) a twelfth-century minuscule containing all four Gospels with the commentary of Theophylact, and (b) two leaves from a tenth-century majuscule lectionary, containing portions from John's Gospel, as well as two portraits of the evangelists, taken from a different manuscript. There is a description in I. Hutter, *Corpus der byzantinischen Miniaturenhandschriften*, vol. v, *Oxford College Libraries*, Stuttgart, 1997). Before this manuscript came to Corpus Christi College, it belonged successively to two of the founding fathers of Greek scholarship in England, namely William Grocyn and Thomas Linacre. The manuscript was described in H.O. Coxe, *Catalogus codicum mss. qui in collegiis aulisque Oxoniensibus hodie adservantur* (2 vols., 1852), as well as in older catalogues, and yet somehow it had been overlooked. A. J. Brown, 'The Gospel Commentary of Theophylact and a Neglected Manuscript in Oxford', *NovT* 49 (2007), 185–96.

The moral is that the extension and improvement of the *Liste* cannot be assumed to be dependent upon the activities of its editors alone. Every user of this work is encouraged to enquire in libraries which they happen to visit whether they have New Testament manuscripts. Libraries may have their own unpublished catalogues of manuscripts or supplements listing more recent finds. This is a useful way of looking for possible items. (Advice on the way to describe any new find is given in 2.3 below.) As well as looking for new finds, researchers also provide a service by communicating any corrections or supplementary information to the editors (e-mail intf@uni-muenster.de).

1.3.3 Richard

Successful study of manuscripts depends upon the ability to marshal and synthesise a number of tools of different kinds. The *Liste* provides the starting point, a reference number and some basic data. The next stage is to build on this basic descriptive information, and the usual place to go to will be the library catalogue. Apart from providing a check on physical data given in the *Liste*, a catalogue may provide information about provenance (the place or places in which the manuscript was kept before reaching its present location), previous owners, and contents (remember that the *Liste* focuses on the New Testament, but a manuscript containing some of it may also contain other works, and this information may be significant in understanding it). A full catalogue will indicate the precise folio on which each book of the New Testament it contains begins and ends, as well as describing the ancillary material. In order to locate the hundreds of catalogues in which Greek New Testament manuscripts are described, one needs the assistance of the essential catalogue of catalogues, called Richard after its first editor, but now edited by Olivier.

J.-M. Olivier, *Répertoire des bibliothèques et de catalogues des manuscrits grecs de Marcel Richard*, 3rd edn (Corpus Christianorum), Turnhout, 1995 (1st edn, Paris, 1948; 2nd edn 1958; Supplement 1, 1964). 2,507 items are listed by place, with notes indicating the manuscript numbers listed in a catalogue, and other helpful notes.

The degree of information in a catalogue will vary greatly. A modern catalogue produced by a professional bibliographer will provide very detailed information indeed. An older one (for example of the nineteenth century) may give no more than a class-mark, a date and a summary list of contents.

1.3.4 The Bibliography

The next place to go after Richard is to Elliott's *Bibliography*.

Elliott, *A Bibliography of Greek New Testament Manuscripts*, Cambridge, 1989; 2nd edn, Cambridge, 2000. Updates, *NovT* 46 (2004), 376–400; 49 (2007), 370–401.

This work provides an entry for manuscripts in the *Liste* by their Gregory–Aland number, giving references to a range of sources including facsimiles, photographs, transcriptions, collations, monographs, journal articles and specialist catalogues. Further useful features include a five-page general bibliography (covering text-types, introductions to NT textual criticism, library catalogues and other bibliographies), a general bibliography at the beginning of each class of manuscripts and a section on unregistered manuscripts. Again, users can make their own annotations, and again the compiler is grateful for further entries and corrections.

The *Bibliography* acts as a hub, from which one may branch out in various directions, depending on one's interests. But one should avoid looking too exclusively in a single direction too quickly, for example by following up information about its text to the neglect of the manuscript's palaeography or information about its origin and provenance.

1.3.5 The Leuven Database of Ancient Books

A very valuable resource for ancient documents is the online LDAB, available at http://ldab.arts.kuleuven.be/. It currently lists 11,240 Greek and Latin literary texts, listed by accession number, collection, and ancient archive, with many other fields for sorting such as work, century, material and book form. It also offers the opportunity to make graphs of the data found. In the words of the Preface, it 'attempts to collect the basic information on all ancient literary texts, as opposed to documents. On 1 January 2006 it included 10,826 items, dating from the fourth century BC to AD 800 and incorporating authors from Homer (eighth century BC) to Romanus Melodus and Gregorius the Great (sixth century AD), including 3,671 texts of which the author can no longer be identified' (http://ldab.arts.kuleuven.be/ldab_text_help.php).

1.3.6 Reproductions

Whatever one's interests, the ideal is to see a reproduction of some or all of the manuscript. Reproductions may generically be called surrogates, which covers facsimiles, microform and digital images. The best of these is a facsimile edition. Such facsimiles have hitherto been in printed form, so they have traditionally been produced only for the most interesting manuscripts, since they have been expensive to make. Some of the major Greek manuscripts are available in facsimile. For the rest, it is possible, without too much trouble, to find reproductions of at least one page of most of the papyrus and majuscule manuscripts. The minuscules and lectionaries are another matter. Of course it is possible to access the microfilm collections of Münster (which include virtually all Greek New Testament manuscripts), the Library of Congress films of Jerusalem, Sinai and Athos (available in Washington DC, Claremont, Cal. and Birmingham, UK), or other smaller holdings. And anyone undertaking a thorough survey of a manuscript should acquire a full set of images. But until now it has been difficult to get images of any kind, often even of a single page, of hundreds of the manuscripts. All this is set to change, with the increasingly frequent digitisation of entire collections and their publication on-line. A visit to a few places where this is happening will quickly show how great the change is.

Early Manuscripts of Oxford University (http://image.ox.ac.uk/) includes Gregory–Aland 57 (Magdalene College Gr. 9). The *Codices Electronici Sangallenses (CESG)–Virtual Library* provides images of all the manuscripts in the great collection of the Abbey Library of St Gall (www.cesg.unifr.ch/en/index.htm). This predominantly Latin library includes the Greek–Latin bilingual manuscript 037. The website currently being created by the Codex Sinaiticus Project (www.itsee.bham.ac.uk/projects/sinaiticus/index.htm) will include new digital images.

These collections are derived from new digital images and are of more value than sites which provide digital copies of non-digital originals, such as facsimiles and microfilm, because the image quality is far superior. But non-digital images remain useful in the absence of anything better, and by virtue of their presence on the web make the primary materials available to all researchers.

Individual pages of manuscripts are illustrated in specialist studies designed for use by the codicologist and above all the palaeographer. These include repertories of illuminated and dated manuscripts, and are of a similar standard to the modern library catalogue in the quality and quantity of information which they provide.

Some of the most important tools are: K. Lake and S. Lake, *Dated Greek Minuscule Manuscripts to the Year 1200*, 11 vols., Boston, Mass., 1934–45; A. Turyn, *Dated Greek Manuscripts of the Thirteenth and Fourteenth Centuries in the Libraries of Italy*, 2 vols., Urbana, 1964; Turyn, *Great Britain*; I. Spatharakis, *Corpus of Dated Illuminated Greek Manuscripts to the Year 1453* (Byzantina Neerlandica 8), 2 vols., Leiden, 1981 (611 plates); I. Hutter, *Corpus der byzantinischen Miniaturenhandschriften:*

1–3: Oxford, Bodleian Library, 4 vols., Stuttgart, 1977–82; *4: Oxford, Christ Church,* 2 vols., Stuttgart, 1993; *5: Oxford College Libraries,* 2 vols., Stuttgart, 1997; Gamillscheg, Harlfinger and Hunger, *Repertorium.* For Greek New Testament manuscript collections in single libraries see F.G. Kenyon, *Facsimiles of Biblical Manuscripts in the British Museum,* London, 1900; W.H.P. Hatch, *The Greek Manuscripts of the New Testament at Mount Sinai: Facsimiles and Descriptions,* Paris, 1932; and *The Greek Manuscripts of the New Testament in Jerusalem: Facsimiles and Descriptions,* Paris, 1934.

Manuals of palaeography can be helpful when all else fails. First to be noted is E. M. Thompson *et al., Facsimiles of Manuscripts and Inscriptions,* 2 vols., London, 1873–94 (often abbreviated as *Pal. Soc.*); *Facsimiles of Ancient Manuscripts,* 2 vols., London, 1903–34 (often abbreviated as *New Pal. Soc.*).

For the Greek Bible, manuals include J. Finegan, *Encountering New Testament Manuscripts,* London, 1975 (a few good plates); W. H. P. Hatch, *The Principal Uncial Manuscripts of the New Testament,* Chicago, 1939 (76 plates); and *Facsimiles and Descriptions of Minuscule Manuscripts of the New Testament,* Cambridge, Mass., 1951 (both of these have good sets of plates); B. M. Metzger, *Manuscripts of the Greek Bible. An Introduction to Greek Palaeography,* New York and Oxford, 1981 (45 plates, of disappointing quality); H. J. Vogels, *Codicum Novi Testamenti Specimina,* Bonn, 1929 (25 plates of Greek manuscripts). None of these works can be regarded very highly from the codicological or palaeographical standpoint, but they do have the virtue of providing plates. For genuine expertise in Greek hands and a good selection of New Testament manuscripts, one may recommend R. Barbour, *Greek Literary Hands AD 400–1600,* Oxford, 1981 (110 plates) and G. Cavallo and H. Maehler, *Greek Bookhands of the Early Byzantine Period AD 300–800* (ICSBS 47), London 1987 (126 plates).

There are two works which deserve special mention. The first is G. Cavallo, *Ricerche sulla maiuscola biblica* (Studi e testi di papirologia 2), 2 vols., Florence, 1967 (115 plates). This is a study of the formation and development of the hand in which so many of the most significant manuscripts of the fourth to the sixth century were produced, biblical majuscule. Second is the collection *Paléographie grecque et byzantine,* which contains many valuable contributions.

It is always best to commence the study of a manuscript with whatever images are available, because a look at a page tells one so much about the document, and subsequently about the text it contains. How competent is the scribe? When was it written? How tidy is it? How has it been treated by subsequent users, for example in correcting it? How legible is it? Is it written in a hand which betrays a particular place of origin? Does it have a colophon giving the name of the scribe – and if it does, do we know of other manuscripts produced by the same person? What is known about its provenance and origin?

1.3.7 Catalogues

Once as much information as possible has been gathered from such sources as these, there are others which should be explored. In the first place, there are various specialist catalogues. Some of them are devoted to Greek New Testament manuscripts.

Foremost examples of such works are K. W. Clark, *A Descriptive Catalogue of Greek New Testament Manuscripts in America,* Chicago, 1937; K. Treu, *Die griechischen Handschriften des Neuen Testaments in der UdSSR. Eine systematische Auswertung der Texthandschriften in Leningrad, Moskau, Kiev, Odessa, Tbilisi und Erevan* (TU 91), Berlin, 1966.

Later manuscripts may be written by a scribe who gives his name, and such a document may then often be located in a very precise historical context and linked with other manuscripts. The essential resource here is the index of scribal names prepared by Vogel and Gardthausen. The network of further information available once this is known consists of many kinds of historical research, including studies of monasteries, of intellectual movements, and so forth.

M. Vogel and V. Gardthausen, *Die griechischen Schreiber des Mittelalters und der Renaissance*, Leipzig 1909 (reprinted Hildesheim, 1966); E. Gamillscheg and D. Harlfinger, 'Specimen eines Repertoriums der griechischen Kopisten', *Jahrbuch der österreichischen byzantinischen Gesellschaft* 27 (1978), 293–322. For an example of how scholarship appears when the scribes are the centre of attention, see D. J. Geanakoplos, *Greek Scholars in Venice. Studies in the Dissemination of Greek Learning from Byzantium to Western Europe*, Cambridge, Mass., 1962. Further bibliography on lists of scribes in Barbour, *Greek Literary Hands*, xxxiii. Old catalogues can provide information about a manuscript's history. For research on medieval catalogues, see A. Derolez, *Les catalogues des bibliothèques* (Typologie des sources du moyen âge occidental 31), Turnhout, 1979.

1.3.8 Text und Textwert

The resources so far described provide information about the physical characteristics and script of a manuscript. The next stage is to find out what is known about its text. Elliott's *Bibliography* will tell us whether there are any transcriptions, collations or studies of the text of a manuscript. The series *Text und Textwert* ('Text and textual worth') provides a comprehensive guide to the text of all manuscripts, based on a series of test passages from all the New Testament except Revelation (which, as will appear in due course, has already been comprehensively analysed). Detailed explanation of the material available in the series will be reserved until later (1.9). Suffice it here to say that the series was conceived by the Münster Institut as a means of selecting manuscripts to be cited in the critical apparatus of their major critical edition, the *Editio critica maior*. Test readings (Teststellen) were selected which the limited evidence from existing editions suggested would make it possible to determine the groupings of manuscripts, so that those which had little or no independent value could be eliminated. The readings of all witnesses were ascertained at each of the test passages, and the material then analysed in three main ways – by a description of the types of readings of each manuscript, by a statement of the proportion of readings shared with other manuscripts with a similar text, and by tables correlating the other two ways. Although this was conceived primarily for the purposes of the Institut, and although it has been so far largely ignored, the series provides a unique tool for ascertaining information about the text of every manuscript of which the Institut possesses readable microfilm. Because the material is set out in several different ways, it can be used for more purposes than those employed in Münster (deliberately so).

Text und Textwert der griechischen Handschriften des Neuen Testaments, Berlin and New York, 1987–. The individual volumes (all with this title) are, in order of appearance: K. Aland (ed., with A. Benduhn-Mertz and G. Mink), *I. Die Katholischen Briefe*, 3 vols. (ANTF 9–10), 1987; K. Aland (ed., with A. Benduhn-Mertz, G. Mink and H. Bachmann), *II. Die Paulinischen Briefe*, 3 vols. (ANTF 16–18), 1991; K. Aland (ed., with A. Benduhn-Mertz, G. Mink, K. Witte and H.Bachmann), *III. Die Apostelgeschichte*, 2 vols. (ANTF 20–1), 1993; K. Aland†, B. Aland, K. Wachtel (eds., with Klaus Witte), *IV. Die Synoptischen Evangelien, 1. Das Markusevangelium*, 2 vols. (ANTF 26–7), 1998; *2. Das Matthäusevangelium*, 2 vols. (ANTF 28–9), 1999; *3. Das Lukasevangelium*, 2 vols. (ANTF 30–1), 1999; *V. Das Johannesevangelium, 1. Teststellenkollation der Kapitel 1–10*, 2 vols. (ANTF 35–6), 2005. Still to come are a further series of test readings from passages present in all three Synoptic Gospels and the analysis of John 18 readings (the volumes on John cover the first ten chapters only; the second half of the Gospel is being analysed in association with the International Greek New Testament Project).

There is a detailed explanation of the different sections of the volumes and how to use them in Aland and Aland, *The Text of the New Testament*, 317–32. There are additional features in the Gospels volumes.

A useful paper explaining the workings of the project and setting it in a wider text-critical context is given by Wachtel, 'Kinds of Variants'. D. C. Parker, 'A Comparison between the *Text und Textwert* and the Claremont Profile Method Analyses of Manuscripts in the Gospel of Luke', *NTS* 49 (2003), 108–38, uses the Lucan volumes to apply the Claremont Profile Method (see 5.1.3) and to discuss some theoretical questions.

1.3.9 Which edition uses which manuscripts

One obvious source for textual evidence about a manuscript is its use in an edition of the Greek New Testament. Given the number of editions produced, the complexities of how the manuscripts are numbered by the editors and certain contradictions between the lists of manuscripts given by editors and those which are actually used, the presence of a tool which provides all this evidence is a great assistance. J. K. Elliott's *Survey of Manuscripts* consists of tables indicating for each manuscript whether it is cited in ten editions of the Greek New Testament and three synopses.

Elliott, *Survey of Manuscripts*. See also his earlier study 'The Citation of Manuscripts in Recent Printed Editions of the Greek New Testament', *NovT* 25 (1983), 97–132. The ten editions are Nestle–Aland[26] (Stuttgart, 1979); Bover–O'Callaghan (J. M. Bover and J. O'Callaghan (eds.), *Nuevo Testamento trilingüe*, Madrid, 1977); the three United Bible Societies editions then in existence (K. Aland, M. Black, C. M. Martini (2nd and 3rd edns), B. M. Metzger and A. Wikgren (eds.), *The Greek New Testament*, New York, London, Edinburgh, Amsterdam and Stuttgart, 1966, 1968 and 1975); Merk (A. Merk (ed.), *Novum Testamentum graece et latine*, 9th edn, Rome, 1964); Vogels (H. J. Vogels (ed.),

Novum Testamentum graece et latine, 4th edn, Freiburg and Barcelona, 1955); British and Foreign Bible Society[2] (*H Καινη Διαθηκη*, 2nd edn, London, 1958); Souter[2]; and IGNTP *Luke*. The three synopses are those by Aland (K. Aland (ed.), *Synopsis Quattuor Euangeliorum*, 10th edn, Stuttgart, 1978); Huck–Greeven (A. Huck (ed.), *Synopse der drei ersten Evangelien mit Beigabe der johanneischen Parallelstellen/Synopsis of the First Three Gospels with the Addition of the Johannine Parallels*, 13th edn, rev. H. Greeven, Tübingen, 1981); and Orchard (J. B. Orchard (ed.), *A Synopsis of the Four Gospels in Greek Arranged According to the Two-document Hypothesis*, Edinburgh, 1983). In addition, a dagger against a number indicates that the manuscript was given a number by von Soden and the number underlined means that the manuscript is listed in the Prolegomena to Tischendorf, *Editio octava* (in neither case is it implied that the manuscript is cited in the edition). The book is intended more as a survey of the intentions, scope and consistency of printed editions than as a guide to where readings from a manuscript may be found cited, but it serves this function also.

1.3.10 Resources referring to particular categories of manuscript

1.3.10.1 Resources referring to papyri

There are specialist handlists of papyri which should not be neglected. Van Haelst's *Catalogue* lists all Jewish and Christian papyrus (and parchment) manuscripts in a single referencing system and provides basic information about each. Aland's *Repertorium* lists papyri in the groups Old Testament, New Testament, Varia and Apocrypha. Useful information is provided in the 'Consolidated List of Codices Consulted' at the end of Turner, *Typology*, which includes 83 papyri and 111 majuscules.

Many papyrus collections are large enough to have their own literature. Of most importance to New Testament scholarship are the Oxyrhynchus Papyri, which are dispersed around a number of libraries. As a result each papyrus has its Oxyrhynchus number (abbreviated as P. Oxy. or OP) and a library class-mark.

Van Haelst, *Catalogue*. An online update is provided by Cornelia Römer at www.ucl.ac.uk/Grand-Lat/research/christianpapyri.htm. K. Aland, *Repertorium* (uses the Gregory–Aland numbers for the New Testament; items then known extended as far as No. 88).

For online resources, an excellent place to start is with the University of Michigan's Papyrus Collection, http://lib.umich.edu/pap/. It includes bibliographies and teaching materials.

For papyri see also 1.1.1. See further P. W. Pestman, *The New Papyrological Primer*, 5th edn, Leiden, 1990. Studies focusing on New Testament manuscripts include a series of important studies by E. J. Epp: 'The Papyrus Manuscripts of the New Testament', in Ehrman and Holmes, *Contemporary Research*, 3–21; 'The New Testament Papyrus Manuscripts in Historical Perspective', in M. P. Horgan and P. J. Kobelski (eds.), *To Touch the Text: Studies in Honor of Joseph A. Fitzmyer, S J*, New York, 1989, 261–88; 'The Significance of the Papyri for Determining the Nature of the New Testament Text in the Second Century: a Dynamic View of Textual Transmission', in W. L. Petersen (ed.), *Gospel Traditions in the Second Century. Origins, Recensions, Text, and Transmission* (Christianity and Judaism in Antiquity 3), Notre Dame, 1989, 71–103; 'New Testament Papyrus Manuscripts and Letter Carrying in Greco-Roman Times', in B. A. Pearson *et al.* (eds.), *The Future of Early Christianity: Essays in Honor of Helmut Koester*, Minneapolis, 1991, 35–56; 'The New Testament Papyri at Oxyrhynchus in their Social and Intellectual Context', in *Baarda Festschrift*, 47–68; 'The Oxyrhynchus New Testament Papyri: "Not without Honor except in their Hometown"?', *JBL* 123 (2004), 5–55. All reprinted in Epp, *Collected Essays* as chapters 12, 13, 14, 15, 18, 24, generally with added notes; 'Significance of the Papyri' also reprinted in Epp and Fee, *Studies*, 274–97. A valuable specialist tool is A. Blanchard, *Sigles et abréviations dans les papyrus documentaires grecs* (ICSBS 30), London, 1974. A checklist of the papyri with brief bibliography and notes on their textual character is provided by Aland and Aland, *The Text of the New Testament*, 83–102, and the charts at the back of the book are very useful in correlating the contents of extant papyri with every chapter of the New Testament. H. C. Youtie, *The Textual Criticism of Documentary Papyri. Prolegomena* (ICSBS 33), 2nd edn, London, 1974, gives a valuable insight into the difficulties of editing documentary papyri. The International Association of Papyrologists website has links to about 150 other sites (www.ulb.ac.be/assoc/aip/liens.htm).

For a guide to the Oxyrhynchus locations, see R. A. Coles, *Location-List of the Oxyrhynchus Papyri and of Other Greek Papyri Published by the Egyptian Exploration Society*, London, 1974, and online resources at www.csad.ox.ac.uk/POxy/frame1.htm. Images of papyri online are increasingly common: for links see http://dir.yahoo.com/Social/Science/Anthropology_and_Archaeology/Archaeology/ Egyptology/Papyrology/; many of the sites provide links (e.g. http://scriptorium.lib.duke.edu/ papyrus/#links).

1.3.10.2 Resources referring to majuscules

Majuscule manuscripts have frequently been called 'uncials'. The use of this term, which is a description of a certain style of Latin script, for Greek manuscripts is incorrect, and the proper palaeographical term 'majuscule' should be used. It should be noted that some majuscules, although written on parchment, have a papyrus inventory number (e.g. 0109, a seventh-century manuscript of John, is Berlin, State Museum Papyrus 5010). The reason is that finds of manuscripts mostly on papyrus, especially if they are large collections, generally contain some parchment fragments as well. The papyrus number thus identifies the collection, not the writing material.

The oldest and most extensive and important majuscule manuscripts have been well served with facsimile editions, transcriptions, and detailed studies. Others await this treatment. Comprising as they do the manuscripts produced over a period of six hundred years (fourth to the tenth and even eleventh century), there is a considerable variety of scripts, presentation and textual character.

Resources include D. C. Parker, 'The Majuscule Manuscripts of the New Testament', in Ehrman and Holmes, *Contemporary Research*, 22–42. For old but still frequently informative accounts of manuscripts, see Scrivener, *Plain Introduction*, chapters 4–6. Brief summaries with accounts of the textual character of each manuscript are given by Aland and Aland, *The Text of the New Testament*, 103–28. The chart at the back of the book provides, as for the papyri, a conspectus of all the chapters showing which majuscule is extant.

1.3.10.3 Resources referring to minuscules

There are very many minuscule manuscripts, and the chances of there being a facsimile, transcription, collation or study of any one vary greatly. Some of the oldest, longest known, and most easily available (usually in a western European or American library), and of these those whose texts have aroused the greatest interest, are most likely to have been carefully studied. These include members of families of manuscripts (see 4.3). The unevenness of the coverage is illustrated by two manuscripts made by the same scribe, one of the Acts and Epistles and the other of the Gospels. Both are of great textual significance, but while the one (1739) was studied as long ago as 1899, the other (1582) had to wait a century for the first monograph devoted to it.

B. Aland and K. Wachtel, 'The Greek Minuscule Manuscripts of the New Testament', in Ehrman and Holmes, *Contemporary Research*, 43–60; Aland and Aland, *The Text of the New Testament*, 128–58 gives a selection of plates and basic information derived from modern research on the minuscules. Older discussions, in which too great a value is ascribed to manuscripts on the basis of a selection of readings (and a knowledge of a selection of manuscripts) should be treated with great caution. For 1582 and 1739, see 4.3 and chapters 8–10.

The study of manuscripts always requires an informed knowledge of the culture and epoch from which they come, and for the majority of the minuscules this requires a knowledge of Byzantine history and a knowledge of the resources which make it possible often to locate a manuscript or a group in a particular part of the Greek-speaking world (for example, the ability to recognise a manuscript copied in southern Italy).

The groundbreaking work of J. Irigoin showed that it was possible to use the pattern of ruling in a Byzantine manuscript to establish its place of origin. Scriptoria had their own practices in this regard, in which evidently apprentices were taught the chosen pattern and followed it thereafter. Even if there is no evidence linking a pattern to a location, it is a way of finding connections between manuscripts. Irigoin's discovery has since been advanced in a typology of ruling patterns. As yet, no attempt has been made to apply these patterns to New Testament manuscripts, for example in comparing the ruling patterns of manuscripts known to have similar forms of text.

Another piece of physical evidence is the watermark on a piece of paper. These too have been studied and categorised, so that the watermark will often be an indicator of a place and period of time – not necessarily of the copying of the manuscript, but a place from which the paper came, and a date after which the manuscript was made. Watermarks provide a dating tool for manuscripts written from the end of the thirteenth century onwards.

J. Irigoin, 'Pour un étude des centres de copies byzantins', *Scriptorium* 12 (1958), 208–27. The classification of ruling patterns is provided in J.-H. Sautel, *Répertoire de réglures dans les manuscrits grecs sur parchemin* (Bibliologia 13), Turnhout, 1995.

The standard work on watermarks is C. M. Briquet, *Les filigranes. Dictionnaire historique des marques du papier dès leur apparition vers 1282 jusqu'en 1600. A Facsimile of the 1907 edition with supplementary material*, ed. A. Stevenson (The New Briquet. Jubilee edition), 4 vols., Amsterdam, 1968. See also V. A. Mosin and S. M. Traljic, *Filigranes des XIIIe et XIVe siècles*, Zagreb, 1957; there is a 'Form for Searching Descriptions of Papers and Watermarks' at http://abacus.bates.edu/Faculty/wmarchive/FORM_searches.html.

1.3.10.4 *Commentary manuscripts*

Discussion of the accompanying commentaries and other special features of these manuscripts will be found in Part III, in the sections on the text of different parts of the New Testament. An introduction to the tools useful for all the parts is provided here.

Finding one's way through such manuscripts is particularly complicated. It requires knowledge of the exegetical tradition as well as of the Greek New Testament. We are at a point where a good deal of information has been gathered, but conclusions are less easy to come by. Dating the emergence of the tradition is at any rate possible. As has already been stated, the type of manuscript with which we are concerned is one containing a *catena*, that is, a chain of comments on the biblical text. Such a chain will draw on the writings of several exegetes. It follows that the form of commentary in any manuscript will be older than the date of the manuscript and more recent than the latest writer included.

In addition to sometimes preserving passages from lost works, the value of the commentary manuscripts is that they carry a biblical text and are potentially witnesses to the form of text used by the writer or compiler of the commentary. Because such manuscripts will be copied from other manuscripts of the same commentary, so that a particular form of text accompanies the commentary, it is important to know which of the many different commentaries it contains. Moreover, since each commentary stands in its own place in the history of the commentaries, the biblical text it contains has its starting point in the same place. In short, the biblical texts of manuscripts of a particular commentary are prima facie likely to be closely related. Unfortunately, the Gregory–Aland system of classification does not include any indicator that a manuscript includes a commentary, let alone what the commentary might be, but simply classes it among either the majuscules or the minuscules. This sets the user at a remove from this vital information. It is a real virtue of von Soden's much-maligned and undoubtedly over-complicated system that it provides this information in quite a simple way. To find the commentaries, one has either to go through the *Liste* looking for entries with a K in the statement of contents, or to use von Soden, or to go to the specialist studies of commentary manuscripts.

In order to find one's way around the commentaries, one needs a referencing system for Greek patristic writings. This is found in the *Clavis Patrum Graecorum* (IV.228–59; see 3.2.3).

There is a survey of the history of research by Birdsall in Parker and Birdsall, 'Codex Zacynthius', 124–9. For further general bibliography, see M. Faulhaber, *Die Propheten-Catenen nach römischen Handschriften* (Biblische Studien 4, Hefte 2/3), Freiburg-im-Breisgau, 1899; and *Hohelied-, Proverbien- u. Prediger-Catenen* (Theologische Studien der Leo-Gesellschaft 4), Vienna, 1902; H. J. Lietzmann, *Catenen. Mitteilungen über ihre Geschichte und handschriftliche Überlieferung*, Freiburg-im-Breisgau, 1897; G. Karo and H. J. Lietzmann, *Catenarum graecarum catalogus*, Göttingen, 1902; H. von Soden, *Die Schriften des Neuen Testaments. I. Teil: Untersuchungen. I. Abteilung: Die Textzeugen*, Göttingen, 1911, 249–89; R. Devreesse, 'Chaînes exégétiques grecques', in L. Pirot (ed.), *Dictionnaire de la Bible*, *Supplément* fasc. 3–4, Paris, 1928, coll. 1084–233; Devreesse, *Introduction*, 176–81; G. Dorival, *Les chaînes exégétiques sur les Psaumes*, vol. I (Spicilegium Sacrum Lovaniense 43), Leuven, 1986. Details on particular commentaries are provided in the sections of Part III.

1.3.10.5 Lectionaries

It is customary for anyone writing on this topic to note the paucity of material, and there is no doubt that the lament is justified. Here we are lacking the guidance of *Text und Textwert*, which does not include lectionaries.

Lectionaries are grouped in two ways, by their contents and by the type of sequence. The former is divided between the Gospels and the Apostolos (that is, Acts, the Catholic epistles and Paul's letters). Revelation has never been included in the Orthodox lectionary. The sequences are two: the synaxarion (which follows the Church's year, beginning at Easter) and the menologion (which follows the civil calendar of the Byzantine Empire and starts on 1 September). The menologion contains many non-biblical readings, in particular lives of saints and accounts of martyrdoms on the day of their commemoration, and other writings including ancient texts such as the *Protevangelium Iacobi*.

C. Osburn, 'The Greek Lectionaries of the New Testament', in Ehrman and Holmes, *Contemporary Research*, 61–74, with extensive bibliography; Aland and Aland, *The Text of the New Testament*, 163–70, gives a noticeably shorter introduction to this class of manuscript. There are a number of titles in the series Studies in the Lectionary Text of the Greek New Testament (Chicago, 1933–59). For information on the series, including unpublished work, see A. Wikgren, 'Chicago Studies in the Greek Lectionary of the New Testament', in Birdsall and Thomson, *Biblical and Patristic Studies*, 96–121. E. C. Colwell, 'Is There a Lectionary Text of the Gospels?', *HTR* 25 (1932), 73–84, reprinted in *Studies in Methodology*, 84–96. A neglected study is K. Lake and S. Lake, 'The Text of Mark in Some Dated Lectionaries', in H. G. Wood (ed.), *Amicitiae Corolla. A Volume of Essays Presented to James Rendel Harris, D.Litt. on the Occasion of his Eightieth Birthday*, London, 1933, 147–83. For illuminations see K. Weitzmann, *Byzantine Liturgical Psalters and Gospels*, London, 1980, and 1.2.

On some of the history of the terminology in Greek, see J. D. Karavidopoulos, 'The Origin and History of the Terms "Evangelistarion" and "Evangeliarion"', *Orthodoxes Forum. Zeitschrift des Instituts für Orthodoxe Theologie der Universität München* 7 (1993), 177–83.

For a study indicating how an understanding of the liturgical context of lectionaries and their structure can help textual research, see T. van Lopik, 'Licht uit het Byzantijnse Oosten: liturgische invloed op de tekst van het Nieuwe Testament', in E. de Bijll Nachenius *et al.*, *Heimwee naar de Middeleeuwen*, Leiden, 1989. The same writer has studied some variants whose appearance at a different position in the text may be due to the lectionary rather than to their being interpolations: 'Once Again: Floating Words, their Significance for Textual Criticism', *NTS* 41 (1995), 286–91; 'Tekstkritiek: telt het wegen of weegt het tellen?' *Nederlands Theologisch Tijdschrift* 45 (1991), 101–6 (with English summary).

1.4 LATIN MANUSCRIPTS

1.4.1 Introductory

Before the manuscripts are discussed, it is necessary first to observe that the Latin textual tradition of the New Testament (indeed of the whole Bible) is traditionally divided into two: the Vulgate, a version produced in the years before and after 400, for which Jerome was partly responsible, and the Old Latin, consisting of translations and revisions antecedent to the Vulgate (although the manuscripts and citations of this version are by no means necessarily older than manuscripts and citations of the Vulgate). Because the Old Latin versions provide evidence of ancient and sometimes otherwise unattested readings in Greek (that is, the readings of the lost Greek manuscripts which translators used), they have attracted the most attention, and have been the most thoroughly studied by New Testament textual critics. The textual history of the Vulgate is another matter altogether. The dominant Bible of the western world for over a thousand years, it survives in an estimated ten thousand manuscripts (as opposed to the approximately five thousand Greek manuscripts of the New Testament).

There is no Latin equivalent to the *Liste*. On the other hand, Latin palaeography made remarkable advances in the twentieth century, and it is now possible to locate the precise place of writing of many manuscripts, and as a consequence to chart their relationships more accurately. Although much of the inner history of the Vulgate is of no direct value to the editor of the Greek New Testament, it is of value not only in itself but also for the light which it sheds on many other aspects of the history of the Latin-speaking world. Moreover, the detailed study of one text (even though it is a version) may shed light on another, and this certainly turns out to be the case for the New Testament.

With the exception of the Gospels, there are only a few Old Latin manuscripts for any part of the New Testament, so that the reconstruction of the various forms of text which existed in antiquity is largely dependent on indirect evidence, namely citations of biblical texts by writers. For example, there is only one ancient Old Latin manuscript of Revelation (see 7.4.1). In addition, the study of the available manuscript evidence and the citations makes it possible to identify Old Latin readings in 'mixed-text' manuscripts, that is to say, manuscripts which, although they are for the most part representatives of the Vulgate text, also contain some Old Latin readings. At the same time, some manuscripts classified as Old Latin contain a good share of Vulgate readings. Once these points are fully appreciated, it will be seen that it is impossible to maintain a hard-and-fast distinction between Old Latin and Vulgate manuscripts. We will follow the traditional division, but first I must describe various works which deal with Latin manuscripts of all kinds.

1.4.2 *Tools for the study of Latin manuscripts*

The starting point for all study of the manuscripts is the volumes of E. A. Lowe's *Codices Latini Antiquiores*. This remarkable work is an enumeration of every Latin manuscript written before the year 800. Almost every entry provides at least one illustrative plate, with a description based on a fresh examination of the manuscript in question. The work had its genesis in Lowe's initial experiences in studying Latin scripts, which convinced him that 'it would be impossible to arrive at definitive results without first gathering all the available material, and that only such a comprehensive collection was capable of affording new criteria for dating and placing our oldest Latin manuscripts and of casting new light on the broader question of book production in ancient times' (vol. 1, p. vii). The eleven volumes are divided by country, beginning with the Vatican (1934), proceeding with Great Britain and Ireland (1935, 2nd edn 1972), the two volumes of Italy (1938 and 1947), Paris (1950), the rest of France (1953), Switzerland (1956), Germany in two volumes (1959), and all remaining countries (1963 and 1966). These volumes contain 1,670 separate items, a number brought up to a total of 1,811 by the supplementary volume (1971), which also contains updates to the bibliographies and provides indexes of authors, manuscripts and provenances. In addition to the entries and bibliographies, the introductions to the volumes merit careful study.

Lowe's collaborator for volumes V–IX, B. Bischoff, made as great a contribution in a different way, by concentrating on manuscripts produced at the end of Lowe's period and during the years that followed. It is because these two scholars have laid so secure a foundation that a manuscript's place of origin may often be ascertained with such precision.

Turning to biblical manuscripts, for the period down to the Carolingian epoch we have McGurk's *Latin Gospel Books from 400 to 800*, which provides a detailed description by country and place of 138 manuscripts. There are appendices giving tabulated information on the order and types of prefatory material.

Entries in *CLA* are usually cited as *CLA* with volume (often in lower-case roman numerals) and entry. The original volumes are in a much larger format than the reprints (Osnabrück, 1982, 1988) with clearer plates and are therefore to be preferred. But the reprints did bring a new tool: R. Aris, *An Index of Scripts for E. A. Lowe's Codices Latini Antiquiores*, Osnabrück, 1982. For updates to the whole work see B. Bischoff and V. Brown, 'Addenda to *Codices Latini Antiquiores*', *Mediaeval Studies* 47 (1985), 317–64; B. Bischoff, V. Brown and J. J. John, 'Addenda to *Codices Latini Antiquiores* (II)', *Mediaeval Studies* 54 (1992) 286–307. Those interested in the earliest manuscripts will also need to consult various of Lowe's other writings, especially 'Some Facts about our Oldest Latin Manuscripts', *The Classical Quarterly* 19 (1925), 197–208, reprinted in *Palaeographical Papers 1907–1965*, edited by Ludwig Bieler, 2 vols., Oxford, 1972, 1.187–202 and 'More Facts about our Oldest Latin Manuscripts', *The Classical Quarterly* 22 (1928), 43–62 = *Palaeographical Papers* 1.251–74. The Hill Monastic Manuscript Library has systematically acquired reproductions of the manuscripts cited by Lowe. A listing may be downloaded from www.hmml.org/scholars/catalogue_access/catalog ues_handlists.asp.

Most of Bischoff's papers are collected in *Mittelalterliche Studien: Ausgewählte Aufsätze zur Schriftkunde und Literaturgeschichte*, 3 vols., Stuttgart, 1966–81 and *Anecdota Novissima. Texte des vierten bis sechzehnten Jahrhunderts*, Stuttgart, 1984. Some are translated in *Manuscripts and Libraries in the Age of Charlemagne* (Cambridge Studies in Palaeography and Codicology 1), tr. and ed. M. Gorman, Cambridge, 1994. Also important is *Latin Palaeography. Antiquity and Middle Ages*, tr. D. Ó Cróinín and D. Ganz, Cambridge, 1990. For further detailed studies see, e.g., *Die südostdeutschen Schreibschulen und Bibliotheken*, vol. 1: *Die bayerischen Diözesen* (Wiesbaden, 1974), vol. 11: *Die vorwiegend österreichischen Diözesen* (Wiesbaden, 1980). There is a microfiche edition of the archives of Bischoff and his predecessor Paul Lehmann (1884–1964): A. Mentzel-Reuters (ed.), *Handschriftenarchiv Bernhard Bischoff (1906–1991) und Paul Lehmann (1884–1964) mit einem Verzeichnis der beschriebenen Handschriften von Marcus Stumpf und Zdenka Stoklaskova* (Bibliothek der MGH, Hs. C 1–C 2), Munich, 1997.

McGurk, *Latin Gospel Books*. M. McNamara, *Studies on Texts of Early Irish Latin Gospels (AD 600–1200)* (Instrumenta Patristica 20), Dordrecht, 1990, is a textual study with a chapter on the history of research.

Another resource for the study of some manuscripts significant for the Latin versions is K. Gamber, *Codices Liturgici Latini Antiquiores* (Spicilegii Friburgensis Subsidia 1), Fribourg, 1968 and *Supplementum* (Spicilegii Friburgensis Subsidia 1A), Fribourg 1988. It is a catalogue by work, with indications of manuscripts and editions.

L. E. Boyle, *Medieval Latin Palaeography. A Bibliographical Introduction* (Toronto Medieval Bibliographies 8), Toronto, Buffalo and London, 1984 is an invaluable reference work. It is updated by Electronic Palaeography: a New Bibliographical Website In memoriam: Leonard Boyle, OP at www.geocities.com/Athens/Aegean/9891/palaeog.html.

Among many palaeographical handbooks, note the following: M. P. Brown, *A Guide to Western Historical Scripts from Antiquity to 1600*, London, 1990; Gibson, *Bible in the Latin West*; A. Derolez, *The Palaeography of Gothic Manuscript Books. From the Twelfth to the Early Sixteenth Century* (Cambridge Studies in Palaeography and Codicology 9), Cambridge, 2003.

It is regrettable that a division grew up between palaeography as an academic discipline and calligraphy (rediscovered by Edward Johnson in the early twentieth century). A example of a book by an expert scribe from which the academic may learn is S. Knight, *Historical Scripts. A Handbook for Calligraphers*, London, 1986 [1984]. I once spent a memorable afternoon as the author demonstrated to me the variations of technique and the importance of pen angle as he produced fluent imitations of Greek majuscule and Latin uncial scripts. Another work with an interesting approach, including a history of Latin palaeography and a study of the mechanics of writing, is J. Stiennon with G. Hasenohr, *Paléographie du moyen âge*, Paris, 1973.

The abbreviations in Latin manuscripts are often confusing. For assistance, see A. Cappelli, *Lexicon abbreviaturarum. Dizionario di abbreviature latine ed italiane* etc., 6th edn, Milan, 1990. There is an electronic guide by O. Pluta at www.ruhr-uni-bochum.de/philosophy/projects/abbrev.htm.

Online resources include the website of the Comité international de paléographie latine (http://www.irht.cnrs.fr/cipl/cipl.htm), with bibliographies of catalogues of dated manuscripts arranged by countries and of palaeographical terminology (French, Italian and Spanish).

1.4.3 A brief guide to Latin palaeography

The development of Greek and Latin manuscripts is closely interwoven, each influencing the other. The majority of the oldest manuscripts of the New Testament are written in uncial, a regular and rounded form of writing. It is quite surprising to find exceptions, such as a tiny scrap of John written in the fifth century in the script known traditionally as rustic capital (*capitalis rustica*), now more generally called capitalis. Uncial shows some strong regional characteristics, so that manuscripts can be fairly precisely located, for example to Italy or North Africa. Various forms of half-uncial are also found. Uncial gave way to other distinctive forms of script which, with the distinctive habits of manuscript production favoured in certain areas, make it possible to locate manuscripts of the sixth, seventh and eighth centuries. For example, insular manuscripts (embracing Irish, other Celtic and Anglo-Saxon scripts) follow different rules for the relationship of the hair and flesh sides of the parchment in the folding of the sheets and in the ruling. The study of manuscripts from the beginnings of the Carolingian period onwards is, as has been stated, highly refined in the recognition of local habits.

1.4.4 Tools for the study of Old Latin manuscripts

Many of the most commonly used materials have been produced by the Vetus Latina Institut, Beuron. Beginning a hundred years ago, a parish priest in Munich called Josef Denk devoted almost a quarter of a century to making a card index of all Old Latin citations of the Bible from works written before 800. After his death in 1927, the collection was taken over by the Archabbey of Beuron, and in 1945 Bonifatius Fischer founded the Institut there for the purpose of making a new edition of the Old Latin Bible, to replace the two-hundred-year-old edition of Sabatier (see 3.3.2).

The first volume of the edition consisted of lists of manuscripts and writers whose works contained citations to be included. This was in time to be separated into two sets of lists, one of manuscripts and one of writers, the latter going through a series of revisions and updates.

B. Fischer, *Verzeichnis der Sigel für Handschriften und Kirchenschriftsteller* (*Vetus Latina* 1), 1949. The manuscript list is Gryson, *Altlateinische Handschriften*, vol. 1, 1999. A second volume published in 2004 is devoted to manuscripts of the Psalter. It contains an addenda to volume 1 and an index of manuscripts by place, library and classmark. For the list of writers, see 3.2.3.

A brief history of the Institut and edition is available at http://erzabtei-beuron.de/kultur/vetus_latina.php.

The Old Latin manuscripts are traditionally designated with a lower-case roman letter or letters, sometimes with a superscript arabic numeral distinguishing between the same letter designation (e.g. ff^1 and ff^2, r^1 and r^2). This system ran into the same problems as the use of upper-case letters for Greek majuscule manuscripts, namely that the use of the same siglum for manuscripts of different parts of the New Testament caused confusion and that the sequence became exhausted. The Vetus Latina Institut therefore introduced a numbering system in the 1949 list. The sequence in 1949 ran from 1 to 41 for the Gospels, with eight numbers left blank, followed by the Acts and Catholic epistles, which ran from 50 to 67, the Pauline epistles (75–96). Manuscripts containing more than one of these three divisions of the New Testament are listed in the first collection of the three which they contain. There are no manuscripts containing Revelation only. The Old Testament sequence begins at 100. The 1999 list fills some of the spaces, the sequences now extending to 47, 74 and 96. Each entry contains six sections: H (basic codicological and palaeographical data including date), I (contents), E (editions), Z (critical editions in whose critical apparatuses they appear), T (brief indication of the text type(s) and L (selective bibliography).

In addition to these tools and to the edition itself (see 6.3.5), Beuron has produced a companion series of monographs, 'Aus der Geschichte der lateinischen Bibel'. As of 2006, thirty-seven titles have been published since the first appeared in 1957.

Elliott's *Survey of Manuscripts* includes an appendix on Old Latin manuscripts (pp. 259–80). The same editions of the Greek New Testament are included (Nestle–Aland[26], Bover–O'Callaghan, the three UBS editions then in existence, Merk, Vogels, BFBS[2], Souter[2] and IGNTP *Luke*) and the same three synopses (*Synopsis Quattuor Euangeliorum*[10], Huck–Greeven and Orchard). Two Latin editions, Jülicher's *Itala* and the Wordsworth and White Vulgate (see 3.3.2) are also included. See also the same author's 'Old Latin Manuscripts in Printed Editions of the Greek New Testament', *NovT* 26 (1984), 225–48.

Mention must also be made of the series Old Latin Biblical Texts, consisting mostly of transcriptions of manuscripts, published at Oxford in the late-nineteenth and early-twentieth centuries.

1.4.5 Tools for the study of Vulgate manuscripts

In the absence of a list of all Vulgate manuscripts, the researcher needs to gather information in other ways. It must be recognised that there is always a risk of partial results. It is hoped that the development of an online list of Latin biblical manuscripts to which researchers may add entries will in time improve the situation (see www.vetuslatina.org). Until fairly recently, the first step in looking for Vulgate manuscripts was often the list of witnesses in the Wordsworth and White edition of the New Testament. The situation is better now, at least so far as the Gospels are concerned, since Bonifatius Fischer's study of their text down to the year 900 in 447 manuscripts (see 10.5.2).

It will be seen that as far down as the ninth century, the world of Latin manuscripts is smaller than the world of Greek manuscripts. The description of over 1,800 manuscripts by Lowe was a major task, but one that a determined and skilled individual was able to accomplish. To make a comparable 'Codices Graeci Antiquiores' would be another matter altogether. The vast numbers of papyri recovered in modern times (over

Table 1.1

Century	Greek	Old Latin	Vulgate
II	2	N/A	N/A
III	36	0	N/A
IV	38	2	N/A
V	55	13	3
VI	75	7	19
VII	51	8	22
VIII	60	19	90
Total	317	49	134

Note: Manuscripts dated across two centuries are counted in the later one.

Table 1.2

Century	Old Latin
IX	19
X	10
XI	6
XII	2
XIII	4
XIV	1

four and a half thousand published from Oxyrhynchus alone) is one reason for this.

The number of Greek and Latin New Testament manuscripts for the second to the eighth Christian centuries are shown in table 1.1. For the period 400–800, that is after Jerome had made his revision of the Gospels, we have 241 Greek and 181 Latin manuscripts. It is clear that the number of extant Latin manuscripts from the eighth century onwards is far higher than from earlier centuries. By contrast, it is only from the tenth century that the number of extant Greek manuscripts increases dramatically.

A list of all the numbers of Old Latin manuscripts for subsequent centuries (to qualify, a manuscript must have a number in the Gryson list) can be seen in table 1.2. These tables give us some picture of the Latin manuscripts down to the ninth century, and of their general character.

Beyond that, study grows more complicated since it is evident that most of the estimated remaining 9,500 manuscripts are still unaccounted for. Of these, we cannot rule out the possibility that some may prove textually valuable (take the example of a manuscript dated to about 800 in the National Museum, Budapest containing an important version of the text of Paul, whose value was only discovered recently; see 8.5.2). The business of piecing together the history of the medieval Vulgate text progresses by many independent studies of small parts. For the purposes of this book we have ventured far enough into the medieval west – with the exception of the Gospel Harmony tradition, which will be discussed separately (10.7).

For annotated bibliographies accompanying accounts of the early and medieval Vulgate, see de Hamel, *The Book*.

Latin biblical manuscripts, like Greek ones, often contain commentaries. They also contain a wide range of prologues. A guide to both of these has been provided by Stegmüller's *Repertorium*. The prologues can be as useful as the forms of text in recognising the groupings of manuscripts, as can other ancillary material such as the chapter lists normally found in Latin manuscripts. This is not true of Latin manuscripts only. The ancillary text in every language may prove as important as the biblical text itself in finding textual groupings.

Stegmüller, *Repertorium*. Among specialist studies of the prologues, see D. De Bruyne, *Préfaces de la Bible latine*, Namur, 1920.

1.5 SYRIAC MANUSCRIPTS

The Syriac manuscripts can be dealt with rather more briefly here, the details of research being given in the various chapters of Part III. This is because of the complicated situation with regard to the different Syriac versions. Not only are they more in number than the division into two textual forms (Old Latin and Vulgate) of Latin manuscripts, but the situation also differs for different sections of the New Testament.

In brief, there is the

Old Syriac version, best understood in the Gospels, since the only two manuscripts of the version contain these alone;

the Peshitta, containing all the New Testament except for 2 Peter, 2 and 3 John, Jude and Revelation, which are not in the Syrian canon. The great majority of manuscripts contain this version, the 'Vulgate' of the Syrian Church;

the Philoxenian, a revision of the Peshitta carried out in 508, of all twenty-seven books;

the Harklean, a scholarly revision of the twenty-seven books of the Philoxenian version, carried out by Thomas of Harkel and finished in 616;

the Christian Palestinian Aramaic, usually classified among the Syriac versions, of uncertain origin but predating the sixth century, and extant only in a very incomplete form, namely parts of the Gospels, Acts, most of the Pauline letters and 2 Peter.

Some of the principal tools for textual analysis consist of synoptic arrangements of these versions such as Kiraz, *Comparative Edition of the Syriac Gospels* (10.5.1) and the Münster *Das Neue Testament in syrischer Überlieferung*, of which three volumes have appeared (8.5.1, 9.3.3.2). Based on new manuscript resources and patristic evidence and with detailed prolegomena, the major Catholic letters (i.e. all those included in the Peshitta) and those of Paul have been published.

While Greek and Latin texts, whatever their date and whatever the script in which they were produced and transmitted in manuscript form, are printed and written today in a single script, Syriac printed New Testament books may be found in one of three scripts. Estrangelo is the oldest of the three. The name might be derived from the Greek στρογγύλος, 'rounded', 'neat', but this is a long way from certain. It is the script in which the Old Syriac Gospel manuscripts are written. The other two scripts owe their separate existence to the division between those Syrian Christians who accepted the decisions of the Council of Chalcedon and those who did not, preferring the views of Nestorius. There are exceptions, but by and large the former used the Serta script. This was traditionally sometimes called Jacobite, a term to be avoided as somewhat pejorative, and Maronite among the Syrians of India. The third script is Madnhaya ('eastern'), also called Nestorian (again a term to be avoided) and Assyrian. Serta is found mostly within the Roman empire, Madnhaya further east. A fourth kind of writing should be mentioned, the use of Syriac scripts for copying Arabic texts. Known as Karshuni, this practice began in the seventh century when the Arabic language had begun to dominate but Arabic scripts were hardly known. It has continued in use ever since.

Thus far we see at least as great a degree of variation in script as among Greek or Latin manuscripts, since the difference between Estrangelo and Serta is as great as that between the Greek majuscule and pure minuscule or between Latin uncial and minuscule. Whether it is because there is less variation between the manuscripts of each of these three scripts, or because research has taken a different course, the kind of historical analysis of scripts provided by a Thompson or a Bischoff is absent. The primary palaeographical tool for the study of Syriac manuscripts is Hatch's *Album of Dated Syriac Manuscripts*. There is no monograph devoted to the history of Syriac palaeography.

The most recent work (too recent to be used in the writing of this book) is S. P. Brock, D. G. K. Taylor and W. Witakowski, *The Bible in the Syriac Tradition* (Gorgias Handbooks 7), Piscataway, 2006 (there is also a Syriac translation by E. Aydin, Piscataway, 2002), chapter 3; W. H. P. Hatch, *Album of Dated Syriac Manuscripts*, with a new Introduction by L. Van Rompay, Piscataway, 2002. Hatch was an enthusiastic researcher, but his palaeographical skills were somewhat limited. Several dozen Syriac manuscripts are illustrated in E. Tisserant, *Specimina Codicum Orientalium* (Tabulae in Usum Scholarum 8), Bonn, 1914. The Schøyen Collection website provides some images of Syriac scripts, which at any rate offers a brief overview: www.nb.no/baser/schoyen/4/4.4/46.html. There are four plates in H. J. Vogels, *Codicum Novi Testamenti Specimina*, Bonn, 1929. S. P. Brock (ed.), *The Hidden Pearl: the Syrian Orthodox Church and its ancient Aramaic Heritage*, 3 vols., Rome, 2001 covers manuscript studies. There is an equivalent to Richard in Syriac studies: A. Desreumaux, *Répertoire des bibliothèques et des catalogues de manuscrits syriaques*, Paris, 1991.

For information on collections, see J. Simon, 'Répertoire des bibliothèques publiques et privées d'Europe contenant des manuscrits syriaques', *Orientalia* 9 (1940), 271–88, listing libraries and their catalogues.

1.6 COPTIC MANUSCRIPTS

There are a number of different Coptic versions. Here the determining factor in classifying them is not the text form, as we have seen with Latin and Syriac manuscripts, but the dialect in which they are written. The naming and taxonomy of these dialects have changed since the nineteenth century, and care must be taken in using the terminology used in text-critical works. The following will be encountered at one point or another in the following pages:

Sahidic (known in older scholarship as Thebaic), in which most New Testament manuscripts are written down to the ninth century;

Bohairic (known in older scholarship as Memphitic), used in northern Egypt, becoming the dominant form of the language and the liturgical choice of the Coptic Church from the eleventh century;

Fayyumic (also known in older scholarship, notably for us in Tischendorf, *Editio octava*, as Bashmuric) was spoken in the Fayyum, on the west bank of the Nile south of Cairo;

Middle Egyptian (also known as Oxyrhynchite, since it was spoken in that area, is rather similar to Fayyumic;

Akhmimic was spoken around the town of Akhmim in Upper Egypt, flourishing in the fourth and fifth centuries;

Sub-Akhmimic (also called Lycopolitan) is very similar to Akhmimic; a dialect known simply as 'V'.

There is a useful Selected Bibliography on the Coptic Language at http://online.mq.edu.au/pub/AHPG897/biblio.html.

It is rather discouraging to read an article which begins 'What surveys of Coptic palaeography do exist are almost exclusively concerned with the hands of literary texts, the dating of which is a notoriously difficult affair' and goes on to cite another scholar's statement that 'dating Coptic texts is still a very rough art and provides a rather insecure foundation', and to turn to another which offers the view that 'Coptic palaeography, in the narrow sense of the precise science of dating Coptic manuscripts according to the form of their script, does not yet exist'.

Quotations from L. S. B. MacCoull, 'Dated and Datable Coptic Documentary Hands before AD 700', *Le Muséon* 110 (1997), 349–66, p. 349 and note 1 citing R. S. Bagnall, *Egypt in Late Antiquity*, Princeton, 1993, 240; L. Bentley, 'Towards a New Coptic Bibliography', in T. Orlandi and F. Wisse (eds.), *Acts of the Second International Congress of Coptic Studies*, Rome, 1985, 149–58, p. 152.

The following are also to be noted: H. Hyvernat, *Album de paléographie copte*, Paris, 1888; V. Stegemann, *Koptische Paläographie*, Heidelberg, 1936; T. Orlandi, 'Definition of Textological Data for Coptic Texts', *Polata Knigopisnaya* 17–18 (1987), 96–105. A good source for Coptic bibliography of all kinds is T. Orlando (ed.), *Coptic Bibliography*, produced under the auspices of the Unione Accademica Nazionale, 1989.

L. Hyvernat, 'Pourquoi les anciennes collections de manuscrits coptes sont si pauvre', *RB* 10 (1913), 422–8

The surveys of Coptic palaeography which do exist are almost exclusively concerned with the hands of literary texts, the dating of which is a notoriously difficult affair. The earliest Coptic palaeography book was produced as an accompaniment to the author's work on Coptic martyr acts and is literary-oriented as a matter of course. Nearly eighty years later Maria Cramer's *Koptische Paläographie* (Wiesbaden, 1964), undertaken in connection with the early 60s Coptic art boom sparked by exhibits in Essen and Paris, remains both literary in scope and so error-filled that it has been described as useless. Only Viktor Stegemann's *Koptische Paläographie* (Heidelberg, 1936) included some documents in its illustrations and alphabet charts. Recent work on Coptic palaeography, like so much of what was conceived of as 'Coptic studies' in general, has revolved around the Nag Hammadi codices and their bookhands.

Of course, since the interest here is in literary texts, one might feel that the situation is not so bad, except that datable documents contribute to the dating of literary texts. One of the problems is the absence of fixed dates. MacCoull describes six documents, the earliest dated 535/6 and the latest 625. This is simply not enough material to work with. Layton reports that the earliest dated colophon in a Coptic manuscript is from AD 888/9. Another guide is the other script of bilingual manuscripts, especially where that other script is Greek. To make matters worse, Coptic scripts seem to have continued in use for long periods of time. There does not seem to be quite the amount of development and regional variation which has been detected in Greek and Latin manuscripts. Or is it that the methodology for recognising fine details has yet to be developed? Is Coptic palaeography just awaiting its Montfaucon or its Traube, or will it always remain problematical?

Layton calls for an organised programme in five steps: making a list of all manuscripts; collecting data on all dated manuscripts; storing the data in a database; making a chronological album of all dated and datable manuscripts, and finally publishing the data from the database. This sounds a good approach, but it should be noted that it does not offer much hope for the manuscripts of the earlier centuries, precisely the period which for the New Testament scholar is likely to be most interesting.

The situation is much more encouraging when one comes to the cataloguing of Coptic manuscripts of the New Testament, as will be seen in 3.3.4. One feature of this cataloguing should be mentioned here. Coptic manuscripts have often been broken into parts before sale (for commercial reasons), being acquired by a number of buyers. As a result, some manuscripts have been catalogued as a number of separate items in different libraries. The most notable example is 070, which had eleven separate entries in the first edition of the *Liste*. The recognition that separate items belong together cannot always be taken safely on the grounds of palaeographical judgement alone. Format and contents also play a part. In the example of 070, the presence of page numbers makes the task comparatively straightforward.

F.-J. Schmitz, 'Neue Fragmente zur bilinguen Majuskelhandschrift 070', Münster *Bericht für die Jahre 1979 bis 1981*, 1982, 71–92.

I.7 MANUSCRIPTS IN MORE THAN ONE LANGUAGE

Bilingual manuscripts of New Testament writings are not uncommon, and there are even some which are trilingual. It is easy to find out about those of which Greek is one language, since the *Liste* always indicates bi- and trilingual manuscripts in the statement of the contents of a manuscript. In short, there are

24 Graeco-Latin manuscripts
39 Graeco-Coptic manuscripts
16 Graeco-Arabic manuscripts
3 Graeco-Old Slavonic manuscripts
1 Graeco-Armenian manuscript
1 Graeco-Turkish manuscript
Total, 84 manuscripts

There are two trilingual manuscripts, one being Graeco-Latino-Arabic and the other Coptic-Graeco-Arabic.

There is a full list in Parker, *Codex Bezae*, 59–69. My list of Graeco-Coptic manuscripts (p. 60) needs revising in the light of changes to active numbers (mostly through the recognition that separate fragments are parts of the same manuscript) and new additions in the second edition of the *Liste*. Down to Entry 46 it remains unchanged. From there on, read:

47. 0276 + *l*962 + *l*1353a
48. 0298
49. 0299
50. *l*143 + *l*964a + part of *l*1353
51. *l*961
52. *l*962 + 0276 + part of *l*1353
53. *l*964 (formerly *l*964b)
54. *l*965 + 0114
55, *l*1355
56. *l*1602 + *l*1566 + *l*1678
57. *l*1604
58. *l*1606
59. *l*1614
60. *l*1739
61. *l*1741 + part of *l*965 + *l*1994
62. *l*2283
63. *l*2284

The Graeco-Armenian manuscript (256) is partly trilingual, there being an Italian column in the Catholic epistles and the first four chapters of Revelation.

Finding information about manuscripts in pairs of languages which do not include Greek is less straightforward. However, the study of such copies reveals information about the reception of the New Testament into new cultures. One of the leading examples concerns the Gothic version which, while it is translated from the Greek, has also a relationship to Latin. This is seen in various phenomena: that several of the few extant Gothic New Testament manuscripts are Latino-Gothic bilinguals, in the general appearance and various characteristics of Codex

Argenteus (the principal manuscript of the version) and in features of the translation. How far there is direct interference of the Latin in the Gothic rendering of the Greek is debated, but it seems clear that it cannot be ruled out. Another important group of bilinguals are those in which one language is Arabic. There are a number of Arabic versions and revisions, and the bilinguals are a useful tool in studying them.

B. M. Metzger, 'Bilingualism and Polylingualism in Antiquity; with a Check-list of New Testament Manuscripts Written in More than One Language', in W. C. Weinrich (ed.), *The New Testament Age: Essays in Honor of Bo Reicke*, Macon, 1984, II.327–34.
 On the Gothic, see further 3.3.10; on the Arabic, 3.3.8.

There are two basic formats in which bilingual manuscripts are presented: either in parallel columns or with an interlinear translation. The former has various possibilities. Usually the Greek is on the left; there can be either one or two columns to the page, and if there are two then the two texts can either occupy a column of the page each, or each have a page to themselves; the lines can be written either in full column blocks or in sense-lines (in which case the two texts are truly parallel to each other). The interlinear version may be either part of the original manuscript production or a separate process (the interlinear version with which readers are most likely to be familiar is that found in the Lindisfarne Gospels, which was added by one Aldred in the tenth century).

Particularly important bilingual manuscripts which will feature in Part III are Codex Bezae (see 9.2.2), Codex Laudianus (9.2.2), and a group of manuscripts of Paul (8.4).

1.8 MANUSCRIPTS CONTAINING THE ENTIRE NEW TESTAMENT

The great majority of New Testament manuscripts, in Greek and in many other languages, contain only one part of the four possible sets of Gospels, Acts and Catholic epistles, Paul and Revelation. Most manuscripts contain only the Gospels. There are some manuscripts which contain two or more of the four groups. A small number contain all of the twenty-seven New Testament books, some of them with additional literature. Others contain all but Revelation, and there are various other combinations.

The correct number of Greek manuscripts containing the entire New Testament appears to be sixty-one. Of these, between six and eight contain (or contained) the entire Bible.

1.8.1 Ancient Greek manuscripts

It is a remarkable fact that the fourth-century Christian book was so much more than a first hesitant attempt at the parchment codex. Evidence that the papyrus format began slowly with the initial experiment of the single-quire codex was noted in 1.1. But from the fourth-century copies, Codex Sinaiticus and its contemporary Codex Vaticanus, we have two parchment manuscripts that are superior to most other parchment manuscripts of any date, in the quality of the materials as well as in the skill of the execution. From the fifth century survive two more manuscripts of an almost equally high standard. This is followed by a period of five hundred years from which we have no complete Bible.

To produce a single codex containing the entire New Testament writings in a single-quire codex would have been impossible. Only with the introduction of multiple gatherings could codices begin to realise their potential. But even so, a papyrus codex did not have the capacity for more than a part of the New Testament. The fragility and short lifespan of papyrus is often stated too highly. It was in fact a tough and flexible product. But it certainly does not compare in strength with animal skin. This is apparent when one compares the physical dimensions of papyrus and parchment codices. We have already seen that P66, at 14 cm × 16 cm, is more normal and that the largest papyrus is 19 cm × 31 cm. A parchment page is stronger and can therefore have a much bigger format. The capacity led to the codex becoming a legally recognised format from the early third century, so that the great legal digests of Theodosius and Justinian were each called a codex. The four ancient (certainly or possibly) complete Bibles make full use of the opportunity:

01: 38 × 43 cm
02: 26 × 32 cm
03: 27 × 27 cm
04: 27 × 32 cm

It is necessary to say a little about each of them in turn.

For the legal usage of the word 'codex', see Thompson, *Introduction*, 51. For the fourth-century biblical manuscripts generally, see T. S. Pattie, 'The Creation of the Great Codices', in J. L. Sharpe and K. Van Kampen (eds.), *The Bible as Book: the Manuscript Tradition*, London and New Castle, Del., 1998, 61–72 (dealing with 01, 02 and 03).

01 (Codex Sinaiticus, ℵ) is divided between four locations: St Catherine's Monastery, Sinai (where all of the manuscript was kept from antiquity

until the nineteenth century); Leipzig University Library (41 leaves of the Old Testament); the National Library of Russia, St Petersburg (whither much of it, including the entire New Testament, was taken in 1859); and the British Library, London (all of the St Petersburg leaves except for a few fragments having been bought from the Soviet Government in 1933). The manuscript was produced by at least three scribes. Its original contents were the Septuagint, without 2 and 3 Maccabees, and the Greek New Testament with the *Epistle of Barnabas* and the *Shepherd of Hermas* (it is lost completely after Mandates 4.3, so we do not know whether it contained any further texts).

Milne and Skeat, *Scribes and Correctors*; S. McKendrick, *In a Monastery Library. Preserving Codex Sinaiticus and the Greek Written Heritage*, London, 2006. This is the first publication to contain illustrations of the manuscript from all four locations in which it is now held. There is a German version based on this, with different illustrations as far as other manuscripts are concerned: U.J. Schneider (ed.), *Codex Sinaiticus. Geschichte und Erschliessung der 'Sinai-Bibel'*, Leipzig, 2006. A. C. Myshrall, 'Codex Sinaiticus'; Jongkind, *Codex Sinaiticus*; A. Rahlfs, *Verzeichnis der griechischen Handschriften des Alten Testaments*, rev. D. Fraenkel, vol. 1, *1, Die Überlieferung bis zum VIII. Jahrhundert* (Septuaginta. Vetus Testamentum Graecum Supplementum), Göttingen, 2004, 190, 201–6, 324–5, 330–2, 359–61. For an account of a forger's false claim to have written the manuscript, see J. K. Elliott, *Codex Sinaiticus and the Simonides Affair. An Examination of the Nineteenth Century Claim that Codex Sinaiticus was not an Ancient Manuscript* (Ἀνάλεκτα Βλατάδων 33), Thessaloniki, 1982.

02 (Codex Alexandrinus), written by either two or three scribes in the fifth century, contained the Septuagint with the *Psalms of Solomon* (to be precise the *Psalms of Solomon* are listed in the table of contents, but are no longer extant), the New Testament and 1 and 2 Clement.

The bibliography on this manuscript is surprisingly sparse. It deserves a new full-scale study. Milne and Skeat, *Scribes and Correctors*, 91–3; S. McKendrick, 'The Codex Alexandrinus, or the Dangers of Being a Named Manuscript', in McKendrick and O'Sullivan, 1–16; Fraenkel, *Verzeichnis*, 221–6.

03 (Codex Vaticanus), of the same period as 01, contains the Septuagint without the books of Maccabees (this is generally considered to have been an oversight). In the New Testament we have the Four Gospels, Acts and Catholic epistles, and the Pauline letters. Since the manuscript is lost from Hebrews 11.4 onwards, we cannot know whether it contained Revelation, or what other books may have been present. The Alands have suggested that it originally contained Revelation and writings of the Apostolic Fathers. Elliott considers it never to have contained Revelation. Because of this gap in our knowledge, in my view we should speak of seven rather than eight complete Greek Bibles among the manuscripts.

J. K. Elliott, 'The Distinctiveness of the Greek Manuscripts of the Book of Revelation', *JTS* 48 (1997), 115–24. Martini, *Codice B alla luce del papiro Bodmer XIV*, contains a description of the manuscript and the history of research, 1–41. See also J. N. Birdsall, 'The Codex Vaticanus: Its History and Significance', in McKendrick and O'Sullivan, 33–42; T. C. Skeat, 'The Codex Vaticanus in the Fifteenth Century', *JTS* 35 (1984), 454–65, repr. in *Collected Biblical Writings*, 122–34; J. K. Elliott, 'T. C. Skeat on the Dating and Origin of Codex Vaticanus', in Skeat, *Collected Biblical Writings*, 281–94; Fraenkel, *Verzeichnis*, 337–44.

P. B. Payne has recently drawn attention to a feature in the manuscript which he believes to be an indicator of ancient textual criticism. This is the appearance of a pair of dots side by side in the margin opposite places where there is a textual problem. The description of these as 'umlauts' is graphic but inappropriate. The use of points in critical sigla in antiquity is found in the διπλῆ περιεστιγμένη, the ὀβελός περιεστιγμένος and the ἀντίσιγμα περιεστιγμένον, but the textbooks seem to be silent on this precise phenomenon (e.g. Gardthausen, *Palaeographie* (1979), II.411–12 (2nd edn; 288–90 in the 1st edn); Devreesse, *Introduction*, 74). Perhaps δίστιγμα would be a more appropriate term. Payne has withdrawn from his initial suggestion that a horizontal line was also part of this feature, correctly acknowledging the possibility that this may be a paragraph marker (παραγραφός). Examples of passages containing significant variants where the mark is found include Jn 7.52 (see 10.10.4) and 1 Cor. 14.33 (see 8.9.1). Until a fuller study is available, the whole matter remains open. See further P. B. Payne and P. Canart, 'The Originality of Text-Critical Symbols in Codex Vaticanus', *NovT* 42 (2000), 105–13, citing his earlier papers and the response of C. Niccum; P. B. Payne, 'The Text-critical Function of the Umlauts in Vaticanus, with Special Attention to 1 Corinthians 14.34–35: a Response to J. Edward Miller', *JSNT* 27 (2004), 105–12.

04 (Codex Ephraemi Rescriptus) is a palimpsest and, as is the usual result of a book being dismembered, scraped and reused to make a new one, it is no longer complete. It contains parts of the wisdom books of the Septuagint and all of the books of the New Testament except for 2 Thessalonians and 2 John. It does not have any additional books, and, though we cannot be absolutely sure that it never contained any, it is not impossible that this is a copy which contained the Septuagint and the New Testament, with no other writings, perhaps the second of a two-volume set, the first having contained the historical writings and the prophets. This claim must, however, be treated with more caution than is usually shown. Tischendorf drew attention to differences between the hands of the Septuagintal and New Testament portions, which are certainly the work of different scribes, concluding that it was nevertheless all one manuscript. The manuscript is of course disbound, being reconstituted into a new copy. This means that once the scripts have been differentiated it becomes harder to prove all the leaves to have been from a single manuscript. The evidence that it does will lie in a comparison of the page layout (which cannot be conclusive) and the fact that all is used for the one new manuscript (which is circumstantial).

Typical of the illogical statements made about this manuscript since Scrivener's *Plain Introduction* is the observation of Kenyon, *Our Bible and the Ancient Manuscripts*, 143 (unchanged in the 1958 revision by A.W. Adams, p. 206): 'The original manuscript contained the whole Greek Bible, but only scattered leaves of it were used by the scribe of St. Ephraem's works, and the rest was probably destroyed.' For Scrivener, see *Plain Introduction*, 1.121–4; Fraenkel, *Verzeichnis*, 313–15. Swete, *Introduction*, 129, is a rare authority to indicate the possibility of doubt that 04 is a single manuscript.

All these codices were of a de luxe quality and were conceived on a grand scale. While Codex Sinaiticus is easily the largest, none of them is small. The use of teams of scribes (at least three for 01, at least two and perhaps three for 02, at least two for 03, and two for the extant portions of 04 (if one grants that it is a single manuscript)) also reveals the size of the task.

The evidence from these extensive surviving witnesses indicates that the single codex New Testament was exceptional in their own times, and unheard of in the succeeding period. To be precise, they are four out of seventy-two parchment continuous-text manuscripts dated before the sixth century. But is this again an example of the shortage of ancient manuscripts distorting our picture? How many odd volumes of sets do we possess? After all, of about three hundred majuscule manuscripts, the greatest number consist of only a few sheets. However, the facts (such as they are) militate against the likelihood that there were ever many complete New Testaments.

Aland and Aland, *The Text of the New Testament*, 83; according to the Alands, of the 299 manuscripts listed in 1989, only 104 comprise more than two folios, and only 18 with a number higher than 046 have more than 30 (pp. 78–9).

Arguments against any of the fragmentary manuscripts being part of entire New Testaments or complete Bibles, are as follows:

(1) I have not personally seen any evidence of quire signatures in extant books indicating that they may have been a part of a whole New Testament.
(2) In the ninth and tenth centuries, from which many manuscripts survive undamaged, there are none. This encourages us to believe that the same *may* be true of the seventh and eighth centuries, from which fewer manuscripts have survived.
(3) All fragmentary majuscule manuscripts contain text from only one of the sets of Gospels, of Paul, of Acts or of the Catholic epistles or of Revelation.

Why did this style of book not gain ground, but rather fade away? One possible answer may lie in parchment production. Even the wonderfully fine parchment of Codex Sinaiticus runs into a number of separate volumes, and a considerable overall thickness. And the coarser parchment which typifies the later majuscule period would have made a complete Bible even more unwieldy. Thus, the abandonment of fine parchment may have rendered the one-volume Bible unviable.

Table 1.3

Contents	Old Latin MSS	Vulgate MSS
Whole Bible	–	4
New Testament	–	3
Gospels	27	117
Gospels, Acts, 3 John (+ other texts)	1	–
Acts	2	3
Acts, Catholic epistles, Revelation	1	2
Acts, Revelation	–	1
Paul	2	20
Paul, Catholic epistles	1	1
Catholic epistles	3	3
Catholic epistles, Revelation	–	2
Revelation	1	1
Total	38	157

The view that there was an early Christian edition of the New Testament, in which certain standard features were imposed on the entire set of texts, has been advanced by D. Trobisch, *The First Edition of the New Testament*, New York and Oxford, 2000. This interesting thesis requires more detailed investigation. See my review, *JTS* 53 (2002), 299–305.

1.8.2 Ancient Latin manuscripts

At first glance, the situation appears to be no different from what has been shown already. An examination of the data in *Codices Latini Antiquiores* (i.e. manuscripts written before the ninth century) yields the results shown in table 1.3. The fragmentary nature of the Latin Bible is reflected in the piecemeal growth of the Vulgate, to whose New Testament Jerome contributed only the Gospels. The concept of the Pandect, the complete Bible, seems to come from the long-lived Cassiodorus (*c.* 490–580). He made manuscript copying an important part of the work of the monastery which he founded at Vivarium near Naples in 554. In this place three kinds of complete Bible were made, including one in nine volumes. While the monastery did not survive into the eighth century, its influence continued, most notably through the production at Monkwearmouth-Jarrow in Northumbria in the early eighth century of three Bibles, planned by Abbot Ceolfrid. Of these one, Codex Amiatinus, survives in its splendour almost undamaged. A few fragments survive of

Table 1.4

	Total	Bible	New Testament
Greek	203	3	–
Latin	194	4	3

another. They turn up in several places in modern times and are known as the Bankes Leaf, the Middleton Leaves and the Greenwell Leaf. The third is completely lost. The fourth complete Bible is the now partially lost Léon, Arch. Cath. 15, of the seventh century.

P. Meyvaert, 'Bede, Cassiodorus, and the Codex Amiatinus', *Speculum* 71 (1996), 827–83.

Three manuscripts usually described as complete New Testaments deserve more detailed description. The first is Codex Fuldensis, dated precisely to 547, unusual in its Diatessaronic form of the Gospels (see 10.7) and in being the first manuscript to contain Laodiceans among Paul's letters (see 8.3). The second is written in cursive minuscule of the first half of the eighth century, and in Lowe's judgement was written 'certainly in France and probably in the north' (*CLA* V.679). In fact the question of the original contents cannot be answered, since it breaks off at Hebrews 7.12. The third manuscript is also of the eighth century. Because its whereabouts have been unknown since at least 1959, detailed comment is impossible. It was probably produced in the Moselle region.

The manuscript identifications are: Fulda, Landesbibliothek Bonifatianus 1 (*CLA* VIII.1196); Paris, Bibl. Nat. Nouv. Acq. Lat. 1063 (*CLA* V.679); Braunsberg, Lyceum Hosianum 2° 5 (*CLA* VIII.1071). Lowe noted that 'The codex has suffered much from water and mice.'

If we compare Greek and Latin parchment manuscripts produced before about 800 (i.e. all Greek manuscripts dated in the *Liste* as VIII/IX or earlier and all manuscripts included in *CLA*), we find the figures shown in table 1.4. We may thus see that a complete Bible is equally rare in Greek and in Latin, and that a complete New Testament on its own is unheard of in Greek, and in Latin is as rare as a complete Bible.

1.8.3 Ninth-century Latin Bibles

There is a greater number of complete Latin Bibles from the Carolingian period. In the Theodulphian recension (see 1.1.2.8) we have the codices

Table 1.5

Century	Complete NT	Number of NT MSS	%
X	1	127	0.79
XI	6	437	1.37
XII	2	588	0.51
XIII	8	573	1.4
XIV	19	539	3.53
XV	11	249	4.42
XVI	5	140	3.6

Theodulphianus, Aniciensis, Hubertanus, and others; from Alcuin's recension Vallicellanus, while of manuscripts with a Spanish text we have Codex Cavensis; from Ireland, there is the Book of Armagh, made in 807 (this manuscript contains texts relating to St Patrick as well).

1.8.4 Byzantine Greek New Testaments

At a slightly later period we see complete New Testaments in Greek again. The analysis of the contents of these witnesses takes a little investigation. For, while the *Liste* tells us that they contain all the New Testament and indicates if they are a complete Bible, it requires the library catalogue to tell us what else they may contain, and to gather the codicological details which may cast light on the manuscript's original form. Microfilm may be necessary to find out about the hands, and even then it is possible that only an examination of the manuscript itself will tell us what we need to know, namely whether it is a composite manuscript.

Taking the information in the *Liste*, the number of manuscripts which are described as containing the entire New Testament, by the century given for their copying, are shown in table 1.5. In fact, the total is misleading. Several of the manuscripts are written in hands of different dates and are thus separate manuscripts which happen to be bound together. An example of this is 180: the Gospels are twelfth century; the rest is dated 1273. 1857 and 1140 are of a similar character. Others are manuscripts to which Revelation was added later: 209 is a fourteenth-century copy of the Gospels, Apostolos and Paul to which Revelation was added in the fifteenth century; 1668 was written with the same original contents in the eleventh century, Revelation being supplied from a printed copy in the sixteenth century. It is not obvious without further research whether the later part was written to complement the older, or whether the two were only bound together at a subsequent point.

The oldest of these minuscules is 1424, a manuscript now in Chicago. It is a commentary manuscript for the most part (Chrysostom for the Gospels, Theodore, Severian and Theodoret for Paul). The writings are in the order Gospels–Acts–Catholic epistles–Revelation–Paul. The colophon is interesting for the way in which the collection of works is described:

Ἐγράφη τοίνυν ἡ παροῦσα βίβλος τῶν ἁγίων τεσσάρων εὐαγγελίων τῶν τε πραξέων καὶ τῶν καθολικῶν ἑπτὰ ἐπιστολῶν μετὰ καὶ τῆς ἀποκαλύψεως ὁμοῦ καὶ τῶν δεκατεσσάρων ἐπιστολῶν τοῦ ἁγίου καὶ πανευφήμου καὶ οἰκουμενικοῦ διδασκάλου παύλου ...

A few of these manuscripts are complete Bibles:
  G.–A. 205 and 205abs (see 4.3)
  G.–A. 218
  G.–A. 582 (not indicated as such in the *Liste*; the Septuagint part, which is extensive but not complete, is numbered 106 in A. Rahlfs, *Verzeichnis der griechischen Handschriften des Alten Testaments* (Mitteilungen des Septuaginta-Unternehmens der Akademie der Wissenschaften in Göttingen 2), Berlin, 1914, the equivalent to the *Liste*; entries indicated below as e.g. Rahlfs 44).
Others are plausibly complete Bibles with one or more volumes missing:
  G.–A. 664 with Rahlfs 44 (containing the Octateuch and historical books) may be the first and last (third?) volumes of a Bible.
  G.–A. 33 / Rahlfs 198 is possibly the second volume of a set (ninth century). The Septuagint part contains the Prophets.
  Rahlfs 1914 is two volumes (Vatican Library, Gr. 2106 + Venice, Biblioteca Marciana Gr. Z.1), perhaps of a three-volume set, the New Testament being either lost or unidentified (ninth century). For the second volume, see Fraenkel, *Verzeichnis*, 372–4.
  Vatican Library, Gr. 1 (Rahlfs 55) may be the first volume of a Bible. It was written in about 940.
  I am grateful to Dr Scot McKendrick, Head of Westen Manuscripts at the British Library, for this information.

1.8.5 Syriac manuscripts

In the absence of the tools which would supply this information easily, one must gain an impression how one may. Of the forty-two manuscripts cited in Pusey's edition of the Peshitta Gospels (see 10.5.1), only five contain the entire New Testament. They are spread widely through time, one being fifth/sixth century (his 17), one late seventh (33), one dated 768 (16), and two late twelfth (12 and 42). The late-twelfth-century manuscript numbered 12 is exceptional in containing twenty-seven and not twenty-two books. The others have the books of the Syrian canon (see 1.5). The edition of the Peshitta version of the Pauline letters by B. Aland and Juckel yields another manuscript (roughly thirteenth century) in addition to Pusey's 16 and 17 – one out of an additional eleven witnesses. Their edition of the (greater) Catholic epistles adds one out of eight new manuscripts. Altogether from the three editions, seven out of sixty-one manuscripts contain the whole Syriac New Testament. This indicates a situation analogous to that of Greek and Latin witnesses.

It is not so easy to find out about the Harklean. Only three manuscripts are cited by Aland and Juckel in their editions. Two (Oxford, New College 333, eleventh century, and Cambridge U.L. Add. 1700, dated 1169–70) are complete New Testaments (with the twenty-seven book canon).

Aland and Juckel, *NT in syrischer Überlieferung 1*; *NT in syrischer Überlieferung 2*. Pusey and Gwilliam, *Tetraeuangelium*.

1.8.6 Coptic manuscripts

Since Coptic manuscripts have often been sold in small lots (see 1.6), it is particularly hard to piece together the information. Fortunately the *Biblia Coptica*, covering both the Old and New Testaments, is a valuable source of information here. Manuscripts containing selections such as sa 16[lit] and the lectional selections of course do not count. There are no manuscripts which even remotely qualify among the 560 Sahidic items listed. Nor can one find any potential complete New Testaments among the items listed in the Münster *Liste der koptischen Handschriften des Neuen Testaments* (3.3.4).

1.8.7 The medieval west

Moving back to the west in the Middle Ages, the character of the Latin Bible underwent a great change with the growth of the schools and the emergence of the universities. There are again technological developments. In the earlier period only very large Bibles were produced. Then in the thirteenth century the new technology took two forms: the development of a script small enough to change the economics of the writing material, and of a production system geared to putting a copy into the hand of every student. We may here see how the desire and the technology accompany each other: the schools require the essential textbook, and the technology makes it possible.

de Hamel, *The Book*, chapters 3 ('Giant Bibles of the Early Middle Ages') and 5 ('Portable Bibles of the Thirteenth Century').

1.8.8 The Renaissance and the printing press

Some of the later manuscripts listed in 1.8.4 are associated with the circle of Cardinal Bessarion. The production of complete Bibles and New Testaments may owe something to his desire to bring about a reconciliation between the Greek and Latin communions. His copies are Greek manuscripts following the western custom of including the entire Bible, or at least the entire New Testament. But, so far as Paul's letters are concerned, there are fourteen of them, with no room for 3 Corinthians or Laodiceans. This was in line with the work of the humanists, who showed that these texts were spurious, thus reducing the Pauline corpus to the number of letters which it contained in Greek manuscripts. It is hardly surprising that for Erasmus and his contemporaries, the natural way in which to edit the Greek New Testament was as a purified Latin canon. And yet another technological innovation – the printing press – gave this format a circulation and a popularity that proved irresistible.

1.8.9 Conclusion

The full story of the complete Greek New Testaments and Bibles has yet to be told, whether they were initially complete and became partial copies, or whether they began as smaller entities and were augmented, along with the motivation and circumstances of their creation. What has been offered here is no more than a collection of hints.

   The most significant observation is the role of technological innovation in the growth of the concept of the entire New Testament (or even the entire Bible) contained in a single codex, and indeed in the growth of the individual collections comprising the New Testament. It was seen in 1.1–2 that only with the birth of the codex was it possible to collect all of Paul's letters together in one volume, and that the formation of that collection and of the Four Gospels flourished once the multiple-quire construction had been developed. The possibility of the entire New Testament in one, with the Old Testament included, came from the adoption of parchment with the size to contain so much text, yet of fine enough quality to keep weight and thickness to a minimum. For Greek manuscripts in the Byzantine period, it was the introduction of minuscule that made such a production possible again. In the west the development of small-format Bibles made them normative, and it was on this that the pioneers modelled their concept of the printed Bible and New Testament. So it was that a phenomenon which was a rarity in the ancient and Byzantine Greek worlds has become the norm.

One consequence of the rarity of the complete New Testament is that manuscripts containing it, both Greek and Latin, tend to contain composite forms of text, derived from the different text forms of the collection of exemplars which had to be assembled before the copy could be made. Thus, in Part III we will find that the manuscripts containing the New Testament, or even those containing several of its constituent collections, are of varying importance and quality in the form of text they contain.

For example, there are a number of manuscripts which are Old Latin in part and partly Vulgate:

> 67 (the Léon Bible already mentioned) is a palimpsest, the primary text seventh century, mostly Vulgate, but 1–2 Macc., the Catholic epistles and Acts are Old Latin.
> See *CLA* XI.1636; Gryson, *Altlateinischen Handschriften* I.106. The manuscript is a palimpsest. It was written 'doubtless in Spain, to judge by the presence of Visigothic symptoms' (Lowe). It was reused in the ninth century to copy Rufinus' version of Eusebius' *Church History*.
> 7 (G/g¹ Sangermanensis) is Old Latin for Oratio Salomonis, Tobit, Judith, Canticles, 1 Maccabees 1.1–14.1, Matthew, and Vulgate for the rest. It is early ninth century.
> 86 (A manuscript copied in Milan and still nearby). Although copied as late as the early tenth century, its text of Paul is a pure fourth-century Milanese text.
> 6 (c, Colbertinus), is Old Latin for the Gospels and Acts, and Vulgate for the rest of the New Testament. It was written in the twelfth/thirteenth century.
> 51 (gig, Gigas), of the thirteenth century, is Old Latin in Acts and Revelation, Vulgate for the rest of the Bible. This remarkable manuscript contains the *Etymologiae* of Isidore, Josephus' *Antiquities*, Cosmas of Prague's *Chronicle of Bohemia*, and other texts.

Among Greek manuscripts, 1739 is one of the most important witnesses to the text of Paul, but is of less value in Acts and the Catholic epistles, which make up the rest of it. Codex Alexandrinus is a witness to a form of the Byzantine text in some places but not all.

I.9 USING THE MATERIALS: A TEST CASE

With so many sources of information: the *Liste*, Elliott's *Bibliography*, Richard, facsimiles, catalogues, *Text und Textwert* and all kinds of specialist studies, it should be possible to find out at least something and sometimes quite a lot about any Greek New Testament manuscript. A randomly selected example will illustrate how one should go about gathering information both about a manuscript and its text.

Suppose I want to find out about minuscule 724. Turning to the *Liste*, the information given is

   e   1520   Pg/Pap   203   1   22   14,2 × 10   Wien, Österr. Nat. Bibl., Suppl. gr. 175

So we know that according to the *Liste* it contains the Gospels, was copied in 1520, is written on a mixture of parchment and papyrus, has 203 folios, one column and twenty-two lines, each folio measuring 14.2 cm high and 10 cm across, and is in Vienna. 'Österr. Nat. Bibl.' is expanded on page 504 as Österreichische Nationalbibliothek, the Austrian National Library. Suppl. gr. is the collection 'Supplementum graecum', and within it our manuscript is Number 175.

Going next to Richard, we find that the catalogue of the Vienna Suppl. Gr. manuscripts is by Hunger:

H. Hunger and C. Hannick, *Katalog der griechischen Handschriften der Österreichische Nationalbibliothek*, vol. IV: *Supplementum Graecum*, Vienna, 1994.

The page and a half of entry in question partly confirms and partly corrects the *Liste*. The number of folios given is 208, but there is a note explaining that five of these are endpapers, so there is no discrepancy in terms of the number of leaves containing the text. The list of contents states where each Gospel begins and ends, and it records that the manuscript also contains (Folio 6r-v) the lives of the evangelists by Dorotheus. A reference tells us that this work was edited by von Soden (1.307–8). Dorotheus of Tyre seems to be an otherwise unknown writer. The work is described in Theophylact's commentary on the Gospels as Ἐκ τῆς τοῦ Δωροθέου μάρτυρος καὶ Τυρίων ἐπισκόπου Συνόψεως (Migne, *PG* 123 includes the lives of Mark, Luke and John).

Further information reveals not only the date but also the name of the scribe (all on Folio IIIr): Ammonius Levinus, a latinising of Lieven van der Maude, who lived from 1485 to 1556, a Carthusian scholar of Bois-Saint-Martin near Grammont in Flanders. Also on FIIIr is an ex libris recording that a lawyer called Gulielmus (William) Rentier gave (back?) the codex to the monastery on 16 June 1619. Further information about the page layout and the watermarks, along with some other description, leaves one with a very clear picture of the origin of this manuscript. A cross-reference to Gamillscheg, Harlfinger and Hunger, *Repertorium* (the volumes for Great Britain) gives further literature on the scribe, who moreover is to be found in Vogel and Gardthausen (p. 15). Their entry indicates that Lieven van der Maude was responsible for a manuscript now in Dresden (Sächsische Landesbibliothek 304) of works by Gregory of Nazianzus which he made in 1540.

We now have detailed information on the production, including an exact date, a scribe about whom a certain amount is known, and a place. The next stage is to collect information on the text. Reference to Elliott's *Bibliography* adds only one reference to what we have already discovered, and this is to von Soden, 132. This directs us to Section 132 in volume II of von Soden (pp. 743–4). He states that it is one of a group which he calls 'K-Mss of μ^5 strongly influenced by μ^6'. This is not the moment to go into the complexity of von Soden's work, or we will lose sight of our manuscript. Suffice it at present to say that von Soden classified manuscripts by an analysis of John 7.53–8.11, and that μ^5 and μ^6 are two groups within the mass of Byzantine manuscripts (which he designates K). The groups are described on pages 487–90. Since von Soden numbered the manuscript ε530, we have to be on the lookout for this symbol. The description of the μ^5/μ^6 group on pages 743–4 links our manuscript especially closely (so far as one can determine from what is written) with von Soden's manuscripts ε513 δ600 ε703 ε704 ε707 ε708 ε800. These translate into the following Gregory–Aland numbers:

525, a fifteenth-century bilingual manuscript (Graeco-Slavonic)
296, a sixteenth-century manuscript possibly copied from a printed edition (according to the *Liste*)
956, a seventeenth-century manuscript in Mount Athos
963, another of the same (dated to 1636)
1629, the same, from another monastery (dated 1653)
1086, the same, from a third monastery (dated 1648)

What is ε800? It should be an eighteenth-century Gospel manuscript. Apart from a cross-reference to this page in his index, I cannot find any other mention of such a manuscript, nor is this or a similar number found in the tools for changing von Soden into Gregory–Aland numbers. There may be an explanation which I have overlooked, or it may be an error. Such a problem is not unexpected to the user of von Soden.

We thus have in von Soden's view a group of late manuscripts. It is now necessary to see whether *Text und Textwert* corroborates this picture. It is certainly immediately clear that these manuscripts are all Byzantine in text (hardly very surprising, given their late date). Because of this, *Text und Textwert* does not give information about the relationships between 724 and other manuscripts. We would have to work that out for ourselves. Because that takes longer, I will deal only with the two manuscripts which von Soden most clearly associates with 724, namely 525 and 296.

The way to proceed is to tabulate the information about distinctive readings in these three manuscripts. Because the aim of *Text und Textwert* is to separate Byzantine readings from non-Byzantine ones, the emphasis is on three types of reading:

2:     readings which are the form of text from which all others are derived
1:     Byzantine readings, different from 2:
1/:   Byzantine readings which are also the form of text from which all others are derived

But the volumes give us other information as well. These are

Subvariants of 1: or 2:	places where the manuscript in question has a variation on the form of text
Distinctive readings	alternative readings to 2: 1: and 1/:
Singular readings	places where the manuscript has a reading found in no other manuscript
Corrections	places where the manuscript has been corrected (it is not indicated whether the corrections (if there is more than one) are all by the same hand, nor are subsequent corrections distinguished from ones by the scribe)

The correlation of this material gives us a profile for the chosen manuscript which may then be compared with other profiles. To return to 724, and starting with Matthew. It is extant for all sixty-four test passages. In these it has

Reading 2:	twice (32, 64)
Reading 1/:	19 times (numbers of passages not listed)
Reading 1:	43 times (numbers of passages not listed)
Subvariants:	1K:14, 1C:59
Two corrections:	9:2, 64:1

The information about the subvariants means that at test passage 14 the manuscript has subvariant 1K, that is Variation K on the 1: reading. The corrections are at test passage 9, where the correction adopts the 2: reading (it is the original reading which has been used in the calculation of the overall text, as is clear from the information about test passage 64, where the original text follows the 2: reading, which has been corrected into conformity with the 1: reading).

The next stage is to tabulate the information about 724 in Matthew with that provided by 296 and 525 (see table 1.6).

There is too little information in this table to go on. However, it is also worthwhile to find the number of manuscripts supporting the 2: readings,

Table 1.6

Reading type	Number of Teststelle	724	296	525
2:	32	x	x	x
	64	x		
Subvariants	1K:14	x		x
	1N:53		x	
	1I:56			x
	1C:59	x		x
	1I:64		x	
Singular	56:1I			x
	64:1I		x	
Distinctive	1:3		x	
Corrections	9:2	x		
	64:1	x		

Note: x indicates that the manuscript has the reading.

Table 1.7

Reading type	Number of Teststelle	724	296	525	Support
2:	32	x	x	x	590 MSS
	64	x			195
Subvariants	1K:14	x		x	18
	1N:53		x		162
	1I:56			x	1
	1C:59	x		x	7
	1I:64		x		1
Singular	56:1I			x	
	64:1I		x		
Distinctive	1:3		x		155
Corrections	9:2	x			180
	64:1	x			1,369

Note: x indicates that the manuscript has the reading.

Table 1.8

Reading type	Number of Teststelle	724	296	525	Support
2:	34	x	x	x	146 MSS
	88	x			141
	119		x	x	17
Subvariants	1D:69		x		90
Distinctive	11:3		x		5
	21:3	x	x	x	219
	26:3	x	x	x	160
	27:3	x			225
	67:3			x	158
	75:3	x			58
	84:3			x	8
	134:3	x			630
	150:11			x	501
Corrections	64:1/			x	1,403

Note: x indicates that the manuscript has the reading.

the subvariants and the distinctive readings. The same information about corrections might (if one were lucky) cast some light on the manuscript's subsequent history. This information is given in the Collation Results, after the list of manuscripts supporting each reading. Adding them in another column gives the results shown in table 1.7.

Probably the most interesting evidence here is the agreement of 724 and 525 in the rarely attested variants 1K:14 and 1C:59. The agreement of all three in Reading 2: at test passage 32 is weakened by the high level of support (about a third of the total number of 1,806 manuscripts included in the volume). All we can say is that von Soden's case, whether it be true for John or not, plausibly holds at least some water when we come to try it out in Matthew. But it is certainly more worthwhile to test it in John. The results from the 153 test passages in John 1–10, covering 1,987 manuscripts, are shown in table 1.8.

This evidence rather weakens von Soden's case for a special link between these manuscripts throughout John 1–10. It does show several very interesting places: the distinctive reading of 296 at test passage 11, shared with only four other manuscripts, and of 525 at test passage 84, with seven others.

So what have we discovered about 724? Enough to have a very good idea about it, when it was made, by whom and where, along with the beginnings of an understanding of how it fits into the textual history of the Gospels. What we are still lacking is an image. That will require a trip to Münster, or even to Vienna, or else the placing of an order with the photographic department of the library. Finally though, we can enquire whether it has been cited in any edition. Reference to Elliott's *Survey* reveals that 724 was listed by both von Soden (which we already knew) and by Gregory's Prolegomena to Tischendorf, *Editio octava* (Gregory examined the manuscript on 23 August 1886). Of the other editions, the only one to cite it is Nestle–Aland[27], where it was introduced in the seventh printing.

CHAPTER 2

Practical skills in the study of manuscripts

2.1 INTRODUCTION

All the data in the Greek New Testament, and thus in the English Bible, have been collected by means of the collating or transcribing of manuscripts. Without this process, there would be no editions and and no informed translations. It is a task as fundamentally necessary to reading the text as the learning of the Greek language. It seems reasonable to suggest therefore that everyone who studies the New Testament, certainly as a student working with the Greek text, should have some basic knowledge of how collating and transcribing is done and should indeed gain a little experience. It used to be the case that many teachers of Greek or of the New Testament required a collation exercise of their students. One does not hear of it so often these days. But it is a valuable experience: the student has to learn to read a Greek hand and to get to grips with a manuscript, to come to terms with the simple yet rigorous demands of being accurate in an essential task. It is good for one's humility, too. Accuracy is everything – but if human beings were accurate transcribers of texts, there would be no need for the exercise!

There are people who would certainly make excellent collators who never find out – because none of their teachers has ever given them the opportunity to try. If the students do not learn, they will certainly not be able to pass the skill on when they in turn become teachers. This chapter (especially sections 2 and 3) is therefore partly intended to provide a basic framework which could be used in any teaching situation, or by anyone starting work on manuscripts.

It is all written from the point of view of Greek manuscripts of the New Testament. The majority, *mutatis mutandis*, could be used for manuscripts in other languages or of other texts.

2.2 VISITING A LIBRARY

Some libraries are understandably cautious about over-use of precious objects. It is reasonable to use a surrogate as much as possible. But where you can demonstrate that there is good reason for you to examine the witness itself, a library will generally make it available. Reasons may include examining ink colours in order to distinguish between correctors or to study illumination, checking whether the writing material is paper or parchment, looking at watermarks, making a thorough description, or because images are either not available or inadequate. The last reason might be due to the nature of the manuscript: palimpsests are sometimes very hard to read in reproduction, while damaged papyrus or parchment fragments may need studying in three rather than two dimensions if one is to interpret them accurately, and holes in a sheet of parchment may lead one to read text on the page beyond instead of that which one was intending to read.

Not all manuscripts are available in reproduction. But when they are, and if a piece of research requires access to a number, perhaps in different libraries and countries, and the justification for looking at originals is not strong, then either the acquisition of microfilm, or a visit to Münster or any other centre where all the resources are available is the best use of time and money.

A few useful tools may be mentioned. One is to take a strip of paper, lay it down the page and write the number of every third line (three is easier than five for counting the other numbers) on it. This makes it possible to find any line on the page quickly, and to check the number of lines on any page. A more sophisticated item, for which one is dependent upon the library, is the microscope. This is essential for detailed study of damaged materials such as ancient papyrus and parchment fragments.

There are some short cuts for finding one's way around a manuscript, in the absence of modern chapter and verse numbers. Nestle–Aland prints (in the inner margin in italics) the chapter divisions 'most widely used in the manuscripts' (p. 78*). These provide the means of finding a passage anywhere in the New Testament. For the Gospels, it is easier to use the Eusebian apparatus. If you are looking for Mark 13.14 in your manuscript, look in Nestle–Aland for the Eusebian paragraph number (which is the arabic number in upright type 142). Look for 142 in the margin of the part of the manuscript containing Mark, and you will find Mark 13.14. For this you need to know Greek numerals up to 355 (the highest Eusebian paragraph number), so as to be able to recognise ρμβ as 142. If you have forgotten your Nestle, and want to look at a parallel passage in another Gospel, you can do so by referring to the appropriate Canon Table at the front of the manuscript (in this case Table VI; see 10.3.1). The same principles apply for manuscripts in other languages. The Eusebian apparatus is found in hand editions of the Latin New Testament, but not in the British and Foreign Bible Society's Peshitta Syriac.

If it is difficult to find a passage or if what you are looking for is missing, it is important to check that the leaves have been bound in the correct order.

Light is very important. Libraries often have various special tools available, including ultraviolet and infrared lamps. But, although many modern reading rooms use artificial light, there is no substitute in my view for good natural light. Sometimes a manuscript becomes far more easy to read when the sun comes out. Most remarkably, some palimpsested majuscules of John's Gospel in St Petersburg were virtually illegible in all lights except for the period in the early morning when (in late June) the sun was coming low through the windows. As the sun rose in the sky, the ink slowly faded as though the writing were magic runes.

2.3 HOW TO DESCRIBE A MANUSCRIPT OF THE GREEK NEW TESTAMENT

The instructions on which this section is based are to be found among the International Greek New Testament Project papers. They had been written by a former editor, K. W. Clark, for the guidance of collators on the project. I have revised it in a number of ways. When inspecting a manuscript it is particularly important to record information which is unlikely to be obvious from a surrogate, such as the dimensions, materials, ruling and information about the covers. As well as using this as a template for describing a manuscript which is either completely new or unknown to New Testament scholarship, this document will also function as a training exercise, and could be used in a palaeography class or for individual practice.

Looking at a good modern catalogue (for example the Hunger catalogue of Viennese manuscripts used in 1.9) is a good way of organising material. Libraries all have their own sets of rules for cataloguing, but there are also forums for discussion. Guidelines for cataloguing in compliance with the TEI (Text Encoding Initiative) should be followed in recording data for electronic presentation.

L. Burnard, R. Gartner and P. Kidd, 'The Cataloguing of Western Medieval Manuscripts in the Bodleian Library: a TEI Approach with an Appendix Describing a TEI-conformant Manuscript Description', August 1997, at http://users.ox.ac.uk/%7Elou/wip/MS/. For this and other useful links, see the website 'Some links concerning medieval manuscript cataloguing, databases, etc.' at www.ucl.ac.uk/~ucgadkw/mscat.html.

Any intensive study of a manuscript begins with a detailed description, which in the course of its study is completed through illustration (Ist die Handschrift gefunden, so orientirt man sich durch eine detaillirte Beschreibung, die im Verlaufe der Arbeit durch Beispiele vervollständigt wird). (Gardthausen, *Palaeographie*, 1st edn, 440)

(1) Library
> Location (including local address)
> Library number of MS
> Name of librarian and contact details
> Various catalogue numbers (former and current, here and elsewhere)
> Previous library or owners

(2) Type of MS
> Continuous text, lectionary, or type of service book, etc.
> Composite contents or unity? One hand, or more?
> Title or description of contents – extent of text – complete or mutilated?
> Lost portions identified elsewhere?

(3) Elementary statistical description
> Size of folio in centimetres (the α measurement). Indicate whether there is evidence that the MS has been trimmed
> Overall size of total writing space (the β measurement)
> Number of columns of writing
> Width of column (in centimetres) if more than one column and width of space(s) between columns
> Number of lines in a column
> If text layout is cruciform or other shape
> In case of old majuscule manuscripts, average number of letters to a line and height of letter
> (Measurements should be taken at several places in the MS at random, since variation is sometimes found in different portions of a MS. Turner (*Typology*) argued that the width should always be given before the height. Most catalogues give height first, and it is best to follow suit.

(4) Number of folios
Does the MS contain one (or more) numeration of folios or pages? By scribe or others? In what characters? Correct or erroneous? If possible, pencil-in the correct numeration, but do not erase any earlier numbers (KWC): **only after full discussion with an authorised librarian** (DCP).

(5) Arrangement in quires (regularly eight folios – irregularity should be especially noted)

> Numeration of quires: where is the number placed?
> by scribe or (an)other(s)?
> in what characters?

(6) Defective quire arrangement noted and described
  Quires completely lacking
  Quires with specified folios missing
  Quires or leaves bound out of order
  Replacement leaves need a complete separate description

(7) Materials
  Parchment (vellum), paper, or papyrus (note any special quality or characteristics); or mixture, such as parchment for outer sheet of gathering and paper for the inner ones
  Arrangement of hair and flesh sides (is Gregory's Rule observed?)
  Ruling form (see Lake corpus (1.3.6); Irigoin; Sautel (1.3.6))
  Watermarks (describe, copy, match with Briquet (see 1.3.10.3))
  Colour, paper (oriental, oiled or western)
  Ink – black, brown, red, gilt, silver, faded, well preserved
  Covers – wood or cardboard
  Leather (what kind), plain, stamped (blind or gilt)
  Cloth (silk, velvet, tapestry), or paper
  Metal adornments (plates, bosses, clasps) described
  Printed title on cover or spine, or on edges of leaves
  Cover guards
  Book plate
  Condition of the codex

(8) Date
  Hand (description of palaeographic criteria) or hands – majuscule or minuscule
  Above or below the line
  Upright or sloping
  Large or small

Square, angular, round
Regular, irregular
Enlarged letters, taller letters
Breathings square or round, *iota* adscript or subscript
Covers (provenance, by whom)
Colophons (scribal or not), dates of later notes
Textual provenance

(9) Contents
Language(s)
Canonical text (Four Gospels, Praxapostolos, New Testament, with or without apocryphal writings, Evangelion, Apostolos)
Order of books
Special points of text, e.g. Pericope Adulterae, end of Mark, Romans doxology, 1 John 5.7
Lacunae noted (explicit, incipit in each case, giving chapter, verse and letters either side of the gap)
Supplied text

(10) Miniatures, headpieces, illuminated initials (with folio numbers)
Colours used
Description of iconographic criteria (e.g. portrait? seated or standing? architectural background? text illustration, or what story, etc.)
Index of contents with folios numbered
Cryptic
Easter Table

(11) Equipment
Commentary (whose?)
Letter of Eusebius to Carpianus
Eusebian canon tables
Kephalaia
Hypotheses (single or double)
Inscription (form, if unusual)
Subscription
Stichoi
Verses
Tract of Dorotheus on the 70 and 12, etc.
Ammonian section numbers in margin
Eusebian canon numbers in margin
Lectionary Equipment in margin
Titloi

Quire numbers, location

Folio enumeration by previous owners

Lectionary tables, synaxarion, menologion (complete?)

Apodemia Paulou

It may not be possible to recognise texts such as the Tract of Dorotheus or the Apodemia Paulou on the spot if one is not familiar with them. If it is not, then record the incipit (the first six or seven words) for later clarification. Do this for each collection of texts and for each Gospel and letter in case several are represented.

Quire arrangements, textual lacunae, and missing folios must correspond, thus also reconstructing the original form of the codex.

(12) Colophons, with location noted (transcribed and translated if possible), date, scribe, ownership, cursing, prayer, repair, and so forth.

(13) Textual Importance

Previously collated (when?, by whom?, what conclusions?)

Type of text, if known; family, if known; otherwise sample collation, or selected critical readings preferably corresponding to Teststellen

(14) History

Provenance (binding, colophon, hand, saints' days in the menologion, miniatures)

Loss of leaves, or covers

Repair

Owners known (colophons, bookplates, catalogues)

Dealers handling it (sales catalogues)

Recent direct source, date of acquisition, present location

(15) Bibliography

Identified in catalogue listings (Scrivener, Gregory, Von Dobschütz, *Liste*, etc.)

Identified in Library catalogues

Identified in Sales catalogues

Critical notices (textual, iconographic, palaeographic)

Periodicals

Collation published

Facsimile published

Sign your description of the MS, and record the date of your examination.

2.4 HOW TO MAKE A PAPER COLLATION OF A MANUSCRIPT

The paper collation held sway as the preferred method for recording the text of manuscripts until recently. It is no longer the preferred method – the electronic transcription is that. But there remain various circumstances under which paper collations might be required. There are those who prefer them for some reason. And then one might find oneself in a library without power or without a computer. So everyone, however unlikely they think it is that they should use it, should know how to make a paper collation.

The following is based upon a document 'Rules for Collators' which I wrote in 1990 for collaborators working for the International Greek New Testament Project. It assumes that you are making a number of collations for an edition or piece of research.

A collation is a list of differences between a manuscript and a printed base text. It is the most compendious way of recording the text of a witness, since it will be known that at every point where no variant is recorded, it agrees with the base text.

The word is used differently in the world of Bibliography, where it describes the collecting of data about the format, quire composition, and other details of a printed book.

(1) Preparation
  (i)   To state the most obvious, all collations must be made against the same base text. What this is should be stated in brief on each collation. The precise edition and printing should be stated (e.g. Nestle–Aland²⁷, 8th printing, 2001; *Textus Receptus*, Oxford, 1873).
  (ii) If you are making a number of collations, it might be worth devising a simple form to attach to each one, to make sure that you record all relevant information. This should include
       your name
       the date of the collation (beginning, end)
       the date(s) of checking
       the manuscript collated (Gregory–Aland number or similar, library and class-mark)
       the form of the collation source (the manuscript or type of surrogate)
       any transcriptions or other collations which you have consulted

(iii) If possible, always use the same size of paper throughout the collation and for all collations. The collation is easier to consult if you leave a blank line between verses. Put the chapter number, and the name or number of the text being collated, at the top of *every* page. Number every page. Put the verse number before the first recorded variant of each verse. The object in this is to be absolutely sure that neither you nor anyone coming after you could be confused in any way.

(iv) It may be necessary to find your way round the manuscript first, if, for example, it is bound with the leaves in the wrong sequence. Anything like this that you do, keep notes. Record what folio the text you are collating begins on in the manuscript.

(v) Equip yourself with a writing implement, such as a black pencil, strong enough to show clearly when photocopied.

(2) Making the collation

(i)   The normal way in which to present the collation is

      reading of base text] reading of witness

      The minuscule 70 reads βηθανια at John 1.28, where the Textus Receptus has βηθαβαρα. Present as

      βηθαβαρα] βηθανια

      It is necessary to indicate clearly the difference between addition and omission. ADD or + serves for the former, OM for the latter. A change in word order is best represented by writing all in full. For example,

      ουκ ειμι εγω] εγω ουκ ειμι

      Sometimes of course there are multiple types of change, but it is best to keep the variation units as short and economical as possible in the collation.

(ii) If a word comes more than once in a verse in the base text, indicate which occurrence is meant by placing a supralinear number above it.

(iii) Decide at the beginning what kinds of divergencies you are going to record for all the manuscripts you are collating, and be consistent. Remember that the more you record, the longer it will take. The following classes of variation might not be worth recording

punctuation
accentuation
itacisms and other spelling variations
movable *nu*
abbreviations for the *nomina sacra*
other abbreviations, diaereseis

It all depends on whether these things are necessary or not. With regard to the *nomina sacra*, it can be convenient to make a separate list of the normal forms that occur. Then only give the form in the collation if it differs from the norm.

The recording of accentuation might be worthwhile either if a difference in meaning were involved, or in editing a Byzantine text. Its value in editing an unaccented text such as a New Testament writing is highly doubtful, and accents are best ignored.

One does not record the kinds of abbreviation that occur in manuscripts, such as two letters written together in a majuscule at the end of a line, or ligatures in minuscule manuscripts.

The general rule is that you are recording data that will be of value in establishing the relationship between the manuscripts, not all the data about the manuscript you are collating. If you wanted to do the latter, you would make a transcription.

(iv) Record superscriptions, subscriptions and colophons.

(v) Record corrections, indicating them by * for the scribe, C* for auto-correction by the scribe, and C, C1, C2, and so on for later hands.

If the first hand has a divergence from the base text which is removed in a correction, record it as, for example,

βηθαβαρα] βηθανια * (text C)

There are various ways that you can record corrections more subtly if you wish. For example, where a correction just consists of an erasure and could have been by anyone, record it as

word] erased (or eras.) s.m. – s.m. standing for *secunda manu* (Latin meaning 'by a second hand').

Only use C1 and C2 if you are going to distinguish consistently between different hands. This is not usually possible to do with black-and-white reproductions.

(vi) Record lacunae by [ ]. For example, if a manuscript has a hole where the four central letters of βηθαβαρα would be expected, record it as

βηθαβαρα] βη[ ]ρα

If there were doubt as to a reading, you could also put in the likely number of letters. This is not really possible with many minuscule hands, but is more straightforward with majuscules. For example

βηθαβαρα] βη[5]α

is a way of saying that βηθανια is more likely to have been in the manuscript than βηθαβαρα. On the other hand

και παλιν ειπεν αυτοις] και [5] αυτοις

records clearly that there is no room for παλιν and ειπεν. Of course ειπεν with παλιν omitted is more likely than the other way round, but you have recorded what is present rather than guessed what might have been there. If a lacuna covers several words or more, just give the extant parts of the first and last words – so long as it is clear what piece of text is meant. If there is doubt (for example, if the word sequence comes more than once in the verse), be more specific either by indicating word numbers or giving more text.

If a whole verse or chapter is missing, the abbreviation DEF is a useful way of stating it. It is better to record DEF at every lacuna and state its extent – otherwise you or someone else might subsequently think that your collation was unfinished.

(vii) Where a letter is damaged but possible to reconstruct, place a dot under it.

(viii) The abbreviation *vid.* (Latin meaning 'it seems' or 'apparently') can easily be used carelessly. It is best not used at all in a collation.

(ix) If you choose, you can indicate briefly where on the page an addition or marginal note appears (e.g. i/m = in the margin, b/l could mean between the lines).

(x) Finally, you should keep separate notes on any matters of interest that strike you.

(3) If in doubt

If collating a minuscule manuscript that is new to one, perhaps written in an unfamiliar style, it is worth making a list of abbreviations and any other distinctive features, along with where they come. If you are uncertain about any (for, example, which reading it follows in a word ending variation which it abbreviates), gathering information in a number of places will eventually lead you to the answer.

(4) Lectionary manuscripts

There are two extra rules for collating lectionaries.

(i) It is highly advisable to record the sequence of lections, since this might be significant in establishing relationships between manuscripts.

(ii) There are standard incipits (Latin for 'it begins' turned into an English noun in the plural). You can indicate the number which the manuscript has at the beginning of a lection rather than write it out each time. The six listed by the International Greek New Testament Project are

I   τῷ καίρῳ ἐκείνῳ

II   εἶπεν ὁ κύριος τοῖς ἑαυτοῦ μαθηταῖς

III   εἶπεν ὁ κύριος πρὸς τοὺς ἐληλυθότας πρὸς αὐτὸν Ἰουδαίους

IV   εἶπεν ὁ κύριος πρὸς τοὺς πεπιστευκότας αὐτῷ Ἰουδαίους

V   εἶπεν ὁ κύριος

VI   εἶπεν ὁ κύριος τὴν παραβολὴν ταύτην

One has also to be careful to record whether a passage is absent simply because it was not included or because there is a lacuna in the manuscript.

(5) Correcting

All collations need checking! The amount of time you have for repeated checking will depend upon the size of text and number of manuscripts, balanced against the importance of the witness and other factors in your life. A minimum of one check is required. It can be useful to mark your corrections in a different colour pencil or pen, to keep track of your changes.

(6) Collaborative projects

Running a project with more than one collator requires more stringent conditions, in order to reduce inconsistency to a minimum. Possible ideas to bear in mind are

use of a different collator to make a check of a collation

clearly set out guidelines for everyone to follow

standard cover sheets for transcriptions

training sessions for collators

(7) Collating non-continuous witnesses

It is possible to make collations of other witnesses (the case of lectionaries has already been given). Greek patristic citations could be given in the form of variants from the base text. But particular care would have to be taken to show the beginning and end of the citation, along with a reference to the place where the writer cited it. One would need also to state the edition of the writer used, and to note any variants in the manuscript tradition of the writer.

One could do the same with a version (or citations in another language), retroverting the text back into Greek. This is of limited value for the study of the version, being of use only for the study of the form of Greek text from which it seems to have been translated, but is sometimes used in the study of the Greek text in order to locate versional materials within the textual history. The greatest problem in collating this material is that what is represented will inevitably be partial. Only certain types of information could be confidently gathered, so the quality of data is less well defined than in the collation of a Greek manuscript. However such information is gathered, it is probably best brought into an apparatus of Greek witnesses only at the very end of the making of an edition.

The image shows a page of a collation by T. S. Pattie for the International Greek New Testament Project. ☛ (14)

It takes a lot of work to get used to all the ligatures and abbreviations to be found in Greek minuscule manuscripts, and in addition to making personal lists from the beginning, the following are worth mentioning: A. N. Oikonomides, *Abbreviations in Greek Inscriptions: Papyri, Manuscripts, and Early Printed Books*, Chicago, 1974 brings into one volume: M. Avi-Yonah, *Abbreviations in Greek Inscriptions* (first published in *The Quarterly of the Department of Antiquities in Palestine*, 1940); F. G. Kenyon, 'Abbreviations and Symbols in Greek Papyri' (pp. 154–6 of Kenyon, *Greek Papyri*); T. W. Allen, *Abbreviations in Greek Manuscripts* (Oxford, 1889); and G. F. Ostermann and A. E. Giegengack, *Printer's and Translator's Elementary Information on Classical and Modern Greek and Abbreviations in Early Greek Printed Books* (Washington, DC, 1936). Gardthausen, *Palaeographie* (1979) also has plates with examples.

2.5 HOW TO MAKE AN ELECTRONIC TRANSCRIPTION OF A MANUSCRIPT

Before describing how an electronic transcription is made, the fact that it is a new tool requires that something be said about its value.

Ever since the making of the first critical apparatus, scholars have faced the daunting task of doing all the work afresh every time they make an edition. Traditionally, a manuscript was collated (see 2.4) against a base text. The sets of collations were then manually amalgamated into a single apparatus. The material is generally only useful for that editor, since the information was expressed as a list of differences from the printed text. To take the data and express it as a fresh list of differences from a new editorial text is only possible if the first editor has included not only every single variation of the manuscript from the base text, but also every lacuna in the manuscript. It is also a very difficult task in which mistakes are easily made, and has the further drawback that it leaves the new editor totally dependent on the accuracy and method of the predecessor. The difficulties may be seen in the description of the editions of Revelation in the approximate period 1750–1850 (7.2).

Moreover, by listing only the differences, an editor draws attention to the variant reading as a feature of the manuscript in relation to other manuscripts, while omitting material which may seem to be of little or no value to the textual critic, but will certainly be of interest to anyone interested in manuscripts as artefacts and in the way the text was presented.

The transcription can solve these three problems. Once a transcription has been made, it can be made available as open source, for new editors to use as they choose. They can check it and add features to it without having all to do again. The transcription is complete, in that it consists of a precise letter for letter transference of the text of the manuscript into an electronic format, with an indication of all lacunae. It also provides a declaration of the layout of the manuscript by a system of tagging quires, folios (recto and verso), columns, lines, *ekthesis*, indentation, and so on, by means of which a great array of data can be studied and codified. Finally, an apparatus may be created by electronic comparison of the witnesses (which must then be made into a critical apparatus by the editor), and the results exported to a database for further editing and publication in whatever formats are preferred, print as well as electronic.

This new method has also opened the field to a degree of cooperation which was never possible in the days of separate methods of paper collations. The literature telling the history of the relationship between the Münster Institut and the International Greek New Testament Project and their predecessors shows this. Since 1997, the Münster Institut and the International Greek New Testament Project have been developing a common system for making electronic transcriptions. Today's technology facilitates partnerships which also leave room for individual expression, so that the International Greek New Testament Project is making an edition of John with Münster as part of the print

Editio critica maior, while making its own electronic website, and the associated *Vetus Latina Iohannes* can make a print edition in the precise style and appearance of the Beuron Vetus Latina edition at the same time as making a web version with different features. It is also possible to share transcriptions, so that the International Greek New Testament Project John majuscules edition and the United Bible Societies' Byzantine text of John share some transcriptions while producing totally independent texts and apparatuses. In the same way the Codex Sinaiticus Project has taken an existing transcription made in Münster and added to it features such as Eusebian numbers, and more detailed layout information.

For bibliography on these editions, see 6.1.1 and 6.4.

The goal of accurate transcriptions which can form the basis of future editions, leading to a situation where New Testament textual scholars will be able to spend more time studying the data and less time doing the preliminary work is arguably the most important achievement of the electronic edition. For it to be achieved, all scholars wanting to make a contribution need to adopt the same methodology. This chapter is written in the hope that it will set a standard for all editors of New Testament manuscripts to follow, and with the request that those wanting to make transcriptions should not spend time making decisions which have already been made, but instead should use and develop what has been done already.

Any reader who feels sceptical is invited to visit two websites which are home to editions making use of this approach – the 'digital Nestle–Aland' and the 'New Testament Transcripts' Prototype' at the Münster Institut's website and the International Greek New Testament Project's Johannine majuscules, the Byzantine Text of John, the Vetus Latina Iohannes, the Digital Codex Sinaiticus, and the Protevangelium Iacobi, all accessible through the website of the Institute for Textual Scholarship and Electronic Editing at the University of Birmingham.

The pages which these editions show on screen are in XML. At present the transcription is made by typing the transcription in plain text, so that what the transcriber sees looks very different from the end result. In a few years, this will no longer be the case, since a new web-based program is being developed which will show the reader on screen the XML output. In the meantime, and in order to explain the theory, the rules which have been followed are set out below. The current software consists of Collate, which is used for making electronic collations of transcriptions, and

Anastasia, an XML publishing system. They have been used for many years in a number of pioneering editions in other fields, especially Chaucer's *Canterbury Tales*. Collate is not the only software available. It is notable that while Collate is a Macintosh program, Morrill and Lewis developed a PC program inspired by Collate in the early 1990s for the use of collators contributing to the International Greek New Testament Project. This program was called Manuscript.

One of the most important things is that the tagging system (and indeed the whole concept of Collate) is compliant with the Text Encoding Initiative. The TEI provides a standard set of rules for all stages in creating digital texts. This saves people having to invent rules all over again when they become editors, it offers compatibility between projects, and above all it has the goal of ensuring that the texts which we have taken so much time to produce will transcend obsolescent software and will be readable for future generations. The current guidelines (TEI P4) were published in June 2002.

Further information and links to the projects are available at
(www.uni-muenster.de/NTTextforschung/)
www.itsee.bham.ac.uk
www.iohannes.com
The same site provides the text of a number of articles describing the system, and the way it is being used for New Testament editing. The first part of a presentation by Wachtel and Parker describes how their collaborative use of Collate began (www.itsee.bham.ac.uk/online/2005_SNTS_Wachtel-Parker.pdf). For The Canterbury Tales Project, see www.canterburytalesproject.org/index.html. I have discussed the theory and significance of electronic transcribing in 'Through a Screen Darkly: Digital Texts and the New Testament', *Journal for the Study of the New Testament* 25 (2003), 395–411. For the TEI, see www.tei-c.org/.

A transcription is made by adapting a base text of the selected text in the appropriate language. In Greek this base text conveniently is the Textus Receptus, which generally needs less alteration than a critical edition to be conformed to the manuscript's text. It must contain the book, chapter and verse number tagged. It is helpful if it also contains the *nomina sacra* in abbreviated form. The transcriber compares a few words of the manuscript image (or the manuscript itself) with the base text, and wherever there is a difference, alters the base text. Location markers (usually folio, column and line) are entered by means of tags – F 100r, C 1, L1, and so on. A simple return displays a new line on the screen of course, but this is not so robust or secure a way as tagging the new line. Corrections are also entered, with the text of the first hand and the subsequent correction or corrections all tagged. That is the essence of it. There are several other important points to remember. One is to use an absolutely safe way of naming the file, which will record of which manuscript it is a transcription, as well as the status of the file. Another is to back it up safely. Equally important is to ensure accuracy. The International Greek New Testament Project and the Digital Codex Sinaiticus use a system of double transcriptions: two transcriptions are made, ideally by two different people. Only one of them has the layout tagging entered. Collate is then run to make a collation of the two. All discrepancies are shown in the resulting collation. The text is verified, and the transcription containing the layout tags is corrected. This file is then saved under a name which indicates its status. The double transcription is an effective way of eliminating error, so long as both initial transcriptions are of a sufficiently high quality for the two transcribers to be unlikely to make the same mistake independently.

Certain rules have to be set at the beginning of a transcription project:

(1) How much detail to include, such as punctuation and diacritical marks

(2) Whether to reproduce or expand abbreviations. A base text with the *nomina sacra* will save changing these (unless a manuscript has different forms). There is little point in including the ligatures in Byzantine manuscripts. Latin will require decisions about the representation of various common features such as the æ diphthong and *e caudata* ('e with a tail'). A vital rule to remember here is that the more such detail one adds, the more complicated the process of editing the collation will be. There is a balance to be struck, and decisions about the best use of available resources have to be made.

The transcription process is very different from collating. The collation process is strongly based on the location of variant readings from the base text, and pays comparatively little attention to the whole page of the manuscript. Transcription uses the base text only as a short cut to making the copy of the manuscript, and becomes much more interested in the representation of the scribe's whole achievement. It is soon obvious that a scribe had a freedom that the maker of a print or electronic version cannot dream of, the freedom to make any shape of any size anywhere on the page. This artistic license (and the manuscript is like a work of art) can only be represented in a very limited way. It is almost inevitable that the new electronic transcriber will soon become taken with a desire to represent everything that is visible on the page – ink marks that might be smudges, stained areas, possible spaces in the text, letters of an unusual size or shape or out of alignment, changes in ink colour, ligatures. This desire will in time give way to a recognition that this aim cannot be achieved and be replaced with a pragmatic recognition that the main virtues are consistency and accuracy in representation of the most important data. It will always be possible for someone to add more detail at a later date.

Electronic transcribing is an excellent mental discipline, better certainly than collating, because it requires consistent thinking on the part of the transcriber. Any inconsistency, and it will show up very quickly once the collation program starts running.

It is possible to add notes in the transcription, but it is preferable to detach them from the beginning. There should be two accompanying files: a commentary file, which contains the transcriber's private notes and queries, and a file of notes intended for publication (containing a cross-reference to the place in the transcription). Both should have names clearly associating them with the transcription file. At first, it is advised to provide a status note at the beginning of the transcription repeating the manuscript identification, recording the transcriber, the date of working and the stages of revision. Once the transcription is complete, this note should be removed and placed in a separate documentation file. Placing comments in these three separate files leads to more effective and quicker production of the apparatus.

Finally, success is dependent upon setting up the right structures at the outset:

rules for transcribing
file naming
directory structure
an efficient and safe system of storage and back up. If this is forgotten, hours of work may be lost

The computer age has shown up some anomalies in the Gregory–Aland number system (described in 1.3.1). A list of the example of classes of manuscript given there sorted automatically, or a folder containing a transcription of each, would place them in the order

0108
108
L108
P108

replacing the approximately chronological order which makes some kind of scientific sense and is the one used by all scholars with an order based upon the workings of the machine. In order to combat this, a six-digit system has been developed by the Münster Institut, and adopted by the International Greek New Testament Project, with one (probably temporary) modification. The first digit is 1, 2, 3 or 4: 1 if it is a papyrus, 2 if it is a majuscule, 3 if it is a minuscule, and 4 if it is a lectionary. The next four numbers are the given numbers of the catalogue, with zeros as required for numbers below one thousand. The final number indicates a supplement (any supplement being transcribed as a separate file in an electronic edition): if a zero appears then the text is the copying of the original scribe (most manuscripts only consist of this), 1 a first supplement, and so forth. The number 5 indicates that the manuscript is a known copy of a numbered manuscript (this is the equivalent of the superscript abs (= 'Abschrift', 'copy') in the *Liste*. Thus the four manuscripts listed above are given the numbers

```
101080 = P108
201080 = 0108
301080 = 108
401080 = L108

302050 = 205
302055 = 205^abs
```

The modification adopted by the International Greek New Testament Project in its study of all manuscripts of John's Gospel was to indicate commentary minuscule manuscripts with an initial 5, so that 301080 (which is such a manuscript) is numbered 501080. The drawback with this is that the 3 and 5 sequences are no longer complete in themselves.

This last matter apart, the numbers, being of a single type (all numerical) and size (6 digits) will always display in the preferred order in electronic format. This new standard should be used for file names and formal purposes in electronic editing, but the shorter letter and number system should be publicly displayed, in the critical apparatus or in discussion.

In the same way, the electronic version of the Vetus Latina list as used by the Vetus Latina Iohannes Project consists of three digits, such as 001 for number 1, and so on.

2.6 HOW TO MAKE A PAPER TRANSCRIPTION OF A MANUSCRIPT

It sounds increasingly improbable that anyone would transcribe a manuscript with pencil and paper today, since the advantages of working electronically are too great. In fact there are various conditions under which it would be a definite advantage – not necessarily at the end of making one, but certainly at the beginning. Suppose one is making a transcription of a rather difficult papyrus, extant in only a single leaf. You need to look at the papyrus, to put it under a microscope, to hold it to the light. There might even be text at different angles, or you might want to sketch the shape of the page and imitate the letter shapes to get a sense of the available space. All this is much easier to do if you are recording your work on a sheet of paper, since it is more manoeuvrable and less bulky than a computer. It is quite possible that you will transfer the transcription to a computer later. You would be much less likely to make a paper transcription of a whole, perfectly legible manuscript, because today you could do it more efficiently by adapting an electronic base text (see 2.5). By making a paper transcription, you would be making a copy of the copy, and all the errors of transcription would become yours. If you did, this is how you would go about it.

Most of Tischendorf's greatest achievements were transcriptions of manuscripts. The volumes of his *Monumenta Sacra Inedita* were made, incredibly, in the following way. Tischendorf made a complete transcription, line by line and page by page, of the manuscript, with everything laid out on the page as he saw it. The printer composed from this new manuscript, and the edition was made. There are examples among his papers in Leipzig University Library. The one I saw broke one of the cardinal rules I am about to provide – he nowhere indicates which manuscript he has transcribed!

You need a cover sheet, as in the advice for making a paper collation. You also need writing materials. You must state what manuscript it is.

The process of transcribing is the same as making an electronic transcription, without the tagging. To be precise, you still need a tagging system, to indicate the difference between the first hand and a correction, for example. You can place different kinds of brackets around each state of the text, but this will become difficult if there are several different correctors at work. Alternatively, you can mark the first-hand reading, and set the corrections either in the margin or at the bottom of the page.

Traditionally, some transcriptions of manuscripts ignored the page layout of the original. This is a pity, and probably the easiest way to proceed is to keep the layout of your manuscript; writing it out one can easily follow the approximate position of running titles, page or quire numbers, and so on. Writing each page of the manuscript on a separate sheet is also helpful.

An accompanying sheet of paper for notes and queries is important.

For other rules of presentation, see 2.4.

CHAPTER 3

Other types of witness

3.1 INTRODUCTION

It is customary to divide the witnesses to the New Testament text into three types: Greek manuscripts, the versions and patristic citations. This is a reasonable classification from the point of view of the study of variant readings, and especially for the editor of a text. But it is worth pointing out at the beginning of this survey that there is an important way in which there is only one type of witness to the text – copyings of some or all of it in a manuscript. One might categorise these manuscript copyings in various ways: as manuscripts in Greek and manuscripts in other languages; as manuscripts of the whole text and manuscripts of a part of it in a different context; or using both, so that they were placed in one of four categories: as manuscripts of all the text in Greek, of all the text in another language, of some of the text in Greek or of some of the text in another language.

3.2 PATRISTIC CITATIONS

3.2.1 Editions of patristic writings

All the works of every early Christian writer were of course transmitted in manuscript form, and it is important that these works also should be properly edited from the manuscript sources. Not so many such editions exist as we would like, and too often we are dependent upon old editions made from a handful of manuscripts, and these not necessarily ones which a critical editor would wish to use. Even where a critical edition exists, the editor (an expert in patristics rather than the textual problems of the New Testament) has not necessarily been aware of the particular problems pertaining to the citations. But the proper study of biblical citations is of value for two reasons: because they provide evidence of the text known to the writer, and because they illuminate the interpretation and reception of the text.

The critical study of the manuscripts and transmission of patristic texts should not be neglected by the New Testament scholar. Using a Father's citations wisely requires an understanding of the problems associated with his text. Moreover, such studies can improve one's understanding of ancient textual transmission. One may single out M. Bévenot, *The Tradition of Manuscripts. A Study in the Transmission of St Cyprian's Treatises*, Oxford, 1961. Among studies illustrating different aspects of relevant research in earlier volumes of TU are J. Bidez, *La tradition manuscrite de Sozomène et la Tripartite de Théodore le Lecteur* (TU 32.2b), Leipzig, 1908 and B. Dombart, *Zur Textgeschichte der Civitas Dei Augustins seit dem Entstehen der ersten Drucke* (TU 32.2a), Leipzig, 1908. Another example of relevant research is W. Höllger, *Die handschriftliche Überlieferung der Gedichte Gregors von Nazianz*, vol. I: *Die Gedichtgruppen XX und XI*; vol. II: *Die Gedichtgruppen I* (Studien zur Geschichte und Kultur des Altertums NS Series 2, Forschungen zu Gregor von Nazianzen 3 and 4), Paderborn, Munich, Vienna and Zurich, 1985–6.

Patristic authors are also a source of all kinds of information about early Christian books. See, e.g., J. O'Callaghan, *El papiro el los padres grecolatinos* (Papyrologica Castroctaviana. Studia et Textus 1), Barcelona, 1967.

In addition to writings by individuals, the category of 'patristic citation' also includes citations of Scripture in liturgical texts, the acts of Church Councils, apocryphal texts and acts of martyrs – in fact everything documentary from early Christianity except for the New Testament writings themselves. These other forms of citation are a less rich source of information than the main bulk, which consists of writings by individuals.

Some Church Fathers were not reluctant to have their thoughts written down, and where a work achieved such popularity in later centuries that it was frequently copied, perhaps hundreds of times, their editor is faced with a monumental task, which must begin with finding and cataloguing the manuscripts and then analysing their relationship in order to understand the history of the text. Only then can the work of editing proper begin. At any rate there are editions, even if not all of them are very good, of the vast majority of Greek and Latin authors. In the case of works in other languages there may be no edition at all, so that they must be studied in manuscript copies.

Given these problems, why are quotations of New Testament writings so often studied and cited by textual scholars? The answer lies in the fact that the quotation may be a transcript of the manuscript which the Father had open beside him, or at the very least may tell us something about the text as it was written in that manuscript. If it is, then we have what is as good as a copy of at least a small part of the manuscript which Origen, Cyprian, John Chrysostom or Augustine was using. We have few manuscripts of the age of Chrysostom and Augustine, and fewer still of the age of Origen and Cyprian. If the writer is from a yet earlier date, if we are dealing with Tertullian, Clement of Alexandria, or back in the second century with Justin Martyr or the Apostolic Fathers, we potentially have glimpses of the text of the second century, a period from which only fragments of New Testament manuscripts survive. Moreover, if we can find similarities between the text as it is quoted by a particular Father and the text as it stands in known manuscripts, we have a link which allows us to connect a manuscript with a place and an era. This is a tantalising prospect. It is, however, one beset with ifs and buts. Before we go any further these ifs and buts must be set out.

3.2.2 *Evaluating citations*

1. An author might have written in the second century, but the manuscript copies of his writings are likely to be many centuries more recent.

2. We need to know how carefully the manuscript tradition of the writer we are studying has preserved the text as it was first quoted by the writer and set down by his amanuensis. It is plausible to suspect that later scribes might, perhaps unconsciously, have altered a citation to conform to the text as they knew it best. Where a lot depends on a particular form of words, this may be less likely, since it might make nonsense of the argument. How confident we may be about the outcome of our consideration is not only in our hands. If we are dependent upon an old edition, which may have used late manuscripts, we may be forced either to leave the problem open or to have recourse to whatever manuscripts we may be able to find for ourselves in order to cast more light upon the matter.

3. Once we have found out as much as we may reasonably require of ourselves, it is necessary to study the author's habits and categorise the citations. Generally speaking, the author may be offering an adaptation, an allusion, or a genuine quotation. An adaptation might be the use of a biblical phrase turned around in some way. A preacher might take the text 'The kingdom of God is within you' (Lk. 17.21) and refer to it repeatedly in a homilectical style in the words 'The kingdom of God is within us.' No one would suppose that this was in the codex used by the speaker. An adaptation might also change the general grammatical structure of a sentence to conformity with the writer's own sentence. An allusion is a glancing reference to some biblical wording, and again one must expect some alteration, but even such a phrase may be of value if it reveals that the author knew a form of a word or a phrase of the biblical text which also exists in another form. For the versions, it may

show knowledge of a word found in part of the manuscript tradition. Finally, we have citations which intend to quote explicitly from the biblical text, and do so, possibly at length. Here we must still remain cautious if any distinctive wording appears. It might be the result of faulty quotation from memory, or in the case of the beginning of a quotation might be, for example, the use of a conjunction for the sake of the writer's own argument. Of most value are the following places:

(i)   When the writer uses some phrase such as 'my codex here says ...'
(ii) When the writer states that some codices read such-and-such, but other codices read something else.
(iii) Where the writer cites a text more than once and cites it consistently (and for no purpose of his own argument).

These are the places with which a study of the writer's citations must begin, since they can provide a framework for a better understanding of the rest.

Houghton has drawn the distinction between 'primary citations', in which the author makes reference to a codex, and 'secondary citations', where he cites from memory. H. A. G. Houghton, *Augustine's Text of John. Patristic Citations and Latin Gospel Manuscripts*, Oxford, 2008.

4. It is worthwhile also to consider the kind of work in which the citation occurs. Even poetic references can be of value on occasion (there are examples in the Kontakia of Romanos Melodus). Quotations in commentaries fall into a particular category. It is necessary to study the citations as they appear at the beginning of a passage of discussion (the lemma) and the citations as they are cited in whole or in part in the course of the exegesis. Differences between the two need to be studied and accounted for, so that a decision may be made as to which is more likely to have been in the author's codex. In the case of commentaries, we sometimes find that later scribes, and even modern editors, have supplied the biblical text at the beginning of a section. I name no names here – let the users ascertain for themselves whether what is in the edition is in the manuscripts.

Books of testimonies, notably Cyprian's *Ad Quirinum* (*CPL* 39), come into a special category, since Scripture is cited extensively, most plausibly by being copied straight out of a codex. This is extremely valuable evidence.

Another special set of circumstances is the citation of the Old Testament in the New. Here the New Testament version of the passage may have been adapted (either by the Father or in the manuscript tradition) to a form of the Old Testament text which was more familiar to the later writer.

5. The chronology of a writer should be understood, and it must be recognised that when one speaks of an author having a codex, that codex might have changed, certainly if two writings are separated in time or even in place, and even if a different copy of the Scriptures was picked up 'from the last time that a quotation was made. Such codices might have happened to be rather different from each other at the passage in question, so that if it is quoted twice in different wording, we have no way of knowing whether the cause is due to a difference between the codices or because one (or both) citations were the result of a lapse of memory.

Once all of an author's citations have been studied, it should be possible to form some opinion as to his habits of citation, and the likelihood of his having cited accurately, and, if so, on what occasions he is most likely to have done so. Where there is room for uncertainty, that uncertainty must be acknowledged.

Translations of patristic writings into other languages need to be treated in their own way. A translator may either make his own translation of the citations, perhaps to reproduce the biblical text used by the author more closely, or use an existing version in the receptor language. In either case the results can be important, in the first instance by preserving evidence of some details of the text used by the original author, and in the second by testifying to a form of text in the secondary language. This may be significant even where the original author wrote in a language other than Greek (for example, a translation into Greek of a Syriac text may provide useful information about the Syriac New Testament known to the author and about the Greek New Testament known to the translator).

For a series of introductory articles, see the following in Ehrman and Holmes, *Contemporary Research*: G. D. Fee, 'The Use of the Greek Fathers for New Testament Textual Criticism', 191–207; J. L. North, 'The Use of the Latin Fathers for New Testament Textual Criticism', 208–23; S. P. Brock, 'The Use of the Syriac Fathers for New Testament Textual Criticism', 224–36. Other studies include J. Duplacy and M. J. Suggs, 'Les citations grecques et la critique du texte du Nouveau Testament: le passé, le présent et l'avenir', *La Bible et les pères, Colloque de Strasbourg, 1969*, Paris, 1971, 187–213, reprinted in Duplacy, *Études*, 123–49; Duplacy also discusses methodological questions with respect to R. W. Muncey, *The New Testament Text of Saint Ambrose* (TS 2.4), Cambridge, 1959 in 'Citations patristiques et critique textuelle du Nouveau Testament. Àpropos d'un livre récent', *Recherches de science religieuse* 47 (1959), 391–400, reprinted in Duplacy, *Études*, 15–24; G. Visonà, *Citazioni patristiche e critica testuale neotestamentaria. Il caso di Lc 12,49* (Analecta Biblica 125), Rome, 1990; B. D. Ehrman, 'The Use of the Church Fathers in New Testament Textual Criticism', in McKendrick and O'Sullivan, 155–655. G. D. Fee's shorter writings on citations are collected in Epp and Fee, *Studies*, part VI. B. M. Metzger, 'Explicit References in the Works of Origen to Variant Readings in New Testament Manuscripts', in Birdsall and Thomson, *Biblical and Patristic Studies*, 78–95, reprinted in Metzger, *Historical and Literary Studies* (NTTS 8), Leiden, 1968, 88–103; 'Patristic Evidence and the Textual Criticism of the New Testament', *NTS* 18 (1971–2), 379–400, reprinted in Metzger, *New Testament Studies*, 167–88; 'The Practice of Textual Criticism among the

Church Fathers', in E. A. Livingstone (ed.), *Studia Patristica XII* (TU 115) Berlin, 1975, 340–9, reprinted in *New Testament Studies*, 189–98; 'St Jerome's Explicit References to Variant Readings in Manuscripts of the New Testament', in E. Best and R. McL. Wilson (eds.), *Text and Interpretation: Studies in the New Testament Presented to Matthew Black*, Cambridge, 1979, 179–90, reprinted in *New Testament Studies*, 199–210.

After the evidence has been collected and sifted, there should be a body of quotations, small or large depending on the author's output and the extent to which Scripture is cited, which may be taken as evidence of the biblical text known to him. This evidence may then be compared with the manuscripts of the language in which the author wrote. The results will illuminate the transmission of the New Testament text and may be cited in a critical edition.

3.2.3 Tools for the study of patristic writings

In order to negotiate the authors and texts, the textual scholar needs to make use of two sets of materials: tools of patristic research and tools dedicated to the listing and study of patristic citations of the Bible.

One of the main sources of basic information are the patrologies, handbooks to patristic writings. My recommendation for the study of Greek and Latin writings is the five volumes of Quasten.

Quasten, *Patrology* (full details in list of abbreviations, p. xxiii). Further useful works include F. L. Cross (ed.), *The Oxford Dictionary of the Christian Church*, 3rd edn, ed. E. A. Livingstone, Oxford, 1997, and Kannengiesser (1.3–113 covers the history of research and describes primary tools for study). For Syriac writers, see I. Ortiz de Urbina, *Patrologia Syriaca*, Rome, 1958; supplement in *Orientalia Christiana Periodica* 27 (1961), 425–33; 2nd edn Rome, 1965. For a very recent guide to Syriac literature on a wide range of topics, see S. P. Brock, *Syriac Sources and Resources for Byzantinists*, www.byzantinecongress.org.uk/paper/III/III.1_Brock.pdf. Regular bibliographies on Syriac literature are provided by S. P. Brock in *Parole de l'Orient*: 4 (1973), 393–465 (for the years 1960–70); 10 (1981/2), 291–412 (1971–80); 14 (1987), 289–360 (1981–5); 17 (1992), 211–301 (1986–90); 23 (1998), 241–350 (1991–5); 29 (2004), 263–410 (1996–2000). The first four of these have been reprinted in *Syriac Studies: a Classified Bibliography (1960–1990)*, Kaslik, 1996. *Hugoye: Journal of Syriac Studies* is a source of up-to-date information. Finally, attention should be drawn to the very recent work by S. P. Brock, *An Introduction to Syriac Studies* (Gorgias Handbooks 4), Piscataway, 2006.

For Coptic, T. Orlandi, 'Patristic Texts in Coptic' in Di Berardino, *Patrology: From Chalcedon to John of Damascus*; A. S. Atiya (ed.). *The Coptic Encyclopedia*, 8 vols., New York, 1991. (Note that di Berardino's volume also contains a section by S. J. Voicu on 'Patristic Texts in Armenian (5th to 8th Centuries)'.)

Once a general picture has been formed of the writings of an author, their date and character, along with bibliographical information, one needs a tool which permits simple and secure identification of individual items. This is provided by a *Clavis* (Latin for 'key'). Such a work provides a numbered entry for each writing by every author ordered by date. The author entries are in chronological order. In addition to the incipit (the first words of the work, permitting identification), there is basic information about the available editions, any versions that exist, various notes and references to selected secondary literature. The Greek *Clavis* is known in short as *CPG*. The Latin equivalent is referred to either as Dekkers (after its original compiler) or by the abbreviation *CPL*.

While it is possible to identify every writing by its *Clavis* number, this would be inconvenient for the user of a critical study or edition, since one would need either to have a prodigious memory for numbers or to spend one's time referring to the *Clavis*. Moreover, numbers are usually reserved for manuscripts: citations need to be shown differently. The next requirement therefore, especially for a critical edition, is a simple and unique abbreviation for each author and work. The hand editions such as Nestle–Aland, which refer only to an author, contain lists of their own abbreviations. The Latin patristic scene is served with the comprehensive system devised by the Beuron Institut, now available through Gryson's *Répertoire Général*.

This replaces H. J. Frede, *Kirchenschriftsteller: Verzeichnis und Sigel* (*Vetus Latina* 1/1), 1981 and its updates (H. J. Frede, T. Kainthaler and R. Gryson (eds.), *Kirchenschriftsteller: Verzeichnis und Sigel. Aktualisierungsheft* 1999 and H. J. Frede, J. Hermann and R. Gryson (eds.), *Kirchenschriftsteller: Verzeichnis und Sigel. Aktualisierungsheft*, 2004). A typical abbreviation is HIL tri (Hilary of Poitiers on the Trinity, the author being in upper-case and the work in lower-case letters. The edition used in the compilation of citations is also given (there is a regular process of updating these). In the Vetus Latina edition, the abbreviation is followed by an indication of the reference in the work (book, chapter, section, etc.). The work provides information on dates and places of composition where these are known, and describes various complicated matters such as the sermon output of individual authors, including cross-referencing them with duplicates attributed to another author (many sermons were wrongly attributed to Augustine of Hippo in later times). Translation literature is also included. The system is followed by the International Greek New Testament Project's apparatus to Luke's Gospel (6.1.4.1, 6.3.3).

It is worth pointing out that the Latin *Clavis* contains 2,314 entries, while its Greek counterpart has more than three times as many, so that, as with the early manuscripts, the Greek evidence is considerably greater.

There is nothing quite like this for citations in other languages. The International Greek New Testament Project's edition of Luke used the abbreviations in Lampe's *Patristic Greek Lexicon* for Greek Fathers. The *Editio critica maior* editors devised their own set of abbreviations. They are typically somewhat longer than the Beuron system. Only the author is stated in the critical apparatus, the precise citation by work and reference being given in the supplementary volume. The International Greek New Testament Project devised its own abbreviations for the few Syriac Fathers it cited in Luke.

G. W. H. Lampe (ed.), *A Patristic Greek Lexicon*, Oxford, 1961, xi–xlv.

The study of patristic citations needs all these tools. But the most basic requirement is a list of citations. Citations by biblical book, chapter and verse and citation by author are both important. It should be clear by now that the bare listing of all forms of wording of a given verse in all the Fathers would be useless. The *Biblia Patristica* progresses chronologically, with listings of citations in canonical order, authors being listed alphabetically within a verse. This is valuable for the patristic scholar and exegete, but editors of the New Testament and researchers on the New Testament text of particular authors have chosen to go about it in their own way. A model approach is again shown by the Vetus Latina Institut. A huge card index was compiled. The sequence is by book, chapter and verse. Each card contains the reference and form of citation in a single work. This index is held in Beuron. A set of digital images is now available commercially, and an electronic database is also in preparation commercially. A regular process of updating the cards from new editions continues. It is worth noting that there are two ways of collecting citations from a writer. One is to use the index, if there is one. The other is to read through all his writings, noting all places where there is a reference to a biblical text (this is made easier if citations are printed in a different font, although in those circumstances the editor should not be trusted until proved worthy).

J. Allenbach *et al.* (eds.), *Biblia patristica. Index des citations et allusions bibliques dans la littérature patristique*, Paris, vol. I: *Dès origines à Clément d'Alexandrie et Tertullian*, 1975; vol. II: *Le troisième siècle (Origène excepté)*, 1977; vol. III: *Origène*, 1980; vol. IV: *Eusèbe de Césarée, Cyrille de Jérusalem, Épiphane de Salamine*, 1987; vol. V: *Basile de Césarée, Grégoire de Nazianze, Grégoire de Nysse, Amphiloque d'Iconium*, 1991; vol. VI: *Hilaire de Poitiers, Ambroise de Milan, Ambrosiaster*, 1995; vol. VII: *Didyme d'Alexandrie*, 2000.

Today any such index of citations should be made in a database, for two reasons. Such a database will permit fast and sophisticated sorting and searching of citations, and it will also be in a format for outputting into the database for a critical apparatus. The format of database devised by the International Greek New Testament Project for its editions of John is intended to be suitable for citations in any of the languages in which editions are being made (Greek, Latin, Syriac and Coptic), with the possibility of searching either the entire database or a single language or other subset. It contains the following fields:

(1) Book
(2) Chapter in double figures (e.g. 01, 09, 10)

(3) Verse in double figures
(4) Work Author in standard abbreviated form
(5) Work Title in standard abbreviated form
(6) Work Reference (the book, chapter or paragraph of the citation)
(7) Edition (editor's name and date, or series and volume number)
(8) Page Number of the edition (and line number if lines are numbered in it)
(9) *Clavis* Number
(10) Introductory Formula (the text preceding the citation)
(11) The text of the citation. Interruptions by the author are included in angled brackets
(12) Manuscript variants as attested in the edition of the writer
(13) Category: CIT (verbatim), ADAPT (adaptation) or ALL (allusion)
(14) Cross reference (for cross-referencing to related works, e.g. Latin translations of a Greek Father, using the *Clavis* number of the related text)
(15) Comments by the transcriber
(16) Transcriber's initials
(17) Date of entry (with tracking of corrections)

The Greek database is a revision of the card index originally compiled by G. D. Fee and assistants, including comparison with the card index in the Münster Institut made for the *Editio critica maior* and further checking with printed editions. The Latin database is taken from the Beuron card index, with slight revisions. Both the Coptic and the Syriac databases are fresh compilations from the patristic editions.

Preparatory tasks associated with the International Greek New Testament Project have included detailed studies of individual writers. The New Testament in the Greek Fathers is a continuing series, each studying an individual writer's citations in either some or all of the New Testament. H. A. G. Houghton has studied the Johannine citations in the writings of Augustine, and other contributors to the Vetus Latina Iohannes Project have made a special study of the citations of Tertullian, Hilary and others.

B. D. Ehrman (to 1998), M. W. Holmes (since 1998) (ed.), *The New Testament in the Greek Fathers. Texts and Analyses*, Society of Biblical Literature:

  Vol. 1, B. D. Ehrman, *Didymus the Blind and the Text of the Gospels*, 1986.
  Vol. ii, J. A. Brooks, *The New Testament Text of Gregory of Nyssa*, 1991.
  Vol. iii, B. D. Ehrman, G. D. Fee and M. W. Holmes, *The Text of the Fourth Gospel in the Writings of Origen*, vol. i, 1992.

Vol. IV, D. D. Hannah, *The Text of I Corinthians in the Writings of Origen*, 1997.
Vol. VII, R. L. Mullen, *The New Testament Text of Cyril of Jerusalem*, 1997.
Vol. V, J.-F. Racine, *The Text of Matthew in the Writings of Basil of Caesarea*, 2004.
Vol. VI, C. D. Osburn, *The Text of the Apostolos in Epiphanius of Salamis*, 2004.

Note also C. P. Cosaert, 'The Text of the Gospels in the Writings of Clement of Alexandria', unpublished PhD thesis, University of North Carolina at Chapel Hill, 2005.
   There are many older studies of the citations in individual writers. I select P. M. Barnard, *Clement of Alexandria's Biblical Text* (TS 1.5.5), Cambridge, 1899; W. Sanday and C. H. Turner, *Nouum Testamentum Sancti Irenaei* etc. (Old Latin Biblical Texts 7), Oxford, 1923. A more recent work to be noted is M. Mees, *Die Zitate aus dem Neuen Testament bei Clemens von Alexandrien* (Quaderni di Vetera Christianorum 2), Bari, 1970.

3.2.4 Three special cases

Three special cases require further discussion. The first is the recovery of biblical citations from a writer whose works are known only at second hand. The most famous instance is Marcion, whose writings are only preserved as they are cited by his opponents, most notably Tertullian. Apart from such extreme instances, there is no shortage of instances of writings surviving only in quotations by other writers, or in a *catena* (here the study of commentary manuscripts of the New Testament and the study of citations come together). On these occasions, it is important to study the secondary source, its purposes and its style of quotation, before making a decision.

For Marcion and literature, see 8.3 and 10.8.

   The second case is the citation of the New Testament by the earliest susbsequent Christian writers. The further back one travels in the second century, the more uncertain matters become. There are two reasons for this. The first is that quotation habits were different, being more free and less easy to categorise, so that the writings of the Apostolic Fathers tend to contain allusions which are not always certainly references to New Testament writings. The second is that the forms of text known to second-century writers were frequently different from those found in later manuscripts. As a result of this second reason, we cannot always be sure that what seems to us a free allusion is not a more or less careful citation of an otherwise unknown form of the text. What is one to make of material in the *Didache* bearing a similarity to material in Matthew? What is one to make of the fact that it is often unclear which writings were known to which Apostolic Fathers? How is this material to be related to the Greek manuscript tradition? These questions, although they are unfortunately either overlooked or played down by New Testament scholarship in

general, press hard upon anyone wishing to claim that the oldest forms of
the manuscript tradition of the New Testament writings are also forms of
text dating from the beginning of the second century and earlier.

Petersen, 'Textual Traditions Examined'; J. K. Elliott, 'Absent Witnesses? The Critical Apparatus to
the Greek New Testament and the Apostolic Fathers', also in Gregory and Tuckett, 47–58, and other
writings in the same volume dealing with particular authors; J. Verheyden, 'Assessing Gospel
Quotations in Justin Martyr', in *Festschrift Delobel*, 361–77. For problems of the second-century text,
see especially 10.11.

The third case concerns apocryphal writings. In the past fifty years,
much has been written on the relationship between some of these writings, notably *The Gospel of Thomas*. Have non-canonical forms of text
influenced the manuscript tradition of the canonical text? It will be seen
that the problem is different from those arising out of the study of
patristic citations, these being drawn from works which are commentaries, dogmatic treatises, sermons, and so on. An apocryphal text is of the
same genre as the text which it might affect. J. K. Elliott has addressed
this question, concluding that the only instances by which he is convinced
are two passages in 2 Timothy where the *Acts of Paul and Thecla* has
influenced the text (one manuscript at 3.11 and two at 4.19).

J. K. Elliott, 'The Influence of the Apocrypha on Manuscripts of the New Testament', *Apocrypha* 8
(1997), 265–71.

3.3 THE STUDY OF THE VERSIONS

3.3.1 Introduction

Chapter 1 offered introductions to the manuscripts of the three languages
into which the New Testament was first translated. Part III will provide
details on the versions of the different sections of the New Testament.
This section will describe the main tools and some of the broader
problems relating to the older versions.

As with the citations, it is important that this introduction to the
versions is read with what has been written about manuscripts in mind.

The versions are sometimes divided between the eastern and the
western. A distinction is also drawn between primary versions, translated
directly from the Greek, and secondary versions, translated from a primary version. The interest in this section is on both, down to around the
year 1000. Versions are valuable both as witnesses to the biblical text from

which they are derived and for the study of many aspects of the culture in which the translation is made, including language, exegesis, interpretation and book history.

General studies: K. Aland, *Die alten Übersetzungen*; the contributions are from a colloquium held at Bonn, 20–22 May, 1970; Metzger, *Early Versions*; Vööbus, *Early Versions;* chapters in Ehrman and Holmes, *Contemporary Research.*

Increasing attention has been paid in recent years to the problems inherent in reconstructing the Greek texts from which versions were derived. It has sometimes happened that scholars have found versional support for readings in Greek manuscripts without considering other explanations. It is now beginning to be more fully recognised that a variant might have arisen within the textual tradition of the version, that the form of words might be due to the grammar and morphology of the version, or that there might be more than one possible reconstruction of the Greek from which it was derived.

There are difficulties in representing versional witnesses in an edition of the Greek New Testament. It is certainly not always convenient for the user if all versions are given in their original language, since very few people will know all of them. Traditionally, this problem was solved by translating the version into Latin (for the example of Walton's Polyglot, see 6.1.2). There is another risk here, of much detail being lost in translation into Latin, which has then to be compared with the Greek. Sometimes another language, such as English or French, has been used, with similar difficulties. There is no solution to these problems. The scholar has to be cautious, to be guided by expert opinion, and to indicate the difficulties.

For a study of the problems of representing a version in a Greek apparatus, see P. J. Williams, *Early Syriac Translation Technique and the Textual Criticism of the Greek Gospels* (TS 3.2), Piscataway, 2004. A discussion of the limitations of each versional language discussed in rendering the Greek is provided by Metzger, *Early Versions*. The *ECM* uses double arrows and other sigla to indicate that a version could support two or more Greek readings.

With regard to versions other than the Latin, Syriac and Coptic, it should be noted that I have no knowledge of any of the languages, have never undertaken any research upon them, and am dependent wholly upon secondary literature in the western languages with which I am familiar. The most that the reader could hope for from me is therefore a report on research which is to some extent at third hand. As I promised in the Introduction, I shall avoid repeating information which has been provided elsewhere by those who are qualified to write on these matters, and I offer no more than the briefest of summaries and reference to literature which I have found helpful.

3.3.2 *The Latin versions*

Research has not been able to maintain the rigid distinction between Old Latin and Vulgate witnesses. The fact that many manuscripts are of mixed type has already been mentioned. There are other considerations. Jerome's Vulgate was a revision of an existing text, and in any case in the New Testament did not extend beyond the Gospels. The origins of other parts remain unclear, and we will find some surprising silences in the authorities on this matter. Finally, many writers deal with both Old Latin and Vulgate together. For these reasons, the two will be taken together in this summary of materials covering the modern history of research.

There are a number of general studies, of which Fischer's survey stands as a milestone between previous and subsequent research. Among the monographs, a classic but dated (in particular by subsequent advances in palaeography) study is by S. Berger. It goes as far as the Carolingian period. H. Quentin, *Mémoire sur l'établissement du texte de la Vulgate* is more of a series of extended essays than a full treatment. He uses a discussion of the classification of manuscripts to set out his 'règle de fer', the grouping of manuscripts in threes. There is a long chapter on the sixteenth-century editions, and discussions of a number of groups of manuscripts.

Fischer, 'Das Neue Testament in lateinischer Sprache'; for further research by Fischer, see the volumes of collected papers, *Lateinische Bibelhandschriften im frühen Mittelalter* (GLB 11), 1985 and *Beiträge*. For more recent surveys see J. K. Elliott, 'The Translation of the New Testament into Latin: The Old Latin and the Vulgate', *ANRW* 11, *Principat* 26.1, Berlin and New York, 1992, 199–245; J. H. Petzer, 'The Latin Version of the New Testament', in Ehrman and Holmes, *Contemporary Research*, 113–30.

S. Berger, *Histoire de la Vulgate pendant les premiers siècles du Moyen Âge*, Paris, 1893 (reprinted Hildesheim and New York, 1976). H. Quentin, *Mémoire sur l'établissement du texte de la Vulgate*, vol. 1: *Octateuque* (CBL 6), Rome and Paris, 1922.

F. P. Dutripon, *Vulgatae editionis Bibliorum Sacrorum Concordantiae*, 9th edn, Paris, 1838 (a twentieth-century reprint was made by Olms) is superseded by B. Fischer, *Novae concordantiae Bibliorum sacrorum iuxta Vulgatam versionem critice editam*, 5 vols., Stuttgart, 1977. A. Schmoller, *Handkonkordanz zum griechischen Neuen Testament* 7th edn, Stuttgart (n.d.) 1989 indicates the words used in the Vulgate for each entry; T. A. Bergen, *A Latin–Greek Index of the Vulgate New Testament Based on Alfred Schmoller's* Handkonkordanz zum griechischen Neuen Testament *with an Index of Latin Equivalences Characteristic of 'African' and 'European' Old Latin Versions of the New Testament* (Resources for Biblical Study 26), Atlanta, 1991 turns this around and provides a Latin–Greek key to Schmoller.

The history of editions of the Old Latin begins with Sabatier in the first half of the eighteenth century. His *Bibliorum sacrorum latinae versiones antiquae seu Vetus Latina* appeared in three volumes at Rheims (1743–9). The contemporary Beuron Vetus Latina edition is the 'new Sabatier'. Details of individual volumes are given in the relevant places in Part III. So far the volumes to have appeared contain Ephesians to Revelation. John is in preparation, as is Acts. An edition of the three Synoptic Gospels together is projected. Introductions to editions of Romans and 1 Corinthians have been published.

For the Vulgate, the major edition remains Wordsworth and White, based upon a number of manuscripts, and including the prefaces and other ancillary material. Begun by Wordsworth and White, carried on by the latter, with the assistance of other scholars, and finished by H. F. D. Sparks, the whole process of publication spanned sixty-five years.

Wordsworth and White, *Nouum Testamentum* 3 vols.: vol. 1, J. Wordsworth and H. J. White, *Quattuor Euangelia*, Oxford, 1889–98; vol. 11, J. Wordsworth† and H. J. White, *Epistulae Paulinae*, fasc. 1, *Romans*, ed. White, 1913; fasc. 2, *1 Corinthians*, ed. White, 1922; fasc. 3, *2 Corinthians*, ed. White and A. Ramsbotham, 1941; fasc. 4, *Galatians and Ephesians*, ed. White, 1934; fasc. 5, J. Wordsworth† and H. J. White† with H. F. D. Sparks, *Philippians*, ed. White and Sparks, *Colossians, 1 Thessalonians, 2 Thessalonians, Argumenta in Epistulam ad Timotheum primam*, ed. Sparks, 1937; fasc. 6, J. Wordsworth† and H. J. White† with H. F. D. Sparks and C. Jenkins, *1 Timothy, 2 Timothy, Titus, Philemon*, ed. Sparks, 1939; fasc. 7, *Hebrews*, ed. Sparks, 1941; vol. 111, J. Wordsworth and H. J. White† with H. F. D. Sparks and A. W. Adams, *Actus Apostolorum – Epistulae Canonicae – Apocalypsis Iohannis*, fasc. 1, J. Wordworth and H. J. White, Acts, 1905; fasc. 2, J. Wordsworth† and H. J. White† with H. F. D. Sparks, A. W. Adams and C. Jenkins, *Catholic Epistles: James, 1 Peter, 2 Peter and Jude*, ed. Sparks; *1 John, 2 John, 3 John*, ed. Adams, 1949; fasc. 3, J. Wordsworth† and H. J. White† with H. F. D. Sparks, *Apocalypse of John*, 1954.

The most useful smaller edition is one of the entire Bible published by the German Bible Society, sometimes called after the name of its principal editor, Weber. It is now in its fifth edition. An edition of the Latin New Testament edited by B. Aland and K. Aland is issued by the same publisher.

Weber, *Biblia Sacra*; B. Aland and K. Aland (eds.), *Novum Testamentum Latine*, 2nd edn, Stuttgart, 1992.
An edition of the New Testament produced by H. J. White with a brief apparatus is now out of print: J. Wordsworth and H. J. White, *Nouum Testamentum Latine secundum editionem Sancti Hieronymi, Editio minor*, ed. J. White, Oxford and London, 1911.

3.3.3 The Syriac versions

Because the situation with the Syriac versions varies so much between different parts of the New Testament, there are very few tools which apply to all parts. This section must therefore be brief, the majority of the information being reserved for the various chapters of Part III. Only for one version do we have an edition spanning the entire New Testament. There have been editions of the Peshitta available since the sixteenth century. The one currently in use is a hybrid, since the editors decided to provide the text of the books not included in the Peshitta canon from elsewhere. Thus the minor Catholic epistles (2 Peter, 2 and 3 John and Jude) and Revelation are taken from Gwynn's editions of what is agreed to be the Philoxenian version of these books (see 7.4.2 and 9.3.3.2). For the rest, the text is based upon work carried out by G. H. Gwilliam and J. Pinkerton. There is no apparatus.

The New Testament in Syriac, London, 1919. An edition is now published by Gorgias Press: *Syriac New Testament and Psalter*, Piscataway, 1998. The Harklean version was edited by Joseph White, but in two separate editions, the Gospels being published in 1778 and the Praxapostolos in 1799–1803 (see 9.2.3.1, 9.3.3.2 and 10.5.1). For the oldest printed editions, see recently R. J. Wilkinson, 'Immanuel Tremellius' 1569 Edition of the Syriac New Testament', *Journal of Ecclesiastical History* 58 (2007), 9–25; *Orientalism, Aramaic and Kabbalah in the Catholic Reformation. The First Printing of the Syriac New Testament* (Studies in the History of Christian Traditions 137), Leiden, 2007 (deals with the 1555 *editio princeps*); *The Kabbalistic Scholars of the Antwerp Polyglot Bible* (Studies in the History of Christian Traditions 138), Leiden, 2007.

Some of the principal problems involved in the study of the Syriac has been the identification of the different versions. The details of the relationship between the Philoxenian and Harklean remain unclear. The problem of evidence for an Old Syriac version outside the Gospels is confused by the question as to whether a reading which is not attested by the main tradition of the Peshitta is necessarily an Old Syriac reading, since study of the Peshitta has shown that this version was not the product of a single event but developed into a more fixed form over a period of time.

3.3.4 *The Coptic versions*

There are two catalogues of Coptic manuscripts, each with its own numbering system. The *Biblia Coptica* is a register of Sahidic manuscripts for the entire Bible. Each fascicle contains a detailed description and a plate of every witness. The other catalogue is produced in the Münster Institut.

Biblia Coptica; F.-J. Schmitz and G. Mink (eds.), *Liste der koptischen Handschriften des Neuen Testaments, 1: Die sahidischen Handschriften der Evangelien* (ANTF 8), Berlin and New York, 1986; *2.1* (ANTF 13), Berlin and New York, 1989; *2.2* (ANTF 15), Berlin and New York, 1991. The third volume contains updates on preceding entries. There are 355 entries.

The most extensive editions of the Coptic remain those of George Horner, in two series, published between 1898 and 1924.

Horner, *Northern Dialect*; Horner, *Southern Dialect*. For use of single manuscripts in the edition of the Bohairic, see 6.1.4.3.

Another tool is L. T. Lefort and M. Wilmet, *Concordance du Nouveau Testament sahidique*, vol. I: *Les mots d'origine grecque* (CSCO 124), Louvain, 1950 (Lefort); vol. II: *Les mots Autochtones, 1* (CSCO 173), 1957; *2* (CSCO 183), 1958; *3* (CSCO 185), 1959 (Wilmet).

3.3.5 The Armenian version

After the Latin Vulgate, Armenian manuscripts are said to be the most numerous of any version, Rhodes' catalogue containing 1,244 entries. The version is also an early one: translations of the books were made in the early fifth century. For the most part, they seem to have been translations from an Old Syriac form of text, only Revelation having been taken from the Greek. There are no manuscripts of this oldest form of text, known as Arm 1, there having been a revision after the year 431 on the basis of Greek copies. This second version, Arm 2, is represented in the manuscript tradition, but the fact that the oldest manuscripts date from the ninth century means that there is debate about the degree to which they genuinely represent the oldest forms.

There is no critical edition of the Armenian. The edition of the whole Bible made by Zohrab and published in 1805 is not satisfactory. As Alexanian points out in his survey, a critical edition is urgently needed.

E. F. Rhodes, *An Annotated List of Armenian New Testament Manuscripts*, Tokyo, 1959; Y. Zōhrapean, *Astuacašuč' Matean Hin ew Nor Ktakaranc'*, Venice, 1805; J. M. Alexanian, 'The Armenian Version of the New Testament', in Ehrman and Holmes, *Contemporary Research*, 157–72. V. Nersessian, *Armenian Illuminated Gospel Books*, London and Wolfeboro, 1987; M. E. Stone, D. Kouymjian and H. Lehmann, *Album of Armenian Paleography*, Aarhus, 2002.

3.3.6 The Georgian version

The Georgian version is closely tied to the Armenian, the earliest versions having been translated from it. The Gospels and Paul's letters had been translated by the end of the fifth century. Later versions were revisions against Greek originals, and bring the version towards the Byzantine text.

Metzger, *Early Versions*, 182–214; J. N. Birdsall, 'The Georgian Version of the New Testament', in Ehrman and Holmes, *Contemporary Research*, 173–87; J. N. Birdsall, 'Georgian Studies and the New Testament', *NTS* 29 (1983), 306–20, reprinted in Birdsall, *Collected Papers*, 197–213. B. Outtier, 'Essai de répertoire des manuscrits des vieilles versions géorgiennes du Nouveau Testament', *Langues Orientales, Anciennes, Philolologie et Linguistique* 1 (1988), 173–9, lists eighty-nine manuscripts; 'Compte rendu d'une mission d'étude sur les manuscrits géorgiennes (19.IX–10.X.1992)', *Revue des Études Géorgiennes et Caucacasiennes* 8–9 (1992–3), 237–9.

3.3.7 The Ethiopic version

The New Testament was translated from Greek into Geʻez, a language now only used liturgically. The first translations were probably made in the fourth to fifth centuries. The majority of the three hundred or so manuscripts date from the sixteenth century onwards. Only for the Gospels are there any older than the fourteenth, one or two possibly pre-dating the thirteenth. Study of the Gospels has identified several text forms.

R. Zuurmond, 'The Ethiopic Version of the New Testament', in Ehrman and Holmes, *Contemporary Research*, 142–56. J. Weitenberg (ed.), *The Leiden Armenian Lexical Textbase*, www.sd-editions.com/LALT/home.html (includes Gospel of John in Armenian).

3.3.8 The Arabic versions

In spite of their cultural significance, the Arabic versions are insufficiently understood. Current research on the Gospels indicates a series of translations and revisions made variously from Greek, Syriac (Peshitta), Bohairic and Latin copies, these different linguistic sources reflecting particular phases in the history of Arabic-speaking Christianity. The earliest extant manuscripts date to the second half of the eighth century.

On Arabic literature in general, see G. Graf, *Geschichte der christlichen arabischen Literatur*, 5 vols., Vatican City, 1944–53 (there is a simple guide to its use at www.lib.umich.edu/area/Near.East/MELANotes6970/graf.html). Metzger, *Early Versions*, 257–68; Vööbus, *Early Versions*, 271–97. For the Gospels, see S. H. Griffith, 'The Gospel in Arabic: an Enquiry into its Appearance in the First Abbasid Century', *Oriens Christianus* 69 (1985), 126–67; most recently H. Kachouh, 'The Arabic Versions of the Gospels: a Case Study of John 1.1 and 1.18', in J. D. Thomas (ed.), *The Bible in Arab Christianity* (The History of Christian–Muslim Relations 6), Leiden and Boston, 2006, 9–36. For manuscripts see G. Vajda, *Album de paléographie arabe*, Paris, 1958; J. Pedersen, *The Arabic Book*, tr. R. Hillenbrand, Princeton, 1984; F. Déroche (ed.), *Manuel de codicologie des manuscrits en écriture arabe*, Paris, 2000.

3.3.9 The Slavonic version

There are different names for this version – Old Church Slavonic, Slavonic, or Slavic. The translation is associated with the brothers Cyril (826–69, who changed his name from Constantine) and Methodius (815–85). The former was responsible for the formation of the Glagolitic alphabet, the first Slavic alphabet, the Cyrillic alphabet quickly superseding it. They were responsible for translations of the Gospels (in either continuous-text or lectionary form) and the Apostolos. The oldest manuscripts date to the tenth and eleventh centuries. The version continues in use in the Russian Orthodox Church. A critical edition is awaited (for the Gospel of John, see 10.5.4).

A. Alexeev, 'The Last but Probably Not the Least: the Slavonic Version as a Witness of the Greek NT Text', in E. Konstantinou (ed.), *Methodios und Kyrillos in ihrer europäischen Dimension*, Berne, 2005, 247–60; H. P. S. Bakker, *Towards a Critical Edition of the Old Slavic New Testament. A Transparent and Heuristic Approach* (University of Amsterdam doctoral dissertation), Amsterdam, 1996.

3.3.10 The Gothic version

The Gothic version was a translation from the Greek by Wulfila (also spelt Ulfilas and Ulphilas), a man who, having grown up a Goth, was briefly Archbishop of Constantinople shortly after 351, returning as a missionary to the Goths, making his translation of the Bible and dying in 383. The New Testament survives only partially: we have the four Gospels and thirteen of Paul's letters (there are no copies of Hebrews). Of these, only 2 Corinthians is complete. The principal manuscript of the Gospels is Codex Argenteus ('the silver codex'), a purple manuscript which is sixth-century and probably of Italian origin. There are two manuscripts of the epistles, both palimpsests of the sixth century (for descriptions, see *CLA* 3.364, 365).

The Wulfila Project website (www.wulfila.be/) contains a number of resources, including revisions of the major editions of the manuscripts, linguistic materials and bibliographies. The relationship between the Latin and Gothic versions is significant, both in terms of manuscript production (for example, there is a strong similarity in appearance between Codex Argenteus and the Old Latin Codex Brixianus) and linguistically (see P. H. Burton, 'Assessing Latin–Gothic Interaction', J. N. Adams, M. Janse and S. Swain (eds.), *Bilingualism in Ancient Society. Language Contact and the Written Text*, Oxford, 2002, 393–418; 'Using the Gothic Bible; Notes on Jared S. Klein "On the Independence of Gothic Syntax"', *Journal of Indo-European Studies* 24 (1996), 81–98).

3.3.11 Other versions

For versions in Nubian, Persian, Sogdian, Caucasian, Albanian, Anglo-Saxon, Old High German and Old Saxon, the reader is referred to Metzger's *Early Versions*. The relevant chapters in the second volume of the *Cambridge History of the Bible* are a starting point for the histories of medieval European vernacular versions. The new translations of the Reformation and beyond are described in the third volume of the same work. None of these versions is of direct value for the study of the ancient text (for versions of the Diatessaron and other harmonies, see 10.7).

The evidence for a Thracian version is so slight as to leave doubt as to whether it ever existed.

G. W. H. Lampe (ed.), *The Cambridge History of the Bible*, vol. II: *The West from the Fathers to the Reformation*, Cambridge, 1969; S. L. Greenslade (ed.), *The Cambridge History of the Bible,*. vol III, *The West from the Reformation to the Present Day*, Cambridge, 1963. A new version in four volumes is currently under way. See also chapters in de Hamel, *The Book*. For the Thracian, see B. M. Metzger, 'The Problematical Thracian Version of the Gospels', in R. H. Fischer (ed.), *A Tribute to Arthur Vööbus: Studies in Early Christian Literature and its Environment, Primarily in the Syrian East*, Chicago, 1977, 337–55, reprinted in Metzger, *New Testament Studies*, 148–66.

3.4 NEW TESTAMENT TEXTS IN OTHER DOCUMENTS AND MEDIA

3.4.1 Greek manuscripts excluded from the Liste

The description of the *Liste* in 1.3.2 stated that one of the criteria for the inclusion of a manuscript (not applied in the case of lectionary manuscripts) was that it should consist of more than excerpts. The application of this criterion to fragmentary papyrus and majuscule manuscripts is very difficult, since it is often either hard or impossible to determine the original extent and character of such a manuscript. It was also noted that there are separate and discontinued majuscule numbers for talismans (0152) and ostraca (0153). Apart from these two categories, there are various other documents not present in the *Liste* which may be textually valuable.

An example of the kinds of problem to be encountered in distinguishing between continuous and excerptive manuscripts is found in the study of those also containing *hermeneiai*, brief sentences at the bottom of the page telling the reader's fortune. In a recent study of eight manuscripts, I concluded that more of them were continuous-text than selections, although one could not reach a certain conclusion in every instance. D. C. Parker, 'Manuscripts of John's Gospel with *Hermeneiai*', in Childers and Parker, *Transmission and Reception*, 48–68. With regard to their textual character, I concluded that 'with caution in certain respects, they deserve to be used alongside continuous-text manuscripts as useful, albeit fragmentary, weapons in the study of the development of the Johannine text' (p. 67).

The papyrus manuscripts of this category are listed in the Aland *Repertorium* (under the heading 'Varia', pp. 323–60) and in van Haelst's *Catalogue* (under various headings, including prayers and magical texts), and electronically in the *Leuven Database of Ancient Books*. These manuscripts are of interest in various ways. As artefacts, they are an important source for the study of the use of Scripture in antiquity. Typically with folds and showing signs of use, they may represent the closest most people came to the Scriptures. Verses carried for protection from the forces of evil were evidently popular. Augustine famously recommended a copy of John's Gospel for a pillow to avoid headaches. This assumed ownership of a codex, which may have been unrealistic for most people. So far as the text is concerned, such citations need to be treated as a possible source of information about forms of text current in early Christianity. It is possible that they will contain traces of adaptation, for example in the way they begin. But they are at least putatively copied from, or ultimately derived from, continuous-text manuscripts. What one cannot achieve with such an excerpt is any kind of stemmatological reconstruction of its place in a manuscript tradition (see 1.3.2). It is this drawback that places it closer to the citational category of evidence.

For an assessment of this category of manuscript, with examples and a list of all such material for John's Gospel, see S. R. Pickering, 'The Significance of Non-continuous New Testament Textual Materials in Papyri', in Taylor, *Studies in the Early Text*, 121–41. A recent study of nineteen manuscript copies containing the Lord's Prayer reflects his belief in the value of manuscripts as 'fingerprints of a bygone time' (T. J. Kraus, 'Manuscripts with the *Lord's Prayer* – They Are More than Simply Witnesses to That Text Itself', in Kraus and Nicklas, *New Testament Manuscripts*, 227–66, p. 231).

Manuscripts which could not be fitted into a stemma might include service books with the Lord's Prayer or canticles, Gospel harmonies, talismans, and so on. Whether evidence from such documents should be included in an edition of the New Testament will be the decision of the editor. The decision must rest on an assessment of the document itself and on the principles according to which the edition is made. It should be remembered that the *Liste* is not intended to distinguish between valuable and useless material, but to be a list of certain classes of manuscripts.

Another kind of citation which is no longer included in the *Liste* is the phrases from the New Testament in the marginal glosses of a seventh-century manuscript of the Octateuch. This manuscript was cited by Wettstein and by Tischendorf. The location of the citations within glosses indicates that this source of information belongs among the patristic citations. The fact that these glosses are in a manuscript of a part of the Bible is not relevant.

See Parker, 'The Majuscule Manuscripts', 26; further details of the passages cited in Scrivener, *Plain Introduction*, 1.134. The passages were published by Tischendorf in *Monumenta Sacra Inedita* (1846, 400ff.). For a plate of the manuscript showing the gloss which included Mk 10.17–18, see Devreesse, *Introduction*, plate XII.

The distinction between manuscripts which should be treated as copies of the text and manuscripts which, containing parts of the text, should either be categorised with patristic citations or treated as special cases, highlights the importance of treating all sources as a manuscript tradition. Curiously, because textual scholars are used to getting information about manuscript from images but information about patristic citations from printed editions, it is easy to think that every manuscript has to be placed in the primary category. Once it is recognised that all our sources of textual information are derived from manuscript sources, it is not so difficult to see that plenty of manuscripts are in the broad citational category rather than similar in character to such a manuscript as P75 or 01.

3.4.2 Inscriptions

In principle, the inscription has great potential as a source of information. While manuscripts are easily moved around, a lump of stone is not (although the mason might be peripatetic). It could provide the best possible kind of evidence about local texts (see 5.1.2 and 5.1.5). Unfortunately, the amount of information is slight, and what information we have is old. (The role of inscriptions in historical research as authenticating events described in documents is well known (for example, the Gallio inscription), and is not our concern here.)

Several recent discoveries illustrate the material. The first is an inscription found on a monument in Jerusalem. 'Absalom's Pillar' was adopted by Christians as the burial place of Simeon, Zachariah and James the brother of Jesus, as various inscriptions on it testify. One contains Luke 2.25 in the following wording:

ΟΘΑΦΟΣΣΥΜΕΩΝΟΣΗΝ (?)
ΔΙΚΑ[Ι]ΟΤΑΤΟΣΑΝΘΡΩΠ
ΚΑΙΓΗΡ[Ω]ΝΕΥΣΗΒΗΣΤΑΤΟΣ
ΚΑΙΠΑΡΑΚΛΗΣΙΝ
Λ[Α]ΟΥ
ΠΡΟΣΔΕΧΣ

This may be interpreted as:

ὁ θάφος (scil. τάφος) Συμεὼν ὃς ἦν (?)
δικα[ι]ότατος ἄνθρωπ(ος)
καὶ γήρ[ω]ν (scil. γέρ[ω]ν) εὐσηβήστατος
καὶ παράκλησιν
λ[α]οῦ
προσδεχ(όμενος)

The reading εὐσηβήστατος (the superlatives are both embellishments) shows knowledge of a form of the text with the reading εὐσεβής. This is attested by 01* 017 036 565 700 1424. The variant εὐλαβής is found in all other witnesses. This is an extremely rare example of an inscription that provides evidence of the knowledge of a form of the text in a particular place and time. The inscription has been dated to the fourth century, and thus it joins Codex Sinaiticus in providing the earliest evidence for this form of the text. It is certainly interesting that an inscription from Jerusalem should support the reading of a manuscript which scholars have often argued was written in Caesarea, but it would be folly to build any theory out of such a tiny scrap of evidence.

Emile Puech, 'Le tombeau de Siméon et Zacharie dans la vallée de Josaphat', *RB* 111 (2004), 563–77. See also E. Puech and J. Zias, 'Le tombeau de Zacharie et Siméon au monument funéraire dit d'Absalom dans la vallée de Josaphat', *RB* 110 (2003), 321–35.

Romans 13.3 is found twice on the floor of the Revenue Office in Maritime Caesarea, in Rooms I and V. This building was in use from the fourth to the early seventh century. In both rooms the text is written within a circle. In Room I (with the original line breaks but with word divisions added) is

ΘΕΛΕΙΣ
ΜΗ ΦΟΒΙΣΘΑΙ
ΤΗΝ ΕΞΟ(Υ)ΣΙΑΝ
ΤΟ ΑΓΑΘΟΝ
ΠΟΙΕΙ

The form in Room V is fuller:

†
ΘΕΛΕΙΣ
ΜΙΙ ΦΟΒΕΙΣΘΑΙ
ΤΗΝ ΕΞΟΥΣΙΑΝ ΤΟ
ΑΓΑΘΟΝ ΠΟΙΕΙ
ΚΑΙ ΕΞΕΙΣ ΕΠΑΙΝΟΝ
ΕΞ ΑΥΤΗΣ

C. M. Lehmann and K. G. Holum, *The Greek and Latin Inscriptions of Caesarea Maritima*, Atlanta, 2000, 100–1 (Entries 88–9) and plate LXIV. There is also a photograph of the second inscription in K. G. Holum, 'Archaeological Evidence for the Fall of Byzantine Caesarea', *Bulletin of the American Schools of Oriental Research*, 286 (May, 1992), 73–85, p. 79 (fig. 4).

Both forms are identical to the text as it is found in the Nestle–Aland. No variants are reported by either Nestle–Aland or Tischendorf, *Editio octava*. Note the itacism in the first inscription (φοβισθαι).

Christian churches of antiquity did not contain inscriptions with biblical citations (e-mail from J. Strange, November 2006). Strange offered the suggestion in the press release announcing the Jerusalem find that 'the ancients apparently believed chiseling Scripture into monuments debased sacred words', but reports that this is a hypothesis not a conclusion. 'It seems odd that churches are not simply full of scriptural quotes. On the other hand, why do we expect that? Synagogues do not, except for Samaritan synagogues, and perhaps this is a clue' (e-mail to the author, 7 November 2006).

D. Feissel, 'La Bible dans les inscriptions grecques', in C. Mondesert (ed.), *La monde grec ancien et la Bible* (*Bible de tous les temps* 1), Paris, 1984, 223–31; L. Jalabert, 'Citations bibliques dans l'épigraphie grecque', in F. Cabrol and H. Leclercq (eds.), *Dictionnaire d'archaeologie chrétienne et de liturgie*, vol. III.2, cols. 1731–56; H. Leclercq, 'Citations bibliques dans l'épigraphie latine', in the same volume, cols. 1756–79.

The lists provided by these writers are due for revision. Such a full list of all inscriptions containing New Testament citations should include inscriptions in other ancient languages. We will then be in a position to assess their significance.

How would one cite inscriptions in an edition of the New Testament? The answer is that they should be classed as patristic citations.

PART II

Textual criticism and editions

CHAPTER 4

Manuscripts as tradents of the text

4.1 INTRODUCTORY

The interest hitherto has been almost totally on the manuscript as a physical entity. The focus now shifts to the texts which the manuscripts contain. That the text is found in manuscripts is not to be forgotten, and the bridge from the manuscripts to the text which best keeps the manuscripts in mind is a study of examples of copying. How accurate were scribes in making a copy? What sort of mistakes did they make? How significant were these mistakes? How many of them were mistakes, and how many intentional alterations? Which of their mistakes did they correct? What sort of corrections did subsequent readers make? In what ways do the physical characteristics of manuscripts cause textual change? How much did scribes alter texts, and how much was it readers who made changes and annotations? How may we observe and quantify these changes, and what sorts of comparisons do we draw between them? What models of scribal activity do we have, and how are these models dependent on our reconstruction of the writing process?

The wording in the title of this chapter is chosen because it does not include a reference to scribal activity. It is true that a scribe wrote down what is on the page. But unless we are able to compare what the scribe produced with the source manuscript, there are limitations to our understanding of scribal activity. Even in what we can deduce, we must consider the role of others besides the scribe in transmitting the text: readers who may have altered the source text; patrons who may have indicated their preferences or requirements; the speaker, if the manuscript was written to dictation. The title avoids these important questions until the right time to face them arrives and seeks to keep the manuscripts in their centre-stage position.

The word 'tradent' requires explanation. It has been used in New Testament textual research by dela Cruz, 'Allegory, Mimesis and the Text' (see 23–5), citing J.A. Sanders, 'The Hermeneutics of

Translation', in H. C. Kee and I. J. Borowsky (eds.), *Removing Anti-Judaism from the New Testament*, Philadelphia, 2000, 43–62. Dela Cruz's definition is 'a person or community that passes on the tradition of the Scriptural text' (p. 23).

In studying the texts of the New Testament writings and comparing the differences, it is essential to remember that the materials we have available to us can be but a fraction of the copies which have been produced. As the French scholar Marcel Richard pointed out, the rate of loss even since the end of the nineteenth century, during a period of great interest in the past, has been very high, with 5 per cent of all known Greek manuscripts destroyed, seriously damaged or lost for a long period of time (mostly either in accidental fires or in war) between 1891 and 1971. The writings of the New Testament were produced in enormous quantities. Yet, even with the papyrus finds of the modern period, the number of extant copies (even very partial ones) is very small – well under a hundred from the period before 400. The significance of this for the study of the texts has been best expressed by Zuntz:

The tradition of The Book is part and parcel of the life of Christianity. It comprises all the manuscripts existing at any given moment throughout the world, with the notes and corrections added to them, the quotations drawn, the versions made from them. You try to visualize the welter of communities small and great everywhere; each of them, and many individual members, have their copies; they use, compare, exchange, copy, and gloss them; and this living process goes on for centuries – a broad stream of living tradition, changing continually and, at any one moment wide and varied beyond imagination. And against this rather overpowering notion of what the tradition really was, you put the comparatively tiny number of old manuscripts and other surviving evidence. Is it surprising that these survivals cannot be brought into a strictly rational relation? On the contrary: it would be surprising if they could. But they are all elements of this broad tradition – you may liken them to pieces of matter carried down by the stream. (*Opuscula Selecta*, 255–6)

M. Richard, 'La recherche des textes hier et demain', in Harlfinger, *Griechische Kodikologie* 3–13, pp. 3–7. For essays on a variety of catastrophes, some man-made and others the result of natural disaster, and their political and cultural significance, see J. Raven (ed.), *Lost Libraries. The Destruction of Great Book Collections since Antiquity*, Oxford, 2004. For a statistical proposal with regard to the loss rate of ancient manuscripts, see M. P. Weitzman, 'The Evolution of Manuscript Traditions', *Journal of the Royal Statistical Society* A 150 (1987), part 4, 287–308. Duplacy has suggested that 'On peut estimer qu'au IVe siècle on copia au moins 1500 ou 2000 manuscrits grecs néotestamentaires' ('Histoire des manuscrits et histoires du texte du NT', *NTS* 12 (1965–6), 124–39, p. 127, reprinted in Duplacy, *Études*, 39–54, p. 42.

G. Zuntz, 'The Text of the Epistles', in Zuntz, *Opuscula Selecta*, 252–68, pp. 255f. (original English version; published in a French translation, 'Réflexions sur l'histoire du texte Paulinien', *RB* 59 (1952), 5–22).

The study of a few examples where we know that a manuscript has been copied from another provides an approach to this broad tradition.

4.2 TWO COPYING EVENTS

A copying event is one way of describing the copying of a text, which might also be called the making of a manuscript. It is appropriate here, because if we can establish that one manuscript has been copied from another, we can observe the event, certainly not as though we were present, but in enough detail to make some judgement as to how the task was undertaken. I begin with two examples which I have studied elsewhere, both concerning pairs of Latin manuscripts.

4.2.1 Codex Mediolanensis and its copy

When studying a Vulgate manuscript which was copied in the sixth century, known as Codex Mediolanensis (Latin for the Milanese Codex) and given the siglum M, I noticed that some leaves of it reduplicated part of the text, and I compared the two sections. It turned out that the best interpretation of the evidence was that the second set of leaves was a tenth-century copy of the older manuscript. I called the newer leaves M^{abs}. My evidence was of two kinds.

(1) From a palaeographical comparison, four points were noticed: (a) the later copy sometimes imitates a distinctive feature of the older hand; (b) the point at which the later copy ends is marked with a cross in the right-hand margin of the older copy; (c) several corrections to the older copy may have been made by the later copyist; (d) in one place a horizontal stroke at a line end was overlooked by the scribe of M^{abs}, resulting in a change of case.
(2) The textual evidence is even more compelling: (a) the two texts share four readings not otherwise attested in any manuscript cited in the critical editions of the Old Latin by Jülicher, and of the Vulgate by Weber and by Wordsworth and White; (b) in twelve other places they share readings with support from only a few other manuscripts.

We thus have evidence of different kinds which together make a very strong case for the later text having been copied from the older one. That being so, we have an opportunity for testing the frequency of change introduced by the copyist. I found thirty places where a change had been made (the twelve noted above, and another eighteen), in a text of approximately 3,200 words. This is a rate of approximately ten changes in every thousand words. Some of these are correction of evident (that is, evident in the eyes of the scribe of M^{abs}) copying errors in M such as misspellings – there are about half a dozen of these. In many others it is the later text that is at fault, making rather typical errors of the copying of John at the time, especially in confusion over the correct verb endings to be used. Only in three places did M^{abs} change a more distinctive reading of M, that is to say, a reading which it shares with few other manuscripts. This amounts to a significant change every thousand words (of course, we would not expect them to be evenly spaced, and in fact they all occur within 292 words (17.1–19)). It is noteworthy that the four unique grammatically possible readings of M are preserved by M^{abs}, so that textually the two copies remain close.

D. C. Parker, 'A Copy of the Codex Mediolanensis', *JTS* 41 (1990), 537–41; For Jülicher, see 10.5.2; Weber, *Biblia Sacra* (on this occcasion I used the 1969 edition).

4.2.2 *The supplementary Latin leaves in Codex Bezae*

My second example is of another pair of Latin manuscripts. The more recent document is that which in the ninth century supplemented some lost pages of the fourth/fifth-century bilingual manuscript Codex Bezae (for Codex Bezae see 9.2.2; these pages are indicated by 5^s, 5 being the Beuron number for this otherwise Old Latin manuscript, the superscript s indicating a supplement). This work was carried out in Lyons (evident on palaeographical grounds). It is possible that the Latin text of this supplement may have been copied from a manuscript currently in Lyons (Bibliothèque Municipale, MS 431) but copied in Saint-Amand in about 860. The Latin supplementation consists of three blocks of text: Matthew 2.21–3.7; John 18.2–20.1; and Mark 16.6–20. The palaeographical evidence here is of two kinds: (a) MS 431 has been corrected at three places to a spelling followed by 5^s; (b) some words initially omitted by 5^s constitute a whole line of text in MS 431. Such an accidental omission, where there is no repetition of a sequence of letters, is more explicable if the scribe overlooked a single line of the source manuscript.

There were eight significant readings in which the text was changed, usually at places where both forms are well attested. Since the three passages amount to 1,735 words (154 in Matthew, 1,371 in John and 210 in Mark), we have a significant change every 217 words, or four in a thousand. But we should be a little more precise. There are none in the page from Matthew, four in the passage from John, and four in Mark. This gives a rate of one difference about every 350 words in John, but one every fifty in Mark. As with the first example, the differences come at varying densities.

The case for d^s being a copy of MS 431 is not as strong as that for M and M^{abs}. Where the second manuscript contains more differences from the first, the case that it is a copy will always be weaker. However, this also means that faithful copies are more recognisable as copies than more divergent ones. It is here that palaeographical evidence comes into its own.

Parker, *Codex Bezae*, 172–3 and bibliography p. 166.

These two examples, both of Latin manuscripts and providing information about Latin scribes of the ninth and tenth centuries, may or may not be typical of copying in general. That there are differences between the examples indicates that it would be a mistake to assume that what is true of one copying event is true of another. That both of these examples come from two places comparatively close to each other (Milan and Lyons) and are perhaps no more than a century apart emphasises that we cannot expect uniform patterns.

4.3 A FAMILY OF MANUSCRIPTS

The next example I take is from the Greek manuscript tradition. It is not an example of one manuscript being copied directly from another, but of three relationships within a family. The family in question here is known as Family 1, and it consists of a group of manuscripts of the Gospels dating from the Byzantine period. It is known as Family 1, because when it was first identified, Gregory–Aland 1 appeared to preserve the text of the archetype most faithfully. Since then, another manuscript, 1582, has come to light, which turns out to supplant 1. The fact that 1582 is two hundred years older, having been copied in 948, is not itself significant, since 1 might turn out to be a more faithful copy of an older form of text. More significant is the fact that 1582 contains a number of marginal notes which stem from the archetype, some of which contain a reading found in 1 when it differs from 1582. Its text in Matthew has been studied in detail by Anderson, and only thirty-four places of variation were found (in five of which the reading of 1 is in a marginal note in 1582). Since there are about 18,800 words in the Byzantine text of the Gospel of Matthew, this constitutes a difference every 550 words, two in a thousand.

The reconstruction of the family tree by Anderson indicates that 1582 is a more exact representation than 1 of the text of the archetype. In her view, 1 and 1582 have a common ancestor intervening between the archetype and themselves, from which 1 is descended through a lost intermediate archetype, from which other members of the family are descended. This is not to say that only one manuscript intervenes between the family archetype and 1582, and two between the archetype and 1, but that *at least* two copying events can be shown to have intervened. That means that the thirty-four differences between 1 and 1582 have arisen in the course of at least two copyings. Altogether, this represents an impressive achievement by both branches of the tradition. There are particular reasons why this may have been achieved. According to some of the marginalia, the form of text represented by the family is that known to Origen.

Lake, *Codex 1*; Anderson, *Family 1 in Matthew*. 1582 was copied by the same scribe, Ephraim, as 1739 (see 8.4).

Within this same family, there are three manuscripts which may be even more closely related in terms of copying events. It has been argued that each is copied from the next older one, so that we have three generations of manuscripts, as it were a grandparent, an offspring and a grandchild. Stemmatically, this is presented as

209

205

205abs

Some brief details on each manuscript are necessary.

205 was written for Cardinal Bessarion (he wrote his name in it) by a scribe called Johannes Rhosus, over a hundred and thirty of whose productions are listed by Vogel and Gardthausen. The precise date of this copy is unknown, but his first dated manuscript was made in 1447 and Bessarion died in 1472. It contains the entire Bible (see 1.8.4 and 1.8.8).

205[abs] is also dated to the fifteenth century.

209 was a copy of the Gospels, Acts and epistles made in the fourteenth century, to which Revelation was added in the fifteenth century.

The stemma presents 205 as intermediary between the two other manuscripts, as a copy of 209, while itself being the source for 205[abs]. That the second case is generally accepted is evident from the manuscript's Gregory–Aland number. This opinion is given by Gregory, having been roundly stated by Scrivener: 'A mere duplicate of Cod. 205, as Holmes clearly saw'. The reference is to Holmes, the editor of the Septuagint, and the same statement was made by Swete. It thus seems at first sight to be a closed case, even though one should be worried that all we have been offered is a series of assertions. It is only when we turn to the Book of Revelation that we find any evidence for the relationship between the two manuscripts. J. Schmid argues that 205[abs] cannot be a copy of 205, because 205 has a considerable number (he lists sixteen) of distinctive errors and small corrections which do not feature in 205[abs].

So far as the New Testament apart from Revelation is concerned, a connection between 205 and 209 had long been suspected. Scrivener records that his contemporary Burgon believed the two to have been 'transcribed from the same *uncial* archetype'. Lake, in the first study of Family 1, reached the following conclusion: 'I was convinced when I studied the question at Venice that 205 was a copy of 209. An hour's work revealed only two or three differences between the manuscripts, and those clearly accidental.' This is yet again a claim without any evidence. We have to go to Revelation and Schmid again to find some hard facts, and from these we learn Schmid's conclusion that 205 and 205[abs] are both descended from a lost 'sister' manuscript' of 209. The phrase 'sister manuscript' I take to mean a manuscript in the same relationship to the family archetype as 209. The resultant stemma is

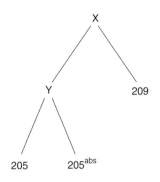

Scrivener, *Plain Introduction*, I.219; Swete, *Introduction*, 151; Schmid, *Andreas von Kaisareia. Einleitung*, 288; Lake, *Codex 1*, xxii.

There are several important lessons to be learned from the history of the study of the relationship between 205, 205^{abs} and 209. The first is the importance of providing evidence. The second is that one cannot assume that because one part of a manuscript is copied from another, the whole must be. Certainly we have three complete New Testaments (two of them complete Bibles), and three manuscripts closely related with regard to their history. But the text of Revelation in 209 may be later than 205 and thus may not be its source. The study of their relationship in the rest of the New Testament is yet to be undertaken. (The situation with regard to the Septuagint is quite different: since 209 has only the New Testament, it is a question only of the relationship between 205 and 205^{abs}.) The statistical evidence of *Text und Textwert* will not help us to discover the stemmatological relationship between all three, since 205^{abs} is excluded (presumably on the grounds that its position in the tradition is known and beyond dispute). But 205 and 209 are present, and an examination of the evidence in the manner which is outlined above (1.9) might help to disentangle this problem.

It is instructive that, while all scholars agreed that these three manuscripts are closely related, we await agreement on the precise nature of their relationship. The analogy of the Milan Latin manuscripts shows that physical evidence may be highly valuable. Textually, the relationship is established, with the listing of agreement and disagreements, in particular at the places where the potential exemplar (source manuscript) has strange or difficult readings.

These four examples are from a comparatively recent period. The further back one goes, with the consequent greater loss of manuscripts, the lower the chance of having two manuscripts so closely related. To repeat Zuntz's words, 'against this rather overpowering notion of what the tradition really was, you put the comparatively tiny number of old manuscripts and other surviving evidence. Is it surprising that these survivals cannot be brought into a strictly rational relation? On the contrary: it would be surprising if they could.' Zuntz was not even thinking of so close a relation as that between exemplar and copy.

How useful might the parallel of the ninth- and tenth-century and late-medieval manuscript copyings be in understanding the manuscript production of the second, fourth, or sixth centuries? Do we have any grounds for gauging the fidelity of scribes to their exemplars, when we are unlikely to have a manuscript even approximately similar to that exemplar? This is evidently a highly important question in the study of the New Testament text. If we could argue that the kind of fidelity shown by the scribes of manuscripts 1 and 1582 was true even of the majority of ancient scribes, we might have grounds for believing that the tradition had been copied very faithfully. There are other grounds for caution in using these examples: all are taken from the Gospels, and it would be careless to assume that what is true of the copying of them will be true of the copying of other books.

This exploration is only one of the ways in which the process of copying could be tested. Another is to look for signs of corrections in manuscripts, in order to assess the degree (1) of self-correction by copyists and (2) of revision by subsequent readers of the text. The study of the two Latin copyings provided some suggestion that a copyist might leave traces in an exemplar. What can we find from the study of corrections?

4.4 CORRECTIONS IN MANUSCRIPTS

E. J. Epp has looked for evidence of manuscript notation among the twenty-eight papyrus and six parchment manuscripts of the New Testament from Oxyrhynchus available in 1997: 'critical signs indicating scholarly editing – those moving beyond the copying process – rarely if ever occur in the New Testament papyri at Oxyrhynchus or in other Christian literature there from the early period'. The twenty-eight papyri represent, of course, a significant proportion of those available to us. It is also the case that of over one hundred papyri now listed, very few are extensive enough for there to be much of a chance of finding any kind of annotation.

A papyrus which does contain annotation is P66 (illustrated in 1.2.1.1). Here an extensive programme of revision has not only corrected many casual slips, but also introduced genuine alternative readings. Fee has listed approximately 450 corrections in the manuscript, virtually all of them the work of the scribe. At the most P66 contains 15,000 extant words. This constitutes a correction every 333 words, or 30 in every 1,000 words.

E. J. Epp, 'The New Testament Papyri at Oxyrhynchus in their Social and Intellectual Context', in *Baarda Festschrift*, 47–68, p. 67, reprinted in Epp, *Collected Essays*, 497–520 with Added Notes (519–20), p. 517. Fee, *Papyrus Bodmer II (P66)*.

There are difficulties with this evaluation of P66, principally the fact that we lack a full list of the corrections. So much of what is written on topics such as this is partial. What is needed is a piece of text where there is enough detailed information to be able to conduct a proper analysis of all the evidence. Fortunately, this is now available in the electronic transcriptions made by the International Greek New Testament Project for their edition of the Gospel of John. They include two categories which are useful here. The first is the complete transcriptions of sixty-six majuscule manuscripts.

Some of these transcriptions are available in print in Schmid, Elliott and Parker, *Majuscules*. All are available electronically at the multilingual electronic edition at www.iohannes.com.

The sixty-six manuscripts date from the end of the third to the beginning of the eleventh century.

III/IV	0162
IV	01 03 0258
IV/V	05 032
V	02 04 026 029 068 0216 0217 0218 0264 0301
VI	022 024 060 065 070 078 086 087 091 0260 0302 0309
VI/VII	083
VII	0109 0210 0268
VIII	07 019 047 054 0101 0127 0233 0238 0256
IX	09 011 013 017 021 030 031 034 037 038 039 041 045 050 063 0211 0290 0306
IX/X	044
X	028 (dated 949) 033 036 0105
X/XI	0286 0299 (the date has '?' against it in the *Liste*)

Forty-one of these manuscripts contain corrections. In table 4.1 the second column gives the total number of places where a correction has been tagged; C* means a place where there is a correction by the scribe; the first column with C indicates the total number of corrections by a later hand, and the next three columns give the breakdown of this total: the second C means places where either there is only one corrector observed in the manuscript or (if the next two columns come into play) those places where it is not possible to distinguish between the hands (e.g. if the correction consists of an erasure). The final column indicates how many times there has been a sequence of more than one correction, that is to say places where a correction has itself been altered (and a few times there is a third level).

Table 4.1

G.-A.	Total	C*	C		C	C1	C2	Multiple
01	517	1	516	=	see below			41
02	30	4	26	=		16	10	
03	34	3	31	=	8	6	17	
04	184	2	182	=	22	46	123	5
05	201	44	157	=	see below			
07	104	8	96	=	92	3	2	1
09	11	0	11					
011	42	1	41	=	23	17	1	
013	36	6	30	=	9	10	12	1
017	57	2	55					
019	50	2	48					
021	16	0	16					
022	27	25	2					
026	1	0	1					
028	33	16	17	=	13	4		
030	8	0	8	=			1	1
031	4	3	1					
032	20	14	6	=	3		3	
033	11	1	10					
034	20	6	14	=	11	3		
036	16	8	8	=	6	2		
037	82	32	49	=		1	1	1
038	134	45	9	=	see below			
039	77	14	63	=	26	30	7	
041	94	4	90	=	87	3	2	2
044	7	0	7					
045	24	14	10	=	6	3	1	
047	10	1	9					
054	14	6	8	=	7	1		
063	1	0	1					
065	2	0	2					
070	6	1	5					
083	9	0	9					
091	4	0	4					
0105	1	0	1					
0109	8	0	8					
0145	1	0	1					
0211	37	2	35					
0233	2	0	2					
0290	2	0	2					
0299	1	0	1					
Total	1,939	265	1,594					

Three manuscripts have more than three correctors differentiated.

01 has a number of correctors, which are named here according to the classification by Milne and Skeat, *Scribes and Correctors*, 40–50:

C*	1	
S1	26	Scriptorium hand
S2	1	Scriptorium hand
Cca	472	Fifth to seventh centuries or from seventh century
Ccb	6	Fifth to seventh centuries or from seventh century
Ccb2	42	Fifth to seventh centuries or from seventh century
Multiple	(41)	(36 of Ccb2 corrections are re-corrections after Ccb)
Total	517	

05 has a total of ten hands described according to the system devised by Scrivener and revised first by Rendel Harris and then by me (F. H. A. Scrivener, *Bezae Codex Cantabrigiensis*, Cambridge, 1864, xxiv–xxix; J. R. Harris, *The Annotators of the Codex Bezae (with some notes on Sortes Sanctorum)*, London, 1901; Parker, *Codex Bezae*, 35–69:

C*	44	
A	27	400–440
B	47	fifth century
C	14	fifth century
D	12	*c.* 450
E	9	450–500
F	4	450–500
H	7	450–500
J1	1	450–500
K	7	indicates corrections which cannot be attributed to a specific hand
s.m.	43	used broadly in the same way as K
Multiple	(14)	
Total	201	

038 has three hands tagged according to G. Beerman and C. R. Gregory, *Die Koridethi Evangelien Θ 038*, Leipzig, 1913, 599–605, as Ca, Cb and Cd:

C*	45	
C	9	indicates corrections which cannot be attributed to a specific hand
Ca	37	
Cb	22	
Cd	26	
Multiple	(5)	
Total	134	

Table 4.2

G.–A.	Corrections per 1,000 words	Number of extant words
01	31	all
02	2	13,900
03	2	all
04	28	6,600
05	15	13,000
07	6	all
09	1	8,000
011	3	15,350
013	2	14,900
017	4	all
019	3	16,000
021	1	all
022	3	10,000
028	2	all
030	0.5	all
032	1	15,000
033	0.5	all
034	1	6,000
036	1	all
037	5	15,800
038	8	all
039	5	all
044	0.5	all
045	1.5	all
083	6	1,450
091	11	349
0109	17	477
0211	2	all
0233	0.3	6,000

These totals are misleading, to the extent that the manuscripts are not necessarily complete. I have therefore counted the approximate number of words in each witness listed in table 4.2 and then calculated the number of corrections per thousand words of text. I have not made the calculations for very lacunose manuscripts with very few corrections in what survives. I have calculated complete manuscripts as having 16,150 words, which is the number in the printed version known as the Textus Receptus. Most witnesses tend to be slightly shorter than this. Note that this calculation does not indicate the number of words affected by corrections, since I have not distinguished between corrections of one word and those encompassing two or more.

The following points are to be made. First, every complete manuscript of John contains corrections. So too do those containing more than the merest fragments of text, as well as some very fragmentary ones. The frequency of corrections varies considerably. At one end of the spectrum, Codex Sinaiticus has thirty-one corrections to every thousand words. Only one other manuscript comes close to such a high number, and this is Codex Ephraemi Rescriptus. Codex Bezae also stands out, not only for the proportion, but also for the unique number of different hands, along with the seventh-century 0109. Apart from 091, the remaining manuscripts have been corrected only very sporadically. The norm is for a manuscript to contain just a few corrections per thousand words, typically in the region of fifty in total for a text the size of John. The numerical average between all the manuscripts is 5.64 corrections per thousand words.

These findings are at variance with the words of Devreesse in discussing Greek manuscripts in general, 'it is not rare to come across manuscripts which show two, three and even six successive stages of correction' (*Introduction*, 86), citing a manuscript of Isocrates.

It is even more surprising to study the nature of the corrections. Myshrall came to the conclusion that the great majority of the C group of corrections are intended to make the text easier to read, with many alterations consisting of revisions of details such as the way words are broken across lines. Likewise, my own analysis of the corrections of Codex Bezae showed that a considerable number of the corrections were slight adjustments of spelling, removal of nonsense, and other minor matters. Several correctors showed particular interest in the correct use of the article. The number of corrections to which I gave attention as significant for the study of the text was about 380 out of 1,400 corrections.

Myshrall, 'Codex Sinaiticus', 776f.; Parker, *Codex Bezae*, 175–9.

Also striking is the general absence of self-correction by the scribe. With the exception of 05, 022 (where virtually all corrections are scribal), 028, 032, 037, 045 and 054 there are few or none. The situation of 01 is different. There are twenty-seven other corrections made at the time of the manuscript's production, and since this was the work of a team, the scribe may have known that his pages would be checked by someone else. Altogether, we have extremes – a few scribes who seem to have checked their own work regularly, and a vast majority who seem to have had either a great confidence in their own accuracy or a lack of interest in the textual quality of their product.

The second approach is in the transcriptions of more than a thousand manuscripts of John Chapter 18, undertaken as part of the process of selecting manuscripts to be included in the International Greek New Testament Project's edition of John. A selected one thousand manuscripts (apart from papyri and majuscules, only complete manuscripts of the chapter were included) yields the following results.

(1) There are 808 words in the Textus Receptus of John 18.
(2) 469 of the 1,000 manuscripts selected for this analysis contain corrections.
(3) There are 1,226 places where corrections have been made.
(4) Manuscripts containing ten or more corrections are as follows (manuscript number in the first column, number of corrections in the second, century of production in the third):

01	23	IV
03	18	IV
04	24	V
61	19	XVI
80	14	XII
90	10	XVI
126	14	XII
276	15	XI
530	27	XI
595	12	XVI
660	11	XII
1059	17	XV
1346	15	X/XI
1357	15	X
1412	11	X
2247	18	XIV
2426	13	XII
2524	19	XIV
2561	19	XI
2661	18	XI

There are thus 332 corrections in 20 of the manuscripts. The remaining 894 are found in 449 manuscripts, an average of about two per manuscript, though in fact 225 manuscripts have only one each.

It will be seen that there are assiduously corrected manuscripts from every period, but that such manuscripts represent a rather tiny proportion of the whole. Of what kind are the corrections? It is difficult to take a sample, because textual change does not fall evenly across the text. I present here all corrections in the first verse of John 18. Silence indicates agreement with the base text, which is the *Textus Receptus*, Oxford, 1873, the wording printed before the square bracket at each place of variation. Note that these are only the corrections, and not the full list of variants.

ειπων] ειπεν 90*
ο ιησους εξηλθε] εξηλθε absent 1574*; εξηλθε ο ιϲ 1574C*
ο] absent 2804*
εξηλθε] εξηλθεν 331* 2661* 2714C; εξηλθεν deleted 2856C
συν τοις] αυτοις 2426*; τοις 2426C
συν] συν absent 1671*; συν εις 1671C
τοις] αυτοις οι*; του 126*
αυτου] absent 1504*
χειμαρρου] [χειμ]αρου P66*; [χειμ]αρρου P66C*
περαν] absent 741*
χειμαρρου] χειμαρου P66* (txt P66C*) 74C 519*
των κεδρων] του κεδρου οι*; των κεδρων οιCca
κεδρων οπου] οπου 1567*; δενδρων οπου 1567C*
κεδρων] κενδρων 2714C 834*; κευρων 760*
οπου] οπυ 59*; absent 1577*
ην κηπος] absent 820*
εισηλθεν] εισηλθον 507* 507C 1781* 2509C

Of the nineteen words in this verse according to the base text, fifteen have been the subject of correction in the manuscripts. This is hardly very surprising. Even though the verse has no syntactical or exegetical difficulties, even though it was never, so far as I know, a focus of controversy in early Christianity, its copyists make obvious mistakes and rather more subtle ones, and its readers try to improve on what was written (see for example the first and second readings of 2426 where the base text has συν τοις).

It is at this point that we recognise how apt Zuntz's statement is. By and large, there are not many corrections in any one manuscript, yet when we put even so historically insignificant a number as a thousand manuscripts together, a good three quarters of the text has been corrected at some point. Not only, it must be stressed, are there many corrections here; there are even more variations of all kinds between the manuscripts, so that there is not a single word unanimously attested. The significance of the degree of copying has been largely overlooked in the study of the New Testament text. In particular the oldest period suffers from a desperate paucity of evidence. To piece together the relationship between the manuscripts of that period can seem like trying to reconstruct a jigsaw picture with ten out of three thousand pieces.

4.5 IS THERE LESS VARIATION IN TEXTS WITH FEWER MANUSCRIPTS?

There is a way of testing the theory that the degree of textual variation is a result of frequency of copying. If it is correct, then there will be more textual variation in books of which there are many manuscripts than in books of which there are fewer manuscripts. The fact that the extant manuscripts are mostly Byzantine does not really matter, since what we are looking for is the impact of frequent copyings on the textual tradition, not for readings of a particular kind. Until very recently there was no easy way of getting this information. Today, however, it can be collected very quickly, since the *Text und Textwert* series list all the readings from virtually all the extant manuscripts at a series of passages across most of the New Testament.

We start with Luke: 1,756 manuscripts were scrutinised. The part of the volumes which concerns us here is the 'Resultate der Kollation', in which the variants and the manuscript support for them are listed. The list groups the readings into main variant forms. Within these main forms are subforms, variants which they believe to be variations on the main variant. To find how many readings there are, therefore, we need to count the subvariants as well as the variants. If we do this, we find that at TS (= Teststelle) 47 (the inclusion or omission of Lk. 23.17) a grand total of sixty variants is listed, the most for any place in Luke. The majority of witnesses (1,284) support the reading ἀνάγκην δὲ εἶχεν ἀπολύειν αὐτοῖς κατὰ ἑορτὴν ἕνα. But there are also thirty-three variations on this reading, twenty-seven of them supported by fewer than five manuscripts and fifteen by only one. As well as the reading which omits the verse, there are a number of other variants and subvariants: Reading 3 has three subvariants; Reading 4 has fifteen; Readings 5 and 6 have one each, and Reading 7 has none. One manuscript has left out verses 16 to 22; another, verses 15 to 17. One hundred and one manuscripts are lacunose at this point. Subtracting these, one illegible manuscript and nine of which the film proved defective in some way or other, 1,643 manuscripts have provided sixty-two different forms of the text at this point (sixty if we except the manuscripts with larger omissions).

Turning to Matthew, the number of manuscripts is similar (1,757), but no Teststelle has as many variant readings as the most complex in Luke. The greatest number is thirty-eight in TS 15 (Matt. 5.44 (2)). There are twenty-six subvariants on the main Byzantine reading (καὶ προσεύχεσθε ὑπὲρ τῶν ἐπηρεαζόντων ὑμᾶς καὶ διωκόντων ὑμᾶς, attested by 1,321 manuscripts). Sixteen are found in only one manuscript. There are four other readings, one with six subvariants, one with one and the others with none. If we take away the 261 lacunose manuscripts and the ones for which the information could not be collected, 1,488 manuscripts provide thirty-eight different forms of the text.

These two examples from the Gospels, where there are over 1,700 manuscripts, need to be tested against other parts of the New Testament. In the Pauline letters, the largest number of readings in Romans is at TS 20 (11.6, mostly different forms of the longer text εἰ δὲ ἐξ ἔργων οὐκέτι ἐστὶν χάρις ἐπεὶ τὸ ἔργον οὐκέτι ἐστὶν ἔργον), with twenty-eight in 608 manuscripts. There are even more variations (thirty) in 620 manuscripts at 1 Corinthians 2.4, all the more striking because what is at issue here is the form of only four words (πειθοῖς ἀνθρωπίνης σοφίας λόγοις). Nineteen of these are found in only one manuscript each. At 1 Corinthians 8.8 (TS 23) there are forty variants listed, while an impressive fifty-eight variants occur in 628 manuscripts at Galatians 5.1 (TS 16, τῇ ἐλευθερίᾳ ἡμᾶς χριστὸς ἠλευθέρωσεν στήκετε οὖν).

Before assessing any possible conclusions, it has to be asked whether there are any methodological flaws in this exploration of the Teststellen. The answer is that there are several difficulties, which almost led me to abandon the experiment. However, this book seeks to discuss questions of method, so I have retained the section as a lesson in the advantages and disadvantages of this approach. First, the number of variants at any one of the places discussed is due to many factors, such as

  the length of the variant, since a longer one will attract more subvariants in the form of spelling variations and accidents of different kinds (although the longest variants in Luke and Galatians are only a word different in length)
  the difficulty of the passage, and its significance
  the number of forms already in existence, leading to confused recollections in the scribal mind; that is to say, where confusion starts it will multiply

Secondly, there is a procedural question as to whether one should be looking for the number of variants and ignoring subvariants, since many of the latter seem rather trivial alterations.

Thirdly, while the number of readings known to us is derived from extant copies, the degree of variety between those copies must be at least partly due to the degree of variation between the copies which are lost.

Fourthly, I have to ask whether the data I have used is fit for this purpose. The Teststellen were not chosen to illuminate the amount of variation, and it is not certain that the places I have listed are really representative of the degree of variation. Unfortunately, the only way in which we could find that out would be by a full collation of the entire text in every manuscript, and it is the impracticability of that which provided us with *Text und Textwert* in the first place.

Fifthly, it is not at all clear how different texts, different copying traditions and different variations can be compared. Is the comparison genuine? What other factors might be at work which keep some frequently copied texts more consistent than others rarely copied?

These, and perhaps other objections, illustrate the problems of all kinds of textual comparison, not just of this experiment. My impression in turning the pages of *Text und Textwert* is that the number of variants is smaller in the Pauline letters than in the Gospels, but this may be affected by the different typefaces and details of presentation between the two volumes and by my presuppositions.

Even bearing these points in mind, are there any useful pointers in what we have seen? The comparison of Galatians 5.1 with Luke 23.17 suggests not. There are sixty variants in the former in 628 manuscripts, and sixty-two in the latter in 1,643 manuscripts. Is it significant that the readings in Galatians are mostly independent readings (thirty-three in number) while in Luke there are only six such readings, the rest being classed as subvariants? Or does this reflect only different interpretations of the evidence by the different editors of the two volumes? At any rate, this piece of evidence must call into question a simple link between the number of extant copies and the numbers of variant readings. This will become a significant factor when the results of this chapter are summarised.

4.6 DID SCRIBES REVISE THE TEXT THEY WERE COPYING?

This has become a pressing question. Reading an older handbook, for example Kenyon's *Our Bible and the Ancient Manuscripts*, one observes that the attribution of all changes in the text to a scribe was unproblematic, because the changes were presented as of little account, being divided between 'Errors of Hand and Eye', 'Errors of Mind' and 'Errors of Deliberate Alteration', with regard to the last of which we are assured that 'The veneration in which the sacred books were held has generally protected them against intentional alterations of the text, but not entirely so' and that 'The intentional alterations of the scribes are, for the most part, verbal, not substantial.' The message which Kenyon conveys is that (1) most scribal changes to the text are accidental and (2) intentional changes are insignificant. In recent years, a different opinion has arisen, which holds that intentional changes are by no means rare or insignificant. According to B. D. Ehrman, the text was altered in order to bring it into conformity with current orthodox theological belief, by the removal of wording which appeared to support heretical views. For example, he argues that at Luke 3.22 the text originally read 'You are my son, today I have begotten you', but that this was changed to 'You are my beloved son, in you I am well pleased', because the first reading supported the beliefs of adoptionists. Our interest here is not in the theory as a whole, but on the mechanics, in particular in the attribution of such alterations to copyists. It is important not to take it for granted, but to examine it closely. In particular the mechanics of copying must be carefully considered.

Kenyon, *Our Bible and the Ancient Manuscripts*, 19–21 (quotations from pp. 20, 21, see also 5.3.3), wording maintained unaltered from the initial editions of the nineteenth century; Ehrman, *Orthodox Corruption*: 'I . . . take my overarching thesis to be established: proto-orthodox scribes of the second and third centuries occasionally modified their texts of Scripture in order to make them coincide more closely with the Christological views embraced by the party that would seal its victory at Nicea and Chalcedon' (p. 275); 'Scribes altered their sacred texts to make them "say" what they were already known to "mean"' (p. 276); Lk. 3.22 is discussed on pp. 62–7. See also the same author's *Misquoting Jesus. The Story behind Who Changed the Bible and Why*, New York, 2005 (e.g. p. 175, closely echoing the previous quotation); Metzger and Ehrman, 259–71, esp. pp. 265–8 ('. . . led some scribes to change . . .' p. 267). A similar approach is taken with regard to readings used for apologetic purposes by W. C. Kannaday, *Apologetic Discourse and the Scribal Tradition: Evidence of the Influence of Apologetic Interests on the Text of the Canonical Gospels* (Text-Critical Studies 5), Atlanta, 2004 (e.g. 'Notice here that the scribe has transformed the . . .' p. 186).

It is important at this point to resolve a question of terminology. Is it appropriate to distinguish between 'accidental error' and 'intentional change'? Would it be better to distinguish between 'conscious alteration' and 'unconscious alteration'? In either way of thinking, on what grounds may we decide what was in a scribe's mind? We cannot ask our scribes, and if we did, how valuable would their explanations be from the modern textual critic's point of view? It is rather surprising that textual criticism, of the New Testament certainly, has failed to consider the contribution of modern psychoanalysis, in particular the concept of the 'Freudian slip', to the understanding of textual criticism. This topic has been studied in a work which so far as I know has passed New Testament scholarship by: S. Timpanaro's *The Freudian Slip*. He studies in particular the examples offered by Freud in *The Psychopathology of Everyday Life*, setting against them many examples from textual criticism, mainly of Greek, Latin and Italian literature.

S. Timpanaro, *The Freudian Slip. Psychoanalysis and Textual Criticism*, London, 1976 (tr. of *Il Lapsus Freudiano*, 1974). The number of alternatives which he suggests (pp. 29–48) for Freud's explanation of a misquotation from a line of Virgil, the omission of *aliquis* from *Exoriare aliquis nostris ex ossibus ultor* (*Aeneid* IV.625), suggests we are advised to be careful in providing explanations.

Granted the intentional alterations, to whom are they due? Did scribes peruse their text for theologically undesirable elements in advance of copying? Did they pay so much attention to the text's meaning that when pained by what they found there they altered it on the spot? The matter is addressed here, because if we were to agree that these intentional changes were the work of scribes, we would have to abandon the assumption that the text we find in a manuscript is intended by its scribe to be a faithful reproduction of the exemplar.

Have we seen any evidence so far in this chapter to support the claim that scribes made intentional changes? In a few manuscripts we have seen frequent corrections by the scribe. We do not have any way of knowing the source of those corrections. Some might have been taken from another manuscript, some from memory, some might have been the result of a careful study of the text. In an analysis of a few passages in P66 and P75, B. Aland concludes that the different characteristics of the scribes leads one to conclude that 'Will man Schreiber und ihre Handschriften als Interpreten des Textes einsetzen, so ist das möglich.' In her view also, readings which had hitherto been treated as accidental errors should be regarded as interpretations of the text. To Aland, the question 'Did scribes intend to be faithful to their exemplar?' must be answered with regard to each scribe. This is dealing with early activity. Dain points out that such a statement as ὡς δυνατὸν ἦν ἐξισώθη τῷ πρωτοτύπῳ ('it was matched as closely as possible to the exemplar') may be found in Byzantine colophons. Once again, we must remember that our manuscripts and their scribes were the product of many different generations and cultures.

B. Aland, 'Sind Schreiber früher neutestamentlicher Handschriften Interpreten des Textes?', in Childers and Parker, *Transmission and Reception*, 114–22. For ὡς δυνατόν, etc., see A. Dain, *Les Manuscrits*, 3rd edn, Paris, 1975, 17.

A scribe copying a manuscript had a number of things to pay attention to: the preparation and quality of the parchment; the preparation of ink and the tending of the pen; the copying of the text, and the keeping of the sheets in order. Where in this process did the opportunity arise for the kind of theological examination of the text required by Ehrman's language? It is quite hard to believe that it could have happened in the middle of the process of copying from one page on to another. It is conceivable that it took place at a preparatory stage, in which the exemplar was examined and read, errors being corrected and changes proposed, this prepared text then being copied. The examples of the corrections (possibly by the copyist) in the Milan and Lyons manuscripts discussed earlier in this chapter might bear this out. But here again, we must not make general assumptions about all copyists at all periods and in all places.

A compelling reconstruction of the process of copying is set out by Dain following Desrousseaux, and it leaves little room for the scribe to change the text. It consists of reading the phrase to be copied and then remembering, repeating and writing it (*Les Manuscrits*, 41–6). For a discussion of this book, see Pasquali, *Storia della tradizione*, 469–80.

Under certain circumstances we can categorically rule out the possibility that the scribe had the intention of altering the exemplar. The Old Latin manuscript Codex Rehdigeranus (l, 11) has been shown to be a precise copy of its exemplar in layout. Written in two columns to the page, the scribe sometimes wrote the two columns concurrently, that is both first lines followed by both second lines, and so on. Mistakes caused by going to the wrong place were rectified by erasure back to the beginning of the error. It is clear that this scribe approached the task as a simple mechanical one – to reproduce in all respects what was on the page of the exemplar. To change the text was not possible for a scribe working in this way.

H. J. Vogels, *Codex Rehdigeranus (Die vier Evangelien nach der lateinischen Handschrift R 169 der Stadtbibliothek Breslau)* (CBL 2), Rome, 1913; A. C. Clark, *The Descent of Manuscripts*, Oxford, 1918, 96–103. Note that the manuscript is now in Berlin (Stadtsbibliothek Preußischer Kulturbesitz Depot Breslau 5). Certain features of Codex Argenteus suggest that it follows the page content of its exemplar. Such a method will have made it easy for the scribe to calculate quires and layout accurately.

4.7 DID SCRIBES WRITE TO DICTATION?

Another matter bearing upon this discussion is the role of dictation in book production. It is certainly very hard to conceive of a process of scribal revision in the middle of taking dictation. The common image is of a group of scribes sitting in a room, all writing down the same text as a dictator reads it out. The image here sounds improbably like a manuscript version of a print run, and it is fanciful so far as the ancient world is concerned.

Its origins may lie in an account in Birt's *Antike Buchwesen* (1882), 'of an ancient publishing house in action, with its hordes of slaves busily writing from dictation' (T. C. Skeat, 'The Use of Dictation in Ancient Book Production', *PBA* 42 (1956), 179–208, reprinted in *Collected Biblical Writings*, 3–32 (cited here), p. 4). For some objections to the dictation theory, see Dain, *Les Manuscrits*, 20–2. While being prepared to admit exceptions, Skeat insists that they *are* exceptions, pointing to a confusion between the process of composing a work (which was done orally in the ancient world) and the process of making copies of that completed work. As Skeat points out, one of the difficulties of Dain's arguments is knowing to what period he is referring (pp. 14f.). It is probable that he is thinking of Byzantine manuscripts. Skeat's interest, on the other hand, is in late antique papyrus and early parchment manuscripts. Again, debate needs to be more specific. That Byzantine scribes generally copied by eye is suggested by the typical portrait of an evangelist, sitting in a scribal posture with the exemplar on a lectern in front of him. ☞ (15)

The debate about dictation is an excellent example of the way in which theories about ancient book production have developed since the nineteenth century. In this instance, one may find a strength and a weakness in every argument on each side of the case. Here are two on each side of the case, if discussion is restricted to manuscripts copied before about 400.

In favour of dictation:

1. The fact that the position of the scribe in the ancient world, sitting cross-legged and writing on the lap, left nowhere for the exemplar to be placed. The well-known colophon in a first-century papyrus of part of Homer's *Iliad* ('the pen, the right hand and the knee wrote me') supports the view that a copyist assumed this position. Against it, as Skeat repeatedly observes, is the fact that nearly all the comparatively rare reproductions of writing in classical antiquity are more likely to represent an author composing. But we do not have any evidence to suggest that a scribe copying worked differently from this or had any extra furniture.

   The manuscript is British Library Pap. 136 (see Skeat, 'The Use of Dictation', *Collected Biblical Writings*, 7f.)

2. There are manuscripts containing features best explained by dictation. Skeat's examples from the ancient world are Codex Sinaiticus and the Morgan Iliad. Both (the former especially in Scribe B) contain many examples of writing words phonetically. Against this is the fact that scribes dictated to themselves (no reading was silent reading in the ancient world), so that errors of dictation may have (indeed, will have) arisen by this means (see Dain's four stages in 4.6).

   It is only fair to say that Skeat has another very specific piece of evidence with regard to Codex Sinaiticus, the reading at 1 Macc. 5.20. For a different opinion on this passage, see Jongkind, *Codex Sinaiticus*, 22, 251f.

In favour of visual copying is

1. The difficulty for a scribe of managing page layout with no template. 'The process of copying from an existing written model is the only one which makes calligraphy possible, which gives the scribe an opportunity to organise the *mise-en-page* and the division into lines, and to allow for illumination' (Dain, *Les Manuscrits*, p. 22, my translation). Against this claim is the observation that because it seems impossible to us, it is not the case that it was impossible to ancient scribes, who certainly possessed techniques and a professional expertise which are now lost.

2. There are a number of arguments produced in favour of visual copying which consist of claims for its superiority in accuracy and economics over dictation. These arguments are all dubious, and Skeat demonstrates their weaknesses. There is a potential confusion between copying to dictation as the norm and producing multiple copies to dictation. I have worked with colleagues in the Principio Project (see 6.4.2.3), where we made manuscript transcriptions with one person reading the manuscript and the other altering the base text to make a copy of the manuscript, and we found this to be both accurate and fast.

In conclusion, there are arguments in favour of each case, and weaknesses in both. Having for long inclined to the visual copying theory with the element of dictation contained in the scribe's repetition of the words, I now hesitate between the possibility that both may have been practised on different occasions, and the recognition that dictation to a single scribe may not be so improbable as I used to think. The fact is, we do not know and cannot do more than construct theories. Yet on these theories we build more theories of the scribal role. In the situation of dictation, we move away from the scribe as the single creator of a manuscript to the theory of a team, a team in which perhaps the dictator prepared the exemplar while the scribe prepared the materials for the copy. Skeat, indeed, draws attention to such a two-man operation in the creation of the copy made in the early fourth century by the martyrs Antoninus and Pamphilus, whose making is recorded in colophons to the books of Ezra and Esther in Codex Sinaiticus:

This volume has been transcribed from, and corrected by, the Hexapla of Origen, as corrected by his own hand. Antoninus, the confessor, collated (ἀντέβαλεν), and I, Pamphilus, corrected (διόρθωσα) the volume in prison, by the favour and enlargement of God. And if it be not presumptuous so to say, it would not be easy to find a copy equal to this copy. (Skeat's translation, 'Use of Dictation', 18)

Far be it from my intention to make matters worse by proposing this as a universal theory for early Christian manuscript production. I take the example for the purpose of arguing that the little and contradictory evidence we have suggests that there was more than one way for a scribe to put a codex together. We must be mindful of this range of possibilities when we discuss the roles of scribes and readers in the creation of variant readings.

4.8 CONCLUSION

This wide-ranging chapter has addressed a number of topics pertinent to the question of how texts fared in the manuscripts in which they were copied.

It began with a study of two examples of copyings of Latin texts in the ninth and tenth centuries. The first (of Codex Mediolanensis) showed one change every thousand words, the second (in Codex Bezae) four every thousand. The example of the Greek manuscripts 1 and 1582 showed that these two manuscripts, closely related but in descent from a common ancestor rather than exemplar and copy, differ twice in every thousand words.

The corrections in twenty-seven majuscule manuscripts of John were then surveyed, and it was found that a few manuscripts had been corrected frequently (five of them more than ten times in every thousand words), and the rest rather infrequently, in fact around the rate of two in a thousand words. Self-correction by a scribe was rather rare.

All the corrections in John 18.1 in one thousand manuscripts were then listed, and it turned out that about three-quarters of the words in the text had been corrected at some point.

The data in the series *Text und Textwert* were then scrutinised, in search of an answer to the question whether there would turn out to be fewer variants in texts attested by fewer manuscripts. The results here were hard to evaluate, but the fact that a passage in Paul showed fifty-eight variants in 628 manuscripts, against sixty-two in 1,643 in a place in Luke, suggests that there is no direct correlation so far as the extant manuscripts are concerned.

Finally, the question whether scribes made significant intentional changes to the texts they were copying was addressed, along with the important question whether or not their mode of copying would have made such activity possible. Here a degree of agnosticism proved necessary.

With regard to the extent of scribal activity as it may be studied through observable copyings and the degree of correction in most manuscripts, the conclusion is that, with a few notable exceptions, whether we are looking at changes to an exemplar, differences between carefully written members of a family, or frequency of correction, the rate of change being made to texts that we can observe is at the rate of fewer than five in a thousand words. In the best examples, this is of the same level of accuracy as is attained by an experienced modern scholar collating or transcribing a manuscript, where a mistake in a thousand words is a good piece of work.

The picture that emerges from this survey does credit to our surviving manuscripts. But it is not the whole picture. It is necessary to describe ways of interpreting evidence before we can formulate a way of understanding the variation in the wording of the texts.

But that is a subject for another chapter.

CHAPTER 5

Textual criticism

5.1 TWO HUNDRED YEARS OF TEXTUAL CRITICISM

5.1.1 Introduction to the topic

The essence of textual criticism is easily understood. It was present in the definition of variant readings in the introduction. Textual criticism is the analysis of variant readings in order to determine in what sequence they arose. A variant reading is one of four kinds of difference, expressed by comparing the text of one witness with that in one or more others:

addition (strictly, the presence of text in one witness or more which is
   absent in one or more other witnesses)
omission (strictly, the absence in one witness or more of text which is
   present in one or more other witnesses)
substitution (a word or words different from those found in one or
   more other witnesses)
difference in the order of the same words

One or more of these conditions can and does occur at once when a number of witnesses differ at a single place.

More pressing at this point are questions regarding ways of comparing material in order to determine the relationships between texts. The reader should have noticed by now that there are fewer references to manuscripts and more to texts. Some of the references to manuscripts (although I have tried to eliminate them) may be references to the form of text carried by a manuscript. We know what a manuscript is, that it is a handwritten object, and therefore three-dimensional, with a weight, an appearance, a feel in the hand and its own smell if it has been in the damp. It is not so easy to describe the text contained in a manuscript. In one way it too is physical and three-dimensional, consisting of ink on the page, although the empty areas of the page also make the text, just as silence is a part of

159

music. But the text in the mind is more than the text beneath the fingers and before the eye, since it includes whatever else the reader associates with it, recollections of past readings in different manuscripts, quotation from sermons, the words of the lector. When we begin to compare the forms of text as they are found in different manuscripts, we are always in danger of confusing the two. Generally speaking, research on handwritings, page layouts and other features of the manuscript is easier than the comparison of texts. In order to understand why, it is time for a brief historical account of approaches.

I do not intend to provide a full history of research on the New Testament text. Views and methods from the past are described at various places in order to illustrate particular points. M. R. Vincent, *A History of the Textual Criticism of the New Testament*, New York, 1899, goes down to B. Weiss. For particular epochs, see: B. Smalley, *The Study of the Bible in the Middle Ages*, 3rd edn, Oxford, 1983; J. H. Bentley, *Humanists and Holy Writ. New Testament Scholarship in the Renaissance*, Princeton, 1983; for the period from the first printed Greek New Testament onwards, Tregelles, *Account of the Printed Text* (includes Tischendorf's second Leipzig edition); Scrivener, *Plain Introduction*, II.175–301 (includes Hort); for the twentieth century, the account by J. N. Birdsall, 'The Recent History of New Testament Textual Criticism (from Westcott and Hort, 1881, to the present)', *ANRW* II, *Principat*, 26.1, 1992, 99–197; A. Gilmore, *A Dictionary of the English Bible and its Origins* (The Biblical Seminar 67), Sheffield, 2000 provides short articles. In addition, one may go to some of the handbooks for compact surveys. Parvis and Wikgren, *New Testament Manuscript Studies* provides a snapshot of the state of research in 1950.

Several bibliographies may also be mentioned here: C. Böttrich, *Bibliographie Konstantin von Tischendorf (1815–1874)*, Leipzig, 1999; for the early twentieth century, B. M. Metzger, *Annotated Bibliography of the Textual Criticism of the New Testament 1914–1939* (SD 16), Copenhagen, 1955.

It is also important to have a knowledge of the history of textual research outside the New Testament. Titles to be consulted include U. von Wilamowitz-Moellendorf, *History of Classical Scholarship*, ed. H. Lloyd-Jones, London, 1982 (German original published in 1921); L. D. Reynolds and N. G. Wilson, *Scribes and Scholars. A Guide to the Transmission of Greek and Latin Literature*, 3rd edn, Oxford, 1991. Studies of particular epochs include R. Pfeiffer, *History of Classical Scholarship. From the Beginnings to the End of the Hellenistic Age*, Oxford, 1968; N. G. Wilson, *Scholars of Byzantium*, rev. edn, London and Cambridge, Mass., 1996; a set of studies helpful to understanding the context of contemporary textual production and manuscripts is M. W. Herren with S. A. Brown (ed.), *The Sacred Nectar of the Greeks. The Study of Greek in the West in the Early Middle Ages* (King's College London Medieval Studies), London, 1988.

I also refer here to several important tools for the study of the printed editions: E. Reuss, *Bibliotheca Novi Testamenti Graeci cuius editiones ab initio typographiae ad nostram aetatem impressas*, Brunswick, 1872, is a catalogue of printed editions of the Greek New Testament; T. H. Darwell and H. F. Moule, *Historical Catalogue of the Printed Editions of Holy Scripture in the Library of the British and Foreign Bible Society*, part 3, London, 1911, includes all other languages.

One other matter to be considered before proceeding concerns the term 'textual criticism'. Is this a useful name for the discipline? The German concept as developed from the nineteenth-century 'Philologie' covers a wider spectrum of historical, linguistic and textual research and method, and it appears more helpful in avoiding a too-narrow concentration upon a single aspect. It is a pity that the English word 'philologist' has a much narrower meaning. Textual criticism has a narrower scope also than 'textual scholarship', which more easily embraces all the topics covered in this book. The word 'textology', developed by Russian scholars to describe the study of the text of certain writers whose works circulated more or less secretly in the Stalinist era, has been adopted for New Testament research by A. Alexeev. When we use 'textual criticism', we need to remember also the range of meaning found in these other terms.

According to the *New English Dictionary*, the word textual first appears in some manuscripts of *The Canterbury Tales* in the line (ironical in the present context):

But for I am a man not textueel I wol noght telle of textes neuer a deel. (Chaucer, *The Manciple's Tale*, l. 131)

The word may be Chaucer's coinage, since it seems to have been unknown to some scribes, who altered it to 'text wel' or 'texted wel'. The first cited occurrence of 'textual criticism' in the *New English Dictionary* is 1859.

5.1.2 Lachmannian stemmatics

The nineteenth-century German philologist Karl Lachmann (1793–1851) was the first person to make a critical edition of the Greek New Testament (a first edition in 1831 and another in two volumes, 1842–50), as well as of other texts. He applied certain principles of analysis which are most famously seen in his edition of the Latin poet Lucretius. In this work he was able to demonstrate the relationship between the principal extant manuscripts, and even to reconstruct the page layout and type of script of the archetype from which they are descended, as well as to determine the script of the ancient manuscript from which the archetype had been copied. A noteworthy feature of this approach is that, while reaching its conclusions on the grounds of textual analysis, it does not overlook the fact that data revealing information about the physical characteristics of lost manuscripts is also very important in understanding the text. For example, the form of script may explain some textual variation on the grounds that a particular letter-form has been misread, while information on the layout may explain the absence of a piece of text in some of the manuscripts. The part of Lachmann's methodology with which I am concerned here was that he looked for agreement in error as an indicator of a relationship between manuscripts. Such a distinctive reading is usefully known in English as an 'indicative error', in German as

a 'Leitfehler', and in Latin as an *error significativus*. An indicative error
may be defined as 'a distinctive reading representing an alteration of the
text which is found in two or more manuscripts and cannot have been
made on two separate occasions'. This could be the absence of a significant block of text which may be ascribed to physical damage or
oversight, or a distinctive revision or set of revisions of the text in a
common ancestor. It is evidence which leads to a statement of the way in
which the manuscripts are related. This relationship is expressed by a
stemma, a family tree, of the manuscript tradition. A further advantage in
this methodology was that it provided a method of collecting evidence
that was both convenient and consistent. It required the listing of all the
differences in each witness from a base text (for collating, see 2.4), followed by a comparison between these lists. The emphasis is therefore
upon the differences between witnesses.

The previous chapter provided several examples of stemmata, indicating the place of surviving
witnesses in the textual history, and indicating missing links with symbols (typically X, Y, or a, b).

In claiming a relationship between the two manuscripts with which
chapter 4 began, I set some store by their agreeing in several distinctive
readings. To a Lachmannian these distinctive readings are indicative
errors. Undoubtedly it is impossible to be a textual scholar and not
owe something to Lachmann in one's way of working. Nobody ever
claimed that Lachmann's techniques as applied to Lucretius were directly
applicable to the whole problem of editing the Greek New Testament,
though it has successfully been applied to parts of the tradition, such as
Family 1. The Lachmannian view could only be applied very broadly to
the New Testament text, but applied it was. If one looks at some classic
diagrams of its evolution, it is hard not to see at least parts of them as
stemmata in which types of text have replaced manuscripts. Throughout
this process, the method of comparison by which such groups were
determined remained the search for indicative error, so that what defined
one group against another was shared readings absent from the other.
This overlooked the rather obvious fact that manuscripts might have
much more text in common than differences.

For Lachmann, see particularly the classic study by S. Timpanaro, *La genesi del metodo del Lachmann*,
2nd edn, Turin, 1981 [1963], now ed. and tr. G. W. Most, *The Genesis of Lachmann's Method*, Chicago
and London, 2005 (for a review discussing the evolution of the work, see E. J. Kenney, *The Classical
Review* 57 (2007), 240–3). See also Pasquali, *Storia della tradizione*, 3–12, 15–21.

   Indicative error is more probable in the tradition of a text which was rarely copied than in one which
is frequently copied. In a frequently copied text, omitted blocks will have been quickly replaced, and
the possibility of changes being made on two or more separate occasions will be much greater.

P. Maas, *Textual Criticism*, Oxford, 1958 (translation of *Textkritik*, 3rd edn, Leipzig, 1957) provides the best-known guide to traditional stemmatological analysis, along with a full guide to the ideal process, nomenclature and sample stemmata. This volume was the Teubner series handbook on textual criticism, until it was replaced in that role by M. L. West, *Textual Criticism and Editorial Technique Applicable to Greek and Latin Texts*, Leipzig, 1973. Guides to these standard procedures with examples and test passages are also found in J. Willis, *Latin Textual Criticism*, Urbana, Chicago and London (Illinois Studies in Language and Literature 61), 1972.

Probably the best-known diagram of the New Testament text is Streeter's 'The Theory of Local Texts', on the same page as his diagram of Westcott and Hort's theory. ☛ (16) Streeter simply calls them 'The Theory of "Local Texts"' and 'Westcott & Hort's Theory' (Streeter, *The Four Gospels*, 26), but the reproduction in Metzger and Ehrman has the title 'Stemma Illustrating Streeter's Theory of Local Texts' (Metzger and Ehrman, 216).

5.1.3 Methods of quantitative analysis

A number of mathematical and statistical models have been developed for the study of the relationship between the texts of New Testament manuscripts, as of other texts. The interest here is in an approach which owes its origins to the American scholar E. C. Colwell. In a series of studies Colwell set out clearly what he perceived to be the problems with the traditional 'stemmatological', 'text-type approach', as well as advancing new theories on ways of grouping manuscripts. He was forward-looking in recognising the need for complete sets of data, but it is becoming apparent today that in accepting the concept of grouping manuscripts, as well as in the nomenclature, he shared the basic concept of those scholars whose methods he wanted to replace. One might say that he took the lines out of Streeter's diagram but kept the language. Perhaps his most important contribution is an article jointly written with E. W. Tune, 'The Quantitative Relationships between MS Text-types', which shows parallels with what has been attempted earlier in this section. Using facsimiles and several transcriptions, the authors made a complete comparison in John 11 of eighteen witnesses, consisting of thirteen manuscripts, the corrected texts of four of them, and the printed Textus Receptus. The article sets out some principles in computing quantitative relationships between manuscripts, provides a table of the percentage of agreements between them (the table is like a mileage chart, except that a high number indicates proximity rather than distance between the two), and studies the effect of the corrections in P66, 01, 02 and 032 on textual relationships. The most significant decision taken by Colwell and Tune in this analysis was to eliminate singular readings. In their view, these readings are 'particularly meaningless for this study', because (1) they tell us nothing about manuscript relationships, (2) they make it appear that other manuscripts are more closely related than they really are and (3) they are probably 'no more than scribal error' (scribal activity again!). Against this, it may be objected that whether a reading is singular or found in several manuscripts may be no more than an accident of history. Certainly, early Christian writers speak of readings as well known which are not present in any surviving manuscript. Rather than distorting the picture, the singular reading is as important as any other reading.

E. C. Colwell, 'The Significance of Grouping of New Testament Manuscripts', *NTS* 4 (1958), 73–92, repr. as 'Method in Grouping New Testament Manuscripts', in *Studies in Methodology*, 1–25; 'Method in Locating a Newly-Discovered Manuscript'; 'Origin of Texttypes'; E. C. Colwell and E. W. Tune, 'The Quantitative Relationships between MS Text-types', in Birdsall and Thomson, *Biblical and Patristic Studies*, 25–32, reprinted as 'Method in Establishing Quantitative Relationships between Text-types of New Testament Manuscripts', in Colwell, *Studies in Methodology*, 56–62; E. C. Colwell, 'Genealogical Method: its Achievements and its Limitations', *JBL* 66 (1947), 109–33, repr. in *Studies in Methodology*, 63–83. For a recent assessment of Colwell, see K. Wachtel, 'Colwell Revisited: Grouping New Testament Manuscripts', in Amphoux and Elliott, *New Testament Text*, 31–43.

The elimination of the singular reading was taken to its ultimate absurdity in F. Wisse and P. McReynolds' application of the Claremont Profile Method to the Gospel of Luke, where it was concluded that 05 (Codex Bezae) was a member (admittedly an exceptional one) of Group B (along with 01 and 03). They add the comment 'That the unique group readings of B and the unique features of D were not taken into account ... has, no doubt, accentuated the relationship' (F. Wisse, *The Profile Method for the Classification and Evaluation of Manuscript Evidence as Applied to the Continuous Greek Text of the Gospel of Luke* (SD 44), Grand Rapids, 1982, 91). Where a manuscript has enough unique readings (as does 05 in Luke), to pass over them is seriously to distort the presentation.

This aspect of the Claremont Profile Method is the more to be regretted because the principle on which it is founded is a very good one. It starts with the recognition that the manuscripts are so inconsistent that few distinctive readings are really 'indicative readings'. It then goes on to say that while two or more related manuscripts will not agree on every reading, they will nevertheless have a common profile of readings. Even though all the readings which make up the group profile may be present in manuscripts of other groups, the profile, the particular set of readings, will be unique to the group.

The theory of the percentage analysis has become more popular in the United States than in Europe. Apart from the development of the Claremont Profile Method, the quantitative analysis has developed into the Comprehensive Profile Method. This approach is used in the series The New Testament in the Greek Fathers to locate the form of text found in a father's citations to the manuscript groups. Descriptions are provided by its principal inspiration B. D. Ehrman, in three places. The method begins with a quantitative analysis and then goes on to profile the witness in a developed form of the Claremont Profile Method, by comparing the witness with a wider range of readings found in the members of a group.

B. D. Ehrman, *Didymus the Blind and the Text of the Gospels* (The New Testament in the Greek Fathers 1), Atlanta, 1986; 'The Use of Group Profiles for the Classification of New Testament Documentary Evidence', *JBL* 106 (1987), 465–86, reprinted in Ehrman, *Studies*, 33–56; Metzger and Ehrman, 238–9.

For a general survey, see T. C. Geer, 'Analyzing and Categorising New Testament Greek Manuscripts', in Ehrman and Holmes, *Contemporary Research*, 253–67.

These approaches have all made a contribution to the advancement of the study of the relationship between the manuscripts. Although they appear different, what they have in common is more significant. First, they all seek to group the text of individual manuscripts. Second, they define the groups in advance and on the basis of partial evidence. The Claremont Profile Method as originally conceived used an initial selection of data to define the group readings. The manuscripts were then collated in each test passage in order to determine the profile. But, given the limited nature of the initial data, it is unlikely that the real group profiles (and therefore the groups themselves) will always be a match. All the methods are in fact based upon a time-honoured view of the New Testament text as divided into groups called 'Alexandrian', 'Western', 'Caesarean', and 'Byzantine'. This nomenclature is explicitly used in the Comprehensive Profile Method, with the added refinement that the first is sometimes divided into 'Primary Alexandrian' and 'Secondary Alexandrian'. Wisse's classification of manuscripts is rather different, since 'Group B' is used for the Alexandrian, while all other groups are either called by von Soden's nomenclature for forms of the Byzantine text or given an appropriate name if they are newly discovered. Colwell's views on group terminology are rather complicated to determine. On the one hand he was quite cautious in the statements he made about text-types, on the other he believed in their existence (this may be seen in the article 'The Origin of Texttypes of New Testament Manuscripts'). Third, all three methods define types and groups on the basis of difference from other groups. In this they remain the heirs of Lachmann, not least in the degree to which the other groups are defined as different from the Byzantine.

Is it possible to find an alternative to this, which defines group relationships on the basis of the whole text as it stands in a manuscript rather than on the basis of a part of it, and which does so moreover on the basis of all the available evidence rather than a pre-determined sample? The answer is that in recent years such a different technique has been developed, and it has been applied with worthwhile results.

5.1.4 Coincidental agreement between witnesses

A major challenge to the concept of genealogically significant readings is the possibility that errors may have arisen independently in two copies. There are various ways in which one can guard against this, for example, by treating only readings so distinctive that their appearance in more than one witness is unlikely to be the result of coincidence. U. B. Schmid has found a way of testing the concept, by an analysis of a modern scholarly study. H. J. Vogels' 1919 publication on Tatian's Diatessaron (see 10.7) lists forty-four readings where the ninth-century Latin manuscript Codex Cassellanus containing a harmony of the Gospels differs from Codex Fuldensis, from which some scholars had believed it to be derived. Vogels believed not only that this showed that Codex Cassellanus was independent of Codex Fuldensis (that is, neither directly copied from it nor via intermediaries), but also that it derived readings from other Latin, as well as Greek, Syriac, Arabic and Armenian witnesses to the Diatessaron. However, twenty-four out of these forty-four readings are not present in Codex Cassellanus at all but are errors in the nineteenth-century edition which Vogels used.

This observation leads Schmid to several points pertinent to this chapter: he playfully but forcefully suggests that the total of 360 errors which have been identified in the edition of Codex Cassellanus cast doubt on the claim of the edition to be a direct copy (an edition) of the manuscript. What he considers to be even more devastating is that Vogels' forty-four readings were 'carefully selected as *genealogically significant* deviations' (p. 133). Vogels' findings remain valid, in that the agreements between the eastern witnesses and the edition of Codex Cassellanus *do* exist – but the forty-four agreements are with a nineteenth-century and not a medieval text. If we seek an explanation for the differences between the manuscript and the edition, the only plausible explanation is that they are due to error. We therefore have to say that it is only by chance that any of those forty-four deviations between the manuscript and its edition happened to agree with the parallels adduced by Vogels. If this is so, then the twenty differences between Codex Fuldensis and Codex Cassellanus in which the latter agrees with eastern Diatessaronic witnesses may also be due to chance.

'What went wrong?' asks Schmid. First, Vogels' list covered sixty-three words, which amounts to only 0.16 per cent of the whole text of the manuscript. This is too little evidence to make a case. Second, Vogels found forty-four agreements, but between different witnesses and witnesses of different kinds. Third, Vogels seems to have assumed that agreements between distant witnesses in rare readings are convincing candidates for genealogical agreement. Against this, Schmid concludes that given the size of the New Testament textual tradition, such agreements are more likely to be accidental.

Schmid, 'Genealogy by Chance!' He several times cites B. J. P. Salemans, 'Building Stemmas with the Computer in a Cladistic, Neo-Lachmannian Way. The Case of Fourteen Text Versions of *Lanselot van Denemerken*', Proefschrift Katholike Universiteit Nijmegen, 2000 (see www.neder-l.nl/salemans/diss/salemans-diss-2000-appendices.pdf). *Lancelot of Denmark* is a medieval Dutch play.

5.1.5 Evolution, genetics and stemmatics

Three main problems assailed Lachmannian stemmatics and led to such scepticism that scholarship resorted to the dull pursuit of counting percentages:

(1) where a manuscript's form of text combined readings from two different sources (what is known as contamination) it is impossible to construct a stemma.
(2) it is possible that two or more witnesses independently made an alteration to the text (see 5.1.4; note that Lachmannianism recognised this and insisted that to be indicative a reading must be one that could not have arisen independently in two different places – but in the case of a text copied as frequently as the Greek New Testament, of how many readings could that be said?).
(3) it is possible that a new variant reading in a branch of a tradition might be 'switched back' to the form from which it was derived, and such a switch would be virtually impossible to detect.

These three problems have been a serious challenge to the viability of Lachmannianism. But they are not a challenge unique to textual criticism. Analogous problems are encountered by geneticists. For example, a scientist studying a 'flu' virus may observe that (1) cross-mutation between strains of a virus may occur, (2) two or more viruses may mutate in the same way independently, (3) a mutated virus may mutate back to a previous form. Moreover, there is an overall similarity in research, since textual scholars and evolutionary biologists are studying the different evolutions of forms which have both strong similarities and marked differences. The development of tools for unravelling genetic fingerprints has included some sophisticated mathematical modelling and software, to enable researchers to detail the DNA of a subject, and then to compare it with other DNA. The important thing to note is that DNA consists of a sequence, so that the statement of an individual's DNA is a full statement rather than a partial list of certain things which make them unique. The methods and software used in the application of these theories are known as phylogenetic.

Since the problems which the textual scholar confronts have also been encountered by the scientist, it has been possible to develop a new form of stemmatics which provides new models of manuscript relationships, based upon complete sets of data. It is possible to treat a text as though it were a DNA sequence, so that what is stated about the text is not an abstraction of selected parts defined as difference from another form of the text, but refers to the entirety of the text.

P. Van Reenen and M. Van Mulken (eds.), *Studies in Stemmatology.* Amsterdam, 1996, 71–103; C. J. Howe, A. Barbrook, B. Bordalejo, L. Mooney, P. M. Robinson and M. Spencer, 'Manuscript Evolution', *Trends in Genetics* 17:3 (2001), 147–52; *Studies in Stemmatology* 11 generally; C. Macé, P. Baret, A. Bozzi and L. Cignoni, *The Evolution of Texts: Confronting Stemmatological and Genetical Techniques* (Linguistica Computazionale 24–5), Pisa and Rome, 2006. For the New Testament, Wachtel, Spencer and Howe, 'The Greek Vorlage of the Syra Harclensis; Wachtel, Spencer and Howe, 'Representing Multiple Pathways'. R. Dawkins, *The Ancestor's Tale. A Pilgrimage to the Dawn of Life*, London, 2004, 133–9, is interesting as an evolutionary biologist's version of how textual critics have used the biologists' tools.

These methods require full sets of data. This is possible as a result of the introduction of full electronically analysable transcriptions of manuscripts (see 2.5).

Once the data are complete in an electronic form, previous forms of textual analysis become redundant. Recent developments in the Claremont Profile Method show why. The use of partial data for determining the group profiles in Luke has been superseded in John. The profiling has been conducted from complete electronic transcriptions of all witnesses, collated automatically, manually revised, and exported to a database. The database program compares the witnesses and it groups them, so that one might say that the group profiles are found at the end of the process rather than the beginning. This provides a check on previous groupings (mostly the work of von Soden), rather than taking them for granted.

The stemmata produced by phylogenetic software are different from the Lachmannian variety in that they are not designed necessarily to show the point of origin of the text, and a vertical line of descent from it. Instead, they typically express the closeness or distance between forms of text spatially, as this example of a group of manuscripts of the Letter of James shows.

☛ (17)

Is there already an analogy between evolutionary biology and textual scholarship in Streeter's theory
of local texts? Is Streeter drawing on Darwin's observations, for example on the differences between
animals and plants in different parts of the Galapagos Islands? He writes that 'it is the circumstance,
that several of the islands possess their own species ..., these species having the same general habits,
occupying analogous situations, and obviously filling the same place in the natural economy of this
archipelago, that strikes me with wonder' (C. Darwin, *Journal of Researches into the Natural History
and Geology of the Countries Visited during the Voyage of HMS Beagle*, London, 2003 (repr. of 3rd edn,
1860, 396). His subsequent discussion of the reasons why this should be, including the significance of
the natural barriers between the islands, has an analogy with the discussion of the degree of movement probable between different Christian centres which has been stimulated by Streeter's theory.
The precise analogy between Streeter and Darwin is found in Streeter's theory that repeated
reproduction of the text in a single locality led to the development of characteristics unique to that
text. This is even natural selection in the sense that Streeter is more likely to have been thinking of
unintentional change than of change made by conscious human intervention.

5.1.6 The Coherence-Based Genealogical Method

The Coherence-Based Genealogical Method is a second form of textual
analysis which has been developed in response to electronic sets of
complete data. Yet in essence it is the application of traditional philological skills, monitored by a computerised record of the scholar's textual
decisions. It uses these resources explicitly to combat the first two of
the three problems (in fact it combats the third as well) in constructing
a stemma listed at the beginning of the previous section: contamination
and coincidental agreement. Recognising that the traditional grand
stemma for New Testament manuscripts would never be possible,
G. Mink had the idea of applying the stemmatological model at each unit
of variation. This is an essentially simple but brilliant stroke. The
stemma, which is known as a substemma, then presents not the relationship between manuscripts (or rather, between the forms of text in
different manuscripts) but the relationship between the forms of text at a
single place of variation. ☛ (18) The decisions may be made on any
grounds. That is, the method is not wedded to a preconceived method.
One might use internal criteria, asking which reading explains the other
readings, determining that a reading is a modification of a certain other
one, and so on; or external criteria, assessing the quality or age of the
witnesses; or any other available criteria. Once this local stemma has been
drawn up the results are recorded in a database, which records the 'textual
flow' from manuscript to manuscript. ☛ (19) For example, a reading
which is present in Manuscript A (and perhaps others) is the source of a
reading in Manuscript B (and perhaps others). This is expressed in the

database as B⇐A. If there are hundreds of manuscripts of a text, differing at scores of places, this information could not be manually recorded in a form which could then be usefully analysed, but in a computer it is simple. Once a number of local stemmata have been made, the database may be studied to discover how consistent the 'textual flow' between individual witnesses is, as well as the overall textual flow logically required by the stemmata. ☛ (20) If it is inconsistent, the decisions made are not necessarily wrong, but need scrutinising. That is, one returns to the local stemmata in order to assess one's initial conclusions. Any subsequent revisions will lead to modification of the overall textual flow.

One may see that there are different ways of describing the coherence: the 'pre-genealogical coherence' of the initial local substemma; the 'genealogical coherence' of the next stage, which moves from the comparison of manuscripts in individual variants to the global stemma, and the 'stemmatological coherence' of the best final result. It is worth pointing out that in a tradition with none of the three problems which have dogged traditional stemmatology, every local stemma should be identical. Even in the actual circumstances of the New Testament text, the more that the substemmata correspond, the better.

Finally, it is worth making the following points:

(1) It is possible to take all the evidence into account: all the variants in all the manuscripts, although one may prefer after initial analysis to limit it to selected manuscripts.

(2) The textual importance of variants is not relevant. It may be the case that less significant variants may be more valuable genealogically. But since there is no absolute measure of textual significance, all variants are treated equally.

(3) The difference between manuscripts and texts is always observed.

(4) While the conventional stemma indicates lost intermediaries (see 5.1.2), the Coherence-Based Genealogical Method dispenses with them, on the grounds that the stemma presents not the descent of copying between manuscripts but the direction of textual flow through the forms of text found in the manuscripts.

(5) The majority of substemmata are easy to draw up.

G. Mink, 'Ein umfassende Genealogie der neutestamentlichen Überlieferung', *NTS* 39 (1993), 481–99; 'Editing and Genealogical Studies: the New Testament', *Literary and Linguistic Computing* 15 (2000) 51–6; 'Was verändert sich in der Textkritik durch die Beachtung genealogischer Kohärenz?', in Weren and Koch, *Recent Developments*, 39–68; 'Problems of a Highly Contaminated Tradition: the New Testament. Stemmata of Variants as a Source of a Genealogy for Witnesses', in *Studies in Stemmatology*, II.13–85 (corrigenda at www.uni-muenster.de/NTTextforschung/Veroeffentlichungen).

html); 'Kohärenzbasierte Genealogische Methode–Worum geht es?', www.uni-muenster.de/ NTTextforschung/ with full bibliography; Wachtel, Spencer and Howe, 'The Greek Vorlage of the Syra Harclensis; Wachtel and Parker, 'The Joint IGNTP/INTF Gospel of John'.

This is the method used in reconstructing the development of the text by the editors of the *Editio critica maior* (6.3.6). Its application in the Catholic epistles is discussed below (9.3.5).

5.1.7 What is a text-type?

One of Colwell's contributions was to offer some definitions of important and easily confused terms, in particular text-type, family, and group. It is easy to define the second and third terms. 'Family' has already been seen to describe a set of manuscripts sufficiently closely related for a stemma to be drawn up and the text of the archetype to be reconstructed, and 'group' to refer to a set of manuscripts which are closely related, but not in such a way that one may either construct a stemma or define the archetype. A text-type is another matter altogether. Consider those listed above: 'Alexandrian', 'Western', 'Caesarean', and 'Byzantine'. Byzantine here means the form of text found in the Byzantine period, having a degree of consistency over against the other groups. But this is a period spanning nearly a thousand years, and it is represented by a very high proportion of the extant manuscripts. It is not surprising to discover that this 'Byzantine' text-type is an overall name for scores of groups, the whole showing some signs of bifurcation. 'Alexandrian', by contrast, refers to a form of text found in a handful of manuscripts (only eight in all three test passages in Wisse's profiling in Luke), and these manuscripts were produced within a much shorter period. As to the 'Western', as it has long been said, the main thing that the manuscripts of this type have in common is that while they differ from those of other types, they differ from each other almost as much. Finally, the term 'Caesarean' has come under considerable scrutiny and even if its existence is granted, it has little more coherence than the Western. The four terms therefore mean very different things. They express nothing geographically, since there are no longer grounds for locating the 'Western' in the west, while the 'Alexandrian' is not necessarily Egyptian, the 'Caesarean' could be from anywhere, and the 'Byzantine' refers to the civilization in which it flourished. What clinches the matter is that there is so great a disparity in size between the different entities. The creation of an Alexandrian text-type out of a dozen witnesses is claiming a great deal from very little. Moreover, these terms were coined and their terms defined before the discovery of papyri from the early twentieth century onwards. Not only this, but they are treated as universally applicable to the New Testament when in truth the situation in each part is different.

In order to understand the situation, it is necessary to consider the development of the text-type concept. It is generally ascribed to J. A. Bengel (1687–1752), who divided the manuscripts and versions into two families: the African, as he called it, included the more ancient witnesses, and the Asiatic the more recent. J. S. Semler (1725–91) renamed the second of these and divided the first into two, so that we have, Alexandrian, Western and Eastern. The theory was considerably expanded by J. J. Griesbach (1745–1812), who used Semler's terminology. Tregelles sums up the theory as follows (I omit phrases indicating that these are not the author's views):

The names assigned by Griesbach to the three *classes* of text were Western, Alexandrian, and Constantinopolitan. The first of these contained the text which in the early periods had been in circulation, and which, through the errors of copyists, required much correction; the Alexandrian was an attempt to revise the old corrupt text, and the Constantinopolitan flowed from the other two ... The critical authorities were ranged by Griesbach under his three recensions; and each was valued, not so much for its absolute evidence as for contributing its testimony as to what the reading is of the *recension* to which it belongs. Thus in forming his text he placed more reliance upon union of *recensions* in attesting a reading, than upon other external evidences. (*Account of the Printed Text*, 84)

For Bengel's edition (*Novum Testamentum Graece*, etc., Tübingen, 1734), see Tregelles, *Account of the Printed Text*, 71; for Semler's *Wetstenii libelli ad crisin atque interpretationem Novi Testamenti*, Halle, 1764, see Metzger and Ehrman, 161–2. For another history of the text-type theory, see R. Kieffer, *Au delà les recensions? L'évolution de la tradition textuelle dans Jean VI*, 52–71 (CBNTS 3), Uppsala, 1968, 5–36.

Subsequent generations also identified a Caesarean text-type in Mark, and possibly elsewhere in the Gospels, and have latterly been inclined to separate some Alexandrian witnesses into a Proto-Alexandrian text-type.

The concept of attaining an older form of text is one which had been anticipated by Richard Bentley (1662–1742) at the beginning of the century. It is also broadly what Westcott and Hort were to follow a century later. Their view of the Syrian text is precisely the same, and the only difference is in their introduction of the Neutral Text, the one on which they relied most heavily in constructing their text. We may see from this very brief outline that the theory of text-types has changed very little for two and a half centuries. It is interesting to note that it was developed as much out of the study of the versions and patristic citations as out of ancient Greek manuscripts, of which very few were available. That is to say, the concept of text-types has survived even though their core membership and the materials for textual research have changed. These are problems to be taken very seriously.

For Bentley, see the words 'the old Greek copies and the old Latin [of the Vulgate] so exactly agree ... that the pleasure and satisfaction it gives me is beyond expression', R. Bentley, *Letter to Archbishop Wake*, 1716, repr. in A. Dyce (ed.), *Richard Bentley. The Works*, London, vol. III, 1838 (repr. Hildesheim and New York, 1971), 477–9, p. 478. See also *Dr. Bentley's Proposals for Printing a New Edition of the Greek New Testament and St Hierom's Latin Version*, London, 1721, repr. Dyce, III.487–96. It is also available in Tischendorf, *Editio octava*, III.231–40.

I also venture to suggest that the theory of text-types was initially worked out with reference to the Gospels alone. It was then applied to other parts of the New Testament by default and without sufficient consideration of possible objections. The theory that the witnesses represent one of the Alexandrian (and latterly the Proto-Alexandrian), the Western, the Caesarean where it may be found or the Byzantine, either wholeheartedly or with a degree of mixture, has been most fully worked out in the Gospels and then often applied elsewhere. One may see this in attempts to find a Caesarean text of the Catholic epistles, as though what was true in the Gospels must be applicable elsewhere.

For the Byzantine text, see also 9.3.5. Arguments presenting the Caesarean Text (with a short history of relevant earlier theories) are first met in Streeter, *The Four Gospels*, 79–108. For a dissident voice see F. C. Burkitt's review of *The Four Gospels* in *JTS* 26 (1925), 278–94, pp. 284–8, to which Streeter partially responded in 'The Washington MS and the Caesarean Text of the Gospels', *JTS* 27 (1926), 144–7; see subsequently K. Lake, R. P. Blake and S. New, 'The Caesarean Text of the Gospel of Mark', *HTR* 21 (1928), 207–404, and also available as a separate volume. There is an elaborate stemma of the text facing p. 325; Burkitt addressed this work also, in 'The Caesarean Text', *JTS* 30 (1929), 347–56. One may see the theory gathering pace with an article by Streeter which makes use of Lake, Blake and New: 'Codices 157, 1071 and the Caesarean text', in R. P. Casey, S. Lake and A. K. Lake (eds.), *Quantulacumque. Studies Presented to Kirsopp Lake by Pupils, Colleagues and Friends*, London, 1937, 149–50. It is interesting to note that my copy of E. Hautsch, *Die Evangelienzitate des Origenes* (TU 34.2a), Leipzig, 1909, whose previous owners are C. H. Turner, P. L. Headley, T. W. Manson and J. N. Birdsall, has had much added support from manuscripts adduced as Caesarean by Streeter and Lake, Blake and New added in the margins. The subsequent theory of a 'pre-Caesarean text' is discussed in L. W. Hurtado, *Text-Critical Methodology and the Pre-Caesarean Text. Codex W in the Gospel of Mark* (SD 43), Grand Rapids, 1981. The Proto-Alexandrian text is first named by Zuntz, *Text of the Epistles*, 156, 250f., 279. For its adoption see Martini, *Codice B alla luce del papiro Bodmer XIV*, 152.

If we then consider the various parts of the New Testament, the future chapters of this book will reveal that the theory of text-types does not apply at all to the Apocalypse; is only applicable strictly in the Pauline corpus where careful research has shown genealogical affiliation, so that

Zuntz's Western Text is the fourth-century archetype of a group of bilinguals; fails to apply to the Acts of the Apostles, because there we seem to have two competing forms of text, one of which appears to have undergone a steady growth, other forms representing various halfway houses; and in the Catholic epistles has never been easily applied, in the absence of a Western Text, and has been found inappropriate in the uniquely detailed stemmatological researches undertaken by the editors of the *Editio critica maior*.

For Zuntz, see 8.10.

Lecturing in 2006, Strutwolf advanced the view that it is time to abandon the concept of text-types altogether. If one considers the frequency with which writers on many of the newly found papyri, from P45 onwards, confessed to the uselessness of the traditional terminology in describing these older witnesses, one wonders why it has taken so long to face the problem. It would be a mistake to reverse the procedure of applying textual models for the Gospels to the rest of the New Testament, by assuming that the failure of the theory of text-types elsewhere means that they should be abandoned here too. But the time has come to take a long and hard look at the question.

Why then are they still in use? There is no single answer to this. But one point must be made, namely that the eighteenth-century text-type model was a means by which New Testament textual scholarship could make use of Lachmannianism even though the texts could not be related in a full Lachmannian stemma. It is now possible to move on, abandoning the concept of the text-type and, with the new tools and methods now available, retelling the history of the text.

A Caesarean text of 1 Peter and 1–3 John was proposed by M. M. Carder, 'A Caesarean Text in the Catholic Epistles?', *NTS* 16 (1970), 252–70, and a Caesarean text of James by C.-B. Amphoux and B. Outtier, 'Les leçons des versions géorgiennes de Jacques', *Biblica* 65 (1984), 365–76. Strutwolf's paper was read at the New Testament Textual Criticism Section of the Society of Biblical Literature Annual Congress in Washington, DC in November, 2006. In addition to drawing attention to historical and methodological problems, he showed how use of the Coherence-Based Genealogical Method has led Münster researchers to abandon the framework and terminology altogether. Sometimes in the past scholars have attempted to link a text-type (or more precisely the recension giving rise to a text-type) to a particular figure. A classic example of this is F. G. Kenyon, 'Hesychius and the Text of the New Testament', *Mémorial Lagrange*, Paris, 1940, 245–50.

It is important to take note of the fact that the Byzantine text is far from being a unity. For one thing, it has a noted tendency to split into two traditions. See K. Wachtel, 'Kinds of Variants'; 'Early Variants in the Byzantine Text of the Gospels', in Childers and Parker, *Transmission and Reception*, 28–47; for the Catholic epistles, see his work cited in 9.3.5. For another, the closer study of the Byzantine tradition reveals a complicated picture of evolving groups and subgroups.

5.1.8 Majority Text theory

The theory of text-types has been used in a particular way by adherents of
the view that the oldest, and indeed generally in their view the original,
text has been preserved in the majority of manuscripts. Ever since the
series of editions which began with Lachmann and ended with Westcott
and Hort, there have been those who reject their historical reconstruc-
tions, arguing instead in favour of the Received Text (although generally a
form of it modified in places where the Received Text differs from the
majority of manuscripts). These views often owe a certain amount to
a priori conviction, lacking arguments which can be either proved or
disproved.

The Byzantine priorist is in an uncomfortable position. If one reads a
survey such as Robinson's, one sees that much of the approach of the
form of Lachmannianism set out by Westcott and Hort has been
accepted. The concept that the form of reading which best explains the
others is primary is accepted, and so is the concept of text-types. It is the
conclusions which are turned on their head. It means that all arguments
on the grounds of critical theory in favour of the Majority Text are
particularly vulnerable when critical theory makes another advance. This
may be seen by the move from the theory of text-types to the application
of more advanced stemmatological methods. Supporters of the Majority
Text will be defending their views on someone else's terms while critical
scholarship will be using another methodology.

In short, the fundamental problem with the Majority Text theory is
not that it is historically wrong, but that it is a pre-critical theory trying to
use critical tools. It will always be an anomaly, a theory from the past for
which its adherents are trying to find new support.

H. A. Sturz, *The Byzantine Text-Type and New Testament Textual Criticism*, Nashville, Camden and
New York, 1984. M. A. Robinson, 'The Case for Byzantine Priority', in D. A. Black (ed.), *Rethinking
New Testament Textual Criticism*, Grand Rapids, 2002, 125–39; M. A. Robinson 'In Search of the
Alexandrian Archetype: Observations from a Byzantine-Priority Perspective', in Amphoux and
Elliott, *New Testament Text*, 45–67; T. P. Letis, *The Ecclesiastical Text. Text Criticism, Biblical
Authority and the Popular Mind*, Philadelphia and Edinburgh, 1997; J. van Bruggen, 'The Majority
Text. Why Not Reconsider its Exile?', in McKendrick and O'Sullivan, 147–53; W. N. Pickering, *The
Identity of the New Testament Text II*, 3rd edn, Eugene, 2003. There is also a Majority Text Society,
with a website and online newsletter (www.majoritytext.org/).

Opposition to Westcott and Hort in the late nineteenth century is encapsulated in J. W. Burgon
(ed. E. Miller), *The Traditional Text of the Holy Gospels Vindicated and Established*, London and
Cambridge, 1896. For an account of a debate on the topic, see J. L. North, 'The Oxford Debate on
the Textual Criticism of the New Testament, held at New College on May 6, 1897: an End, not a
Beginning, for the Textus Receptus', in Taylor, *Studies in the Early Text*, 1–25. For a detailed

presentation of difficulties in Byzantine priority claims, see G. D. Fee, 'The Majority Text and the Original Text of the New Testament', in Epp and Fee, *Studies*, 183–208 (reworking three previous articles).

5.1.9 Textual criticisms?

This chapter has referred occasionally to scholars who have studied or edited texts other than the New Testament. It is worth considering in more detail how New Testament textual criticism can learn from and contribute to other branches of textual research. Two of these branches are to be considered: the criticism of classical texts in Greek and Latin, and the criticism of texts in modern European languages (of which English is the one of which I am most aware). In spite of the fact that the histories of these criticisms are closely entwined, one might wonder how such different traditions can learn from each other, and even whether they represent each other accurately. Take a famous quotation, the words from A. E. Housman's lecture 'The Application of Thought to Textual Criticism', that textual criticism is 'the science of discovering error in text and the art of removing it'. This has been misrepresented (by me as well as by others) as a blend of rigorous scholarship and creative insight. If one studies the whole quotation more carefully and considers the kind of traditions Housman was interested in, it may seem more probable that what he meant was, for example, that the editor of a Latin poet will observe a place where the wording breaks the rules of prosody and may 'scientifically' be observed to be wrong. The restoration of the wording to something both convincing and metrically correct (I suspect very possibly on no manuscript authority) requires art (even poetic skill). Perhaps the classical scholar will correct this interpretation also. At any rate, this blend of science and art is scarcely required of the New Testament scholar.

We may wonder likewise how an editor of works which have circulated as printed editions whose concern is with the activities and customs of the printing house, who may well have access to the author's manuscript, can contribute to the study of the New Testament text.

There are three reasons why textual critics can and do learn from each other. They are all very simple. The first is found in the title of Housman's lecture, 'The Application of Thought to Textual Criticism'. It is always a good lesson in textual criticism to observe other scholars applying thought to the study of the witnesses, the elucidation of the textual tradition, and the establishing of a critical text. One can learn from the classicists, because they are not distracted by thousands of witnesses but have to make full use of the often very limited evidence. One can learn from the editor of modern texts, because often the textual tradition is very complete, perhaps with full sets of the author's working papers, and yet there are many editorial decisions of quite a familiar kind to be made.

The second reason lies in a corollary of the remark that every textual problem is possibly unique: that while it may be unique to your work, it may be bread and butter to someone else, someone editing Thucydides, Manilius, the *Niebelungenlied*, Thackeray, Wittgenstein or James Joyce. One of the benefits from studying other textual criticisms (and talking to other textual critics) is that there is always the chance of finding a solution to a problem.

A third very specific reason is that different traditions bring to the table many different concepts of the editorial task and the place of the author. Is the editor seeking to establish the text of an archetype? or of the text as the author sent it to the printer? or the stages in which the text changed in the author's study? or the many stages by which a text grew through the hands of a succession of writers, perhaps over a number of generations? Do we know how much the printer 'made' the work? Was there an author, and what can the word 'author' mean? Knowledge of many different theories leads to the recognition that some models are not appropriate for New Testament writings, and thus to the opportunity to improve ones that are.

There are also several minor reasons why textual critics should talk to each other. One is that new ideas usually occur to more than one person at once, and discussion of them together can be more effective. Another is in the sharing of information about the tools of the trade, such as new software and new critical theory. Another is the exposure of one's fancies to the cold light of day. Once one has explained them to an expert colleague with no specific knowledge of one's own text, do they remain convincing?

There are certain books which should be known to all textual critics, whatever their specialisation. Many are cited elsewhere in these pages. I note especially: Housman's collected papers, and above all the paper already quoted (A. E. Housman, 'The Application of Thought to Textual Criticism', *Proceedings of the Classical Association* 18 (1922), 67–84, reprinted in J. Diggle and F. R. D. Goodyear (eds.), *The Classical Papers of A. E. Housman*, 3 vols., Cambridge, 1972, III. 1058–69; Pasquali, *Storia della tradizione*; E. J. Kenney, *The Classical Text. Aspects of Editing in the Age of the Printed Book*, Berkeley, Los Angeles and London, 1974, a work which also does the New Testament scholar the service of placing the history of its editing (and especially the status of the Received Text) within a wider framework of textual scholarship (note Kenney's version of the art and science question: 'Textual criticism, then, must be approached and viewed as the art and science of balancing historical probabilities' (p. 146)). In the fields of modern textual editing, writers not mentioned elsewhere who should not be forgotten include Thomas Tanselle (for example, 'Textual Scholarship', in J. Gibaldi (ed.), *Introduction to Scholarship in Modern Languages and Literatures*, New York, 1981, 29–51). W. W. Greg, 'The Rationale of Copy-Text', *Studies in Bibliography* 3 (1950–1), 19–36, repr. in J. C. Maxwell (ed.), *W. W. Greg: Collected Papers*, Oxford, 1966, 374–91, is a text which the New Testament scholar should read and ponder in order to understand why the concept of the edition as a reconstruction of an authorial text is problematical for the New Testament. Another short and influential study is F. Bowyers, 'Textual Criticism', in J. Thorpe (ed.), *The Aims and Methods of Scholarship in Modern Languages and Literature*, 2nd edn, New York, 1970.

Neither should be neglected the textual criticism of other texts more closely connected to the New Testament be neglected. For the Hebrew Bible, see E. Tov, *Textual Criticism of the Hebrew Bible*, 2nd edn, Minneapolis, 2001. For the world of Septuagint studies, see amongst others N. F. Marcos (tr. W. G. E. Watson), *The Septuagint in Context. Introduction to the Greek Versions of the Bible*, Boston and Leiden, 2001 and J. Lust, 'Textual Criticism of the Old and New Testaments: Stepbrothers?', *Festschrift Delobel*, 15–31. Looking ahead from early Christianity, note R. Maisano, 'Filologia neo-testamentaria e filologia bizantina. Riflesioni sulle problematiche comuni e gli indirizzi attuali', *Rendiconti dell'Accademia di Archeologia Lettere e Belle Arte* 71 (2002), 113–29.

The study of other sacred texts has the added importance of revealing some of the particular pressures which may bear upon their editors. See, e.g., G.-R. Puin, 'Observations on Early Qur'an Manuscripts in Ṣanʿāʾ', S. Wild (ed.), *The Qur'an as Text*, Leiden, New York and Cologne, 1996, 107–11 (with bibliography); T. Lester, 'What Is the Koran?', *The Atlantic Monthly* 283 (1999).

The best opportunities to hear other textual critics are at the Society for Textual Scholarship, meeting annually in New York (http://www.textual.org/) and the European Society for Textual Scholarship, meeting annually in Europe (www.textualscholarship.org/ests/). Each has its own journal (*Textual Cultures: Texts, Context, Interpretation* and *Variants*).

This chapter has by no means provided a full survey of the last two centuries of research. It has described some of the main aspects of critical thought, with the aim of illustrating the exciting and important stage of research which we have now reached. It should be clear by now that current scholarship is not seeking to apply past methodologies to new material, but is developing new methodologies as significant as any of the period from Lachmann onwards. I venture to predict that the Coherence-Based Genealogical Method and the use of phylo-genetic software will prove to be equal to any past advance in their significance.

They are important in two ways: for the reconstruction of the history of the text, and in the process of editing that text. These topics are therefore next to be considered.

One other aspect of the development of textual criticism cannot be altogether omitted: the growth of 'canons' to be applied in choosing between different readings in reconstructing the oldest form of text. These canons are associated in their origins with Bengel, although they have a more complicated history. One of the most-commonly cited, *lectio difficilior potior*, is apparently a combination of several rules set out by Griesbach, (see W. G. Kümmel, *The New Testament. The History of the Investigation of its Problems*, London, 1973, 414 (n. 45). There is a set of twelve canons for today in

Aland and Aland, *The Text of the New Testament*, 280–2. How much use such rules are in practice, given Housman's dictum that every situation is possibly unique, has to be considered doubtful. As in medical practice, the diagnosis is far more difficult than the prescription.

5.2 THE HISTORY OF THE TEXT AND EDITING THE TEXT

It is a common misconception that the process of editing the text concerns only the creation of a critical text. The concept of a textual history is also essential. It will not take long to explain these two matters, but a separate section is appropriate, because it forms a bridge between this chapter and chapter 6.

5.2.1 The concept of textual history

Textual history is the history of the changes in wording of a text. Its study has two stages. First is the collection of the information by a study of the witnesses (manuscripts, versions and citations). That is to say, it is the collection of the evidence in order to produce a list of the variant readings. Once this material has been gathered comes the second stage, the examination of the evidence in order to relate the different forms of text chronologically. This is not the same as a chronology of the manuscripts. Of course one could set the forms of text as we find them in the manuscripts in a sequence, but this is no more than stating the *terminus ante quem* for any one form of the text. The text as it is found in a manuscript is a copy of an older form of text. Generally, by comparison, we can sequence such forms of text fairly accurately, not only by finding the witness in which they first appear, but by comparing the different forms of text in order to determine which gave rise to which.

Thus a major critical edition sets out the history of the text, both showing at each point of variation all the different stages through which the text evolved, and providing an overall view of the development of the text. This may include the establishing of different groups and subgroups and families of manuscripts, the recognition of significant stages and phases in the text's life, such as times of editorial activity, and influences and trends in use and understanding of the text. In the case of the New Testament, this process of writing the textual history of the book under consideration includes the separate study of each version, followed by the process of relating the versions to the Greek, and includes also the study of patristic citations and relating them to the manuscript evidence.

The history of the text is a principle for organising the raw data, without which it remains of little value to anyone.

See most recently E. J. Epp, 'It's All about Variants: a Variant-Conscious Approach to New Testament Textual Criticism', *HTR* 100 (2007), 275–308. What has been written here may be considered in the light of the discussion of Ehrman, *Orthodox Corruption* (4.6). I described this and similar approaches as 'narrative textual criticism' (review of Ehrman, *JTS* 45 (1994), 704).

5.2.2 *Editing the text*

Once the history of the text has been written, the editor is in a position to move on to the next stage, making the text itself. The wording of this text will have been established in the writing of the history, since at every point the reading which is deemed to be the source of all the others will be the one selected for the critical text. At the same time, the scrutiny of the text which results from the series of decisions which has been made at each point of variation will lead to a reassessment of the process hitherto (see the procedure used by the Coherence-Based Genealogical Method, 5.1.6).

It is essential at this point to understand what a critically reconstructed text is and what it is not. What it *is*, is the text reached once the editor has decided, at each point of variation, which reading is the source of all the others. This is a decision based upon the known materials. It is *not* the case that this text will necessarily be the 'original' text, however that is defined (for example, as the text as it left the author's hands). The editor's text is essentially a genealogical statement: this is the form of text from which all other forms of text are descended. If we take the analogy of the analysis of human DNA, the comparison of the DNA of a number of individuals may show them all to be descended from a common ancestor. What it will not demonstrate is that the common ancestor was Adam. The distance between the critical text and the beginning of the existence of this text is an important matter for consideration, providing often the biggest unsolved problems in New Testament textual criticism. Whether bridging this gap is the task of the critical editor is another matter, and wisdom inclines to the view that it is not. Rather, this gap is part of the study of the history of the text, which is then resumed.

The text from which all existing forms are descended may appropriately be named the Initial Text. This is in fact the English version of the German 'Ausgangstext', the name for the reconstructed text of the *Editio critica maior*. The first letter of the name in each language provides a siglum which indicates the text's status (I as a Roman numeral one, A as the first letter of the alphabet). What this Initial Text is in relation to any authorial text will be a different matter in each different text, and the third part of this book will attempt to indicate some of the relevant questions as each text is discussed.

It should be noted that the text as it is reconstructed by the editor may not necessarily always follow the text of a known witness. Sometimes it will be decided that two or more extant forms of wording must be derived independently from an initial wording not preserved in any manuscript. The reconstructed initial wording is a conjectural emendation (for a further discussion and examples, see 9.3.6).

This account of the editorial process sets out the essence of what is attempted by the critical edition. In practice, much of the editor's work is taken up with issues of presentation. These will include matters such as orthography and punctuation, on which the witnesses may or may not be a useful guide, as well as of the entire construction of the edition. These are issues which can also predominate in the mind of the user. But to understand the presentational issues, both editor and user have to understand clearly what is being attempted.

There is another topic, or series of topics, also to be considered before the mechanics of the edition can be discussed, namely the wider significance and function of textual criticism. Once these matters have been discussed, the reader will be in a better position to understand the value and character of the many different kinds of editions which are available.

5.3 THE ROLE OF TEXTUAL CRITICISM

J. Neville Birdsall used to quote an eminent scholar who observed to him that he regarded a textual critic in the same way as the man who rods the drains – he was glad he was there, but would not like to do it himself. This frank appreciation of the charms of textual scholarship is at least an appreciation. There are also those who seem unaware that it is even necessary – or that there are drains to be cleared.

There are two misunderstandings in this regard which need clearing up. The first is the belief that the original text of the New Testament has been reconstructed and that the scholar need no longer worry about the possibility that the text may be corrupt. The second, the theme of this chapter, is that the researches and findings of textual critics are only useful to textual critics. In fact textual criticism is no more a discipline existing in its own bubble than is any other. This chapter explores three other 'disciplines' to which textual criticism contributes. The concept of disciplines is not a very satisfactory one, and leads to all kinds of absurd distinctions. Admittedly 'textual criticism' and 'history' and 'exegesis' and 'theology' all have their own goals and character. But none is complete in itself, and all four are studying the same material.

5.3.1 Textual criticism and history

The strongly historical nature of much of the earlier parts of this book, the study of the manuscripts, the versions and citations all show how much textual criticism is dependent upon historical research. The dependence runs the other way as well. The dating and analysis of documents is essential to the historian, evidently so far as primary evidence is concerned, but also in the study of textual development and the study of the impact of forms of the text. A full study of the manuscripts and the text they carry can also be of importance to social historians, linguists studying the development of certain features, and intellectual historians of all kinds. Such a study may provide evidence of cultural links between different places and of expansion and change in a certain area. Where the text has been a highly influential one in a civilisation, the contribution of its textual study to historical research will be all the greater. The role of the Bible in Latin, Byzantine, and eastern Christianity has been great. Time and again, manuscript study and text-editing contribute to the understanding of the wider culture.

One traditional view of textual criticism saw it as 'the lower criticism' (laying the drains?) necessary for the 'higher criticism' to flourish. This higher criticism was the business of establishing matters of the date, authorship and place of writing of the text. In terms of the historical-critical method, both lower and higher criticism provided information which formed the basis of more significant research. It is not hard to see why this understanding of historical research was important a hundred and more years ago, when so much scientific research needed to be undertaken. The New Testament text, which had been printed in a poor form on the unhistorical grounds of dogmatic statements about the divinely inspired character of the Received Text, needed to be edited on critical principles, and nothing else could be done until this was completed. Then, on the grounds of a newly established text, the old traditions and beliefs about dates, authorships and relationships of text could be studied in a historical manner in which the claims and legends of the Fathers and other older opinions on these matters could be scrutinised. From a modern vantage point, such confidence in the scientific accuracy of the historical-critical approach may seem naively optimistic, but that is to overlook how different it was from what had gone before. Today, one cannot say that the researches of lower and higher criticism are complete or that all their questions have been answered. The researches and the questions are as necessary as ever. What has become outdated is the concept of lower and higher criticism, which appears to view historical research as a series of stages on each of which the next storey in the building could be built. Textual criticism does not fulfil this role, since subsequent stages of research may cast new light on some of the problems encountered at the beginning. The concept of the hermeneutical circle may be more helpful to us: the study of the text and other branches of historical research continue to provide each other with answers and fresh questions as patterns of research change and fresh evidence emerges.

5.3.2 *Textual criticism and exegesis*

These two have been described as 'siamese twins' (J. Delobel). There is a simple reason why the exegete of the New Testament cannot afford to ignore the variant readings: they provide some of the earliest commentaries upon the meaning of the text – and often we cannot determine which is the text and which the commentary! That is to say, the variant is an attempt to make the text say what it must mean. This changing of the wording seems rather crass, or even unbelievable today, but we have other ways of saying what we think it means – in a commentary. Is it fanciful to see a connection between these two observations, namely that a large proportion of the variant readings in the New Testament came into existence before about 200, or 250 at the latest, and that the early third century saw the introduction of the commentary on Scripture, pioneered in Alexandria by Didymus and Origen? Once the commentary was available, there was no need to change the text to show its meaning – that interpretation was carried in the commentary, a commentary perhaps written in the margins of the text itself ☛ (21). Thus varying forms of text attest to the way in which the texts were being interpreted.

How should the exegete make use of textual criticism? In the first place, by working with the fullest edition available, and by trying to understand the history of the text and the nature of the critical text that is available. Each is important for a different reason. The full edition matters for the simple reason that it gives the fullest access to the textual variation. Understanding the history of the text matters, because it is significant in understanding what the text is. For example, the textual history of Romans cannot be separated from the textual history of the collected Pauline letters (see 8.9.1). At the same time, the relationship between literary and textual theory with regard to textual history has to be quite clear. There is especially likely to be confusion in this respect with regard to the Gospels. Whatever theories are held with regard to the relationship between the four Gospels, it must be clear that these are literary theories, which are not to be confused with the textual history. The type of edition is important, because exegetes often speak of the critical text as though it were an authorial text even if the editor has made no such claim for it. No editor of the Greek New Testament would claim either the tools or the ability to produce an authorial text (see 5.1.8). Exegetes need to understand the nature of the text on which they are commentating.

At this point I hear the common objection, 'But surely we have more or less what the author wrote; we can tell his style; there may be a few problems of detail, but what of that?' The answer is that what is available is not an authorial text, but the product of a more complicated process in which the author's writings have been preserved but also to some degree changed, for better or for worse, by his readers. It is not just that such a text is like the man who could play all the notes of a piano piece, but not necessarily in the right order. It is that the whole text as it emerges from the period without any surviving manuscripts is already, however subtly, the product of a process of reception and transmission. The very fact that the text has survived tells us that it was to the taste of enough people for it to have been copied and recopied.

Exegesis which was convinced by these suggestions would treat variant readings in a rather different way from that in which they are usually taken. The normal approach is to discuss the different possibilities, to decide which was the 'best' or 'original' and by implication authorial and then to commentate upon it and to ignore the others. The approach which treated the variants as early forms of commentary and accepted also that since we do not absolutely know which was the 'best', then they must all be suspected to be commentaries, would explore the ways in which each contributed to the meaning of the text.

There are some very simple rules which are often ignored but must be followed. Even if an exegete just follows a printed edition and never or hardly ever refers to a variant, the reader still deserves to be told what edition has been used. I could point to some commentaries on the Greek text which, although they are deservedly used and trusted in other respects, nowhere state what that Greek text is.

K. Aland, 'Neutestamentliche Textkritik und Exegese', in K. Aland and S. Meurer (eds.), *Wissenschaft und Kirche. Festschrift für Eduard Lohse*, Bielefeld, 1989, 132–48; J. Delobel, 'Textual Criticism and Exegesis: Siamese Twins?', in B. Aland and J. Delobel (eds.), *New Testament Textual Criticism, Exegesis and Early Church History. A Discussion of Methods* (Contributions to Biblical Exegesis & Theology 7), Kampen, 1994, 98–117. See also various contributions to the *Festschrift Delobel*. For examples of studies indicating the significance of textual changes for exegesis, see J. K. Elliott, 'The Parable of the Two Sons. Text and Exegesis', in *Festschrift Delobel*, 67–77; 'The Divine Names in the Corinthian Letters', in T. J. Burke and J. K. Elliott (eds.), *Paul and the Corinthians. Studies on a Community in Conflict. Essays in Honour of Margaret Thrall*, Leiden and Boston, 2003, 3–15; 'Changes to the Exegesis of the Catholic Epistles in the Light of the Text in the *Editio Critica Maior*', in Sang-Won (Aaron) Son (ed.), *History and Exegesis. New Testament Essays in Honor of Dr E. Earle Ellis for his 80th Birthday*, New York and London, 2006, 324–39.

Sometimes a particular textual form of a passage can have significance not only on the interpretation of a passage but on the development of a concept. One of the most prominent examples is Augustine's understanding of the translation of ἐφ ᾧ as *in quo* at Rom. 5.12 and his use of it to develop his doctrine of original sin. For a discussion of the significance of differences in the Latin renderings of this verse for its interpretation, see B. Harbert, 'Romans 5,12: Old Latin and Vulgate in the Pelagian Controversy', *Studia Patristica* 22 (1989), 261–4.

5.3.3 *Textual criticism and theology*

The idea that there is any relationship between textual criticism and theology has not been very common. The principal reason for this I believe is the condemnation, often fierce and personal, which textual critics received from the early eighteenth century onwards. The Received Text, based although it was upon late Greek manuscripts (and in a number of verses on no Greek manuscripts at all, see 7.2), was generally believed to be the inspired Word of God. Not many such believers were very happy to be told by textual critics that the ancient manuscripts read differently. Since scepticism towards revealed religion began to emerge at the same time, textual critics were caught in the middle. To the atheist or sceptic, the discovery that there was textual variation between the witnesses was evidence that the biblical revelation as conceived by the theologian was a fake. As a result, the reporting of such data was regarded by many defenders of revealed religion as betrayal to the enemy. The results are to be seen as early as the debate caused by John Mill's *Novum Testamentum Graece* of 1707, the first edition to contain an extensive citation of manuscript evidence. ☞ (22) Mill printed the commonly received text, with an apparatus containing about thirty thousand variant readings from manuscripts, versions and patristic citations. This, the most extensive conspectus of the material hitherto, disturbed the theological sensitivities of the age. On the one hand, a clergyman (Daniel Whitby) was grieved and vexed 'that I have found so much in Mill's Prolegomena which seems plainly to render the standard of faith insecure, or at best to give others too good a handle for doubting'. On the other, a free-thinker (Anthony Collins) offers the disparaging comment that Anglican clergy were 'owning and labouring to prove the Text of the Scripture to be precarious'.

D. Whitby, 'Examen Variantium Lectionum Joannis Millii S.T.P. in Novum Testamentum', in *Paraphrase and Commentary on the New Testament* (first published 1703), London, 1710, cited by A. Fox, *John Mill and Richard Bentley. A Study of the Textual Criticism of the New Testament 1675–1729* (The Aularian Series 3), Oxford, 1954, 106. A. Collins, *Discourse of Free-Thinking*, London, 1713, 87, cited by Fox, p. 108.

In this sensitive position, one in which they found themselves by chance and not as a deliberate consequence of their research, textual critics seem to have preferred to emphasise that their discipline caused no theological problems, and was indeed quite untheological in character. It became more convenient to practise the lower criticism in peace and quiet than to draw attention to it. This had two consequences: in the first place, it came generally to be believed that none of the textual variation within the New Testament was theologically significant debate, and that there were no theologically motivated variant readings in the New Testament; in the second, textual criticism itself became a discipline divorced from theological debate.

An exception to this is the strong claims made by defenders of the Received Text for its character as divinely inspired, in the face of critical research and editions. This is essentially an ahistorical attitude, since it consists of an a priori claim that a text which was formed in a haphazard manner by sixteenth-century printers and scholars out of whatever manuscripts they happened to have available, is the only form of text which can be regarded as inspired or authoritative. Because the King James Version was translated from this form of text, these ideas are very closely linked with the fundamentalism which treats this version as uniquely inspired. (By fundamentalism I mean an attitude which refuses to recognise the textually provisional character of all editions.) The defence of this text goes back to the nineteenth century, when there were not lacking those who resisted both the critical texts of Lachmann, Tregelles and Westcott and Hort and the making of new translations such as the Revised Version. There is nothing more to be said about this attitude, based as it is upon uncritical claims.

No discipline should be governed by presuppositions derived from another. But presuppositions have a habit of creeping in whether we are aware of them or not. The example of the continuing defence of the Received Text is that the textual criticism of religious texts is particularly prone to outside influence. We may see this in reluctance to debate text-critical issues in other sacred texts such as the Qur'an, while in a different way the textual study of the Hebrew Bible seems to avoid many pressing problems.

The statement by Westcott and Hort that 'there are no signs of deliberate falsification of the text for dogmatic purposes' is well known. The language used seems designed to exclude the possibility of discussion. Equally striking is the conclusion to the section in Kenyon which was quoted in chapter 4: 'One word of warning, already referred to, must be emphasized in conclusion. No fundamental doctrine of the Christian faith rests on a disputed reading.' Why is a 'word of warning' needed? The shades of Mill, Whitby and Collins seem to hover over the page.

Westcott and Hort, II.282; Kenyon, *Our Bible and the Ancient Manuscripts*, 23 (unchanged in the fifth edition).

In spite of all this, it does not follow that there is nothing to be said about theology and textual criticism. What is most necessary is for theological debate to be informed by text-critical research, and to develop arguments on the basis of what is known about the manuscripts and the textual tradition, not on the basis of attitudes formed before the textual questions had been properly explored.

I have approached these questions in several places, and shall not repeat myself here. I shall address one matter only, which may help to set a single theological question in a text-critical context.

D. C. Parker, 'Ethics and the New Testament', *Studies in Christian Ethics* 10 (1997), 39–57; 'A Reply to Francis Watson', *Studies in Christian Ethics* 10, 62–3 (see Francis Watson, 'On the "Uselessness" of the New Testament: a Reply to David Parker', *Studies in Christian Ethics* 10 (1997), 58–61); 'Et Incarnatus Est', *Scottish Journal of Theology* 54 (2001), 330–43; 'Through a Screen Darkly: Digital Texts and the New Testament', *JSNT* 25 (2003), 395–411; 'Jesus and Textual Criticism', in J. L. Houlden (ed.), *Jesus in History, Thought and Culture. An Encyclopedia,* Santa Barbara, Denver and Oxford, 2003, II.836–41; 'Textual Criticism and Theology', *The ExpositoryTimes* 118 (2007), 583–9.

The obvious significance of the connection between one's wider understanding of history and human society and one's attitude to textual criticism will be more clearly illustrated to someone working in the theological milieu by examples of a quite different point of view. Timpanaro's criticism of Freud in the book discussed in chapter 4 (*The Freudian Slip*) is explicitly offered from a Marxist point of view (see, e.g., pp. 173ff.). See R. S. Dombroski, 'Timpanaro in Retrospect', *Italica* 78 (2001), 337–50. For another Marxist approach, see G. Thomson, 'Marxism and Textual Criticism', *Wissenschaftliche Zeitschrift der Humboldt-Universität zu Berlin, Gesellschafts-und Sprachwissenschaftliche. Reihe* 12 (1963), 43–52. For an example of an approach to New Testament textual criticism with an equally explicit ideology, see the website 'Evangelical Textual Criticism, a Webpage Promoting Textual Criticism of the Bible from the Perspective of Historic Evangelical Theology' (www. evangelicaltextualcriticism.com/), claiming among others for evangelical textual criticism the characteristics that

It approaches the task of identifying the words given by God with reverence and therefore caution.
It approaches the task of identifying the words given by God with a confidence in God's provision.

It is not clear whether this providence is seen in the way in which the text has been preserved or in the work of the textual critic (or both), but in any case the exploration of this idea might furnish an interesting comparison with the arguments which Timpanaro uses in his critique of Freud's determinism.

While the concept of textual authority holds one set of resonances for the theologian, it holds others for the textual critic, and in particular for the editor. An 'authority' in textual language is one way of referring to a witness to the text (in our case, a manuscript or patristic citation). Authority as a concept in textual scholarship can be defined in many different ways. This is because it is dependent upon two things: the nature of the textual tradition and the way in which a particular editor understands the role of making an edition. The description of conceptions of authority by Shillingsburg, whose own experiences of editing have principally been of nineteenth-century English literature, sets this out clearly. He distinguishes between a number of orientations which a scholarly editor may choose. These are the historical, the aesthetic, the authorial and the sociological. For each of these classes of editor, the criteria by which they choose an 'authoritative text' is different.

For the historical orientation, authority 'usually resides in the historical document, warts and all'. Shillingsburg may have in mind an autograph or a single print edition. In the field of New Testament scholarship, this view of authority would locate it in the manuscript copies.

For the aesthetic, it 'resides in a concept of *artistic* forms – either the author's, the editor's, or those fashionable at some time'. At first glance this seems less applicable to New Testament textual scholarship, but it perhaps applies best in the idea of a form of the whole text which is subtly edited, with a consistency to the whole, perhaps the impress of a particular age. The role of the K^r form of the Byzantine text is perhaps the best example, and its possible role in editing is seen in the choice of minuscule 35, a complete New Testament of this form, as the base text for the Byzantine Text Edition of the Gospel of John (see 6.1.5).

'Authority for the authorial orientation resides with the author, though editors do not agree on what that means.' This concept of authority is closest to that held by readers of the New Testament who are not textual scholars, who generally assume that the text in their printed edition is what Matthew, Paul and the others wrote. It is also closest to the traditional ascription of the texts' authority to divine inspiration (or even dictation).

The sociological orientation finds authority in the 'institutional unit of author *and* publisher' (pp. 21, 22, 24, 25). Shillingsburg has in mind the nineteenth-century novel, and again the New Testament equivalent is not obvious. But an equivalent there is. It is the emphasis on the concept of the texts carried by the manuscripts as the product of a process of copying, with its mixture of intended and unintended changes to the text, in which the text is seen not as an authorial product but as the result of a process of reading and rewriting.

These are Shillingsburg's types of textual authority. Applied to the New Testament, it may be seen that they are all practised by textual scholars. Each carries with it a possible way in which the theologian may express concepts of textual authority. Whichever is preferred, the theological argument will only be as cogent as the particular model of text-critical authority which is preferred.

P. L. Shillingsburg, *Scholarly Editing in the Computer Age. Theory and Practice*, Athens and London, 1986, chapter 1.

Theories about the best way of editing a text must be constructed on the basis of sound historical research and well-considered critical practice. Such theories offer a standard against which to judge theological concepts of textual authority. This process is one of the strongest defences available against fundamentalism and bibliolatry. Textual criticism and the discipline of textual editing is a basic requirement of research and reflection. It has nothing to say directly in the world of philosophical and theological reflection, but there is a great deal to be learned from it.

5.3.4 *Textual criticism and the world*

This grand title covers a very simple observation with which this chapter will end. Textual criticism offers an important bulwark against the fundamentalism of all kinds which plays a significant part in so much religious practice that it has even become a factor in international politics and discussion about the relationship between cultures. Much fundamentalism is the default attitude of people who have been given no reason why they should not assume that the form they know of their sacred texts is the only one in existence. While Christianity, with several centuries of textual research to instruct it, has no justification for any kind of fundamentalism, the study of some other sacred texts, in particular the Qur'an, has little tradition and very little current impetus to develop any kind of organised text-critical research. The situation of the textual criticism of the Hebrew Bible, committed to editions of the Massoretic text and with very little ancient material to go on apart from the versions (of which those in Greek are the most valuable) and the documents from the Judaean Desert, is surprising to the New Testament textual scholar, since it seems to tread an uneasy path between traditional texts and modern research. This is a matter to be taken seriously by believers of all faiths who study the Hebrew Scriptures.

Textual criticism both by its nature and by its findings shows fundamentalism to be inadmissible, and has an important role to play in offering an alternative to all world-views which insist on the inerrancy and perfection of texts as a guide through life.

CHAPTER 6

Editions and how to use them

6.1 THE HISTORY OF EDITIONS

6.1.1 Why we have critical editions

The main problem confronting the editor of the New Testament is demonstrably as old as the oldest surviving New Testament documents. The problem is, quite simply, to find the best way of displaying known differences. In the Introduction the difficulties of defining variant readings were discussed. These problems are important to the makers of editions and influence the user's understanding. But they are older than that. Whenever readers and copyists of the texts became aware of a difference in wording, they were faced with similar problems of interpretation. This is evident from one of the oldest manuscripts, the first described in 1.1.2.1. Consider the page of P66 illustrated there. ☛ (23) We find that the scribe provided corrections from a second manuscript, and did so by writing on whatever blank papyrus was available, either between the lines or in a margin. These corrections are better described as alternatives to the first reading, because his method of working allows the reader to see how the alterations stand in relation to the text as first written. There is no question of erasing text on this material. Instead, a system of symbols for transposing ☛ (24) (the single and double oblique strokes), deleting ☛ (25) (in two ways, the hooks around a series of letters and the dots over them) and inserting ☛ (26) material, along with additions on blank papyrus ☛ (27) are used to create a web of variant readings which are both distinguished from the first form of text and woven into it. How easy or difficult the readers of this manuscript found it to use we do not know. What is important to recognise is that the modern reader, puzzled by the details of a critical apparatus, is in the same position as the ancient reader of P66: one is confronted by variant forms of the text. It might be objected that for a manuscript to contain so many corrections is unusual (see 4.4). But it is also true that an edition of any text with a critical apparatus is rare. How many novels are read in critical editions? It is only since the end of the nineteenth century that the most commonly used editions of the Greek New Testament have had an apparatus. But now that one is customary, the problem cannot be ignored.

A variety of other ways in which variant readings are displayed in New Testament manuscripts may be illustrated from one of the major variants in the Gospel of John, 7.53–8.11 (discussed at 10.10.4). This passage is completely omitted in a number of manuscripts (we cannot use P66 as an illustration, since it is one of them, with no sign of the scribe or a reader having known of the passage). The options here are to include the text in its usual place, with or without comment, to exclude it without comment, or to include it outside its usual place. The latter course of action is represented in the sophisticated archetype of Family 1 (see 4.3), preserved for us by the monk Ephraim, scribe of 1582 (see 8.4). ☛ (28) 1582 usually presents alternative readings as marginalia. The Pericope Adulterae, however, is placed at the end of the Gospel, ☛ (29) with a textual note that includes a discussion of patristic attestation. ☛ (30) Here is a different way of handling the problem: instead of being closely related to the text to which it is an alternative, the variant has been placed at a distance from it. At the same time, the fact that the passage is often regarded as a part of John has been acknowledged by placing it immediately afterwards. The story is both included and excluded. Two well-known English versions, The New English Bible and the Revised English Bible, present this passage in the same way. ☛ (31)

Another way to signal inclusion and exclusion is to set the passage in its usual place, but with a symbol indicating a measure of uncertainty. The symbol used is the obelos, one of the series devised by the Homeric scholars of Alexandria. In this example, the ninth-century 045, the obelos stands against every line. ☛ (32) A modern form of this presentation is used in the Nestle–Aland, where double square brackets around the text serve the same function. ☛ (33)

For the obelos and other symbols, see Devreesse, *Introduction* 74 and plate XVI; Gardthausen, *Palaeographie*, II.410–14. The square brackets in Nestle–Aland are explained in the Introduction (German text, p. 7*; English text, p. 50*): they 'indicate that the enclosed words, generally of some length, are known not to be a part of the original [ursprünglichen] text. These texts derive from a very early stage of the tradition, and have often played a significant role in the history of the church.'

The hardest thing to execute is to exclude a piece of text while commenting on its exclusion. The reason is that this is, paradoxically, to *include* it. The problem is solved in some manuscripts by means of a gap, as in this. ☛ (34) Editions and translations which place the passage in a footnote follow a similar course of action.

It is no coincidence that this passage and ones like it pose some of the hardest technical problems facing a maker of an electronic edition.

6.1.2 The transition from manuscript to printed book

These examples of the display of the variant reading are drawn from manuscripts. The most common form of emendation in a parchment manuscript is by erasure, the second reading being written on the erased spot. When a correction is too long to be fitted in (generally the provision of text not copied by the scribe), it is added in a margin. When we turn to the printed texts, we find no change in the situation. ☛ (35) The first edition to contain manuscript variations, Stephanus' of 1550, displayed them in the margin. That is to say, he took the same option as that found in members of Family 1. The reading in the text and the marginal reading are linked by arabic numerals, and the witnesses are distinguished by each receiving a Greek number. There are thus three elements to Stephanus' system:

(1) the arabic numeral linking text and variant, which today is called an 'address'
(2) the marginal reading
(3) the Greek number designating a witness

Stephanus did not invent the system, which is already found in editions by the Italian humanist Politian at the end of the fifteenth century. See M.D. Reeve, 'John Wallis, Editor of Greek Mathematical Texts', in G.W. Most (ed.), *Editing texts / Texte edieren*, Göttingen, 1998, 77–93; 'Lucretius from the 1460s to the 17th Century: Seven Questions of Attribution', *Aevum* 80 (2006), 165–84.

But even earlier, the first printed edition of the Greek New Testament had shown incredible sophistication both in its concept and in its technical execution. This page is from the Complutensian Polyglot ☛ (36), printed in 1514, but published in about 1522. The impressive achievement shows what could be done at an early stage in the development of the new technology. In fact, all the great Polyglot Bibles date from before the end of the seventeenth century. In spite of the massive technological advances of the later centuries, nobody has attempted anything so ambitious again until today (see 3.3.1).

Stephanus' brevity was to become the norm for the printed critical edition, but from the seventeenth century onwards we can observe other formats. Walton's London Polyglot, published in the 1650s ☛ (37), partially abandoned the concept of an apparatus, in which the readings are presented as briefly as possible as alternatives, for a much bulkier but in some ways much more secure presentation, with each witness in full. Of course, there are good reasons for this, and the multilingual version is in its own category. Such an edition aside, the following types of edition may be instanced. They divide into two categories: the presentation of the text (with or without other features) of one or more witnesses in full, and the presentation of the text of more than one witness in a compressed form.

6.1.3 Editions which present the text of one or more witnesses in full

These also divide into different types.

6.1.3.1 A manuscript transcription

The example taken here is Irico's transcription of the Old Latin Gospels Codex Vercellensis, of 1748 ☞ (38) (for a description and image of the manuscript, see 1.1.2.4). This is known as a diplomatic edition. It is the best way of representing as exactly as possible the text of an individual witness. Such an edition is used to study how the text is reproduced at a particular point in its transmission. Whatever apparatus is provided will be orientated to the textual and historical context of the manuscript (Irico includes variants of the manuscript from the Vulgate). Because it contains only one witness, this type of edition is the most suitable for representing 'paratextual' features, namely the layout and such things as running titles, numbering systems, punctuation and initial letters. It is preferable that the edition keeps to the manuscript page for page, though this is sometimes impracticable in a printed edition.

J. A. Irico (ed.), *Sacrosanctus evangeliorum codex S. Eusebii Magni episcopi et martyris manu exaratus ex autographo basilicae Vercellensis ad unguem exhibitus nunc primum in lucem prodit*, 2 vols., Milan, 1748. An example of a transcription which indicates the folios but not the line breaks is H. S. Cronin (ed.), *Codex Purpureus Petropolitanus. The Text of Codex N of the Gospels* (TS 1.5.4), Cambridge, 1899, reprinted Nendeln, 1967. This is not so great a problem, but when the same editorial decision is taken with a palimpsest, a user trying to check the edition against the manuscript may have a difficult task. A. S. Lewis (ed.), *Codex Climaci Rescriptus* etc. (Horae Semiticae 8), Cambridge, 1909, gives the line divisions of the Syriac overwriting, but not of the underlying Greek. The later edition of I. Moir, '*Codex Climaci Rescriptus Graecus*' etc. (TS 2.2), Cambridge, 1956, is superior in providing the full line and page structure of the manuscript.

Sometimes this type of edition uses one or more additional manuscripts to supplement the main text where it is lacking. One has then to be on one's guard against being misled. L. J. Hopkin-James, *The Celtic Gospels. Their Story and their Text* (Oxford, 1934) presents the text of the Chad Gospels, these being replaced by the Hereford Gospels from Lk. 3.8. But it would not be hard to overlook this fact, which is nowhere very forcibly stated, and assume that all is the one manuscript.

6.1.3.2 A presentation of witnesses in parallel columns

This example ☛ (39) is from E.H. Hansell's 1864 edition of the manuscripts 02 03 04 and 05, with symbols cross-referencing variations between them, and sophisticated typesetting to keep the four lines as parallel as possible. It remains a valuable resource for comparing their texts. All layout and most other paratextual information is lost (although this edition does include the section numberings of the manuscripts and could have included their punctuation had the editor chosen to).

E.H. Hansell (ed.), *Novum Testamentum Graece, antiquissimorum codicum textus in ordine parallelo dispositi accedit collatio codicis sinaitici*, 3 vols., Oxford, 1864.

6.1.3.3 A presentation of witnesses in lines above each other

This is best known to contemporary scholarship from the editions of Swanson. Such an edition is easiest to use when each line represents that of a single witness or text-type. Swanson's presentation is more complicated, since each line contains one form of the text as it appears at that place, except that the text of Codex Vaticanus and of whatever witnesses agree with it is always presented on the top line. The support for the readings in the subsequent lines will vary all the time. There are five apparatuses at the bottom of the page containing

statements of lacunae
itacisms and impossible readings
the forms of *nomina sacra*
the lectionary apparatus
section numbering

By combining this information with the main apparatus, it is possible to gain a good picture of the text as it is presented in the individual witnesses. Because the witness list is limited to Greek continuous-text manuscripts or editions (though Clement of Alexandria is included), the editorial task of presentation is comparatively simple. The biggest drawback of this particular edition is the confusion for the reader in distinguishing between forms of text and the text in manuscripts. A problem for the editor (and publisher) is that, as with the Hansell type of edition, there is much repetition of identical text.

Swanson, *Greek Manuscripts*: Gospels in 4 vols., 1995; Acts, 1998; Romans, 2001, 1 Corinthians, 2003; 2 Corinthians, 2005; Galatians, 1999.

6.1.4 Editions which present the text of more than one witness in a compressed form

These too come in a variety of forms.

6.1.4.1 Editions which present only evidence

By this I mean editions which present textual evidence but not a critical edition of the text. Such an edition is more accurately a 'thesaurus of readings'. The biggest example of this in recent years is the International Greek New Testament Project's edition of Luke's Gospel. The apparatus consisted of the evidence from several hundred Greek manuscripts, Greek and Latin patristic citations down to the year 500 and a wide range of versions. At the time, this represented the largest apparatus for any part of the New Testament. The readings are presented as a negative apparatus. The printed text is identical with that against which the materials were collated (*Textus Receptus*, Oxford, 1873). From the editor's point of view, this is much easier to achieve, because the process of realigning such a large negative apparatus to show deviations from a new base text would be very slow and difficult. Other major examples of this type of edition include Hoskier's collation of all Greek manuscripts of Revelation (see 7.2). Before the nineteenth century the total dominance of the Received Text meant that some of even the most significant editions (such as Mill and Wettstein) were of this type: they may have wanted to replace the text with something better, but all their editions were *thesauri* of variants from it.

6.1.4.2 A collation of one or more manuscripts

These will be familiar to many people from several collections by Scrivener. ☛ (40) The advantage is an extremely concise presentation. The difficulties are that the data have to be combined with information from other sources if one is to attain a coherent picture, and that the text forms of the individual witnesses have become fragmented, with little or no information about the physical contexts of the readings. At the time at which Scrivener worked, each of these publications contributed a little to the growth of knowledge. He sought out manuscripts and collated them. His work would then be used by an editor (perhaps Tregelles, perhaps Tischendorf, or Westcott and Hort) as one source among many to compile the material for an edition. This system lasted as long as the total dominance of the Received Text. When everyone printed the same text, a new set of collations could be added into an apparatus with a minimum of difficulty. Once editors began to create their own text, collations had to be adapted to show their differences from the new text, and this was a great deal more difficult. Even so, the collation remained valuable so long as everyone was agreed on the standard against which to collate. As soon as it was abandoned (e.g. by the Critical Greek Testament's editions of Matthew and Luke, which collated against Westcott and Hort, and by the Münster Institut, which adopted its own critical text for all collating work) this way of working could no longer hold.

F. H. A. Scrivener, *A Full and Exact Collation of about Twenty Greek Manuscripts of the Holy Gospels* etc., London, 1853; *Adversaria Critica Sacra*, Cambridge, 1893, is similar in character. Scrivener, *Augiensis* combines the presentation of a single witness (1–284) with collations (285–563). The Introduction was also published separately as *Contributions to the Criticism of the Greek New Testament*, Cambridge and London, 1859. Another example is Lake and New, *Six Collations*.

6.1.4.3 A full edition with both critical text and apparatus

There is one example *par excellence* of this, the most advanced form of edition. Tischendorf's *Editio octava* set out to provide not just a full apparatus but one with comment and judgement included. ☞ (41) He writes in what is virtually a new language, a combination of Latin abbreviations, manuscript symbols, variants expressed as briefly as possible, and different fonts. Moreover, Tischendorf virtually talks to the reader in such a way that he can alternate between a negative and a positive apparatus. Take (at random) the example of Matthew 22.25. The first variant is presented as a negative apparatus

δε: D q om

The second is a positive one:

γημασ cum [list of witnesses] ... ς γαμημασ cum [list of witnesses]
The formula 'text–cum–witnesses–...–siglum for Received Text–text–cum–witnesses' distinguishes it from a negative apparatus.

It has to be said that Tischendorf's apparatus is better than his critical text. He had come across Codex Sinaiticus since his seventh edition (1859), and his text was too strongly influenced by this manuscript.

Other important examples of this type of edition include von Soden's Greek New Testament, the Wordsworth and White edition of the Vulgate, Pusey and Gwillam's edition of the Syriac Peshitta, and most of the hand editions (see 6.2.1).

Von Soden; Wordsworth and White; Pusey and Gwilliam, *Tetraeuangelium*; Tischendorf, *Editio octava*.

Notice should be made here of a type of edition which, although it contains an apparatus, does not have a critically reconstructed text, but offers the text of individual manuscripts. An example is Horner's edition of the Bohairic Coptic version, where a number of incomplete manuscripts have been used to give a complete text.

Horner, *Northern Dialect.*

6.1.4.4 Editions presenting a number of text-types
The classic modern examples of this are editions of the versions, such as Kiraz's Syriac Gospels and the Vetus Latina edition. The editor has used the manuscript and citational data to reconstruct a number of critical texts. The data are then aligned in an apparatus showing support for the different critical texts. Because of the particular circumstances of different versions, some such editions may in fact present the text of individual manuscripts (e.g. the Old Syriac) and a critical text (e.g. the Peshitta) in the same edition and in the same way.

Kiraz, *Comparative Edition of the Syriac Gospels; Vetus Latina.*

6.1.4.5 Editions presenting a particular class of manuscript
There are several editions dedicated to manuscripts which fall in a single category. Most frequently, these are either the oldest manuscripts of the New Testament or the papyri. Such editions may contain plates, transcriptions and notes. Sometimes they are based upon fresh examination of the originals, sometimes they are a compilation of existing editions, sometimes they are a mixture of the two.

K. Hirunuma, *The Papyri Bearing the New Testament Text*, 2 vols., Osaka, 1994–8 (in Japanese); *NT auf Papyrus I*; *NT auf Papyrus II*; Elliott and Parker, *Papyri*; Schmid, Elliott and Parker, *Majuscules.*

6.1.5 Editions of the Received Text, the Majority Text and the Byzantine Text

I place these editions in a separate category, although in content, method of construction and in purpose they probably ought not to belong together. With regard to content, there are actually three types of edition which are sometimes, in the case of two of them mistakenly, described as editions of the Byzantine Text.

Editions of the Received Text are reprintings of one of two possible texts: the Stephanus edition of 1550 and the Elzevir edition of 1633 giving the *textum ab omnibus receptum* ('the text accepted by all'). This is the one which has been printed the most often, more recent printings being intended for the use of scholars in collating manuscripts. For example, hundreds of fascicles of parts of the New Testament were printed for the International Greek New Testament by photographic offset from an Oxford 1873 printing (*Textus Receptus*, Oxford, 1873). Sometimes this text is printed not for such purposes but out of a belief in the superiority of the text. Such a view often connects the Received Text with the King James Version. This is true of the Trinitarian Bible Society's edition, the society stating:

It is a faithful representation of the text which the church in different parts of the world has used for centuries. It is the result of the textual studies of conservative scholars during the years both before and after the Reformation, and represents for the most part over 5,000 available Greek manuscripts. The Society believes this text is superior to the texts used by the United Bible Societies and other Bible publishers, which texts have as their basis a relatively few seriously defective manuscripts from the 4th century and which have been compiled using 20th century rationalistic principles of scholarship. (www.trinitarianbiblesociety. org/site/principles.asp)

Ἡ Καινη Διαθηκη. *The New Testament. The Greek Text Underlying the English Authorised Version of 1611*, London, n.d. The text is in fact from F. H. A. Scrivener (ed.), *The New Testament in the Original Greek According to the Text Followed in the Authorised Version together with the Variations Adopted in the Revised Version*, Cambridge, 1902 [1894]. This is an adaptation of Beza's edition of 1598 (see Scrivener's preface for the problems of reconstructing a single Greek text as the source).

The difficulty with claiming the authority of the Received Text as that of the majority of witnesses is that it often does not follow the majority. To resolve this problem, attempts have been made to produce a genuine Majority Text. Since we do not know what every manuscript reads in every place, the text is that of manuscripts which the editors consider to be safe choices as representatives of the majority.

M. A. Robinson and W. G. Pierpont (eds.), *The New Testament in the Original Greek According to the Byzantine/Majority Textform*, Atlanta, 1991; revised edition as *The New Testament in the Original Greek: Byzantine Textform 2005*, Southborough, 2005; Z. F. Hodges and A. F. Farstad (eds.), *The Greek New Testament According to the Majority Text*, Nashville, 1982.

Editing the Byzantine Text without regard for questions of the reading of the majority of manuscripts is another matter altogether. Belief in the Majority Text is the result of the history of western scholarship. In the Greek Orthodox Church one is discussing the text as it has been received through the tradition. It is in this spirit that the edition made and still used by the Orthodox Church, the Patriarchal Edition, was produced in 1904.

In fact the Byzantine Text is not a unity, but itself developed and sometimes is divided between two forms of text. What is still lacking is a critical edition of the Byzantine text which will illustrate this development in a way that is of value to communities which use it. A prototype which sets out to meet this need is an edition of the Gospel of John prepared by R. L. Mullen. It uses the minuscule 35 as its base, and contains an apparatus citing manuscripts and Church Fathers to illustrate the variants within the Byzantine text.

B. Antoniades (ed.), Ἡ Καινη Διαθηκη, Constantinople, 1904. Mullen, Crisp and Parker, *John*, with an electronic edition which provides transcriptions of all the manuscripts and a database of the patristic citations at http://itsee.bham.ac.uk/iohannes/byzantine/index.html. For an account of Orthodox views of the tradition, see J. D. Karavidopoulos, 'The Interpretation of the New Testament in the Orthodox Church', in C. Landmesser, H.-J. Eckstein and H. Lichtenberger (eds.), *Jesus Christus als die Mitte der Schrift. Studien zur Hermeneutik des Evangeliums*, Berlin and New York, 1997, 249–62.

6.1.6 Editions which move from print towards the electronic edition

Two editions in recent times have led the move from the traditional print edition towards new ways of presenting the material.

6.1.6.1 The Editio critica maior

The Münster Institut's *Editio critica maior,* ☞ (42) 'the New Tischendorf', combines several traditional features and, adding its own innovations, seems the apotheosis of the critical edition. The use of a variant address corresponds to Stephanus' system. Here it is a lower-case italic letter. The addition of the numbering of words of the critical text with even numbers (the odd numbers representing spaces) to the address means that the variants can be clearly listed in one place, and the supporting witnesses below. In the apparatus the use of three dots (not in the same way as Tischendorf, though with the same result) allows the editors to function with an apparatus that is both negative and positive. The use of different types of arrow to indicate ambivalent evidence and the removal of some information to a supporting fascicle are the other main new features. The sigla of the apparatus attain the greatest consistency and simplicity yet, with only numbers used for majuscules, and all others devised according to a single set of principles.

The success of this edition is due to its being an electronic edition, even if it is one printed on paper. It is an electronic edition because the print form was generated from a database. Considered from the point of view of electronic editing, the role of the critical text is interesting. If we consider both it and the International Greek New Testament Project volumes (see below), we might say that the function of the text given above the apparatus is as a series of hooks from which to hang it.

As an electronic edition, the *Editio critica maior*, particularly in its final fascicle of the Catholic epistles, contained an apparatus which was derived from transcriptions of the Greek manuscripts.

6.1.6.2 The International Greek New Testament Project

In the early 1990s the International Greek New Testament Project (IGNTP) editors had been feeling their way independently towards an edition which in one important respect was the same as an electronic edition: the presentation of the same data in multiple formats. This volume presents the data in three ways: as transcription, as critical apparatus, and as image. If we take the example of a particular witness, we can see how each presentation provides different information about it.

The transcription ☛ (43) provides the editors' reconstruction of the precise text of the witness, with diacriticals and any punctuation, line by line, with the difference between extant and reconstructed text clearly marked, and disagreements with previous editors noted. The apparatus ☛ (44) takes this evidence, sifts out the diacriticals and punctuation, and by using a section listing the lacunae in the manuscripts creates a negative apparatus, with all variants from the base text set out in their place. Finally, the plate ☛ (45) provides a check on the two previous presentations, as well as a display of the witness's appearance as an artefact.

Elliott and Parker, *Papyri*; Schmid, Elliott and Parker, *Majuscules*.

6.1.6.3 Marc Multilangue

Another edition currently in preparation is the *Marc Multilangue* Project, which has the goal of presenting the evidence for second-century forms of text, using Greek, Latin, Gothic, Coptic, Georgian, Armenian, Arabic, Christian-Palestinian Aramaic, Syriac and Slavic manuscripts. '*Marc Multilangue* does not aim to produce an edited text or texts. Rather, it aims to present the existing documentation in an attempt to enable the history of the changing text to be recognised.' The prototype pages provided in the article cited shows Mark 1.40–5, with Greek and Latin evidence. The Greek consists of transcriptions of the texts of six manuscripts (05, 032 and 038 followed by 01, 03 and 02), with an apparatus beneath. This is followed by a Latin prototype, consisting of the texts of manuscripts 2, 4 and 5, and an apparatus of readings in the other Old Latin witnesses. Finally, there is a French translation of each individual form of text. The preparation of the material follows traditional (rather than electronic) methods.

The project is described by three of its editors in J. K. Elliott, C.-B. Amphoux, and J.-C. Haelewyck, 'The *Marc Multilangue* Project', *Filologia Neotestamentaria* 15 (2002), 3–17. Quotation from p. 4, sample pages on 13–17. See also C.-B. Amphoux, 'Une édition "plurielle" de Marc', in Amphoux and Elliott, *New Testament Text*, 69–80, which is a description as much of the author's own textual theories as of the project. See also the summary of materials by C.-B. Amphoux *et al.*, 'Évangile de Marc. Recherches sur les versions du texte', *Mélanges de science religieuse* 56 (1999), 1–93.

In some ways the project shows affinities with the IGNTP papyri edition and older works such as Mansell, in the provision of complete transcriptions. But, unlike the former, there is no attempt to reproduce the formatting and layout of the manuscripts, the texts being provided with diacritical marks and modern punctuation. This approach also has some similarities with the electronic editions based upon complete transcriptions to be described in the next chapter. The translation of the Greek, Latin and other languages back into French raises two interesting questions. In the first place, it seems designed to allow scholars to move between the different languages, so that the French will provide a key for comparing, say the Greek and the Georgian, the two French versions differing only to show what the editors consider to be a difference in the Greek *Vorlage* of the Georgian. The second question concerns access to the data in a scholarly edition, since the French also makes the results of the research available to any interested Francophone, much as Walton's Polyglot was intended to interpret the versions for those not trained in oriental languages. The project is thus both a scholarly edition and an attempt to broaden access to the academic study of the texts.

6.1.7 Conclusion

This has not been intended to be an exhaustive survey. No doubt there remain other types of print edition I have not mentioned. I have tried to describe why we need critical editions, what they can achieve, and how they can do so. The next sections will discuss some practicalities of the edition in more detail.

The print edition has for some decades been straining under the weight of the modern critical edition. The rigour of editorial method and the sheer numbers of witnesses which have now to be cited in order to provide a full account of the history of the text are a severe challenge to traditional technology. As a result, the tried and tested technology is no longer the editor's first choice. That which is replacing it will be described in 6.4.

Once an editor has selected the format a projected edition is to take, there are further questions which need to be addressed. These include the status of disputed readings in a text and the question of the degree of detail which the edition should seek to attain. Both of these matters are of great importance to the user, who should always seek to ascertain what the editor has done.

On the former, see E. Güting, 'Der editorische Bericht als Kommentar zur Textkonstitution und zum Apparat in Editionen des Neuen Testaments', *Editio* 7 (1993), 94–108; on the latter, W. J. Elliott, 'The Need for an Accurate and Comprehensive Collation of All Known Greek NT Manuscripts with their Individual Variants Noted *in pleno*', in Elliott, *Studies*, 137–43. See further G. D. Fee, 'On the Types, Classification, and Presentation of Textual Variation', in Epp and Fee, *Studies*, 62–79.

6.2 THE PURPOSES OF EDITIONS

Editions are made for many different purposes. Take the example of a novel, Jane Austen's *Pride and Prejudice*. It exists in a number of different editions and formats: the hardback scholarly edition by R. W. Chapman (1923 and still in print), in his edition of all the works (there is a slightly altered hypertext version of this on the web at www.pemberley.com); numerous paperback editions including Oxford World's Classics and Penguin Popular Classics. There are also handsome volumes which may or may not be textually reliable (Chapman is both handsome and scholarly). They all serve different purposes, seeking to meet the different ambitions of different users. The critical edition, which goes back to the original sources, is essential, since between Chapman and the first edition is a chain of transmission going back to the work's completion in 1813 and the first edition (1813). A crucial point in this chain was the third edition of 1817, which confused the work by obliterating the original three-volume construction. Thus Chapman's edition is a significant restoration of the work's original printed shape. But in some ways it might not suit every modern user: a critical edition of a text may use the spelling and punctuation of important authorities, or archaic printing conventions. A paperback edition designed for the general reader might fail in its purpose if it followed suit, by placing unnecessary obstacles in the way. For example, the Chapman edition of Jane Austen uses catchwords, which would be out of place in a Penguin edition. In the same way, virtually all printings of the King James version of the Bible adopt modern spelling. This is true also of editions of Shakespeare (there are Wells editions in both modern and old spelling).

R. W. Chapman, *The Novels of Jane Austen. The Text Based on Collation of the Early Editions*, 5 vols. 3rd edn, 1932 (*Pride and Prejudice* is vol. 11); S. Wells, G. Taylor *et al.*, *William Shakespeare. The Complete Works*, 2nd edn, Oxford, 2005; *William Shakespeare. The Complete Works, Original-spelling Edition*, Oxford, 1986.

Rico, the editor of Don Quixote, suggests that the concept of the scholarly edition is a contradiction: 'either it is *scholarly*, or it is an *edition*'. He observes that a critical edition, especially a hypertext edition, interrupts the literary work at every word. F. Rico, 'Scholarly Editions and Real Readers', *Variants* 5 (2006), 3–14.

A reading text needs to be a good reading text, so its production will not be a mechanical matter, an editor having at every point to decide how to interpret and how far to alter the critical text.

The same variety of editions applies to the texts of the New Testament. Apart from the importance of translations in the public and private reading of the text, editions of the Greek and ancient versions are many, as the previous section made clear.

6.2.1 The printed scholarly edition, major, minor and in hand

The question was once asked at a scholarly conference how an *editio maior* differs from an *editio minor*. The only answer I could think of was that it is bigger. The *editio minor* is a reduction of an *editio maior*, in which the text is left unchanged, but the apparatus has been reduced (by either citing fewer witnesses or including fewer variants, or both) or even removed altogether. The prolegomena are also either reduced or excluded. The hand edition is a separate enterprise altogether. It is an edition which is convenient to handle and which cites its evidence in as compact a form as possible. Examples will help.

An example of an *editio minor* is von Soden's small version of his New Testament, misleadingly called a hand edition. Whereas his *editio maior* runs in all to 3,138 pages (2,203 of prolegomena and 935 in the text volume, of which 893 are text and apparatus), his *editio minor* (in a slightly smaller format) has 466 pages (434 being text and apparatus).

Von Soden; H. von Soden, *Griechisches Neues Testament Text mit kurzem Apparat (Handausgabe)*, Göttingen, 1913.

The Nestle–Aland and United Bible Societies Greek New Testaments are both hand editions, that is, they are convenient editions with an extensive but not an exhaustive apparatus. But they are not *editiones minores*, because neither is derived from an *editio maior*. Once the *Editio critica maior* is completed, it is currently intended that both will become *editiones minores* derived from it, with an identical text and their own smaller and more compact versions of the apparatus.

Sometimes the relationship between an *editio minor* and its parent is more complicated. The Wordsworth and White Vulgate *editio maior* is in three quarto volumes with a total of 2,140 pages. It contains full introductions, and text and apparatus not only of the entire New Testament text but also of the paratextual material such as chapter lists and prefaces. The *editio minor* has 620 duodecimo pages. However, the *editio minor* was published before parts of the *editio maior* had been started. Thus, only parts of it are an *editio minor*, the remainder being a hand edition.

What are the reasons for two editions together, *editiones maior* and *minor*? Commercially, a simpler spin-off improves the commercial success of a big edition. It also makes some of its achievements available to a wider public. The part which the *editio minor* makes available to the public is the critical text. The texts of the Cambridge critical editions of D. H. Lawrence's novels, for example, are available in popular paperback form. In terms of the improvement of the reading public's experience of the text, an expensive and large scholarly work is less likely to make an impact than a cheap and convenient copy.

A less convincing reason is that a scholar will find a hand edition more convenient even for quite serious work. It is true that most New Testament scholars today seem to spend their working lives using only a hand edition. But a hand edition will not necessarily be more convenient for a textual scholar, who is likely to spend as much time as possible working with the fullest sources available.

What are the risks of using a small edition? Simply, the scholar who uses nothing else will be missing a great deal of information necessary for a full and informed reading of the text. The historian, exegete or theologian (see 5.3.1–3) who uses only a small edition will be the poorer for it.

What is the ideal edition? For the *editio maior*, the plea has often been made for an edition which would contain all the variants in all the manuscripts, errors, nonsense readings, spelling errors, everything. The true electronic edition will provide that (see 6.4). But whether everything is included, or whether a selection is made by the editor in advance, a structure is necessary. A huge mass of data might be comprehensible to someone who has compiled it, living with it for a long period of time.

Anyone else needs signposts, or else has to be prepared to learn the routes
and put up their own.

What about the ideal *editio minor*? There are two things to think
about. In the first place, one may wish to use the one with the best critical
apparatus. Here, for the Greek text, there is a clear edition of preference,
the Nestle–Aland[27]. There are frequent reprintings incorporating new
data, and no other edition has so much information compressed into
so small a compass.

The types of edition described in this and the previous section serve a
number of different purposes. Sometimes a hand edition, or even a good
reading text, will be a suitable medium for certain types of reading
and study. On its own, however, the *editio minor* affords only samples
of material. No scholar should get into the bad habit of working always
with one single edition. Regular exposure to different editions, both
minor and major, is essential for all students of the New Testament.
Without it, they get used to a restricted number of variants and one form
of text.

6.2.2 The printed reading edition

This may be dealt with rather briefly, since it has become rather rare in
recent times. In the nineteenth century Westcott and Hort set out to
produce a good reading edition based upon good authorities, which could
be used in schools and colleges and by clergy, and this is almost what their
volume of text amounted to. There is no critical apparatus, except for a
few marginal notes of variant readings on each page. A smaller-format
edition without even these was also printed. Editions of the Received Text
have also generally lacked an apparatus and functioned as reading editions
(many were published until the later part of the nineteenth century). The
Trinitarian Bible Society's edition is a plain reading text (for both
see 6.1.5). Some editions with their own text had only a brief apparatus
(for example, the British and Foreign Bible Society's 1904 edition and
Souter's edition of 1910), so that they are best described as reading
editions. The same was true from the beginning of the Nestle edition,
whose apparatus has grown and developed into what it is today. The
United Bible Societies Greek New Testament also functions rather like a
reading edition, with the text divided into sections with English titles and
(in its earlier editions) a very readable typeface, although its apparatus
makes it into something of a hybrid, since it has few variants but detailed
attestation.

(British and Foreign Bible Society) Η Καινη Διαθηκη. *Text with Critical Apparatus*, London, 1904 (the text is based on Eberhard Nestle's first, 1898, edition); *Second Edition with Revised Critical Apparatus*, London, 1958 (a revision of the first by Erwin Nestle and Kilpatrick); B. F. Westcott and F. J. A. Hort (eds.), *The New Testament in the Original Greek*, London, 1885 and often reprinted. Pp. 541ff. contain an abridged version of volume II of the main edition; Souter[1], Souter[2].

6.3 THE PRINCIPAL PRINT EDITIONS AND HOW TO USE THEM

Major editions are not always easy to use. The apparatus may be written in Latin, and the editor may be bad at explanations. But reading even a difficult apparatus is a matter of practice, and the best way to learn how to use one is to take time to study it. Dipping into occasional readings will not achieve the same familiarity. Treat an apparatus as a very condensed story, and read it so as to expand it into something perfectly clear. One could do this by writing everything out in a narrative form.

Fortunately, others have provided guides to editions before me, and where these exist I will direct the reader to them.

6.3.1 Tischendorf's eighth edition

The *editio octava critica maior* was published in two volumes of text (the Gospels in the first and the rest of the New Testament in the second). Tischendorf himself provided a key in two forms. At the beginning of the first volume there are the following lists

sigla of majuscule manuscripts of the Gospels (pp. IX–XIV)
sigla of the versions (XV–XVI)
abbreviations for Church Fathers (XVI)
other abbreviations (XVI)
sigla for editions (XVI)

There is also a leaf without any number on either recto or verso which gives most of the same information again in summary form (in my copy, this is bound in immediately before the first page of text, but I suspect that its position may vary).

At the beginning of volume II (in my copy) are two unnumbered leaves, listing similar material under the heading 'Notantur interim'. These are

Four lists of sigla of majuscule manuscripts, referring respectively to Acts, the Catholic epistles, the Pauline epistles and the Apocalypse sigla of the versions

The other abbreviations and sigla are unchanged from the Gospels. It should be repeated that Tischendorf's manuscript sigla are not always in use today, in particular that the minuscule numbers are only likely to be the same for the Gospels (see 1.3.1). When working with Tischendorf in other parts of the New Testament, one of the conversion tables should be used. Tischendorf's apparatus is written in Latin, so even the list of sigla will be of little use to one who knows none. Usually, however, a small Latin dictionary will provide an explanation for the abbreviated words. Here is a list of those given in the first leaf of sigla, the three columns providing the abbreviation, the Latin word for which they stand, and the English meaning:

al	alii	others
aliq	aliquot	some
	aliquoties	several times
c.	cum	with
mu	multi	many
pm	permulti	very many
pler	plerique	most
pauciss	paucissimi	very few
et.	etiam	also
evgg/evgll	evangelistaria	lectionaries
rell	reliqui	the rest

One way of getting to know this apparatus is to study it in conjunction with one more familiar, comparing the ways in which the material is presented. However daunting it may appear initially, practice is all that is needed to make its study easy.

I take the example of Mark 9.2 (on pp. 303–4 of Tischendorf's edition). ☛ (46)

The first block concerns whether μετά or μεθ᾿ should be read, the difference being the scribal rule with regard to the form of μετά before an aspirated vowel. μετά is read by אB C D L Δ, that is by 01 03 04 05. The statement in brackets 'minusc non notati' means that the differences in minuscules have not been included. The support for μεθ᾿ is ς A N X Γ Π unc⁹ al pler. The letter ς (stigma, not to be confused with ς, the final form of sigma) stands for the Received Text, which (being a printed edition) is always placed before the reading; the other witnesses are 02 022 033 036 041, nine other majuscules (unc = unciales, Tischendorf's Latin for majuscules) and most other manuscripts, namely the majority of minuscules. If we go back to the first reading, we may infer that a small number of minuscules read μετά.

The vertical bar indicates that we move on to the second reading. Here he first gives an abbreviated form of the printed text, παρα-λάμβανει ὁ Ἰησοῦς, then states that A (02) changes the word order to ὁ ῑ̅ς̅ παραλάμβανει, giving the *nomen sacrum* as it is in the manuscript.

The third reading concerns τὸν Ἰάκωβον, read by 01 02 03 04 (vid means apparently, i.e. there is some uncertainty as to what precisely it reads) 05 019 022 041 nine other majuscules and most other witnesses (al pler); τόν is omitted by 033 036 037 and many other manuscripts (al mu).

The fourth reading is similar, and concerns the presence or absence of τόν before Ἰωάννην. Here a number of minuscules are cited in support of the reading including it (1 33 69 124 and 'al sa mu' (*alii satis multi*), which we might translate as 'plenty of other manuscripts'; it is omitted by Griesbach, Scholz, Lachmann and Tischendorf (his seventh edition; like the symbol for the Received Text, other editions are placed before the reading) and many other witnesses. The following symbol in brackets indicates an explanation with the double colon, the following 'll pp' standing for 'loci parallelli', namely parallel passages in other Gospels, so that we know that in his view the cause of the omission is harmon-isation to other Gospels where the word is absent (for harmonisation, see 10.10.2).

The fifth reading concerns the word ἀνάφερει. Two witnesses read ἄναγει: 05 and 2^pe. The latter siglum indicates one of the manuscripts in St Petersburg collated in the edition by von Muralt. The Gregory–Aland number is 565 (details of von Muralt's work in Elliott, *Bibliography*, *ad* 565). There is no place of reference that I know of to identify these ^pe numbers. Tischendorf then cites some Latin evidence for the alternative word. 'Latini: it ^pler vg *ducit* vel *duxit*, k* *inseruit*' means: Latin witnesses: most Old Latin witnesses and the Vulgate read either *ducit* or *duxit*, and the first hand of k (Codex Bobbiensis) reads *inseruit*.

The sixth reading may be made into the following narrative: 'To my reading ὑψηλόν (by the way, two Old Latin manuscripts, a and k, read *altum* and five others, f g^1 g^2 (it appears) l and q with the Vulgate have *excelsum*), manuscripts 01 52 124 and the lectionary 19 add λίαν, and similarly the Old Latin manuscripts b c ff^2 i n read *altissimum* [Tischendorf is indicating that the superlative form reflects the pre-sence of λίαν in the Greek *Vorlage*]. But there are several other variants to be considered: 52, 255 and L19 with the Sahidic omit κατ' ἰδίαν μόνους, six others omit μόνους, as do the Syriac in Schaaf's edition, the remaining Coptic and the Ethiopic. Of Latin manuscripts, b c f g^1 (apparently) i l² and the Vulgate render κατ᾽ ἰδίαν μόνους with *seorsum solos* (c has *secreto* instead of *seorsum*); a number of other manuscripts which have *seorsum solus* are listed as well as one with *solus cum solis.*'

The seventh reading concerns an addition. What Tischendorf writes is that before μετεμορφώθη (for which 05 reads τατεμορφώθη), 13 and some other manuscripts insert ἐν τῷ προσεύχεσθαι αὐτόν (565 reads ἐγένετο ἐν ... and some read αὐτούς), and we have a citation from Origen (3, 559 is the reference) which supports this reading. Finally the double colon is followed by the suggestion that this addition is from the Lucan parallel.

The verse ends with a citation from Origen bearing on the last two words of the verse.

No further proof of the conciseness that Tischendorf achieved is needed than the observation that it has taken me 750 words to write this commentary on seventeen lines of his apparatus.

6.3.2 Von Soden's editio maior

The Alands' handbook provides a description and an explanation of how to use von Soden's edition, with a sample page.

Von Soden. The Greek text and apparatus are in volume IV. Images of the entire work are available at www.csntm.org/PrintedBooks.aspx (but I could not find the preface to volume IV). Aland and Aland, *The Text of the New Testament*, 40–2. For references on tools for converting von Soden's sigla for Greek manuscripts into Gregory–Aland numbers, see 1.3.1. It is also helpful to know that von Soden provided a list of the manuscripts in his edition by the holding libraries (pp. 45–80, with an update on pp. 2137–40) which affords another form of cross-reference. He also (pp. 81–94) gives concordances between his sigla and those of Stephanus, Walton (the 'London Polyglot, 1657'), Fell (Oxford, 1675), Mill (Oxford, 1707), Bengel (Tübingen, 1734–), Matthaei (Riga, 1782–8), Birch (Copenhagen, 1788), Scrivener (the lower-case letters used separately in Scrivener's collections of collation of 1853, 1859 and 1893), and of Wettstein and his successors.

6.3.3 The International Greek New Testament Project's edition of Luke

The International Greek New Testament Project's edition of the papyri of John is simple to use and needs no special comment. The edition of Luke is a far bigger and more complicated edition, and it merits a few additional comments to what is provided in the explanation at the beginning, full and clear though it is.

Its character as a negative apparatus has already been noted (6.1.4.1). This means that (orthographic variation and nonsense readings apart) the text of every Greek manuscript may be reconstructed. This is because of the DEF sections in the case of manuscripts and the patristic index in the case of citations. The DEF sections (DEF stands for 'deficient') are of two types. One at the beginning of each chapter lists the witnesses totally lacking in it. Those in each verse list the witnesses which, while present at some point in the chapter, lack that verse. Where a witness is found in neither the chapter nor the verse list, the user knows that silence in the apparatus means that the witness follows the base text, and so can reconstruct the text precisely. The system also works well for Greek patristic citations which are treated as citations and not as adaptations. The patristic index for each verse lists the references to every citation of the work by an early Christian writer, indicating the first and last words of the base text to which the citation corresponds, listing more precise citations and adaptations separately. Inclusion in the index and silence in the apparatus again indicate support for the base text. But the system does not work so well for Greek patristic citations classed as adaptations and for versional evidence, since here silence in the apparatus does not necessarily mean agreement with the base text, but may indicate no more than uncertainty. It follows that this class of evidence must be used with care.

It should also be noted that there is one inherent difficulty in citing patristic evidence in every edition of the Gospels, and especially any of the synoptists, namely that it will not infrequently be impossible to determine which of them an author is citing. Of course either an explicit statement (unless the author is working from memory) or a context will clarify the situation (of course there is little question if the work is a commentary on a single Gospel). Otherwise, the doubt will remain. The Luke edition is generous in its inclusion of material, with the consequence that it is always worth checking it for possible evidence when studying a variant in another Gospel with a parallel to Luke.

One difficulty in working with this volume, which includes the readings of about two hundred Greek manuscripts in a negative apparatus, is working out which manuscripts support the base text. A simple solution is to make photocopies of the card insert listing all the witnesses, and each time one studies a variant to take one of these copies, write the variant at the top of the page, and cross out all the witnesses cited in the apparatus, including the chapter and verse DEF sections. The remainder will be those which support the base text.

Parvis and Wikgren, *New Testament Manuscript Studies* is a collection of studies produced as American scholars began work on the IGNTP. Further bibliography at www.theology.bham.ac.uk/parker/IGNTP/biblio.htm.

6.3.4 *The Nestle–Aland 27th edition*

One sometimes hears of teachers who are reluctant to introduce their students to anything in the Nestle–Aland beyond the text, ignoring not only the apparatus but also the accompanying materials, on the grounds that these things will be too difficult for them. This is mistaken. Understanding this edition is no more difficult than any of the other skills needed to become competent in biblical studies, and is easier than some – for example, the mastering of languages, complex exegetical questions and extensive bibliography. To use only the text block is not only to miss the chance to use other features but also fundamentally to misunderstand what is presented. This 'working text' is only comprehensible along with what goes with it. What features are there?

Both the table of contents and the Introduction are in German and English. The latter describes the edition and lists all the abbreviations and symbols in it. There is also a blue card insert which explains the abbreviations. Unfortunately this is currently in Latin, but future editions will provide them in either English or the first language of the country where a copy is sold.

After the Introduction comes Eusebius' *Epistle to Carpianus* and the Canon Tables (see 10.3.1). Between these and the first page of text is another table of contents giving the page number on which each book of the New Testament begins. Matthew begins on page 1, all previous pages having been numbered as 1*, 2*, and so on.

☛ (47)

Taking a double page of text, the following features are present. Predominant is the text block, in the largest type. Beneath it is the apparatus, indicating variant readings and the support for them. A system of symbols placed in the text block and repeated in the apparatus keys the variants into the text. In the outer margin are parallels to other texts (mostly but not exclusively biblical). The inner margin contains two features: the Eusebian apparatus, consisting of an arabic number above a roman one (see 10.3.1), and the standard κεφάλαια (chapters, see 10.3.2) in italic arabic numbers at the beginning of each new chapter. The same elements are found throughout (except of course that the Eusebian apparatus is confined to the Gospels).

The five appendices are the most neglected part of the edition – mistakenly, as my description will show.

Appendix 1 is a list of all Greek and Latin manuscripts cited in the edition. For the Greek manuscripts (pp. 684–713) it gives the

Gregory–Aland number, a date, the holding library, and the contents (by book, chapter and verse for the papyri, majuscules and some minuscules, with a dagger for other minuscules). The statement of lacunae for the extensive majuscules is fuller than the *Liste* provides, so the tool is useful for manuscript study. After the list (on p. 714) is a list of manuscripts represented by the siglum 𝔐 (i.e. the majority). The list of Latin manuscripts (in fact all are Old Latin) contains the same types of information (with the traditional letter and the Beuron number), in the sequence Gospels (715–16), Acts (717), Paul (717–18), Catholic epistles (719) and Revelation (720).

The second appendix (pp. 721–49) is headed *Variae Lectiones minores e codicibus graecis quos apparatus criticus in parenthesi exhibet* ('minor variant readings of Greek manuscripts which are bracketed in the critical apparatus'). Sometimes a manuscript is cited in the apparatus in brackets. This means that although it broadly supports the reading which it is stated to attest, it does not have precisely the same text. The precise text it has at this place is what is given in this appendix. This appendix is thus essential for a full understanding and for any really careful analysis of the text.

The third appendix (pp. 750–71) lists differences between some major editions (Tischendorf's eighth), Westcott and Hort (with their marginal readings), von Soden, Vogels, Merk, Bover and Nestle–Aland[25]. This tool is valuable on its own. If used in conjunction with Scrivener's edition listing the differences between the Received Text and Lachmann, Tregelles and Tischendorf one may chart the varying decisions of most of the important editions of the critical era.

The fourth appendix is, I suspect, better known. It is a list of all the references cited in the outer margins, arranged by work (pp. 772–808). Note that for the Old Testament it distinguishes between citations from Hebrew and citations from the Septuagint.

Finally, there is a list of all symbols, sigla and abbreviations, explained in Latin (pp. 809–12).

6.3.5 *The Vetus Latina*

The Vetus Latina edition looks more complex than it really is. This is because instead of having a single critical text it presents all the text-types at the top of the page. ☛ (48)

What is present is, first, the Greek text from the Nestle edition which was current at the time at which the volume was being edited. This is intended as a point of reference, not as a reconstructed Greek text behind any Old Latin version. Beneath are the text-types as they have been reconstructed, with the symbol » where they agree. Sometimes where there is variation between the witnesses to a text-type, the reading of one is set in smaller type beneath. There are then two blocks of apparatus. The first contains the variant readings and the manuscript and patristic support for them. The second contains the full text of all patristic citations, arranged alphabetically by author and work for each verse, with a reference to the edition as well as to the book, chapter and paragraph numbers of the work.

6.3.6 The Editio critica maior

The explanations for its use in the Introduction to James (in German and English) are comprehensive and clear, and there is little need to say more. Attention should again be directed to the further information (each text fascicle is accompanied by one containing 'Supplementary Material')

> lists of sigla
> lists of manuscripts
> further information about the Byzantine manuscripts and text
> further information about the lectionaries
> lists of lacunae
> lists of patristic citations
> further information about the versions
> an additional apparatus
> explanations of places in the main apparatus where witnesses are
>   marked as ambiguous

6.3.7 Synopses

Among the printed synopses, two should be singled out. One presents the same text and apparatus as the Nestle–Aland. The other is the modern replacement of the standard edition, Huck. This, edited by H. Greeven, attempts to pay particular attention to variants caused by harmonisation, and thus significant for the comparison of the Gospels. Neither is difficult to use, and this section will be restricted to two observations.

The first is to emphasise again the importance of using the apparatus. The extra effort of comparing two or three or four columns, each with the printed text of a Gospel, may seem enough. But the printed text is a version made by a modern editor, and to explore properly the way in which the Gospel texts were influenced by each other in antiquity, it is also necessary to be aware of the variants in the apparatus. It is the difference between working on paper and working three-dimensionally.

Second, one should not use only a single synopsis. Looking at another will provide a fresh perspective on the evidence. Greeven's text-critical judgements are not always the same as those by the editors of Nestle–Aland, and they should be considered.

K. Aland (ed.), *Synopsis Quattuor Evangeliorum, locis parallelis evangeliorum apocryphorum et patrum adhibitis*, 15th edn, Stuttgart 1996; 3rd corrected impression, Stuttgart 2001; A. Huck (ed.), *Synopse der drei ersten Evangelien mit Beigabe der johanneischen Parallelstellen. Synopsis of the First Three Gospels with the Addition of the Johannine Parallels*, 13th edn, rev. H. Greeven, Tübingen, 1981. Also to be mentioned are: J. B. Orchard (ed.), *A Synopsis of the Four Gospels in Greek Arranged According to the Two-Gospel Hypothesis*, Edinburgh, 1983 (introductory essay in English and German). This is an example of a synopsis based upon a particular solution to the synoptic problem. The theory that the construction of a synopsis is biased towards the literary theories of its editor is disputed. A. Poppi, *Sinossi dei quattro vangeli*, vol. 1. *Testo*, 14th edn, 2004, contains not a critical text but a lightly revised version of Codex Vaticanus, so that the comparison is between the different Gospels in a single manuscript. For a discussion of relevant issues, see G. D. Fee, 'Modern Textual Criticism and the Synoptic Problem; On the Problem of Harmonization in the Gospels', in J. B. Orchard and T. R. W. Longstaff (eds.), *J. J. Griesbach: Synoptic and Text-critical Studies 1776–1976* (SNTSMS 34), Cambridge, 1978, 154–69, reprinted in Epp and Fee, *Studies*, 174–82. See also 10.2.

6.3.8 Some other hand editions

Although the twentieth century has been increasingly dominated by the Nestle editions, there are some others which must be mentioned. The most commonly used is that produced by the United Bible Societies, now in its fourth edition. Conceived for the use of Bible translators, its apparatus gives more information about fewer variants. It presents the same text as Nestle–Aland[27].

The editions of Merk, Bover and Kilpatrick differ in that they are the work of individuals rather than of teams. They are of interest in presenting a different text, according to the views of their editors, and deserve study simply in order to observe different minds at work.

B. Aland, K. Aland, J. Karavidopoulos, C. M. Martini and B. M. Metzger (eds.), *The Greek New Testament*, 4th edn, 5th printing, 2001 [1st edn, 1966]; A. Merk, *Novum Testamentum Graece et Latine*, 11th edn, Rome, 1992 [1st edn 1933]; J. M. Bover† and J. O'Callaghan, *Nuevo Testamento trilingüe*, Madrid, 1977 (Bover's Greek text first appeared in 1943 and his Latin in 1974); G. D. Kilpatrick's incomplete edition appeared in a series of fascicles under the title *A Greek English Diglot for the Use of Translators*, London, 1958–64 (books edited were the four Gospels, General Letters, Romans, 1 and 2 Corinthians, the Pastorals and Hebrews). He was also responsible (with Erwin Nestle) for the second edition of *Η Καινη Διαθηκη*, London, 1958 (first edition, 1904).

For the manuscripts used by Merk and Bover, see the work by Elliott, *Survey of Manuscripts* (see 1.3.9).

6.4 CRITICAL ELECTRONIC EDITIONS

6.4.1 Their purpose and definition

The first section of this chapter presented a number of ways of editing ancient documents, and drew attention to their different strengths. It was seen that traditionally the diplomatic edition contained the most information for interpreting forms of the text found in individual manuscripts, and the critical apparatus the best synthesis and systematisation of all material. The ideal is an edition which combines these two approaches. This is achieved by the electronic edition. Basic to the concept is the complete transcription of all witnesses. The starting point thus brings together what have traditionally been two separate activities. This has the further result that the basic material, the transcription, will remain available for subsequent editors.

Setting aside the quite different mechanism of the electronic processor, we should compare the concepts behind the electronic edition with those behind the creation of the manuscript and the print edition. Comments on some of the strengths and weaknesses of the electronic edition in comparison with previous types of edition will be offered later in this section.

For a survey of the earlier stages in the adoption of computers in the field, see R. A. Kraft, 'The Use of Computers in New Testament Textual Criticism', in Ehrman and Holmes, *Contemporary Research*, 268–82. To his bibliography one may add K. Aland, 'Neutestamentliche Textforschung und elektronische Datenverarbeitung', in Münster *Bericht für die Jahre 1977 bis 1979*, 1979, 64–84, already indicating plans to use computer technology in the *Editio critica maior*.

But first of all, I should try to define what a critical electronic edition is not: it is not an on-line version of a printed edition. Many texts available on the web are simply that, electronic versions of print editions (often with no proper description of what it is). Sometimes they are no more than a pdf. Such a thing as this is a print edition where the onus of printing it rests with the end-user instead of with the publisher. This is the case whether such an edition is a machine-readable version of an edition first made available in print or has been made on and for the computer. By contrast, the critical electronic edition is a new edition made with electronic tools, containing the fully searchable text in which the primary evidence of the documents is the source from which the critical apparatus is generated.

I forebear to name any examples of an edition electronically available which is simply a pdf. Instead I mention a halfway house, an edition which is quite sophisticated in terms of what may be done with it, but which has been produced using the computer as a word-processor, namely the apparatus available with the Accordance software, produced in the Center for New Testament Textual Research, New Orleans Baptist Seminary (www.accordancebible.com/ and http://nobts.edu/ CNTTS/Default.html).

For a randomly selected example of a text made available electronically without any statement as to what it is, see the Latin Vulgate at www.fourmilab.ch/etexts/www/Vulgate/, which is simply headed 'Latin Vulgate' and described elsewhere as 'Saint Jerome's AD 405 Latin translation of the Bible' (at www.fourmilab.ch/). For the reasons why this statement is unsatisfactory, see 3.3.2.

Sometimes scholars express anxiety about the making of electronic editions, fearing that they may take critical decisions out of the hands of humans. This is not the case, since a critical electronic edition is no different from any other kind of edition in being controlled by the editor at every stage of its production. The computer may be used to generate certain kinds of output automatically. But the generating process and the output are always open to the editor's intervention.

6.4.2 Case studies

The following account is based upon editions made in the Institute for Electronic Editing and Textual Scholarship and in the Institut für neutestamentliche Textforschung. The software we use is not the only software available for making an electronic edition, and ours are not the only possible ways of working, but the projects are most of the major ones in progress. Most of them include either a critical text, or a critical apparatus, or both. One, however, is a uniquely detailed edition of a single witness.

All the following editions are based upon the same method. It begins with the transcription of the witnesses. Here the editions show slightly different interpretations of the distinction which W. W. Greg made between 'substantives' and 'accidentals', the first being the words of the text and the second its surface features. Each manuscript is transcribed twice. The Collate program makes a list of differences between the two, which are then reconciled to produce an accurate version. All the transcriptions are then automatically collated by the Collate program. This first rough collation will be accurate in terms of recording the differences, but unsatisfactory from the editor's point of view in how the differences are expressed. The editor will need to work through the transcription, making decisions which are then imposed on the software, with regard to determining the beginning and end of each unit of variation, and making a filter which offers the option of suppressing orthographical and non-sensical variants. Such an apparatus of variants forms the basis of what is visible in the editions listed below. Further stages may include the making of databases of patristic citations, and the exporting of the collation into a database so that the patristic and versional data may be added to the final apparatus. Of course, what is produced is a fully searchable electronic set of texts which make it possible for the user to study any word or form in any manuscript. In addition, the database may be used to conduct phylogenetic analysis of the relationship between the witnesses (see 5.1.5).

For the software used and the theory behind it, see P. M. W. Robinson, 'Is There a Text in These Variants?, in R. J. Finneran (ed.), *The Literary Text in the Digital Age*, Ann Arbor, 1996, 99–115; writings by Robinson and B. Bordalejo in publications of various texts (see www.itsee.bham.ac.uk/publications.htm).

6.4.2.1 The virtual Codex Sinaiticus

The significance of Codex Sinaiticus as a manuscript of the very greatest importance not only for the New Testament text, but in the history of the book, has already been discussed (1.1.2.3). Through the accidents of history between the 1840s and 1930s the manuscript ceased to be united in the place where it had been preserved for centuries, so that today there are portions of it in four locations (St Catherine's Monastery on Mount Sinai, the British Library, Leipzig University Library, and the National Library of Russia). The electronic edition makes it possible to bring together fresh digital images, an electronic transcription, a detailed physical analysis and explanation, commentary, and research in a single website, in fact as a virtual Codex Sinaiticus. The iconic status of this manuscript has justified a project which is testing to the full the opportunities offered by digital technology in a collaboration between the four libraries, with other partners responsible for parts of the work. Currently in development, the website will be complete in 2010. The Codex Sinaiticus Project transcription seeks to transcribe every meaningful ink mark on every page of the manuscript, the whole being linked at the line level to the digital images.

www.itsee.bham.ac.uk/projects/sinaiticus/index.htm. For digital facsimiles, see P. M. C. Robinson, 'Making and Publishing a Manuscript Digital Facsimile', in B. Plachta and H. T. M. Vliet (eds.), *Perspectives on Scholarly Editing / Perspektiven de Textedition*, Berlin, 2002, 127–49.

6.4.2.2 New Testament Transcripts Prototype and the digital Nestle–Aland

Münster's New Testament Transcripts Prototype presents transcriptions of up to twenty-six significant manuscripts, keeping their format with regard to page layout, including column and line breaks, but without including any other text such as running titles, and substituting nu for the superlinear line. The principal choices for the user are between viewing a manuscript transcription (either in its own layout or by chapter) and an apparatus based upon an automatic collation of these witnesses against the Nestle text, which will either display or conceal original spellings. The digital Nestle–Aland[28] contains the manuscript transcriptions from NTtranscripts, to which it adds the Nestle–Aland apparatus, a Printed Edition view and a small New Testament lexicon. There is also the potential to link further material to the symbols (e.g. references of patristic citations, versional readings).

This edition is planned to combine the degree of information about variants packed into the printed Nestle–Aland apparatus with the different kind of information provided by transcriptions of the leading witnesses. Users will be able to have the best of both worlds by comparing the apparatus with selected manuscripts.

http://nttranscripts.uni-muenster.de/; there is a guide at http://nttranscripts.uni-muenster.de/guide.html. For the digital Nestle–Aland, see http://nestlealand.uni-muenster.de/. Release is planned for 2008.

6.4.2.3 *The Principio Project's edition of the majuscules of John*

The Principio Project's edition of the majuscules of John has a higher level of information about paratextual elements than New Testament Transcripts, since it adds running titles, and some other layout features such as *ekthesis* and punctuation, but without Eusebian apparatus. This reflects its development out of the earlier edition of the Johannine papyri, as well as its relationship to the printed volume of the majuscules. Both the electronic and the print volume apparatuses were created by making an automatic collation of a full set of transcriptions, and then editing it. In the final stages of editing, the two forms of the edition were treated separately.

Schmid, Elliott and Parker, *Majuscules*, and www.iohannes.com. D.C. Parker, 'Manuscripts of the Gospels in the Electronic Age', *Restoration Quarterly* 42, 221–9; 'The Text of the New Testament and Computers: the International Greek New Testament Project', *Literary and Linguistic Computing* 15 (2000), 27–41; 'The Principio Project: a Reconstruction of the Johannine Tradition', in Amphoux and Elliott, *New Testament Text*, 21–9; 'Electronic Religious Texts: the Gospel of John', in L. Burnard, K. O'B. O'Keeffe and J. Unsworth (eds.), *Electronic Textual Editing*, New York, 2006, 197–209; Wachtel and Parker, 'The Joint IGNTP/INTF Gospel of John'.

6.4.2.4 The Gospel according to John in the Byzantine Tradition
The purpose of the Byzantine Text Project was described in 6.1.5. Technically, it was possible to achieve within its time frame because of its relation to the Principio Project. Some of the transcriptions are shared between the two (in fact the editors made their material available to each other), although the purpose, base texts and apparatuses of the two editions are quite independent. As with the edition of the majuscules of John, the print and electronic versions were generated together, but the final revision took place separately. The electronic version is able to provide all the evidence lying behind the apparatus, with a full set of transcriptions and the text of the patristic citations. This printed version has a claim to be the first New Testament edition to be produced from the basis of electronic transcriptions.

Mullen, Crisp and Parker, *John* and http://itsee.bham.ac.uk/iohannes/byzantine/index.html.

6.4.2.5 Vetus Latina Iohannes
The Verbum Project transcriptions of Old Latin manuscripts of John have a similar level of detail to those of the Principio Project, and in addition frequently include chapter lists and other prefatory material in the manuscripts. This electronic edition, consisting of transcriptions and an apparatus, is the foundation for further editions, one printed and one electronic: the former will be the edition of John in the Vetus Latina edition. The other will be the Latin component of www.iohannes.com. Materials too bulky to include in a print volume, such as the full texts of patristic citations, will be provided.

The Verbum Project: www.iohannes/vetuslatina/index.html.

6.4.2.6 The Virtual Manuscript Room
This tool will develop an area combining information about manuscripts of all kinds with images and links to further materials such as transcriptions. Developed jointly in Münster and Birmingham, it is conceived as a project with no limits: information about manuscripts of all kinds and of all texts will be eligible for inclusion. The concept is of an opportunity to bring together existing knowledge and create a structure for the addition of new information as it is gathered.

These editions could have been described at much greater length, but they are better understood by using them than by reading about them.

6.4.3 Advantages and disadvantages of the electronic edition

The advantages:

(1) Editors will no longer have to start again at the beginning every time previous editions become outdated (see 6.1.4.2 for the way in which evidence used to be compiled and 7.2 for the example of Tregelles' edition of the Apocalypse). By contrast, these editions can be updated by the addition of new manuscript transcriptions or the revisions of existing ones. It is also possible to use the same basic material (transcriptions) to make different editions (see the example of the IGNTP edition of the majuscule manuscripts of John and the Byzantine Text Edition). Likewise, the transcription of the New Testament of Codex Sinaiticus made in Münster for the Nestle–Aland[28] has been adapted for use in the Digital Codex Sinaiticus Project, and both compared with the transcription made for the John majuscules.

(2) We can use the structure of the software to produce more accurate editions. That is to say, mistakes in a web-based edition can be rectified without the need for a new printing or for a list of errata. (This is not an advantage which is necessarily part of the electronic edition, but of the web edition. A CD-ROM would still require a revised impression to remove errors.)

(3) The apparatus to the critical electronic edition allows the user access not just to the end result but also to all the basic data which the editor has collected, in the form of all the transcriptions of the documents. It is therefore transparent, in that the editorial decisions may be reviewed by the user. This also serves the purpose of providing the user with more information to help in understanding the material.

(4) Images may be combined with the transcriptions, so providing the user with the opportunity to assess the transcriptions on the basis of the material from which they were made, as well as offering also the opportunity to study the manuscripts. Such images should by preference be new digital images rather than copies of older surrogates.

The image is closely linked to the transcription in the editions of the Canterbury Tales Project, the edition for which the software described was first developed. See www.canterburytales project.org/.

(5) The transcriptions are modular in concept. That is to say, anything omitted (such as Eusebian numbers and canon tables, punctuation or

prefatory material) can be added to a transcription at a later date or by another user.

(6) The edition is built from a database which stands between the transcriptions and the output of the apparatus. Such a database makes possible the creation of sophisticated search and analysis tools. From this we can connect to other databases, for example online editions of early Christian writers, to broaden the context and accessibility of our work.

(7) The transcriptions are designed to be freely available to anyone wishing to augment them.

These are some advantages. But everything also has disadvantages. I point to two.

(1) The pioneering character of current editions makes them hungry of resources, and often the first achievements have taken longer than would have been required to publish a conventional print edition. But already improving tools and methodologies and greater experience are overcoming these problems. And the fact that the electronic edition is creating transcriptions which will be useful for longer should be set against the resources required to make them.

(2) A commonly raised uncertainty is the question of the long-term maintenance and survival of complicated electronic editions. The parchment codex is a fairly robust survivor in most conditions. Papyrus, which needs very dry conditions, does not do as well. We do not know how well the electronic edition will compare. In one respect it has the potential to survive in as many copies as a print edition. Since a manuscript is unique, the destruction of a single copy will be a significant loss. The preservation of multiple CD-ROMs and duplicate websites is much safer. It is not in this, but in its readability, that the danger may lie. Will today's media be readable in fifty years' time? The solution to such problems may lie partly with future generations, but today's pioneers of the critical edition must take their precautions. Every electronic edition should be made in a format that is universally agreed, marked up using the agreed standards of the Text Encoding Initiative (TEI, see 2.3, 2.5), with the additional conventions for New Testament manu-scripts and editions that have been developed in Birmingham and Münster.

6.4.4 Conclusion

Today's makers of critical electronic editions are pioneers. To future generations their efforts may appear rather inadequate. At present there are ways in which digital texts still mirror printed codices rather closely, just as the earliest printed texts look remarkably like contemporary manuscripts. It seems likely that in time the similarity will become fainter. In one respect the text in a computer has a technology which predates the codex: in the act of scrolling, it is a roll.

The practical demands of making critical editions of all kinds are great. There are added problems when one is making the first critical electronic editions. It is only possible when one has a team of researchers with complementary skills working within a well-conceived framework. There is a great need for cooperation. Here the formal agreement between the Münster Institut and the IGNTP to collaborate is essential to their achievements.

There is a risk in a pioneering period such as today's, namely that time and resources are wasted by small groups of scholars or individuals 'reinventing the wheel', and devising new software and methodologies. There is a better alternative to this approach. It is to join in with projects which are already under way and achieving results. If everyone interested in making editions were to throw in their lot with the methodology which has been described here, we would have within our grasp the possibility of making available machine-readable fully searchable transcriptions of at least the more significant documents of all periods of the manuscript transmission. We would also be able to use all the available resources for further development of the software as ideas and technology develop. This chapter ends therefore with a plea to everyone interested in making electronic editions: please seek partnership with the world's two leading New Testament editing projects: those of Münster and the IGNTP.

For a collection of essays on a wide range of issues, see Burnard, O'Keeffe and Unsworth (eds.), *Electronic Textual Editing* (a pre-print publication version is available at www.tei-c.org/Activities/ETE/Preview/index.xml); P. M. H. Robinson, 'What Is a Critical Digital Edition?', *Variants* 1 (2003), 43–62.

See also G. Bornstein and T. Tinkle (eds.), *The Iconic Page in Manuscript, Print and Digital Culture*, Michigan, 1998; J. J. McGann, *Radiant Textuality. Literature after the World Wide Web*, New York and Basingstoke, 2001; P. M. H. Robinson and H. Gabler (eds.), *Making Texts for the Next Century, Literary and Linguistic Computing* 15 (2000).

On Coptic texts, see T. Orlandi, 'Definition of Textological Data for Coptic Texts', in W. R. Veder (ed.), *International Data Bases for Medieval Manuscript Studies (Polata Knigopisnaja. An Information Bulletin Devoted to the Study of Early Slavic Books, Texts and Literatures* 17–18 (1987)), 96–105.

PART III

The sections of the New Testament

CHAPTER 7

The Book of Revelation

7.1 INTRODUCTION

There are several reasons why I begin with Revelation. In the first place, because there are fewer manuscripts of Revelation than of any other part of the New Testament, and because they and their relationships have been very fully studied, the materials are more manageable, and it will be easier to observe the nature of successful research. In the second, the section on the history of research with which this chapter begins functions as a microcosm of that of the whole New Testament. This is because the story of the text of Revelation from the Renaissance down is a simpler version of the same broad sequence of events. In the third, Revelation bears out one of the themes of this section of the book, namely that the genre of a text, its composition and the reasons for which it was both written and read have a direct effect upon the character of its textual tradition. It may not be coincidental that the relationships between the manuscripts of Revelation, a work which is in various ways unique among the New Testament writings, is defined in a different way from those of the rest of the New Testament. Certainly, one may see the influence of its genre on some of the textual variants discussed below.

7.2 THE HISTORY OF RESEARCH

See also the historical survey by J. Hernández Jr., *Scribal Habits and Theological Influences in the Apocalypse. The Singular Readings of Sinaiticus, Alexandrinus, and Ephraemi* (WUNT 2nd series 218), Tübingen, 2006 (pp. 10–48) which has appeared since I wrote the following pages.

The printed text of Revelation got off to a very bad start. It is a well-known story that Erasmus had only one manuscript available to him in Basle and that it lacked the last six verses of the book. He therefore had recourse to translating his Latin text into Greek. The resultant text of course has only accidental similarities with the forms of text present in the manuscripts (apart from his memories of any Greek manuscripts which he might have seen previously). It is perhaps less generally known that Erasmus suffered from a more general difficulty in using this manuscript: it is a commentary manuscript of the kind which contains the biblical text within (and indistinguishable from) the commentary text. ☛ (49) The result was that Erasmus was frequently unable to find the necessary Greek text (or the text which he expected on the basis of his Latin text) and made a retroversion on each such occasion. What is more surprising is that much of this retroversion survived in the Received Text. It was only with the critical editions of Lachmann, Tregelles, and Westcott and Hort that the text was freed from these oddities.

Erasmus' manuscript was 2814, a twelfth-century manuscript with the commentary of Andreas. Full details are provided by Schmid, *Apokalypse Kommentare* (see below, p. 239), 1–6. For the text of the last six verses in the edition of Erasmus, along with the Complutensian text and that of the editor, see S. P. Tregelles, *The Book of Revelation in Greek, Edited from Ancient Authorities; with a New English Version and Various Readings*, London, 1844, xxxv–vii.

Given such a start, it was never going to be very difficult for a critical editor to do better. The first steps were taken by S. P. Tregelles in 1844. We find him attempting to set the text of the book on a firm footing in two respects, first by verifying readings. He states that by collating the manuscript variants listed in a number of editions from Wettstein onwards, he was able to make a collection of forty thousand references to manuscripts (p. xxix). This work was a compilation of information from a number of late eighteenth- and early nineteenth-century collections of variant readings. It did not include a re-examination of the manuscripts. Secondly, Tregelles drew up a set of critical principles, based upon his study of the textual variants. He recognised already the importance of a principle which he expressed in these words: 'The authority of *ancient* MSS. (A. C.) is superior to that of the whole mass of *modern* copies' (p. xxx) (A = 02, Codex Alexandrinus; C = 04, Codex Ephraemi Rescriptus).

Tregelles was fortunate with 04 because, although he was dependent in his researches upon Wettstein's collation, he was able to use Tischendorf's transcription of it (Leipzig, 1843). Altogether, he drew upon three majuscule and 92 minuscule manuscripts. He also cited seven versions: Latin, in both Old Latin and Vulgate forms; Coptic (which dialect is unstated); Ethiopic; Syriac, in a version about which he could not be more specific, but thought 'may perhaps be assigned to the sixth century' (p. xxviii); Armenian; Arabic (using two versions, one found in Walton's Polyglot, the other in an edition of 1616); and the Slavonic. Almost all this information he seems to have taken from the printed editions of

Wettstein and Griesbach. The exception is for the Latin versions, where he also cited manuscripts from the edition of Matthaei, along with a collation of Codex Amiatinus which had been published in 1840, and one of the Vetus Latina manuscripts (65, cited from Griesbach's *Symbolae Criticae*).

There was thus a mass of information available from collations in editions, often very informative editions, by scholars such as Wettstein, Griesbach and Matthaei. The information was passed on, with no doubt a few errors removed and a few new ones introduced (for the reusing of collations, see 6.1.4.2).

Tregelles was right in treating 02 and 04 as significant, although it is worth pointing out that they were the *only* ancient Greek manuscripts available to him (01 was not yet known in Europe). This was noticed by Scrivener, who commented:

> As it is admitted on all hands that the text of the Apocalypse is less satisfactorily represented in our printed editions than that of any other part of the New Testament, I deeply regret that scholars should have published a revision of it, even within the last few years, without having previously sought to add to our existing store of materials, or at least to test their accuracy. (*Augiensis*, lxxviii)

Scrivener, *Plain Introduction*, 2, 184 and note 1 for a list of the Erasmian readings in 22.16–21. He also (p. 185) draws attention to places elsewhere in the New Testament where Erasmus did the same thing. Tregelles, *Revelation in Greek*, also provides a list of changes between the 1550 edition of Stephanus (which followed Erasmus) and the 1624 Elzevir edition, the first appearance of the 'Received Text', as the publisher was pleased to call it at his second edition of 1633.

Tregelles' edition was the first to break with the Received Text, Lachmann's edition of Revelation appearing in 1850. Tregelles edited the Apocalypse again thirty years later in the last fascicle of his better-known *Greek Testament* (1872). In this edition he used fewer manuscripts: five majuscules, including Codex Sinaiticus (from a collation made by F. H. A. Scrivener), along with 02 and 04, and eight minuscules, along with two Latin, two Coptic and a Syriac manuscript, with the Armenian and Ethiopic versions. Some patristic citations are also included.

In the improvement of information about readings, a major step forward was taken in the very same year with the second volume of Tischendorf's *Editio octava critica maior*. We regularly find forty minuscules being cited in support of a reading (not all by number, but some with such a phrase as al²⁰). There is extensive reference to citations in early Christian literature.

The edition of Westcott and Hort in 1881 presented a form of text very similar to those of Tregelles and Tischendorf, as may be seen from

Scrivener's extremely useful collation of five editions against the Received Text. Their discussion of the text of the Apocalypse (II.260–4) shows them attempting, with some difficulty, to find their categories of Neutral, Alexandrian and Western Texts among what they admit are 'new and troublesome conditions of evidence'. 'Not only is B [03] absent, but historical landmarks are obscure and familiar documents assume a new position' (p. 260). They conclude:

> We are by no means sure that we have done all for the text of the Apocalypse that might be done with existing materials. But we are convinced that the only way to remove such relative insecurity as belongs to it would be a more minute and complete examination of the genealogical relations of the documents than we have been able to accomplish, nor have we reason to suspect that the result would make any considerable change. (p. 262)

F. H. A. Scrivener, *Η Καινη Διαθηκη. Novum Testamentum Textûs Stephanici AD 1550*, Cambridge and London, 1877. The editions collated against it are Beza (1565), Elzevir (1624), Lachmann (1842–50), Tischendorf (1865–72) and Tregelles (1857–72), with the readings placed in the margin by Lachmann and Tregelles and in square brackets by all three critical editions (readings where they hesitated between alternatives also indicated).

Westcott and Hort's desired 'more minute and complete examination' was to be achieved, but not for many years. Two works were to achieve a proper understanding of the 'genealogical relations of the documents'.

The first was a task which, while it was easier for this than for any other part of the text, was nevertheless a signal achievement. It was H. C. Hoskier's weightily named (and weighty in bulk) *Concerning the Text of the Apocalypse. Collations of All Existing Available Greek Documents with the Standard Text of Stephen's Third Edition together with the Testimony of Versions, Commentaries and Fathers. A Complete Conspectus of All Authorities*, 2 vols., London, 1929 (usually known as *Text of the Apocalypse*). Hoskier's abilities as a critic were not great – his prejudices were too strong. But he was an accurate and well-organised collator, and it is for these qualities that his work is to be admired.

Hoskier is not alone, in the nineteenth-century scholarship to which his views belong or among writers of other times, in such observations as (discussing 241) 'by the Providence of God, our received text has come down fairly pure' (I.137). It is in other really surprising statements that the weaknesses of his views are shown; for example, on 2020, a late-fourteenth-century manuscript: 'The base of all is really old syriac. It has been tampered with a great deal, but it seems to derive from a MS or MSS having graeco-syriac-latin affinities of a very early date' (I.89). Throughout there is plenty of opinion, much of it unjustified, some of it general views on the New Testament or matters concerning belief. Even more unexpected is Hoskier's report of a form of text of 21.4 communicated by a medium (although he does add the phrase 'for what it may be worth'): 'the only example of which I have cognisance of spirit-communication from an entity who was a bit of a textual critic, or at any rate one who was acquainted with various readings' (1.xxxviii). Was he serious? How would one apply Lachmannian principles to readings arising from what he calls 'psychic (or intercosmic) phenomena'?

The work contains the following parts:

Volume I:

an Introduction of seventy pages, mostly unreadable, but with several useful lists, including one of 'Rarer Greek Synonyms' found in the manuscripts (pp. xxix–xxxii) and one of readings in the 'elder authorities' (papyri and majuscules) not found in any minuscule (xlviii–lxiv)

a Catalogue and Description of the Manuscripts, comprising two papyri (P18 and P24), nine majuscules (01 02 04 025 046 051 052 0163 and 0169) and 230 minuscules, a total of 241 manuscripts. Twenty manuscripts were listed but not used. The manuscripts are classified in groups. These groups are listed on pp. 7–12.

Volume II:

a critical apparatus of the witnesses, largely but not wholly Hoskier's own work (e.g. 385 and 522, see 1.56).

The most valuable parts of this are the manuscript descriptions and the apparatus. Probably the greatest weakness of the whole work is the organisation, above all the lack of any coherent explanation of his methodology in grouping manuscripts. Some statement of all this appears abruptly in volume I, pages xxxiiff. But none of it is easy to negotiate. In the light of later research, it is surprising that Hoskier paid very little attention to the grouping of manuscripts containing the Andreas Commentary.

Elliott, 'Manuscripts Collated by H. C. Hoskier', provides tables to convert Hoskier to Gregory and Gregory to Hoskier numbers. The twenty unused manuscripts are listed in J. K. Elliott, 'The Distinctiveness of the Greek Manuscripts of the Book of Revelation', *JTS* 48 (1997), 115–24, p. 123, n. 14.

The next important event was the discovery and publication of a new extensive ancient manuscript of Revelation, the Papyrus Chester Beatty III, numbered P47. The first transcription, by F. G. Kenyon, appeared in 1934, and a volume of plates was issued in 1936.

Research on the Greek text was advanced more dramatically by Josef Schmid than by anyone else. His most important contributions were published in two waves, in the early 1930s and in the second half of the 1950s.

His publications are best understood as a series (spanning thirty-seven years), dealing with all aspects of the Greek manuscript tradition: J. Schmid, 'Zur Textüberlieferung des Oekumenios-Kommentars zur Apokalypse', *Biblische Zeitschrift* 19 (1931), 255–6; 'Der Apokalypsetext des Chester Beatty ℌ047', *Byzantinische und Neugriechische Jahrbücher* 11 (1934–5), 81–108; *Der Apokalypsetext des Arethas von Kaisareia und einiger anderer jüngerer Gruppen*, Athens, 1936. The four-part article of 1936 is almost a monograph in itself: 'Untersuchungen zur Geschichte des griechischen Apokalypsetextes. Der *K*-Text', *Biblica* 17 (1936), 11–44, 167–201, 273–93, 429–60; 'Unbeachtete Apokalypse-Handschriften', *Theologische Quartelschrift* 117 (1936), 149–87; 'Der Apokalypse-Text des Kodex 0207 (Papiri della Società Italiana 1166)', *Biblische Zeitschrift* 23 (1936–7), 187–9; 'Die handschriftliche Überlieferung des Apokalypse-Ausleger und Oikumenios der Bischof von Trikka', *Byzantinische und neugriechische Jahrbücher* 14 (1937–8), 322–30; 'Die handschriftliche Überlieferung des Apokalypse-Kommentar des Arethas von Kaisareia', *Byzantinische und neugriechische Jahrbücher* 17 (1939–43), 72–81; 'Zur Textkritik der Apokalypse', *ZNW* 43 (1950–1), 112–28. Then come the three major volumes: *Studien zur Geschichte des griechischen Apokalypse-Textes*, vol. 1: *Der Apokalypse-Kommentar des Andreas von Kaisareia. Text*, Munich, 1955, *Einleitung*, Munich, 1956; vol. 11: *Die alten Stämme* (Munich, 1955). These three are discussed by Colwell, 'Origin of Texttypes', 50. Another early report and judgement is G. D. Kilpatrick, 'Professor J. Schmid on the Greek Text of the Apocalypse', *VC* 13 (1959), 1–13. The series of articles then resumes with three updates, one on Oecumenius and finally two on manuscripts not included in his previous studies: 'Der Apokalypse-Text des Oikumenios', *Biblica* 40 (1959), 935–42; 'Unbeachtete und unbekannte griechische Apokalypsehandschriften', *ZNW* 52 (1961), 82–8; 'Neue griechische Apokalypsehandschriften', *ZNW* 59 (1968), 250–8.

The most significant event since Schmid's last work has been the publication of a second extensive early papyrus, P. Oxyrhynchus 4499 (P115, see 7.3), which confirms his theories.

This history encapsulates that of the rest of New Testament textual research: a period of valiant attempts to produce a Greek text, based on limited resources and rudimentary critical principles (the sixteenth to seventeenth centuries); a phase of discovering resources in European, then African and Asian libraries (eighteenth to early nineteenth centuries), leading into a stage combining this with the development of critical methodology (second quarter of the nineteenth century onwards); and the discovery of more, often much older, manuscripts, interpreted on nineteenth-century critical foundations (twentieth century).

7.3 THE MANUSCRIPTS

First, some general comments are in order. According to Elliott, in 1997 there were 303 manuscripts of Revelation: 6 papyri, 11 majuscules and 286 minuscules. Since then, the number has gone up by three (one papyrus, one majuscule, one minuscule) to a total of 306.

Elliott, 'The Distinctiveness of the Greek Manuscripts of the Book of Revelation'; 'Manuscripts Collated by H. C. Hoskier'; see also 'The Greek Manuscript Heritage of the Book of Revelation', [no editor], *1900 Ετηρις της Αποκαλυψεως Ιωαννου*, Athens, 1999, 217–26.

Table 7.1

Century	Copies of Revelation	Number of all other NT MSS
II	1	1
III	1	35
IV	6	31
V	4	50
VI	0	71
VII	1	45
VIII	1	36
IX	2	68
X	15	130
XI	34	404
XII	29	559
XIII	27	546
XIV	64	475
XV	57	192
XVI	39	101
XVII	14	no figures
XVIII	5	no figures

The most obvious difference from other parts of the New Testament is that there are no lectionaries, for the simple reason that Revelation has never been a part of the Greek lectionary. The status of this text is further demonstrated by the fact that so many of its copies are part of collections of non-biblical material. For example, 2050 also contains a collection of ascetic sermons, writings of John Chrysostom, and eight other works; 2329 is bound up with Hippolytus on Daniel. The same applies to forty other manuscripts. According to Metzger, the material in these manuscripts includes lives of saints and theological writers such as Pseudo-Denys and Justin.

See Hoskier, *Text of the Apocalypse*, I.xxvii. For a summary list of the contents of thirty-seven of the manuscripts, see B. M. Metzger, 'The Future of New Testament Textual Studies', in McKendrick and O'Sullivan, 201–8, pp. 205–6.

It is also striking that there are a larger number of manuscripts of Revelation from the late Byzantine and early Ottoman period than is the case in the rest of the New Testament, as table 7.1 shows.

Half of the total number of manuscripts were copied between the fourteenth and the sixteenth centuries. The number of all other manuscripts of the New Testament from the same centuries is just under one third. The difference for the fifteenth and sixteenth centuries is even more marked – 96 for Revelation, 293 for the rest of the New Testament: one third of all such manuscripts compared with just over a tenth. The fall of the Byzantine Empire, with the ensuing Ottoman rule, was a traumatic period for the Greek world. The Book of Revelation, with its coded message of Christian endurance in a hostile world, became a valuable text, as may be seen from a number of commentaries produced in the early centuries of Ottoman rule. The fact that printing Greek books was very tightly controlled by the new regime ensured that manuscript copying continued. This is partly why Revelation, so scant in copies from every century but the fourth and fifth, seems – if the numbers of extant manuscripts is any guide – to have grown in favour slightly from the tenth century, more strongly from the fourteenth. Many of the later manuscripts contain a commentary, providing either a traditional interpretation if it was one of the three older commentaries (see below) or a veiled application of the text to the present circumstances if it was one of the new commentaries produced in the early Ottoman period.

The dates of manuscripts are taken from the chart in Aland and Aland, *The Text of the New Testament*, 82.

It is necessary now to say something about a few of the most important manuscripts. First, it should be reported that Codex Vaticanus is absent (see 1.8.1). There is a fifteenth-century supplement which replaces the missing portion of Hebrews and Revelation (which has been given its own Gregory–Aland number, 1957).

The oldest manuscript is P98, dated tentatively to the second century. All that survives is part of Chapter 1, verses 13–20.

P47, the Chester Beatty papyrus, remains the oldest of our extensive witnesses. The surviving pages contain 9.10–17.2 on ten leaves. It has the appearance of a quickly written hand, with a rather broad pen, and a tendency to run letters together. Highly calligraphic it is not, but it is very well set out, with a perfect left margin, straight lines and a regular right margin. The top of each page is damaged so that the first few lines are incomplete, and the bottom outside corner of the page has gone, but there are about fourteen complete lines on each page. There is little punctuation. A few corrections have been made. It is usually dated in the third century (with a question mark by Turner, *Typology*, 148). There seems to be no thorough palaeographical study of this codex.

The other important papyrus is P115, edited by J. Chapa and published with detailed palaeographical and textual notes and complete plates in 1999.

It is dated to the late third or early fourth century. It contains pieces of Chapters 2, 3, 5, 6 and 8–15 on nine leaves, all of them highly fragmentary. But it is often possible to form a judgement as to its text in variants consisting of longer inclusions or omissions of text by calculating the amount of lost text between the fragments. It is written in 'a medium size, right-sloping (sometimes upright), rather informal hand, rapidly but regularly written' (Chapa in Gonis, Chapa *et al.*, p. 10). This is much as I described P47, so far as the speed is concerned, but in execution this is a better hand altogether. As will be seen below, it is an important witness to the text.

N. Gonis, J. Chapa *et al.*, *The Oxyrhynchus Papyri 66*, London, 1999, 10–35 and plates III–VIII, XI–XII; D. C. Parker, 'A New Oxyrhynchus Papyrus of Revelation: P¹¹⁵ (P. Oxy. 4499)', *NTS* 46 (2000), 159–74; J. Chapa, 'Il Papiro 115: Qualcose in più del numero della bestia', in E. Bosetti and A. Colacrai (eds.), *Apokalypsis. Percorsi nell'Apocalisse in onore di Ugo Vanni*, Assisi, 2005, 311–33.

01, Codex Sinaiticus, has, as elsewhere, been extensively corrected, and these corrections play an important part in Schmid's reconstruction of the text. According to Hernández (following Milne and Skeat), the book has been corrected by Cᵃ, Cᶜ (only in Ff 325r–v, 1.1–3.5), Cᶜ* (7.11 onwards), as well as by correctors in the scriptorium.

02, Codex Alexandrinus, is a very important witness to the text of Revelation. The traditional definitions of 'Alexandrian', 'Western' and 'Byzantine' have been abandoned here in the face of Schmid's more precise definitions, and the reader who has any preconceptions that this manuscript is an early witness to the Byzantine text must abandon them forthwith.

04, Codex Ephraemi Rescriptus is a witness to the same form of text as 02. It was proposed by Lyon that the Apocalypse is written in a different hand from the rest of the New Testament. Not all of Lyon's proposed emendations to Tischendorf's work on the manuscript have been accepted, and this suggestion needs revisiting. At present it must be regarded as no more than a possibility.

R. W. Lyon, 'A Re-examination of Codex Ephraemi', unpublished PhD thesis, St Andrews, 1956; 'A Re-examination of Codex Ephraemi Rescriptus', *NTS* 5 (1958–9), 260–72.

These constitute our most important early witnesses. There are very few other majuscules. Complete are 025 (Codex Porphyrianus) of the ninth century, and 046 of the tenth. Fragmentary copies are listed in table 7.2.

All other manuscripts are minuscules.

Table 7.2

G.–A.	Century	Contents
0169	IV	3.19–4.3
0207	IV	9.2–15
0308	IV	11.15–16, 17–18
0163	V	16.17–20
0229	VIII	18.16–17, 19.4–6, a rewriting over a Coptic text
051	X	11.15–13.1; 13.3–22.7; 22.15–21
052	X	7.16–8.12

7.4 THE VERSIONS

7.4.1 *The Latin versions*

Our knowledge of the Latin tradition down to the end of the first millennium is now soundly based, thanks to the edition of the Vetus Latina. A fuller explanation here will illustrate the principles and significance of the edition as a whole.

R. Gryson (ed.), *Apocalypsis Johannis* (*Vetus Latina* 26/2), 2000–3.

The edition uses ninety-one manuscripts. Twelve are pure Old Latin witnesses: 51, 54, 55, 58, 74 (a single folio), 251, 259, 262, 271, 330, of which two are pre-Carolingian, 55 (h, the fifth-century Fleury palimpsest, containing fragments of Acts, the Catholic letters and Revelation) and 251 (the Luxeuil Lectionary written in about 700). 51 is the celebrated Codex Gigas (see 1.8.9).

A few manuscripts have a mixed text (forms of text containing both Old Latin and Vulgate readings), including 51. Only three witnesses with a Beuron Vetus Latina number (51, 54 and 58) are complete, with the consequence that the editor of the text is heavily dependent upon citations in works of Latin writers. More than 230 such writings are cited.

The editors find eight Old Latin text-types, and three mixed types. The Old Latin are placed in four groups as

(1) **X** (Tertullian) and **Y** (Victorinus)
(2) **K** (55 and Cyprian), **C** (lemmata of Primasius' commentary), and **A** (the replication of Primasius in Augustine, *De Civitate Dei*, 20.1–21.5a only). These are all African.

(3) **S** (the text of Tyconius' commentary), for which Caesarius is also important, and which some of the later exegetical tradition also attests.

(4) **I** and **J** are European texts, produced by revision against Greek evidence. **I** represents the text of Codex Gigas (included in the apparatus only from 2.13, since it is Vulgatised at the beginning). **J** is a late form of **I**, found in the lemmata of an early-sixth-century form of Victorinus' commentary (which had lacked lemmata in its first form). **J** appears in Chapter 1 and is also used for later citations by European authors which are not certainly Type **I**.

The Vulgate text (**V**) used is that of the Stuttgart edition. The alternative would have been the Wordsworth and White edition, which follows the text of White's *editio minor*. But Gryson considers it to rest upon too narrow a base and to contain unconvincing textual decisions (*Apocalypsis Johannis*, p. 90). The older Vulgate copies are Codices A (Amiatinus, early eighth century), F (Fuldensis, finished 547), and G (Monte Cassino, Arch. della Badia 271 K, around 700). Of these G is the least contaminated by Old Latin readings, although it loses value by being rather carelessly copied. Altogether the edition finds seventeen types of Vulgate text.

The mixed types are **T**, **G**, **D**. All come from remoter parts of Latin-speaking Christendom. **T** represents the Spanish tradition, which maintained its connections with North Africa when the rest of Europe had lost contact, and whose liturgical tradition was conservative. **G** stands for north-east Gaul in the pre-Carolingian period. Here there is the influence of a mixed text with Old Latin readings from various traditions, as well as readings which agree with Greek witnesses. Third, Old Latin readings in D, the Book of Armagh (early ninth century) are classed as **D**.

In spite of this variety of groupings, most of the text-types can only be partially reconstructed. There are rarely more than three text-types attested in the apparatus. These are usually **C** or **K**, **S** and **I**, with **V** as a constant.

7.4.2 *The Syriac versions*

There is no evidence of any translation of the Apocalypse into Syriac before the making of the Philoxenian version in 508. Thus there is no Old Syriac version and no Peshitta. The Philoxenian was first published in 1897 from a single copy.

J. Gwynn (ed.), *The Apocalypse of St John, in a Syriac Version Hitherto Unknown*, Dublin, 1897. The text is printed in the more commonly available British and Foreign Bible Society's *The New Testament in Syriac*, London, 1919. For information on manuscripts, see Clemons, *Index of Syriac Manuscripts*.

The book is also extant in the Harklean version, which has not been critically edited, although it was printed long before the Philoxenian, having been published from a manuscript in Leiden University Library in 1627 and included in subsequent editions of the Syriac New Testament. The case for the identification of this version with the Harklean was set out by Gwynn in his edition of the Philoxenian: the essential point is that a manuscript of the same translation in Florence (Bibliotheca Laurenziana 724) contains a colophon stating that the preceding text is the Harklean version.

Ludovicus de Dieu (ed.), *Apocalypsis Sancti Johannis ex Manuscripto Exemplari e Bibliotheca Clariss. Viri Iosephi Scaligeri deprompto* etc., Leiden, 1627. For a study of the Harklean see I. R. Beacham, 'The Harklean Syriac Version of Revelation: Manuscripts, Text and Methodology of Translation from Greek', unpublished PhD thesis, University of Birmingham, 1990. The identification of the two versions is vigorously defended by Zuntz, *Ancestry*, 19, 45, n. 2 (also citing other literature).

7.4.3 *The Coptic versions*

The material here is even slighter. The Biblica Coptica lists only one manuscript (sa 519), which has been variously dated between the fourth and sixth centuries. There are also Sahidic lectionary manuscripts (for example, Vienna, Austrian National Library, K 2658 + 9723 + 9724).

Horner, *Northern Dialect*, vol. IV.

7.5 THE COMMENTARIES

The majority of minuscules are closely associated with the commentary tradition. There are three commentaries from the first millennium. The oldest extant is by Oecumenius (*CPG* III.7470), about whom little is known. He appears to have been a contemporary of Severus of Antioch (*c.* 465–538), so the commentary may be fairly safely dated to the first half of the sixth century. The commentary became known to western scholarship in modern times (the report describing it was published in 1901). The latest editor lists nine principal manuscripts of the commentary, and another twenty-nine partial witnesses. Of the twenty-nine, some overlap in contents with manuscripts of the two other commentaries shortly to be described.

F. Diekamp, 'Mitteilungen über den neuaufgefundenen Commentar des Oekumenius zur Apokalypse', *Sitzungsberichte der preussischen Akademie der Wissenschaften zu Berlin* 43 (1901), 1046–56; M. de Groote (ed.), *Oecumenii Commentarius in Apocalypsin* (Traditio Exegetica 8), Leuven, 1999.

Oecumenius' comments are not the oldest extant ones on the book. There is a collection of longer and shorter notes on difficult passages drawn from the writings of Clement of Alexandria, Irenaeus and Origen (*CPG* I.1468). The surviving fragments were published under a somewhat misleading title by C. Diobouniotis and A. Harnack, *Der Scholienkommentar des Origenes zur Apokalypse Johannis* (TU 38.3), Leipzig, 1911. For details and further bibliography, see Quasten, *Patrology* II.46 and *CPG* I.167.

The most common commentary, found in approximately one third of all the minuscules of Revelation (some lack the commentary but their text is of the kind on which the commentary was written), is that by Andreas (*CPG* III.7478), written when he was Archbishop of (Cappadocian) Caesarea (563–614). Schmid lists III manuscripts; 83 are in the commentary's original form, which he divided into twelve groups (nine manuscripts, including 025, could not be grouped). There are thirteen manuscripts of an abbreviated version of the commentary, and fifteen which contain scholia. Schmid drew up stemmata of the groups and related them to each other. As a result of this study of the textual history he was also able to reconstruct in considerable detail the text used by Andreas when he was writing the commentary. So, although so many of these manuscripts were copied in the fifteenth and sixteenth centuries, they are valuable witnesses to a late sixth-century form of the text.

The third commentary is that of Arethas of Caesarea (*c.* 860–after 932). Schmid lists fifteen manuscripts (*Biblica* 1936, 13; *Die alten Stämme*, 27).

Arethas made use of Andreas' work, as Andreas had of Oecumenius' work (de Groote provides a synopsis of parallels). The commentaries of the early Ottoman period make use of this ancient tradition, in particular of Andreas. Manuscripts of these later commentators are ignored by the *Liste*, with the partial exception of Maximos of the Pelopponese (died *c.* 1630). His writing is known from four manuscripts, of which two are in the *Liste* (2114 and 2402, both now bracketed; a third, Athos, Iviron 605, had the old Gregory number 173 and the fourth is Athos, Panteleimon 556).

Schmid, *Andreas von Kaisareia. Einleitung*, 97–8; A. Argyriou, *Les exégèses grecques de l'Apocalypse à l'époque turque (1453–1821). Esquisse d'une histoire des courants idéologiques au sein du peuple grec asservi* (Εταιρα Μακεδονικων Σπουδων Επιστημονικαι Πραγματειαι, Σειρα Φιλολογικη και Θεολογικη 15), Thessaloniki, 1982. The other exegetes studied by Argyriou are Zacharias Gerganos (died a little after 1631), Christophoros Angelos (*c.* 1575–1638) and George Koressios of Chios (*c.* 1570–1633).

Further commentaries of the period and later are, so far as I am aware, not included in the *Liste* and do not provide any contribution to our knowledge of earlier forms of the text.

There is also a well-defined tradition of Latin commentary writing, in which similar dependence of later writers on their predecessors may be observed. The work by the Donatist Tyconius was written in about 400 (*CPL* 710). Next (around 550) comes Primasius (*CPL* 873; Stegmüller, *Repertorium*, 6988). From the eighth century come three important commentaries: Bede's made in about 703–9 (*CPL* 1363, Stegmüller, *Repertorium*, 1640); from the middle of the century we have an anonymous Irish work falsely attributed to Isidore of Seville (*CPL* 1221; Stegmüller, *Repertorium*, 3461, 5271) and from about 785 the commentary of Beatus (Stegmüller, *Repertorium*, 1597). Berengaudus wrote around the middle of the ninth century (Stegmüller, *Repertorium*, 1711; cited by Hoskier as Pseudo-Ambrose).

R. Gryson, 'Les commentaires patristiques latins de l'Apocalypse', *Revue théologique de Louvain* 28 (1997), 305–7, 484–502.

7.6 THE TEXT FORMS

At the end of his researches Schmid concluded that there are two ancient text forms, and two more modern ones. The two older forms he found were represented by P47, 01 and Origen, and 02, 04 and Oecumenius (to which P115 has now been added). This second form is superior. The two more recent forms are the Andreas text and the K-Text. The latter was von Soden's name for a large group of Byzantine manuscripts. Schmid (in his 1936 *Biblica* articles) placed the eighty-seven manuscripts in eighteen groups (the number in each is to be augmented from his later work). In this volume and in his study of Andreas, Schmid grouped two thirds of the manuscripts. The value of this work may be seen from the crowning volume of his work, *Die alten Stämme*. In more detail, the support for the different forms is as follows:

P47/01 text:
  P47 01 0169 0207

02/04 text:
  P18 P24 P115 02 04 0163 (and 025 has a layer of readings of this text)
  Oecumenius' text (best represented in 2053 2062)

Minuscules with an old text form (following neither consistently) grouped (*Die alten Stämme*, 24f.) as:

911 (cited by Schmid as 2040) 1006 1841
1611 1854 2329 2050 2344
2351 2030 2377 and 792 (this last has a layer of K readings)

Andreas:
manuscripts with the commentary text as detailed above (7.3) (111 manuscripts)
Georgian version

K-Text:
other minuscules as detailed above (87 manuscripts)

Mixed Andreas and K-Text groups:
Arethas' text (15 manuscripts)
Family 104/336 (10 manuscripts)
The Complutensian Group (36 manuscripts)
Family O (13 manuscripts)

Of the minuscules with an old text form, 2053 and 2344 are most highly rated. For each of his forms of text, Schmid provides a list of typical readings with comments.

It was observed at the beginning of this chapter that the relationships between the manuscripts of Revelation may be expressed in a different way from those of the rest of the New Testament. The difference lies in the way in which Schmid has set them in groups, and in particular in the way in which he expressed the relationship between the two ancient groups. By observing how this relationship may be applied to the practical problems of finding the form of text from which the others are descended in each place of difference, much may be learned about the practice of textual criticism.

7.7 TEXTUAL CRITICISM

7.7.1 General considerations

Where the manuscripts group as consistently as do those of Revelation, the task of determining the reading from which the others are derived proceeds in two ways. In the first place, the reading of each form of text is noted. For example, the agreement of the members of the two old groups (P47/01 and 02/04) against Andreas and K would immediately provide a good argument in favour of their reading. If, on the other hand, one found one of the old groups and one of the later on each side of the case, one would be driven to internal evidence, that is, the question as to which of the two readings seemed more likely to be secondary. For example, a grammatically superior reading is likely to be an attempt to make a better reading text. The study of the quality and character of readings across the entire book leads to the opportunity to comment on the overall quality and character of each text form. Schmid concludes that the 02/04 text (for which we also now have P115) is the best form, once its errors have been eliminated, and that 02 is a superior witness to 04. For example, at 18.3 02 04 Oec 1611 omit τοῦ οἴνου, an error described by Schmid as blatant carelessness (*Die alten Stämme*, p. 93). Of course, not all the main witnesses of this form of text are complete, and where P115 and 04 are absent, one has to make decisions on the basis of 02 and the minuscules.

The manuscripts containing the two old forms of text do not always agree with each other, and where they split up, perhaps agreeing with another group, the situation has to be weighed again. Schmid lists the places where 02 and 04 differ, and to this I have added the places where P115 agrees with both, one or neither of these two. The role of P115 in assessing readings where 02 and 04 differ is particularly important, since its age gives it a certain claim to be taken seriously until it is found wanting. In my assessment, P115 and 02 almost always have a better form of text when they agree against 04, while P115 and 04 are right about half the time when *they* agree against 02.

A large part of Schmid's second volume is taken up with a study of linguistic usage in the book. This is another important part of the foundation for a critical edition of the text.

See also G. Mussies, *The Morphology of Koine Greek as Used in the Apocalypse of St John. A Study in Bilingualism* (NovTSuppl 27), Leiden, 1971.

7.7.2 The number of the beast

The variant reading at 13.18 is particularly interesting for several reasons. Apart from its intrinsic exegetical fascination, it poses an unusual problem for the textual critic, in that the best way of applying internal criteria is not obvious when the writer has intentionally concealed his meaning. As a variant discussed by an early Christian writer, it also gives us the opportunity to assess ancient attitudes to such problems.

What is the number of the beast? Six hundred and sixty-six is enshrined in the millenarian fantasies of two millennia. This is because it is the reading of the Andreas and K Texts, and thus of the great majority of copies, so that it is better known. Nineteenth- and twentieth-century discoveries brought us also the P47/01 text to support it (actually P47 is not extant here, so only 01 provides evidence that it was the reading of this text as well). But the same centuries also brought two new members of the 02/04 text. The oldest known member of the group, 02, supports the same reading. But the other two provided the first manuscript evidence for another reading, 616. This variant was already known, since Irenaeus, Bishop of Lyons between about 178 and 200, discussed the alternatives and their meanings in Book Five of his work *Against the Heresies*. It is worth quoting his discussion at length:

I do not know how it is that some have erred following the ordinary mode of speech, and have changed the middle number in the name, deducting fifty from it, so that they have a one instead of a six. Others then received this reading without examination; some in their simplicity, and upon their own responsibility, making use of this number expressing one decad; while some, in their inexperience, have ventured to seek out a name containing the wrong and false number ... [3.] ... There are many names which have this number; which of them the coming one will bear, it is to be asked. But we will not take the risk of making a positive identification of the name of the Antichrist; for if it had been necessary that his name should be unmistakably revealed in this present time, it would have been spoken by the seer of the apocalypse. (5.30.1–3; my translation from the Greek)

J. N. Birdsall, 'Irenaeus and the Number of the Beast. Revelation 13,18', in *Festschrift Delobel*, 349–59. Irenaeus, *Libros quinque adversus haereses*, ed. W. W. Harvey, 2 vols., Cambridge, 1857, II.406–9. Cited in Eusebius, *History of the Church*, 3.18 and 5.8. The Latin translation is fuller, and includes explanations of the two numbers. In Irenaeus' view, the cause of the number 616 was a misreading of ξ as ει.

It is clear that even by the time of Irenaeus there were two well-known forms of the text, or he would not have spent so much time and insisted so strongly on the accuracy of his preference for 666.

Further versions of the number are found in the Latin versions: 617 is read as a variant in the text of the anonymous Irish commentary; 646 is the reading of text-type **D** and two variants in the anonymous Irish commentary (by *metathesis* notes the editor); a variant in Caesarius of Arles (died 542) reads 690. The editor treats this as a subvariant of the reading in text-type **I**.

The application of criteria for selecting the most probable reading when the writer intentionally avoided a self-evident meaning requires the use of historical judgement. The number 616 could be applied, by the ancient practice of gematria, in which letters of names are given a numerical value in order to bring out their symbolism, to the Emperor Gaius (Caligula). His name might have been selected because his attempt to have his statue erected in the Jerusalem temple represented the ungodly power of the Roman state. The number 666 can be interpreted as referring to Nero, whose persecution of Roman Christians after the Fire of Rome might have made him a more obvious choice. Moreover, 666 (both in its repetition of 6, which as one short of the perfect number 7 represents its antithesis, and because it is a triangular number) is more striking than 616. It is probably the fact that it is so much more dramatic that leads one to suppose that an original 616 was replaced by 666 than the reverse. The details of the application of each number will always be a matter for debate (which we may assume was the writer's intention).

7.7.3 Other readings

Among many readings from Revelation which contain interesting text-critical challenges, a few may be selected. At 1.5 the variant offers the choice between λύσαντι and λούσαντι. The words look similar, but phonetically have no connection, so that the possibility of confusion is less than one might at first suppose. Here the fact that the three extant main representatives of the two texts (01 02 04) favour the former provides a good reason with regard to the history of the text since, where they agree, one is justified in using the argument that they represent the oldest form of the text. The variant λούσαντι is intelligible as a change caused by the rest of the sentence, since being washed in the blood of the lamb might be suggested by 7.14. Here an idea attractive to a later reader has to be rejected by the modern editor as too attractive to be plausible.

At 4.3 there is again a choice between two readings which look similar on the page: is the throne encircled by an ἶρις or by ἱερεῖς? The latter is the reading of 01* 02 2329 and a few other manuscripts. Again we have representatives of both texts (04 is not extant). Schmid dismisses ἱερεῖς as an obvious scribal error (*Die alten Stämme*, 73), presumably one suggested by the next verse. Again the text seems to have been influenced by an idea in the wider context. A further explanation may lie in the custom from the time of Constantine (for example, at the Council of Nicaea) of priests to stand around the imperial throne.

Schmid discusses a large number of variants in which the grammar of the work has been improved. The result of this is that the form of text as we now have it is far rougher than the version known in the Byzantine and subsequently the Received Text. It is easy to see how a poor piece of writing or a solecism may have been replaced by a reader or perhaps by a copyist suspecting an error in his exemplar. An example appears at the very beginning, in 1.15. We have the following:

οἱ πόδες αὐτοῦ ὅμοιοι χαλκολιβάνῳ ὡς ἐν καμίνῳ πεπυρωμένος

The last word is read thus in 02 04. The variants are

πεπυρωμένῳ 01 2050 2053 2062 pc
πεπυρωμένοι Andreas' text and the majority of manuscripts

In spite of Schmid's hesitation (*Die alten Stämme*, 245) the second and third reading may be interpreted as false corrections of the difficult πεπυρωμένος, which would then be a reading intending the meaning of the 01 reading but failing to attain it.

The study of these and other problems in the Apocalypse is a good starting point for the practice of New Testament textual criticism: one is not overwhelmed by the evidence, and the causes of the variants are frequently easy to determine. A good way of building up one's critical skills would be by a careful study of the apparatus in Nestle–Aland, referring also to Hoskier's apparatus and Schmid's comments. Someone who has done this will then be in a good position to understand the more complex situations in the rest of the New Testament.

CHAPTER 8

Paul

8.1 INTRODUCTION

The textual criticism of the Pauline corpus, as this letter-collection is generally called, is inseparable from questions of the development and transmission of the collection. The key research questions are the following:

(1) What are the origins of the process of collection?
(2) Do they begin with Paul himself?
(3) How many collections were there in the second century?
(4) What is the relationship between the text of the letters as they are found in the collections and the text of the letters as they circulated independently?
(5) What light does a study of the role of Paul's amanuenses cast on the early history of his letters?

It is not hard to see ways in which these questions are relevant to other matters in the study of Paul's letters. The questions surrounding the formation of the corpus necessarily concern the relationship between the genuine and the deutero-Pauline letters. But to treat them as identical issues would be to assume that our interests and those of the ancients were identical. The fact that Hebrews, a letter which today is universally agreed not to be by Paul, appears in some collections at quite an early date, is a warning against doing so. Another topic of importance to all is the study of the possible role of Paul in the formation of the collection, with the attendant possibility that he was responsible for revision of the text of the letters. If established, this would raise the further possibility that there might be places where two forms of the text were both Pauline. The question about Paul's amanuenses may be relevant to such matters as the consistency of his style and the degree to which he oversaw the detail of his letters.

For a recent comment on the way in which many different Pauline questions should overlap – but rarely do – see S. E. Porter, 'When and How Was the Pauline Canon Compiled? An Assessment of Theories', in S. E. Porter (ed.), *The Pauline Canon* (Pauline Studies 1), Leiden and Boston, 2004, 95–127, p. 95: 'I find it perplexing to note just how little significant insight into this overlap there is in the scholarly discussion.'

8.2 THE WRITING OF THE LETTERS

Although this is not always regarded as a topic appropriate to an introduction to the textual study of the letters, there are good reasons why such a survey as this should begin with the role of the scribe in the production of Paul's letters. In the first place, the study of the way in which the letters were produced is important for an understanding of the formation of collections of the letters. In the second place, it gives the opportunity to study scribal activity so far as the creation rather than the transmission of texts is concerned. The following section will thus present some of the questions which occur to the textual scholar concerning the way or ways in which Paul may have produced his letters.

There are a number of references in Paul's letters which cast light on the process by which he produced them (all citations taken from Nestle–Aland[27]):

2 Thessalonians 3.17: Ὁ ἀσπασμὸς τῇ ἐμῇ χειρὶ Παύλου, ὅ ἐστιν σημεῖον ἐν πάσῃ ἐπιστολῇ· οὕτως γράφω.

1 Corinthians 16.21: Ὁ ἀσπασμὸς τῇ ἐμῇ χειρὶ Παύλου.

Galatians 6.11: Ἴδετε πηλίκοις ὑμῖν γράμμασιν ἔγραψα τῇ ἐμῇ χειρί.

Romans 16.22: Ἀσπάζομαι ὑμᾶς ἐγὼ Τέρτιος ὁ γράψας τὴν ἐπιστολὴν ἐν κυρίῳ.

Colossians 4.18: Ὁ ἀσπασμὸς τῇ ἐμῇ χειρὶ Παύλου.

Philemon 19: Ἐγὼ Παῦλος ἔγραψα τῇ ἐμῇ χειρί.

1 Thessalonians 5.27: Ἐνορκίζω ὑμᾶς τὸν κύριον ἀναγνωσθῆναι τὴν ἐπιστολὴν πᾶσιν τοῖς ἀδελφοῖς.

Colossians 4.16: καὶ ὅταν ἀναγνωσθῇ παρ' ὑμῖν ἡ ἐπιστολή, ποιήσατε ἵνα καὶ ἐν τῇ Λαοδικέων ἐκκλησίᾳ ἀναγνωσθῇ, καὶ τὴν ἐκ Λαοδικείας ἵνα καὶ ὑμεῖς ἀναγνῶτε.

The passages cast light on two questions: how the letters were written and how they were read. The writing involved the use of a scribe. This was a normal practice in antiquity. What was the precise role of the scribe? It is usually stated that the custom was that an author would dictate his words to an amanuensis. The amanuensis could have taken the text down in either longhand or shorthand. It is likely that a fair copy will have been made of this rough draft and dispatched to the congregation which Paul was addressing. Paul will have had the opportunity to check and revise either copy. Of course we have no way of knowing the details of this operation, but the mechanism could have affected several features in the text of the letter. We do not know either how far or how often Paul may have left the details of wording to the amanuensis. Cicero writes on one occasion about the need to dictate to someone who wrote his words out in longhand when he wanted to get a document absolutely right, even though he found this tedious. Usually he gave the task of drafting to his secretary Tiro. We have no way of knowing how important Paul considered any one of his letters to be. On the whole it is assumed that he cared deeply about it. See, for example, the comment of Cranfield about Romans: 'In view of the special importance and special difficulty of its subject matter and also in view of its occasion, it hardly seems particularly unlikely that Paul would dictate his letter to the Roman church.'

C. E. B. Cranfield, *A Critical and Exegetical Commentary on the Epistle to the Romans* (The International Critical Commentary), 2 vols., corrected edition, 2001, 3f.

This seems a straightforward production process so far as most of the letters are concerned. But there is another factor to consider. 1 and 2 Thessalonians, according to the first verse of each, were written by Paul and Silvanus and Timothy. 2 Corinthians, Philippians and Colossians are from both Paul and Timothy (1.1 of each letter). Galatians, even more strikingly, includes 'all the brethren with me' (1.2) in the address. What was the role of each author? Did Paul write it, and the other one (or two) add their names for some other reason, such as strengthening the letter's authority? Did this joint authorship affect the role of the amanuensis, and, if so, how? I draw attention to this only in order to point out that we do not know in detail how Paul's letters were put together.

I have referred to the assistant as an amanuensis, but the word 'scribe' would be accurate. So far as I know, there is no evidence which would allow one to distinguish between the roles of making the first copy of a new text and of copying a text which had already been copied by another (see 4.7). A scribe may have been expected to do either and needed the same skills of being able to prepare the materials and produce a readable text. In the case of the making of a new text, the scribe was responsible for more than one document: the first draft and the fair copy.

The evidence for shorthand from at least the second half of the second century includes the fact that Galen's commentary on dissection seems to have been available in shorthand. See Devreesse,

Introduction, 36. For evidence from the papyri, see Blanchard, *Les débuts du codex*, 4. Later on, Origen in the second century and Basil in the fourth (Ep. 333) made use of shorthand writers. See also E. M. Thompson, *A Handbook of Greek and Latin Palaeography*, London, 1901 (reprinted Chicago, 1966 and 1980), 82f.

O. Roller, *Das Formular der paulinischen Briefe. Ein Beitrag zur Lehre vom antiken Briefe*, Stuttgart, 1933, points out a problem. What was happening in the composition of Rom. 16.21–3? Presumably Tertius added his greeting when he wrote the fair copy.

The second question is one of the letters' reception. Colossians 4.16 refers to the sharing of letters for public reading in the churches of Colossae and Laodicea. (The question of the authenticity of this letter is irrelevant, since we are discussing the reception of the letters which became a part of the Pauline corpus.) This suggests the possibility that more than one copy was made at a very early stage.

The fair copy made by the amanuensis will have served two functions: to provide a clear reading copy for the recipients, and to allow Paul to retain an original. The existence of several copies from the composition and first distribution phases of letters brings us to one of the important questions concerning the formation of the corpus. How would a person making such a collection go about compiling the materials? It seems reasonable to suppose that it would be much easier to work with Paul's archived copies than by trying to get copies from the different destinations to which he had sent them. If this were the case, then we may see how the collected letters will have been derived from different copies from those which were actually received by his correspondents. It must then be accepted as a formal possibility that some of the variants in our manuscripts were the result of corrections of discrepancies between individual copies in circulation and the archived version.

An alternative possibility is that the collection grew up from an early stage through the exchange of letters between churches to whom Paul had written (see Col. 4.16). This is advanced by, for example, the Alands. There is no evidence either way. One is left with a question of probability.

Aland and Aland, *The Text of the New Testament*, 49.

8.3 THE GROWTH OF THE PAULINE CORPUS

Gamble's theory was that early Christian adoption of the codex format stemmed from its use in making Paul's collected letters (see 1.1.1). He argues that this collection into a single volume had to be in codex form, since it would have been too long to be contained in a roll. Thus, a technological innovation was the essential prerequisite of the Pauline collection.

In detail, the argument is as follows. The contents of P46 would run out, by Gamble's calculations, if it were a roll, at 2,806 cm. Even without Hebrews, it would have been 2,400 cm, or 80 feet. His conclusion is that the Pauline corpus must first have been collected in a codex, and is the origin of the use of this distinctive form by the early Church. Gamble, *Books and Readers*, 54–66.

What do we know about the growth of the corpus? In the second century we have evidence of a number of different collections. What happened before that is less certain, and there are several different views. G. Zuntz, in a work which will feature regularly in the coming pages, believed that the corpus came into being in about the year 100, on the grounds that a collection was known to Ignatius a few years into the new century, but not to Clement writing in 96. On the other hand, the Alands believe that references to Romans, 1 Corinthians and Hebrews in *1 Clement* 'reflect the existence in Rome at this time of a collection of Paul's letters'. Small collections in individual churches grew 'by a process of exchange' until finally the Pastorals were added in the middle of the second century and 'the collection of the fourteen Pauline letters was considered complete'. This conclusion runs against the drift of the argument, since the idea of the growth of several small collections could explain the fact that the middle and late second centuries attest a number of different collections, as will be demonstrated shortly.

Zuntz, *Text of the Epistles*. For recent appraisals see M. W. Holmes, '*The Text of the Epistles* Sixty Years After: an Assessment of Günther Zuntz's Contribution to Text-Critical Methodology and History', in Childers and Parker, *Transmission and Reception*, 89–113; E. Güting, 'The Methodological Contribution of Günther Zuntz to the Text of Hebrews', *NovT* 48 (2006), 359–78. Porter's article cited above gives an account and appraisal of different theories concerning the formation of the collection. Aland and Aland, *The Text of the New Testament*, 49.

If we compare the views of the Alands and Zuntz, we see that the Alands' interest lies in the letter collection (Zuntz conceded that Clement knew three letters, but he infers from this that Clement did not know the collection as we have it). To Zuntz what is important is the archetype, the manuscript of the collected letters from which all others are descended. It is a presupposition of Zuntz's theory that he conceives only of a single collection from the beginning and overlooks the possibility of a number of collections, each making a contribution to the subsequent development of the text.

A quite different view has been advanced by D. Trobisch, namely that Paul himself was responsible for the first collection of his letters. He made it by bringing together Romans, Galatians and 1 and 2 Corinthians, and he did so in order to offer a compromise that would put an end to the bitter dispute between the Jerusalem Church and the Paulinists. He had the church of Ephesus in mind particularly, and wanted to justify his actions in his disagreement with the church in Jerusalem. What is now Romans 16 was an addition, intended as a cover note to the Ephesians. This formed a nucleus of the larger collections of the second century.

Die Entstehung der Paulusbriefsammlung: Studien zu den Anfängen christlicher Publizistik (Novum Testamentum et Orbis Antiquus 10), Freiburg and Göttingen, 1989; *Die Paulusbriefe und die Anfänge der christlichen Publizistik*, Munich, 1994; D. Trobisch, *Paul's Letter Collection. Tracing the Origins*, Bolivar, Mo., 2000.

While Trobisch's case is by no means proven, it deserves to be taken seriously, if only because it is a reminder of how few facts there are concerning the origins of the collection. It is only when we come to the middle of the second century that we find any hard evidence.

The oldest collection about which we have any evidence is that of Marcion. His version of Paul, produced in about the middle of the second century (Marcion's dates are usually thought to be 90/100–150/160), consisted of ten letters. He placed them in the order

Galatians
1 and 2 Corinthians
Romans
1 and 2 Thessalonians
Laodiceans (= Ephesians)
Colossians and Philemon
Philippians

Epiphanius states that Marcion put Philemon and Colossians together. See H. Y. Gamble, *Books and Readers in the Early Church*, 61 and note, and Schmid, *Marcion und sein Apostolos*, 286. For a synoptic presentation of the different orders in the ancient witnesses, see H. J. Frede (ed.), *Epistulae ad Philippenses et ad Colossenses* (Vetus Latina 24/2), 1966, 290–303.

If the letters to a single destination and Colossians and Philemon are combined, there are seven units. Schmid concluded that Marcion took over an existing ten-letter edition that was already at least some decades old (284ff.).

The next piece of evidence is the Muratorian Canon, a text which lists and discusses the canonical books. It has traditionally been dated to the late second century, but the view that it is all of a single piece may be questioned. It survives in a single eighth-century Latin manuscript, and there are some difficulties with understanding all that is said. Here is my translation of the section about Paul:

The letters of Paul reveal to anyone who wants to know, from where and for what purpose they were sent. First he wrote to the Corinthians, condemning the schism of heresy; then to the Galatians condemning circumcision; next he wrote at greater length to the Romans, making known the arrangement of the Scriptures and that Christ is their main theme [beginning, origin].

They must be mentioned one by one, because this blessed Apostle Paul, following the arrangement of his predecessor, John, wrote only to seven named churches, in this order: first to the Corinthians, second to the Ephesians, third to the Philippians, fourth to the Colossians, fifth to the Galatians, sixth to the Thessalonians, and seventh to the Romans. Although he wrote twice to the Corinthians and to the Thessalonians, in order to correct them, it is recognised that there is one Church spread throughout the whole terrestrial globe. Likewise John in the Apocalypse writes to seven churches, but speaks to all.

He also wrote one letter to Philemon, one to Titus and two to Timothy out of fondness and love. They are sanctified with honour by the Catholic Church in the ordination of ecclesiastical discipline.

There is extant also a letter to the Laodiceans, and another to the Alexandrians, forged in the name of Paul for the purposes of the Marcionite heresy, as well as many others which cannot be received in the Catholic Church, since gall and honey cannot be mixed.

My translation. For an alternative, see the translation in Metzger, *Canon of the New Testament*, 306f.

This seems to be a compilation from two lists. First it refers only to letters to the Corinthians, Galatians and Romans. The letters are mentioned in a different order the second time:

Corinthians
Ephesians
Philippians
Colossians
Galatians
Thessalonians
Romans

As with Marcion, we have a sevenfold canon. There is also a distinction between letters to churches and letters to individuals, a pattern which we may find also in the oldest extensive, manuscript, P46, dated to about 200. It contains parts of these letters, in the order:

Romans
Hebrews
1 and 2 Corinthians
Ephesians
Galatians
Philippians
Colossians
1 Thessalonians

P46 is a single-quire codex with numbered pages, so that we know that the original quire contained 208 pages. It is generally stated that the amount of space remaining after 1 Thessalonians can only have contained 2 Thessalonians and possibly Philemon. If this was the case, then the manuscript originally contained a collection of ten or eleven letters, in order of descending length. If Philemon was absent, then the collection will have consisted only of letters to congregations. The possibility of such a rationale for a collection is supported by the Muratorian Canon. But there is no way of proving anything about what is no longer present. A small extra quire might have been added at the end. It has also been claimed that the density of writing increases on the later surviving pages, an indication that the scribe had realised that he needed to squeeze more text into the remaining pages.

The theory that P46 never contained the Pastorals has been challenged by J. Duff in 'P46 and the Pastorals: a Misleading Consensus?', *NTS* 44 (1998), 578–90. The theory is worth discussing, since it illustrates some important matters of methodology and argument. He produces two lines of argument to the contrary. The first is that the number of letters per page of the manuscript increases towards the end, for which he produces a graph. This is the weaker argument, because he has taken a short cut to calculate this, namely the use of a computerised version of a printed edition 'adjusted to reflect the spelling used in P46', because the amount of damage to the papyrus makes it impossible to count the number of letters on a page. This is true, but a more trustworthy method is to count the number of letters on every extant line, and use the average of these on a page to reach an estimated figure for those lines which are partly or wholly lost. As it is, this part of the argument must be considered unproven until examined more carefully. In order to establish Duff's claim that this greater number of letters results from the scribe's realising that he was running out of space, it would also be necessary to ensure that this was not a feature of other single-quire codices and unrelated to problems associated with fitting the text into the available space.

Duff's second argument is that there are examples of scribes adding extra sheets to single-quire manuscripts when they have run out of space. The examples of single sheets being added do not provide a convincing analogy, since as Duff admits, P46 would by his calculations require four added sheets. His better examples are two other manuscripts. The first, Nag Hammadi Codex 1, consists of a large quire of twenty-two sheets, followed by an eight and a six. Robinson has suggested that this is due to a miscalculation of space by the scribe. However, one has to wonder whether this is the best explanation, since the error requires mistaking the text's length by two-fifths, and under-calculating not once but twice. The second example is the Toura papyrus of Origen, and again there are some difficulties with taking this as a precedent for P46: in the first place, this manuscript was made in the sixth century, when the codex format had been in use for four hundred years, and had moreover the now well-established parchment codex to follow (in which the use of single-sheet quires or even half-sheet additions to finish a work is commonplace); in the second place, this codex contains several works by Origen, and we cannot be sure that the scribe derived them all from a single exemplar, which is required for a proper comparison with P46 (assuming of course that P46 itself is copied from a single exemplar).

Note that the same set of ten letters, but in the order Romans–1/2 Corinthians–Hebrews–Galatians–Philippians–Ephesians–1/2 Thessalonians–Colossians, is found in the fifth-century Middle Egyptian codex (see 8.5.3 below).

Duff is surely quite right to point to the dangers of arguing with too much certainty that P46 *did not* contain the Pastorals, and he reminds us that we are dealing with something which can never be finally answered. His positive arguments, however, highlight some of the difficulties in the study of ancient documents and their comparison.

For a detailed analysis of Duff's arguments, with further questions about his conclusions, see E. J. Epp, 'Issues in the Interrelation of New Testament Textual Criticism and Canon', in L. M. McDonald and J. A. Sanders (eds.), *The Canon Debate: On the Origins and Formation of the Bible*, Peabody, Mass., 2002, 485–515, pp. 498–502; reprinted in *Perspectives on New Testament Textual Criticism*, 595–639, pp. 613–19.

Codex Sinaiticus, which is the oldest complete manuscript of Paul, shares the canon and order of Athanasius' Festal Letter of 367:

Romans
1 Corinthians
2 Corinthians
Galatians
Ephesians
Philippians
Colossians
1 Thessalonians
2 Thessalonians
Hebrews
1 Timothy
2 Timothy
Titus
Philemon

It is standard from then onwards for Greek manuscripts to contain fourteen letters. But this order was subsequently abandoned, Hebrews being placed after Philemon. Codex Vaticanus, so far as it is extant, shares the order of Sinaiticus. But the manuscript also contains evidence of an older order, since it has paragraph numbers which run sequentially through the epistles, but not in the correct order, those for Hebrews placing it between Galatians and Ephesians.

The development of the canon in the second century may then possibly have included the expansion of a Pauline nucleus. It is clearer that it included three patterns providing different rationales: a set of seven universal letters matching the letters to the seven churches of the Apocalypse (Marcion, Muratorian Canon); the distinction between letters to churches and letters to individuals (Marcion, Muratorian Canon and perhaps P46); and placing the letters in order of descending length (P46). 01 and 03 only partially meet any criteria, except that certainly in 01 they begin in descending order of length to churches, with Hebrews standing between those and the letters to individuals. The order of the paragraph numbers in 03 is harder to understand.

The Greek tradition was to keep to the fourteen letters. The three earliest versions each took a different direction. The canon of the Old Syriac collection had fourteen letters, but not the same fourteen – it omitted Philemon and included 3 Corinthians. Our evidence for this is the Armenian version of Ephraem's Commentary on Paul (*PS*, p. 63), which has the order:

Romans
1 Corinthians
2 Corinthians
3 Corinthians
Galatians
Ephesians
Philippians
Colossians
1 Thessalonians
2 Thessalonians
Hebrews
1 Timothy
2 Timothy
Titus

The Sahidic canon has the same books as the Greek, but a different sequence:

Romans
1 Corinthians
2 Corinthians
Hebrews
Galatians
Ephesians
Philippians
Colossians
1 Thessalonians
2 Thessalonians
1 Timothy
2 Timothy
Titus
Philemon

This is the most common collection and sequence but is not universal in the manuscripts.

The Latin tradition came to favour a fifteen-letter collection, the fourteen of the Greek collection, with the addition of Laodiceans (not the same as Marcion's letter given the same name). The first manuscript to contain this letter is Codex Fuldensis. In the middle of the fourth century, there was a bilingual tradition which seems to have omitted Hebrews, giving a collection of thirteen letters:

Romans
1 Corinthians
2 Corinthians
Galatians
Ephesians
Colossians
Philippians
1 Thessalonians
2 Thessalonians
1 Timothy
2 Timothy
Titus
Philemon

Frede, *Altlateinische Paulus-Handschriften;* R. F. Schlossnikel, *Der Brief an die Hebräer und das Corpus Paulinum. Eine linguistische 'Bruchstelle' im Codex Claromontanus (Paris, Bibliothèque Nationale Grec 107 + 107A + 107B) und ihre Bedeutung im Rahmen von Text- und Kanongeschichte* (GLB 20), 1991. For Hebrews see also W. H. P. Hatch, 'The Position of Hebrews in the Canon of the New Testament', *HTR* 29 (1936), 133–51.

It will be seen that a full coverage of the textual history of the Pauline letters would include sixteen letters, since Laodiceans and 3 Corinthians appear in the corpus in some part of the tradition. In practice this does not happen. For example, Laodiceans is not included in editions of the Latin Bible, perhaps because it is sometimes and not always present in manuscripts. This chapter likewise will confine its discussions to the fourteen letters most commonly included in the collection.

8.4 THE MANUSCRIPTS

There are more manuscripts of Paul than of Revelation, 792 being detailed in the *Liste*. The oldest extensive manuscripts were, until 1934, the fourth-century codices Sinaiticus and Vaticanus. It was on these, especially on the latter, that the nineteenth-century critical text was founded. Although a number of fragments of papyri had already been published, the publication in 1934 of a fairly well-preserved papyrus dated to about the year 200 changed the course of research. The manuscript is one of the Chester Beatty Papyri, now in Dublin. The papyrus is important, not only for the character of its text (which includes places where alternative readings are set side by side), but also for the presentation of the collection and the information which it provides about the history of Paul's letters.

The *editio princeps* was made by F. G. Kenyon, *The Chester Beatty Biblical Papyri. Descriptions and Texts of Twelve Manuscripts on Papyrus of the Greek Bible*, vol III: *Pauline Epistles and Revelation. Text*, London, 1934; *Plates*, London, 1936; *Supplement. Text*, London, 1936; *Plates*, London, 1937. The first studies, raising questions subsequently handled in detail by Zuntz were H. C. Hoskier, 'A Study of the Chester Beatty Codex of the Pauline Epistles', *JTS* 38 (1937), 148–63; *A Commentary on the Various Readings in the Text of the Epistle to the Hebrews in the Chester-Beatty Papyrus* $\mathfrak{P}^{46}$ *(circa 200 AD)* *(Supplementing his Review of the Other Epistles)*, London, 1938.

There are thirty-two papyri, twelve of them dated to the period before about 400. Table 8.1 states their dates as given in the *Liste* and the letters represented in their surviving fragments.

It is a rather curious fact that two of the earliest copies of Hebrews are papyrus rolls. Admittedly, one of them is an opisthograph, so it would be a misunderstanding to seek a connection between the unique (so far as the New Testament is concerned) literary character of this work and the untypical format.

The spread of dates underlines the fact that the advent of parchment codices by no means led to a sudden abandonment of papyrus, which continued to be used for another three hundred years and more.

There is a synoptic edition of the papyri then known (down to P99): *NT auf Papyrus II*. P13 has been studied in detail by P. M. Head and M. Warren, 'Re-inking the Pen: Evidence from P. Oxy. 657 (P¹³) concerning Unintentional Scribal Errors', *NTS* 43 (1997), 466–73. They conclude that the scribe's frequent and obvious ink dipping regularly led him to make mistakes in copying.

Turning to the majuscules,

01 is the oldest complete copy of Paul's letters.

02 lacks only three leaves, breaking off at 2 Corinthians 4.13 γεγραμμ and beginning again at 12.7 υπερβολη.

03 is one of the most valuable witnesses to the text where it is present, but it breaks off at Hebrews 9.14.

04 has Colossians, 2 Timothy, Titus and Philemon in their entirety and is partially extant in all the rest except for 2 Thessalonians (see 1.8.1).

Table 8.1

Date	Papyrus	Book and chapters represented
c. 200	P32	Titus 1, 2
	P46	Chapters of Rom., Heb., 1 and 2 Cor., Eph., Gal., Phil., Col., 1 Thess.
III	P15	1 Cor. 7, 8
	P27	Rom. 8, 9
	P30	1 Thess. 4, 5; 2 Thess 1
	P40	Rom. 1, 2, 3, 4, 6, 9
	P65	1 Thess. 1, 2
	P87	Philem.
	P113	Rom. 2
	P114	Heb. 1
III (end)	P12	Heb. 1 (roll)
	P49	Eph. 4, 5
III/IV	P13	Heb. 2–5, 10–12 (roll)
	P16	Phil. 3–4
	P92	Eph. 1, 2 Thess. 1
c. 400	P51	Gal. 1
	P99	A Graeco-Latin glossary (chapter of Rom., 2 Cor., Gal., Eph. survive)
IV	P10	Rom. 1
	P17	Heb. 9
	P89	Heb. 6
IV/V	P117	2 Cor. 7
V/VI	P94	Rom. 6
VI	P11	1 Cor. 1, 2, 3, 4–5, 6, 7
	P14	1 Cor. 1, 2, 3 (a single manuscript with P11?)
VI/VII	P116	Heb. 2, 3
c. 600	P26	Rom. 1
VII	P31	Rom. 12
	P34	1 Cor. 16; 2 Cor. 5, 10, 11
	P79	Heb. 10
VII (?)	P68	1 Cor. 4, 5
c. 700	P61	Rom. 16; 1 Cor. 1, 5; Phil. 3; Col. 1, 4; 1 Thess. 1; Titus 3; Philem.
X (?)	P118	Rom. 15, 16

015 is a highly fragmentary (forty-one folios only) sixth-century manuscript, whose study is complicated by the fact that portions of it are held by seven different libraries. Its significance rests particularly in the fact that it is a major witness to the Euthalian Apparatus (described in 8.7).

Table 8.2

Date	MS	Book and chapters represented
III	0220	Rom. 4, 5
IV	0185	1 Cor. 2, 3
	0221	Rom. 5, 6
	0228	Heb. 12
	0230	Eph. 6 (Graeco-Latin manuscript)
IV/V	0219	Rom. 2, 3
	0270	1 Cor. 15
V	061	1 Tim. 3, 4, 6
	062	Gal. 4–5
	0172	Rom. 1–2
	0174	Gal. 2 (verso blank)
	0176	Gal. 3
	0201	1 Cor. 12, 14
	0226	1 Thess. 4–5
	0227	Heb. 11
	0240	Titus 1
	0252	Heb. 6
	0254	Gal. 5
	0261	Gal. 1, 4

016 should be a significant witness, being a fifth-century copy of parts of all the letters except Romans, on eighty-four leaves. Unfortunately its fire-damaged state renders much of it illegible.

A number of other fragments of majuscules have been discovered in the past century. Those dated securely to the fifth century or earlier are listed in Table 8.2. 0220 would be a very rare example of a third-century parchment manuscript of the New Testament. It is a date which requires reconsideration: so far as I know, nobody has scrutinised Hatch's original opinion of 1952.

W. H. P. Hatch, 'A Recently Discovered Fragment of the Epistle to the Romans', *HTR* 45 (1952), 81–5, p. 84. For a plate, see Aland and Aland, *The Text of the New Testament*, plate 14.

There is a very important group of Graeco-Latin bilingual manuscripts. The oldest member of the group is Codex Claromontanus (06, formerly known as D^Paul). It was copied in the fifth century, possibly in Sardinia. It contains fourteen epistles. It is set out with the Greek on the left page and the Latin on the right. The text is divided into sense-lines,

that is into short grammatical units. This was the easiest way of presenting the two texts of a bilingual manuscript. The other members of
this group were produced in the west, and most date from the ninth
century. Two of them are direct copies of the Claromontanus, known as
06$^{abs\ 1}$ and 06$^{abs\ 2}$ (the latter is slightly later, being tenth century). Both
contain Greek and Latin, although in the case of 06$^{abs\ 2}$, which consists of
only a few short selections, the two columns do not necessarily contain
the same text. More important are the Codices Augiensis (010, formerly
F^{Paul}) and Sangermanensis (012, formerly G^{Paul}). These two manuscripts
were both produced by Latin scribes who had some difficulty with
copying a Greek text. They are different in format, the former having the
two texts in parallel columns, the latter having the Latin text written
above the corresponding Greek word. Study of these witnesses has led to
the construction of the following stemma:

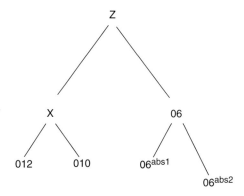

Z is the archetype of the tradition, and it is dated to about the year 350. It
was a bilingual manuscript, copied in sense-lines (like 06). X is a lost
intermediary from which 010 and 012 are descended. Such a stemma does
not necessarily state every copying that took place, but the minimum
necessary to explain the relationship between the manuscripts. Thus,
while the manuscripts date from the sixth century and later, they may be
used to reconstruct a valuable older form of text. According to G. D. Fee,
the archetype of this tradition is even older than mid-fourth century, and
represents the text known to Hippolytus, Bishop of Rome in the early
third century (he was still alive in 235).

Frede, *Altlateinische Paulus-Handschriften*. G. D. Fee, 'The Majority Text of the New Testament and
the Original Text', *Bible Translator* 31 (1980), 113–14 and 'The Majority Text of the New Testament
and the Original Text', in Epp and Fee, *Studies*, 183–208, p. 204.

There are also a number of other interesting Graeco-Latin manuscripts. 0230 is a fragment of Ephesians, produced in the fourth century and thus the oldest example of a Graeco-Latin manuscript of any part of the New Testament. There is also a manuscript which may perhaps be best described as a glossary of Paul, the Greek and Latin equivalents being presented word by word. There is a third group of manuscripts (628, 629, 1918), produced as a consequence of interest in Greek matters on the part of western scholars, dated in the fourteenth century.

For all these bilinguals, see 1.7, and Parker, *Codex Bezae*, 51–69, and literature cited there.

As is the case in every part of the New Testament, the majority of manuscripts are minuscules and lectionaries. To deal first with the former, most of them are manuscripts with a Byzantine form of text.

One of the most important minuscules is 1739, a volume containing Acts and the Catholic and Pauline epistles. It begins at Quire 13, so it is to be assumed that there was a first volume (now lost) containing the Gospels. The manuscript is also known as the Codex van der Goltz, because it first came to attention through the work of E. van der Goltz, one of von Soden's researchers (in a publication of 1899). It was copied by a scribe who combined technical expertise with scholarly credentials. Ephraim, a ninth-century Constantinopolitan, was responsible for a number of manuscripts. They include copies of Polybius, Aristotle, Plato, the Gospels and the Praxaopostolos which are among the most important representatives of their tradition. 1739 is descended from two manuscripts, the one containing Acts and the Catholic letters, and the other Paul. The following discussion concerns only this second ancestor. 1739 contains a colophon describing this part of the manuscript's genesis, which runs as follows:

ἰστέον τὰς ῑδ τοῦ ἀποστόλου ἐπιστολάς. γεγράφθαι ἀ
πὸ ἀντιγράφου παλαιοτάτου. οὐ πεῖραν ἐλάβομεν ὡς
ἐπιτετευγμένου. ἐκ τῶν εἰς ἡμᾶς ἐλθόντων ὠριγέν(ους)
τόμων ἢ ὁμιλιῶν εἰς τὸν ἀπόστολον· εὑρηκότες αὐτὸ συμ
φωνοῦν οἷς μνημονεύει ῥητοῖς· ἐν ταῖς εἴτε εἰς τὸν ἀ
πόστολον εἴτε εἰς ἄλλην γραφὴν ἐξηγήσεσιν ὁ ἀνήρ.
ἐν οἷς οὖν παραλλάττει ῥητοῖς· πρὸς τὰ νῦν ἀποστολικά.
διπλῆν τὴν λεγομένην παρεθήκαμεν ἔξωθεν· ἵνα μὴ
νομισθῆι κατὰ προσθήκην ἢ λεῖψιν ἡμαρτῆσθαι τουτὶ
τὸ ἀποστολικόν· τὴν δὲ πρὸς ῥωμαίους [*sic*] ἐκ τῶν εἰς
αὐτὴν φερομένην τόμων μεταγραψάμενοι. οὐκ ἐχρη
σάμεθα τῆι διπλῆι. ἥτις ἐστιν αὕτη>·

Copied from the collation of the manuscript by K. Lake, J. de Zwaan and M. S. Enslin, 'Codex 1739. Athos, Laura 184 [B ´64] (Greg. 1739; von Soden α78)', in Lake and New, *Six Collations*, 141–219,

p. 199. E. von der Goltz, *Eine textkritische Arbeit des zehnten bezw. sechsten Jahrhunderts, herausgegeben nach einem Codex des Athosklosters Lawra* (TU 17.4, NF 2/4), Leipzig, 1899; J. N. Birdsall, 'The Text and Scholia of the Codex von der Goltz and its Allies, and their Bearing upon the Texts of the Works of Origen, Especially the Commentary on Romans', *Origeniana* (*Quaderno di Vetera Christianorum* 12), Bari, 1975, 215–22; reprinted in *Collected Papers*, 81–6. There is a very clear statement of the manuscript's prehistory in C. P. Bammel, 'A New Witness to the Scholia from Origen in the Codex van der Goltz', in R. J. Daly (ed.), *Origeniana Quinta. Papers of the 5th International Origen Congress* (BETL 105), Leuven, 1992, 137–41, reprinted in C. P. Hammond Bammel, *Origeniana et Rufiniana* (GLB 29), 1996, chapter 2 (no new pagination).

The note begins by stating that 'the 14 epistles of the Apostle were copied from a very ancient exemplar' which has been verified as agreeing with the text of Paul quoted in Origen's surviving commentaries and homilies on the Apostle, while Romans has been copied from his commentary on it.

The manuscript contains many marginal notes, some reporting the results of the comparison of the text with that of Origen, others commenting on points either philological or doctrinal. The beginning of each volume of Origen's commentary is marked in the margin. We thus have a rich and potentially ancient source of readings, and neither text nor marginalia disappoint. We may note, however, that in point of detail, the relationship between 1739 and the very ancient copy is unlikely to be as straightforward as direct derivation. Such a note as the one quoted above is also likely to have been preserved as testifying to a copy's value, so it is possible that there may be one or more intermediaries between the very ancient copy and Ephraim's production. Nevertheless, the number of such intermediaries is less important than the quality of text in the manuscript. 1739 is one of the most telling proofs of the fact that the age of the text contained in a manuscript is not the same as the age of the manuscript. Where an ancient form of text has been carefully preserved through few intermediaries, it may be of more value than the text found in an older manuscript which has gone through many indifferent copyings.

It would of course help us to understand all this better if we had direct access to the Greek of Origen's commentary on Romans (*CPG* 1.1457). Unfortunately, all we have are some fragments and Rufinus' Latin translation. In fact, 1739 is one of our few Greek sources for Origen's text (see 8.6).

A small number of other manuscripts also attest the text to which 1739 is a witness, and Birdsall has constructed a stemma of their relationships, in which in Romans 1739 and 1908, and 0243 (only fragments of 1 and 2 Corinthians and Hebrews extant) and 1739 are derived from a sub-archetype Y, while 424 and 6 are derived from another sub-archetype lacking marginalia.

Birdsall, 'Text and Scholia'; J. N. Birdsall, 'The Two Fragments of the Epistles Designated M (0121)', *JTS* n.s. 11 (1960), 336–8. This article showed that these fragments are parts of two different manuscripts. The Hamburg leaves have since been found to be part of another fragmentary manuscript in Venice and renumbered 0243.

Text und Textwert, however, presents somewhat different evidence, even though it should be borne in mind that the justification for associating one or two of these manuscripts with 1739 is in marginal or interlinear corrections. If we turn to the volume covering 1 Corinthians, and the Hauptliste where a manuscript's closest associates are listed we find these entries at the top of the list:

> 0243, agreeing with 1739 in thirteen out of fourteen Teststellen where it is extant (93 per cent)
> 1506, six out of seven Teststellen where it is extant (86 per cent)
> 04, thirty-three out of thirty-nine Teststellen where it is extant (85 per cent)
> 01, forty-six out of fifty-six Teststellen where it is extant (82 per cent)

Other important witnesses are 03 (79 per cent), 02 (73 per cent) and P46 (57 per cent). 424 does not appear in the list at all, because it is Byzantine in text, and 6 comes quite a long way down, with thirty-one out of fifty-six agreements (55 per cent).

Turning to Romans, 1908 is by no means as close to 1739 as some other witnesses, notably 04 and 048 (both 86 per cent), 1852 (83 per cent) and ten other witnesses, agreeing with it in only 64 per cent of readings.

It is interesting to see how an analysis of all witnesses affects our understanding of the relationship between copies previously thought to be closely associated. Here, previous conclusions are partly justified and partly called into question. A more detailed study of the Teststellen throughout the Pauline corpus would help to resolve these questions.

Turning to the lectionaries, not all of Paul is read in the synaxarion. According to Osburn, selections from Romans, 1 and 2 Corinthians, Ephesians and Hebrews are read in the sixteen weeks between the Monday after Pentecost and Holy Cross Day (14 September). A few selections from the first two of these letters occur in Holy Week. Junack details other Pauline readings in the synaxarion. Also, there are comparatively few lectionary manuscripts. Writing in 1972, Klaus Junack enumerated 2,117 lectionary or lectionary fragments, of which 284 contain readings from the Apostolos (i.e. Acts and the two letter collections) and 91 readings with both Gospel and Apostolos pericopae. (These figures are now out of date, with over a hundred more lectionaries present in the current update to the second edition of the *Liste* than there were in the first.) For these two reasons, the role of lectionaries in the textual study of Paul has been slight indeed. Whether this is justified will only be known after proper study.

C. Osburn, 'The Greek Lectionaries of the New Testament', in Ehrman and Holmes, *Contemporary Research*, 61–74, p. 62; K. Junack, 'Zu den griechischen Lektionaren und ihrer Überlieferung der Katholischen Briefe', in K. Aland, *Die alten Übersetzungen*, 498–591, pp. 500f. (numbers of manuscripts), 522 (Pauline lections).

8.5 THE VERSIONS

8.5.1 The Syriac versions

A basic tool for study is the edition by Aland and Juckel. Their Peshitta text is taken from a fifth/sixth-century manuscript in the British Library (Add. 14470). Patristic citations (placed in chronological order either before, at the time of, or after the Peshitta) and the Harklean (based upon a manuscript in Jerusalem, St Mark 37) complete the text. Twelve Peshitta manuscripts, two Harklean, with lectionaries and representatives of the West Syrian Massora, make up the apparatus.

Although there are no surviving manuscripts, there is some evidence that there must once have been copies of an Old Syriac translation. Kerchensteiner has reconstructed fragments of the text from citations in fifteen sources, principally those of Aphraates, Ephraem and the *Liber Graduum*. The precise origins of this text are unclear. Discussions have included Tatian and Marcion as possible influences on its formation. Kerchensteiner's view is that a consistent form of text may be observed in the fourth century.

The Peshitta version was until recently only available in the text which G.H. Gwilliam and J. Pinkerton prepared for their unfinished edition. Whether the questions surrounding the Peshitta Gospels (see 10.5.1) are relevant to the Pauline letters, has not, so far as I can tell, been ascertained. It seems likely that, just as the view that there is a fixed Latin Vulgate form contrasted with free older versions has been abandoned, so the concept of a single Peshitta text has proved unsatisfactory. Aland and Juckel point to a degree of freedom in the scribal tradition of the fifth and sixth centuries, and they aim in their edition to reproduce what they describe as a 'spectrum' (p. 51). The early copies are recognisable as copies of the Peshitta rather than of any other version, but they are by no means in total agreement with each other.

There are five studies of the Syrian traditions of Paul by doctoral students of Vööbus, but none has been published. Gudorf collated sixty manuscripts of Hebrews. Clemons studied eighteen manuscripts of Galatians, with citations in about fifty works.

We have here too the Harklean, finished in 616. The relationship between it and the Philoxenian version is discussed in detail by B. Aland in her edition of the major Catholic epistles (7–13), and her account applies also to the Pauline letters. Almost all the evidence rests in what may be gleaned from two meagre sources, Philoxenus' own quotations and the Syriac version of the Euthalian material (found in the manuscript British Library Add. 7157).

Aland and Juckel, *NT in syrischer Überlieferung 2*; J. Kerchensteiner, *Der altsyrische Paulustext* (CSCO 315, Subsidia 37), Louvain, 1970. T. Baarda, 'The Syriac Versions of the New Testament', in Ehrman and Holmes, *Contemporary Research*, 97–112, approaches the topic by means of two verses with a wide historical range of variants (1 Cor. 1.27 and Heb. 5.7), and so serves as an introduction to the study of the Syriac text of Paul. For details of the unpublished dissertations, see p. 104. Clemons' research is reported in Metzger, *Early Versions*, 62f. Clemons, *Index of Syriac Manuscripts*. For their conclusions with regard to the Philoxenian, they refer to Brock, 'Syriac Euthalian Material'.

8.5.2 *The Latin versions*

So far as the Old Latin is concerned, although there are more materials than for the Apocalypse, there is still very little manuscript evidence. The following are the most important manuscripts catalogued by Gryson. First, the Latin columns of the bilinguals are numbered as follows:

75 = 06
76 = $D^{abs\ 1}$
83 = $D^{abs\ 2}$
77 = 012
78 = 010
85 = 0230

64, the Freising Fragments, is a manuscript from the second half of the sixth century, probably of African origin. Its text is closely related to that of Augustine.

Lowe initially favoured a Spanish origin (*CLA* IX.1286a), while suggesting Africa, which he confirmed in his discussion of African manuscripts (*CLA* S. p. IX).

89 is the Pauline text of a commentary by an unknown author. The manuscript, dated to around 800, is derived from an Italian exemplar (possibly written in Rome). It is an independent witness to the **D** (i.e. the bilingual) text.

The Vetus Latina edition is complete for Ephesians, Philippians, Colossians, 1 and 2 Thessalonians, the Pastorals, Philemon and Hebrews. The first fascicle of the edition of Romans, listing the manuscripts, appeared in 1996, and the Introduction to 1 Corinthians in three fascicles (1995–8). Work on 1 Corinthians by a new editor is in progress.

Vetus Latina 21, *Epistula ad Romanos*, ed. H. S. Eymann, fasc. 1, 1996; 22, *Epistula ad Corinthios I*, ed. U. Fröhlich, fasc. 1–3, 1995–8; 24/1, *Epistula ad Ephesios*, ed. H. J. Frede, 1962–4; 24/2, *Epistulae ad Philippenses et ad Colossenses*, ed. H. J. Frede, 1966–71; 25, *Epistulae ad Thessalonicenses, Timotheum, Titum, Philemonem, Hebraeos*, ed. H. J. Frede, 1975–91.

In the absence of manuscripts, the reconstruction of text-types is heavily dependent upon citations. As detailed in the Introduction to the editions of Philippians and Ephesians, they are:

(1) **X**, the text of Tertullian (discussed at great length in Fröhlich's introduction to 1 Corinthians, pp. 168–83)
(2) **K**, the African text of Cyprian and the pseudo-Cyprianic writings (in Hebrews a later form **C** is identified)
(3) **D**, the text of the bilinguals, attested in Sardinia by the citations of Lucifer of Cagliari in the mid-fourth century
(4) **I**, a widely attested Italian text, probably made in Rome itself. There are three subforms: **J** (a revision of **I**), **A** (distinctive readings in 64) and **M** (the regional text of Milan). **I** is scarcely available in Hebrews 1–9, and **J** and **A** feature as independent text lines.
(5) **V**, the Vulgate (see 7.4.1)

The authorities are often silent on the origins of the Vulgate text of the Pauline epistles. There is no evidence that Jerome ever revised any part of the New Testament other than the Gospels. But the fact is that there is a form of text from which later manuscripts of the type called Vulgate are descended. In Ephesians and Philippians, it is described by the editor (Frede) as a mixture of **D** and **I** (p. 35). This form of text is first encountered in Pelagius' Commentary on the Pauline epistles, which dates from about 405–10 and was made in Rome. It thus emerges a few years after Jerome's revision of the Gospels. The regional types of the Vulgate are defined in more detail in the most recent introduction (Fröhlich to 1 Corinthians, 223–4, where twelve are listed) than in the earlier volumes.

8.5.3 The Coptic versions

Not all the versions of the Coptic concern us here, since Paul's letters are not attested in some. There are manuscripts of the Sahidic and Bohairic dating from the fourth century, and a copy in Middle Egyptian from the first half of the fifth century contained ten letters (it is a single-quire codex, and lacks Philemon and the Pastorals; see 8.3). This manuscript has been studied by Orlandi, who has noted that it is generally close to the Sahidic in the kind of Greek text from which it is derived.

T. Orlandi, *Lettere di san Paolo in copto-ossirinchita* (Papiri della Università degli Studi di Milano 5), Milan, 1974, with a detailed description, transcription, and a number of plates.

Traditionally, the character of the Sahidic and Bohairic has been expressed in terms of their affinities to the form of text found in the Alexandrian text. The obvious geographical connection has been viewed as explaining this similarity. This hypothesis assumes both that the theory of local texts is reasonable and that 'Alexandrian' has a geographical reference. The fact that the whole theory of text-types is open to question (see 5.1.7), requires also a reconsideration of the way in which the textual character of the Coptic versions is expressed. It is appropriate to redefine it in terms of comparison with manuscripts, and thus to speak of strong similarities (so far as Paul's letters are concerned) with Codices Sinaiticus, Alexandrinus and Vaticanus in particular. The data in *Text und Textwert* offer a further tool for refining the comparison.

The Sahidic and Bohairic were edited by Horner. It goes without saying that there are important materials which were not known to him.

Horner, *Northern Dialect*, vol. III. *The Epistles of St Paul Edited from MS Oriental 424 in the British Museum*; *Southern Dialect*, vols. IV–V: *The Epistles of Paul*.

8.6 COMMENTATORS

Among the patristic citations, the following commentaries are of particular importance for the study of the early stages of the text. Origen's was written before 244 (*CPG* 1.1457). Only fragments in Greek survive (see the discussion of minuscule 1739 in 8.4). For the most part, our knowledge comes from the Latin translation by Rufinus, made in 405/6 and preserved in many manuscripts (eighteen are selected for inclusion in C.P. Hammond Bammel's edition), the oldest of the fifth century.

The homilies of John Chrysostom, in sets covering all fourteen epistles (*CPG* II.4427–4440) were written between 381 and 398 in Antioch. Theodoret of Cyrus (*c.* 393 – *c.* 460) commentated on twelve letters (*CPG* III.6209; von Soden 1.693). The commentary by Oecumenius (see 7.5) survives only in *catena* fragments (*CPG* III.7471). There is also a commentary on the Praxapostolos falsely attributed to him (*CPG* III.7475;

von Soden, 1.694–9). John of Damascus (*c.* 655 – *c.* 750) wrote a commentary on the fourteen letters. Born around the decade 1050–60, and dying after 1125, Theophylact, Archbishop of Bulgaria, wrote commentaries on some of the Old Testament and all the new except for Revelation. It is based upon earlier writings.

The citations in the writings of Patriarch Photius of Constantinople (*c.* 820–93) provide valuable information about the text as it was known to him at an important period in the establishment of the Byzantine text. Nicetas of Heraclea, a deacon of Hagia Sophia in 1080 and later Bishop of Heraclea in Thrace, produced a commentary on Hebrews (see also 10.6). Euthymius Zigabenus lived in the early twelfth century. He wrote commentaries on Matthew, Mark and John (see 10.6) and Paul's letters, drawing on patristic sources.

Of the various commentaries given here, the commentary manuscripts present in the *Liste* include those with a *catena*, some of the manuscripts of John Chrysostom and John of Damascus, and at least theoretically all those by the other writers. The *catenae* have been studied by K. Staab.

For Origen, see C. P. Hammond Bammel, *Der Römerbriefkommentar des Origenes. Kritische Ausgabe der Übersetzung Rufins*, 3 vols. (GLB 16, 33, 34), 1990, 1997, 1998 (vols. II and III posthumously edited by H. J. Frede and H. Stanjek). The manuscript tradition is studied in detail in 'The Manuscript Tradition of Origen's Commentary on Romans in the Latin Tradition by Rufinus', unpublished PhD thesis, Cambridge, 1965; for Photius, see J. N. Birdsall, 'The Text of the Acts and Epistles in Photius', *JTS* n.s. 9 (1958), 278–91; 'The New Testament Text Known to Photius: a Reconsideration', Ἐκκλησία καὶ Θεολογία 1 (1989–91), 181–7; reprinted in *Collected Papers*, 47–54. K. Staab, *Die Pauluskatenen nach den handschriftlichen Quellen untersucht*, Rome, 1926; *Pauluskommentare aus der griechischen Kirche. Aus Katenenhandschriften gesammelt und herausgegeben* (NTA 15), Münster, 1933, repr. Münster, 1984. For lists of manuscripts of different commentaries see von Soden, 1.270–84 and Staab's two books.

The oldest Latin commentary was written in the period between 366 and 378 in Rome (*CPL* 184). The author is unknown, and the soubriquet Ambrosiaster was coined by Erasmus (meaning, that the author is rather like Ambrose of Milan but not Ambrose). Pelagius' commentary (*CPL* 728) has already been mentioned. The ninth-century Irish commentator Sedulius Scotus should also be noted.

H. J. Frede and H. Stanjek (eds.), *Sedulii Scotti Collectaneum in Apostolum*, 2 vols. (GLB 31–2), 1996–7.

8.7 THE EUTHALIANA

Put simply, the Euthaliana consisted of a version of Acts and all the epistles which provided a division of the text into sense units with punctuation and line division according to rhetorical principles, and a collection of paratextual materials, namely prefaces and historical background to the texts. The name associates them with a certain Euthalius, who is now believed to have lived in the fourth century, and about whom it is only known that he was a deacon.

The authoritative study is L.C. Willard, 'A Critical Study of the Euthalian Apparatus', unpublished PhD thesis, Yale, 1970. The only edition of the materials is L.A. Zacagni, *Collectanea monumentorum veterum ecclesiae graecae, ac latinae, quae hactenus in Vaticana Bibliotheca delituerunt ... 4 Euthalii Episc. Sulcensis Actuum Apostolorum, & quatuordecim S. Pauli, aliarumque septem catholicarum epistolarum editio ad Athanasium juniorem Episc. Alexandr.*, Rome, 1698 (pp. 401–end). Other studies include J.A. Robinson, *Euthaliana* (TS 1.3.3), Cambridge, 1895 and Zuntz, *Ancestry*, 77ff., which also discusses the role of the Euthaliana in the formation of the Philoxenian version. There is some evidence that the edition of the fourth century may be the work of one Evagrius (see Robinson, pp. 5ff.). Perhaps Euthalius (whom Zacagni had dated to 458) may have been associated with a later revision (see below). But all is obscure.

For a study of the sense divisions in the manuscripts, see S. Crisp, 'Scribal Marks and Logical Paragraphs: Discourse Segmentation Criteria in Manuscripts of the Pauline Corpus', in P.A. Noss (ed.), *Current Trends in Scripture Translation: Definitions and Identity* (Bulletin of the UBS 198/199 (2005)), 77–87.

The full set of ancillary materials, which Willard divided between major and minor pieces, consisted of

Major pieces:
Prologues (one to Acts and one to each collection of epistles)
Lists of Lections
Lists of Old Testament quotations
Lists of chapters

Minor pieces:
Martyrdom of Paul
Arguments (to each book)
Miscellaneous pieces, consisting of six short pieces of text and subscriptions to the letters
Colophon

It is very rare for a manuscript to contain all of these (181, used by Zacagni, does).

The evidence suggests that Euthalius took over an older edition, consisting of the grammatical divisions of the text (in a form possibly derived from an older paragraph division from which the divisions in 01 03 and the Vulgate manuscripts Amiatinus and Fuldensis may be independently descended), and the lists. Euthalius revised these and wrote the prologues, and possibly the colophon. The other materials were added later.

The colophon is extremely interesting. The form in which it is found in 015 states that the book was compared with a copy in Pamphilus' library at Caesarea. Such a colophon does not refer to the codex in which it is found, but to an earlier one, in this case (as it is believed) one directly arising from the activity of Euthalius himself.

Parts of the Euthaliana survive in several of the versions, notably the Syriac (both Philoxenian and Harklean), the Armenian and the Georgian. Such research has wider benefits. For example, Brock has argued that the Euthaliana also provide a rare glimpse of the Philoxenian version.

Brock, 'Syriac Euthalian Material'. The Armenian was critically edited by A. Vardanian, *Euthalius Werke: Untersuchungen und Texte*, Vienna, 1930. For the Georgian, see J. N. Birdsall, 'The Euthalian Material and its Georgian Versions', *Oriens Christianus* 68 (1984), 170–95, reprinted in *Collected Papers*, 215–42.

8.8 VARIANT READINGS WITH A BEARING UPON THE FORMATION OF THE COLLECTION

The largest textual problem in the Pauline corpus, if one considers the number of words involved, is that which concerns the ending of Romans. This variant may be connected to another problem, the presence or absence of ἐν Ῥώμῃ in Romans 1.7, 15, and even to a third, the presence or absence of ἐν Ἐφέσῳ in Ephesians 1.1. Another passage which may bear upon the same topic is 1 Corinthians 1.2, where it has been suggested that τῇ οὔσῃ ἐν Κορίνθῳ may be an addition. Together, these three passages might be additions in the collected edition in order to identify the letters more clearly.

For 1 Cor. 1.2 see J. Kloha, 'A Textual Commentary on Paul's First Epistle to the Corinthians', unpublished PhD thesis, University of Leeds, 2006, 28–32; Zuntz, *Text of the Epistles*, 91, for a different explanation of the difficult text.

8.8.1 *The endings of Romans*

The problems and textual attestation are explained in full by H. Y. Gamble, Jr., *The Textual History of the Letter to the Romans* (SD 42), Eerdmans, 1977. See also R. F. Collins, 'The Case of a Wandering Doxology: Rom 16, 25–27', in *Festschrift Delobel*, 293–303, with information on the positions taken by leading commentators and an analysis of the form. What follows summarises information in Gamble.

There appear to have been three main forms of the text in antiquity. Although every extant manuscript contains all sixteen chapters, there is compelling evidence that fourteen and fifteen chapter forms also existed.

The main point to note is the varying positions of the Benediction (16.24) and the Doxology (16.25–7).

The three forms are as follows:

(1) A fourteen-chapter form, ending with the Doxology. The evidence is of various kinds. I present it in a little detail, because it illustrates certain kinds of evidence.

  (i)   The chapter headings of some Vulgate manuscripts. These headings are like a table of contents, consisting of a number with a brief summary of the contents of the section. Two ancient systems attest it. One is found in Codex Fuldensis, and consists of twenty-three chapters, the last obviously describing our Chapter 14. Another, found in Codex Amiatinus, contains fifty-one chapters. Chapter L refers to 14.15 and 17 and Chapter LI to the Doxology. So these are headings to a fourteen-chapter form (at least one concluding with the Doxology), to which the last two chapters were then added.

  (ii) The *Concordia epistularum Pauli*, a guide to themes in the letters cross-referenced to the chapter numbering found in Codex Amiatinus, has no themes in Romans after numbers XLII, referring to Romans 14.17ff., and XLIII, cross-referenced to Amiatine Chapter LI.

  (iii) The Marcionite Prologue (a set of Latin prologues to Paul's letters, coming from Marcionite circles) refers to the letter having been written from Athens. This could scarcely be believed by anyone who included 15.25–7; 16.1. It has therefore been taken as evidence for the shorter form.

  (iv) Patristic testimony. Silence is difficult, and one will never be certain whether or not it is significant that the first western writer to refer to Chapters 15 or 16 perhaps dates from the middle of the fourth century (the pseudo-Cyprianic *De singularitate clericorum*, CPL 62).

    (a) Cyprian in his *Testimonia* 3.68, 78 (written before 249) speaks of avoiding heretics without referring to 16.17–19. It is argued that he would surely have used the passage had he known it. Moreover, he nowhere refers to chapters 15 or 16.

    (b) Tertullian refers to 14.10 as 'at the end of the epistle' (*Against Marcion* 5.14, written in about 212 in its final form). This may refer to both Marcion's and Tertullian's text.

(c) Origen, in his *Commentary* on 14.23 says that Marcion removed the Doxology from here, and all the rest of the letter.

(v) The placing of the Doxology and the Benediction in Greek manuscripts is a third indirect indication of a form ending at 14.23, since the Doxology is evidently a concluding formula. The manuscripts show the following variations:

1.1–14.23
1.1–14.23 + 16.25–7
1.1–14.23 + 16.25–7 + 15.1–16.24 + 16.25–7

Gamble discusses here in some detail the varying positions of the Doxology, a piece which many argue to be non-Pauline (it is included in the Nestle–Aland text only within square brackets).

(vi) Gamble associates the fourteen-chapter form with the variants at 1.7 and 1.15. 012 at 1.7 reads τοῖς οὖσιν ἐν ἀγάπῃ θεοῦ, and omits τοῖς ἐν ῥώμῃ at verse 15. The Greek column of 06 is missing, but the Latin conflates the two (*qui sunt romae in caritate dei*). There is a mark in the text between *romae* and *in* which may indicate a marginal note, but unfortunately the margin is torn away here. This evidence, along with the variant ἐν (06*) or ἐπ᾿ (012) before ὑμῖν at 1.15 indicates that the fourth-century archetype of this tradition is a witness to the omission of a reference to Rome in this chapter. A note in the margin of 1739 against 1.7 states that τοῦ ἐν. ῥώμηι οὔτε ἐν τῆι ἐξηγήσει. οὔτε ἐν τῶι ῥητ(ω) μνημονεύει, that is, Origen nowhere reads 'in Rome' in citing this verse in his commentary.

(2) The fifteen-chapter form
The evidence for this is much slighter: P46 has the Doxology at the end of Chapter 15.

(3) The sixteen-chapter form
All the manuscripts contain the sixteen chapters and thus support this form, even though some indirectly testify to another form, by their position of the Doxology and Benediction. The variation in the latter is considerable (some witnesses place it in v. 20, without Amen; some as v. 24 with 25–7; some as v. 24 without 25–7: see the table in Gamble, *Textual History*, p. 131). Such variation in positioning often indicates an interpolation.

What is the substantial difference in content between the fourteen- and sixteen-chapter forms? 15.14–16.23 is directed towards Rome and is concerned with a specific time and set of people. Therefore its removal makes the letter more generally applicable. The removal of references to Rome in 1.7, 15 takes away completely any specific reference to Rome. But it is harder to make this apply to 15.1–13. Could it be that 15.5, 7 seemed to be linked to Rome?

Several explanations of this problem have been offered. They divide into two categories. The first attributes both forms of text to Paul. It is perhaps surprising that the writers about to be cited are by no means our contemporaries. The fact is, they had more to say on these matters than do most of their successors, so they are our best guides.

According to J.B. Lightfoot, who knew of fourteen- and sixteen-chapter forms, they were both from Paul. The first form consisted of 1.1–16.23, omitting both the Benediction and the Doxology. 'At some period of his life, not improbably during one of his sojourns in Rome, it occurred to the Apostle to give to this letter a wider circulation' (p. 319). He changed the two references to Rome in Chapter 1, and 'cut off the last two chapters containing personal matters, adding at the same time a doxology as a termination to the whole'.

An alternative version was proposed by Kirsopp Lake. He starts with the main problem, namely that since 15.1–13 seems to belong with Chapter 14, there would have been no need to excise this passage in order to remove an explicitly Roman application of the letter. He suggests that Paul first wrote a general letter, with fourteen chapters, at about the same time as Galatians. He later altered this to address the Romans, with changes in Chapter 1 and the addition of Chapter 15. Lake thought that Chapter 16 was probably addressed to the Ephesians (many of the names seem to have connections with Ephesus than with Rome).

T.W. Manson proposed that Paul wrote two versions of Romans: the first consisted of Chapters 1–15 (cf. P46), and was sent to Rome; the other consisted of this with the addition of Chapter 16, a covering letter to Ephesus.

J. B. Lightfoot, *Biblical Essays*, London and New York, 1893, 285–374, contains a series of papers on the topic under the title 'The Structure and Destination of the Epistle to the Romans': first by Lightfoot, 'M. Renan's Theory of the Epistle to the Romans', 287–320 (reprinted from *Journal of Philology* 2 (1869), 264ff.). There follows a rejection of his argument by F.J.A. Hort, 'On the End of the Epistle to the Romans', 321–51 (reprinted from *Journal of Philology* 3 (1871), 51ff.). Lightfoot defends his view with vigour in 'The Epistle to the Romans', 352–74 (reprinted from *Journal of Philology* 3 (1871), 193ff.). K. Lake, *The Earlier Epistles of St Paul*, London, 1911; T.W. Manson, 'St. Paul's Letter to the Romans – and Others', in M. Black (ed.), *Studies in the Gospels and Epistles*, Manchester, 1962.

The other possibility is that the shorter version(s) were produced by someone else. Marcion is usually regarded as a likely culprit and has been so at least since the time of Origen, who says that Marcion removed the Doxology from the end of Chapter 14, along with all the rest of the letter (Commentary on 14.23).

The questions discussed above are not only of significance for the textual scholar. I hope that it will be clear why they need to be considered and answered to their own satisfaction by all students of Paul and commentators on his letters. These are important questions for the study of Romans, because discussion about the letter has concerned its character as a theological treatise. Whether one wishes to treat Romans as 'Paul's last will and testament' (Bornkamm) or as a solution for a set of problems in Rome, one will need to tackle the challenge posed by the fact that the letter circulated in different guises: Romans as written only to a single specific church, Romans planned as a multi-destination letter, Romans as a letter first sent to Ephesus and then revised and extended, or else a letter sent first to Rome and then to Ephesus.

8.8.2 The problem of Ephesians

There are two textual problems. The first, that Marcion called it *Ad Laodicenses* ('To the Laodiceans'), has been noted. The second is that a number of manuscripts omit ἐν Ἐφέσῳ from 1.1: P46 01* 03* 6 1739. There is no doubt that the copyists and users of these manuscripts believed the letter to be addressed to the Ephesians – several of them have the subscription 'To the Ephesians', or the like (01 03; P46 has no subscription), or running titles. The issue is how the absence is to be explained.

Is it coincidence that some uncertainty surrounds Ephesians, the letter to a place to which it has been argued Romans 16 may have been more likely to have been sent? And that Marcion, who either knew or created the text with a fourteen-chapter letter form, knew Ephesians as something else?

I leave these questions open, preferring to offer three concluding remarks on this section. First, the evidence for fourteen- and fifteen-chapter forms of Romans is a lesson in the value of indirect evidence, chapter headings, and the like, for textual research. Second, my brief report has focused on the external evidence. The exegete will be better placed than I to combine this with the exegetical problems raised by the textual phenomena which have been described. Finally, the questions which have been raised here are of great significance to the exegete, who has to decide what forms of text it is safe to regard as Pauline, and the editor, who has to develop editorial principles which will deal with the facts of the particular text, or sets of texts, to be edited.

Before turning to that, I shall discuss further variants which, for various reasons, have assumed prominence in recent years.

8.9 OTHER VARIANT READINGS

Out of the host of possible choices, I have selected two readings on the grounds of their intrinsic interest and value as examples of current debate.

By doing this, I neglect here totally many other classes of variant, such as examples of stylistically motivated variants (which are discussed in 10.10.5). For a study of one single aspect of this, see E. W. Güting and D. L. Mealand, *Asyndeton in Paul. A Text-critical and Statistical Enquiry into Pauline Style* (Studies in the Bible and Early Christianity 39), Lewiston, Queenston and Lampeter, 1998. For a study using the thoroughgoing eclecticism described in 10.10.5, see J. K. Elliott, *The Greek Text of the Epistles to Timothy and Titus* (SD 36), Salt Lake City, 1968.

8.9.1 1 Corinthians 14.34–5

Debate about the possibility that these verses are an interpolation has grown over recent years, as the way in which the role of women changed in early Christianity has been exposed to greater critical scrutiny. The fact that Zuntz thought the verses were post-Pauline (though in the archetype of the tradition) already suggests that there is more to this than a current interest.

1. The Evidence

As with the shorter forms of Romans, our evidence is indirect. The most important observation is that a small group of witnesses place the verses after verse 40. These are the Greek manuscripts 06 010 012 88 915, the Syriac Peshitta and the Latin manuscripts 61 89 with Ambrosiaster and Sedulius Scotus. The Latin witnesses are largely the bilinguals, whose agreement takes us back either to the mid-fourth or the third century. The other Latin evidence, including Ambrosiaster's writing between 366 and 378 in Rome, suggests that the reading was widespread in the Latin world. Indeed, as Fee points out, it is the reading of all witnesses except those which represent the Vulgate text, known from about 400 onwards. That is, the only text in the west before 400 placed the verses after verse 40.

The Greek manuscript 88 was copied in the twelfth century and 915 in the thirteenth. Both manuscripts belong to the Byzantine textual tradition. As well as placing the verses after 40, 88 contains a correction (perhaps by the scribe) indicating that they belong after verse 33.

Evidence for the different text forms in Greek in *Text und Textwert* 2.2, Teststelle 50. According to
P. B. Payne, 'Ms. 88 as Evidence for a Text without 1 Cor 14.34–5', *NTS* 44 (1998), 152–6, the
phenomenon in 88 can only be explained by positing that it was copied from a manuscript which
lacked the verses. Payne's argument, however, is weak, indeed part of it seems hopelessly confused. It
is probably safest to posit that the exemplar of 88 had vv. 34–5 after v. 40. Payne has also raised the
possibility that a double dot against the verses in 03 also supports ancient evidence for the omission of
the verses (see 1.8.1). Finally, Payne has argued that the Latin manuscript Codex Fuldensis should be
regarded as evidence in support of the verses' omission: 'Fuldensis, Sigla for Variants in Vaticanus,
and 1 Cor 14.34–5', *NTS* 41 (1995), 251–62.

2. Explanations

Variation in positioning is often a sign of an interpolation. That is why
the evidence concerning the location of the verses is so important.
Perhaps the sentence was first written in the margin as a comment or
addition and then found its way into the text in two different places. The
wider the attestation, the older the interpolation is likely to be. The fact
that it had found its way at an early stage (it is already in P46) into the
Greek tradition and some of the versions after verse 33, and after verse 40
in the widely spread Peshitta and the archetype of the bilinguals, as well as
in some Greek manuscripts (attested only by two Byzantine witnesses)
provides evidence for its early date.

Again, the internal evidence (that comparison with 1 Cor. 11.5 suggests a
fatal inconsistency, that the structure of the sentence is more Pauline without
it, that it disrupts the subject matter, and so on) I shall leave to others.

The interest of these verses text-critically lies in their study. The story
of its research is of a comment by Zuntz largely ignored; a proposal by
Fee which finds an interpolation with the aim of silencing women in the
Christian congregation; the search for external evidence to back up the
internal evidence. It is a search which has to be regarded as in need of
further study. In a paper read in 2006 J. Kloha drew attention to a large
number of other similar dislocations of text in the bilingual manuscripts
of Paul, arguing that the phenomenon is a feature of these manuscripts
and has nothing to tell us about the original authenticity of this passage.
On the one hand, a new approach to the study of the role of women in
early Christianity drew our attention to a textual problem in 1 Corinthians
14, and led to a fresh impetus in research. On the other hand, there has been
a tendency to find more evidence than the material really yields, and
caution is required.

Kloha's paper, using material from his doctoral thesis at the University of Leeds, was read at the New
Testament Textual Criticism Section, Society of Biblical Literature Annual Congress, Washington
DC, 2006. For one of his discussions on the topic, see G. D. Fee, *God's Empowering Spirit*, Peabody,
Mass., 1994, 272–81.

Another passage which has received attention for similar reasons in recent years is Rom. 16.7, which has been dealt with in detail by E. J. Epp, *Junia. The First Woman Apostle*, Minneapolis, 2005. See also 'Minor Textual Variants in Romans 16:7', in Childers and Parker, *Transmission and Reception*, 123–41.

8.9.2 Hebrews 2.9

1. The Evidence

I find the evidence most fully stated in Frede's *Vetus Latina* edition (ad loc.):

Virtually all witnesses read χάριτι θεοῦ

χωρίς θεοῦ is read by the Greek copies 0243 1739*, by some Coptic Bohairic manuscripts, by some manuscripts of the Peshitta, and in the margin of the ninth-century Vulgate copy G in a double-rendering, *sine uel extra deum*. It is also found in citations of the passage by some early Christian writers: among the Greeks Origen (in four out of six citations), Eusebius (not mentioned by Frede, and thus deserves checking), Theodore of Mopsuestia, Theodoret, Theophylact (not mentioned by Frede), and Oecumenius (not mentioned by Frede); among the Latins the evidence is even more fully set out by Frede. I repeat the evidence in some detail, because it demonstrates very well the wealth of information not only about the forms and currency of particular readings and renderings, but also about the Latin exegetical tradition, which the *Vetus Latina* affords. First, citations reading *sine deo*:

1. Ambrose, three times in his work *De Fide* (*CPL* 150), written 378–80 in Milan. In the first two citations, three of the manuscripts of this work read *sine domino*.
2. A work wrongly attributed to Augustine (*CPL* 363), written in Africa around 480–90.
3. Rufinus' translation of Origen's commentary on Romans 3.8, made in 405/6.
4. Vigilius of Thapsus (North Africa) in *Contra Eutychetem* (*CPL* 806), written at or shortly after 480.
5. Fulgentius, Bishop of Ruspe (North Africa), in *Ad Trasamandum*(*CPL* 816), written in about 515 cites it twice.
6. Acts of a council as reproduced in the *Collectio Palatina*, made by a Scythian monk in 532/5 (cites both forms).
7. Pope Vigilius' *Constitutum* (*CPL* 1696, see also *CPG* [IV. 9365]), written in 553, once cites it in the rendering *citra deum* (quoting Theodore of Mopsuestia). This is also found in the Latin Acts of the Second Council of Constantinople, made in 553. The *Constitutum* later refers to the reading *sine deo* as a variant of *gratia dei*.
8. Jerome in his commentary on Galatians (*CPL* 591) refers to manuscripts containing the variant: *in quibusdam exemplaribus legitur, absque deo*.

The reading was virtually unknown from manuscripts until modern times, since both 0243 and 1739 are recent discoveries. But it has had occasional advocates since the sixteenth century, including Harnack (cf. Zuntz, *Text of the Epistles*, p. 34, n. 6). It will be remembered that 0243 and 1739 are closely related, being believed by Birdsall to be derived from an archetype Y (see 8.4). The patristic information shows that, however few surviving manuscripts contain it, the reading was once well known. The fact that it is cited in Latin in several different renderings of χωρίς suggests either that there was more than one revision against Greek texts with this reading, or a quite extensive history of revisions within the Latin tradition.

2. Explanations

How did the variant arise? Which reading gave rise to the other? Bengel in his *Gnomon* took χωρίς to mean 'except'. But the proper meaning of the word should be 'without'. The traditional view was that χάριτι was original, and the other a marginal note qualifying 'subjecting all things' (cf. 1 Cor. 15.27, possibly therefore an example of textual comparison and harmonisation within the *corpus*), which got into the text at the wrong place. Another view suggested that it was what has been called 'uncial error', the mis-recognition of similar word shapes when letters are written in majuscule. Although there are several letters in common, the entire sequence is not similar enough for this to be a convincing explanation. The possible confusion of ΑΛΛΑ and ΑΜΑ is the kind of variant better attributable to this cause.

There is internal evidence against the reading χάριτι. The word χάρις in Hebrews has a different meaning from that in the Pauline writings. It refers not to Jesus' salvific death but to the gift of future salvation (4.16; cf. also 10.29; 12.15; 13.25). If this is the case, one has to look for a reason why the innocuous but unconvincing χάριτι should have replaced χωρίς. In a discussion which provides a good example of the book's method, Ehrman in *The Orthodox Corruption of Scripture* argues that

(1) χωρίς θεοῦ fits in with the theology of Hebrews (see 2.11, 14; 5.7; 12.2f.; 13.13).

(2) Its removal was due to a Christological debate in the second century (it must have been that early, because P46 already attests χάριτι θεοῦ). Gnostics argued that the divine in Jesus abandoned him before the crucifixion. Their opponents rejected this. The original text of Hebrews could be taken as support for the Gnostic view. So someone changed it to an innocuous statement.

J. A. Bengel, *Gnomon Novi Testamenti*, 1st edn, Tübingen, 1742, 903f.; Ehrman, *Orthodox Corruption*, 146–50. Note the way in which some of the Latin writers citing *sine deo* also insist on its orthodox meaning (e.g. Vigilius of Thapsus).

S. P. Brock, 'Hebrews 2.9B in Syriac Tradition', *NovT* 27 (1985), 236–44, citing Philoxenus' view that 'apart from God' was a Nestorian corruption of the Syriac text. He argues that the Peshitta first read 'by the grace of God'. This is not an argument concerning the original Pauline text, So far as the Peshitta is concerned, Brock's findings bear out Philoxenus' opinion.

This variant casts light on the method needed for analysing such a reading:

(1) The examination began with the external evidence, the manuscript support and other attestation. The paucity of manuscript support for one reading was seen to be no argument against it, given (a) the rare value of the Greek evidence and (b) the breadth of attestation across Greek and Latin writers, revealing that it must once have been present in many manuscripts.

(2) Study next moved to the internal evidence, to the author's language, style and thought. This should always take precedence, since the weighing of good witnesses against bad is a meaningless and unthinking process. The only occasion on which the external evidence might carry the day is if there were no other grounds for choosing between two equally good readings. Here an editor should be consistent and follow one of two courses of action: where there is nothing to decide, either follow one manuscript every time, or make one's own (consistent) decision every time.

(3) That reading is original which explains all the others. This simple maxim requires that at each place of decision one has to present a history of the text, stating in what order the different variants arose. In such an instance as this, it is particularly clear that a history of the text is only one part of a much wider history, that of Christian thought and practice. Any convincing history of the text must take this wider history into account, and in return will have a contribution to make to it. Having reached this conclusion at the end of a discussion of a mere two out of the many important readings in the epistles, I turn to discuss what an edition of the letters should be.

8.10 EDITING THE PAULINE LETTERS

The most important decision derives from the different possible ways in which the collection of letters came to be formed. Are all our extant witnesses descended from a first copy of a collected edition of the letters? For this to be the case, it will have had to be a collection containing all fourteen letters accepted in the subsequent tradition. Of course, those manuscripts containing fifteen letters will be composite, their text of 3 Corinthians or Laodiceans being ultimately derived from a different archetype. The options which I can think of are as follows:

(1) All manuscripts are descended from one archetype of a single edition of fourteen letters, and the task of the editor is to reconstruct this text.

(2)   All manuscripts are descended from the same two or more archetypes, between them containing the fourteen letters, which the editor should reconstruct.

(3)   Some manuscripts are descended from the archetype of one collection, some from the archetype of another (or multiple archetypes, as in (2)). Here the editor would have to reconstruct a number of different text forms, before making a final decision as to whether a single earlier form of text from which these were derived could be reconstructed, and whether this is best described under (1) or (2) or (5).

(4)   Some manuscripts are descended from archetypes of collections, while some are descended from manuscript traditions of separate letters predating the formation of a collection, or at least contain readings derived from these earlier manuscript traditions. The same set of editorial procedures would apply here as for (3) and (5).

(5)   All manuscripts are descended from manuscript traditions of separate letters, which may be reconstructed without reference to the formation of any collection.

The question therefore is whether we have a unified tradition, the whole descended from a single point, namely a first collected edition of fourteen letters, or whether the tradition is hybrid. It is only when decisions have been made in this regard that the editorial task will become clear. These questions cannot be answered here, since the letters await the attentions of the *Editio critica maior*. It is possible, however, to outline the most important contribution yet to have been made to the Pauline letters, and to illustrate how it sheds light on these problems.

G. Zuntz's *The Text of the Epistles* is certainly a classic work of text-critical analysis, and along with Westcott and Hort's Introduction is one of the texts which should be read and studied by everyone who wishes to understand such research or to undertake it. Zuntz is in no doubt that the task of the editor is to reconstruct the text of the first collected edition which, as has been stated, he considered to have been formed in about 100. He does not believe that the text of this collection perfectly represents what Paul wrote to his churches (we are not talking here about questions of authenticity). He draws attention to several places where he believes the archetype (the manuscript made by the editor of the collected edition) is corrupt: 1 Corinthians 6.5, where it omitted ἀνὰ μέσον ἀδελφοῦ καί before ἀνὰ μέσον τοῦ ἀδελφοῦ αὐτοῦ, or 1 Corinthians 15.2, where it contained a corruption which makes no sense. In both of these cases, it is plain that an impossible reading has come down to all witnesses (the Peshitta supplies the equivalent of ἀνὰ μέσον ἀδελφοῦ καί at 1 Corinthians 6.5, but as a conjecture). The logical conclusion is that the error lies in the archetype, although he observes that this is 'never quite safe to assert' (p. 16). The archetype also contains interpolations: 1 Corinthians 1.16 and Philemon 19a he considers to be Pauline marginal notes; Romans 7.25b; 1 Corinthians 10.29b–30 and 14.33b–35 (see 8.9.1) he views as post-Pauline interpolations.

Zuntz's study, which deals almost exclusively with 1 Corinthians and Hebrews, proceeds by examining the main witnesses and their character both individually and in relation to each other: P46, 03, 1739, what he calls **W**, the Western Text. His study predated Frede's work on the bilinguals and any of the Vetus Latina editions, but he includes the Greek columns of 06, 010 and 012, with what (without being quite clear) he intends to be the Old Latin text-types (p. 85). It is important in the extreme that he concludes P46 to be a text of excellent quality, once its errors have been removed (this requires more than the discounting of singular readings: see the description of Martini's work in 10.4.3). From this he moves on to discuss various types of variant readings, and then to set his findings against the evidence of second-century writers, before coming to draw his conclusions. Having indicated the problem: that the textual tradition is divided between an eastern and a western branch; that western characteristics, including errors, appear in the eastern branch, and that sometimes such features are found in later but not earlier eastern witnesses; he concludes that both branches are (as he develops the metaphor) derived from 'that great common reservoir, the popular text of the second century' (p. 265). Against this, the Alexandrian attempt to preserve and where possible restore the text was not so much a moment in time, a recension, as a process which began in the second century and continued down to the Euthalian Edition. This philology was, he eventually concludes, present even in the formation of the archetype itself, where he argues that the best understanding of the variants in Romans 1.7, 15 and Ephesians 1.1. can only be explained by the conclusion that the archetype had a blank in the text and the address ἐν Ῥώμῃ or ἐν Ἐφέσῳ in the margin, and thus that the editor had available 'copies descended from the Pauline original as well as others which derived from the particular Roman, Ephesian, &c., exemplars and that he embodied their divergences in his edition' (p. 277). He believes that the variant at 1 Corinthians 1.2 is due to the debated clause having been in the margin.

Zuntz's method is to work by comparison of the witnesses, observing where they agree and where they differ, working back up the stream of tradition towards the source. He practises traditional philology. Whether he gave too much weight to the concept of Alexandrian editors and whether he was mistaken in assuming that there was a single collected edition from whose archetype all our witnesses are descended are questions to consider. The task after Zuntz is to seek answers to these questions, which without his researches would scarcely be before us.

CHAPTER 9

Acts and the Catholic epistles

9.1. INTRODUCTION: ACTS AND THE CATHOLIC EPISTLES AS A UNIT IN THE TRADITION

In the later tradition, Acts and the Catholic letters were generally copied together. In 1989 there were 662 manuscripts of these books, of which 59 contained the entire New Testament, 150 all the New Testament except for Revelation, 46 consisted of partial copies numbering fewer than ten folios, and 407 consisted of Acts and the Catholic letters. It was also a common practice in the Byzantine world to produce Praxapostoloi, manuscripts containing Acts, the Catholic epistles and the Pauline collection. Such a book would contain the Catholic epistles directly after Acts (as would a copy with the Gospels).

Data in Aland and Aland, *The Text of the New Testament*, chart 4 (p. 83). The term Praxapostolos is sometimes used more carelessly to include Revelation as well (i.e. all the New Testament except the Gospels) or for Acts and the Catholic epistles alone (it would be helpful to have a term which unequivocally described these eight texts together).

How early did the custom of putting Acts and the Catholic letters together begin? The data for all sixty-five copies down to the ninth century can be seen in table 9.1.

The oldest copy that we have in Greek with only Acts and the Catholic letters is seventh-century. Before and after that, we see quite a variation in practice. In the third century P45 contains Acts with the Gospels. In the late third or early fourth century P72 contains three of the Catholic letters in what seems to be a miscellany. Then in the fourth and fifth centuries we find the eight texts included in what are usually treated (for reservations, see 1.8.1) as complete Bibles. In 01 the collection comes after Paul and before Revelation; in 02 and 03 it comes between the Gospels and Paul. In all three it comes in the order Acts–James–Peter–John–Jude. Around 400, 05 (Codex Bezae) now contains the end of 3 John (only the Latin) between the Gospels and Acts. There is a lacuna between the

Table 9.1

Date	MS	Book and chapters present
III (beginning)	P23	Jas. 1
III	P9	1 Jn 4
	P20	Jas. 2–3
	P29	Acts 26
	P45	parts of Four Gospels and Acts
	P53	parts of Matthew and Acts
	P91	Acts 2–3
III (end)	P48	Acts 23
c. 300	P38	Acts 18–19
III/IV	P72	*Birth of Mary*, 3 Cor., *Odes of Solomon* 11, Jude, Melito's *Paschal Homily*, fragment of a hymn, *Apology of Phileas*, Pss. 33, 34 (LXX), 1 Pet., 2 Pet.
	P78	Jude
	P100	Jas. 3–5
IV	P8	Acts 4, 5, 6
	P81	1 Pet. 2–3
	01	Bible
	03	Bible
	0189	Acts 5
	0206	1 Pet. 5
IV/V	P50	Acts 8, 10
	P57	Acts 4–5
	057	Acts 3
c. 400	05	Four Gospels, 3 John, Acts (Graeco-Latin)
V	P112	Acts 26, 27
	02	Bible
	04	Bible? (2 John not present)
	048	Acts, Catholic epistles and Paul (all fragmentary)
	077	Acts 13
	0165	Acts 3
	0166	Acts 28, Jas. 1
	0173	Jas. 1
	0175	Acts 6
	0232	2 John
	0236	Acts 3 (Graeco-Coptic)
	0244	Acts 11–12
V/VI	P54	Jas. 2, 3
	P56	Acts 1
	076	Acts 2
	0247	1 Pet. 5, 2 Pet. 1, 2
VI	P33	Acts 7, 15
	08	Acts (Graeco-Latin)
	066	Acts 28
	093	Acts 24–5, 1 Pet. 2–3
	0245	1 Jn 3–4

Table 9.1 (*cont.*)

Date	MS	Book and chapters present
	0246	Jas. 1
	0251	3 John, Jude
	0285	parts of Paul and 1 Pet. 3–4
	0296	1 Jn 5, 2 Cor. 7
VI/VII	0294	Acts 14–15
VII	P74	parts of all eight books
	096	Acts 2, 26
	097	Acts 13
	0209	fragments of Rom., 2 Cor., 2 Pet. 1–2
	0316	Jude
VII/VIII	0157	1 Jn 2
VIII	P41	Acts 17–22 (Graeco-Coptic)
	095	Acts 2–3
	0156	2 Pet. 3
IX	014	Acts (epistles added in X, – 2125)
	018	Catholic epistles and Paul
	020	Acts, Catholic epistles and Paul
	025	Acts, Catholic epistles, Paul and Revelation
	049	Acts, Catholic epistles and Paul
	0120	Acts 16–17, 18
	0304	Acts 6–7
	33	Gospels, Acts, Catholic epistles and Paul

Gospels and this leaf which is too long to have contained the rest of the Catholic letters, but of about the right length to have contained Revelation and the remainder of the Johannine letters. It is possible therefore that this manuscript placed the writings ascribed to John (apart from the Gospel) together between the Gospels and Acts. In the fifth century 048 contains portions of Acts, the Catholic epistles and Paul, and 0166, preserved in the end of Acts and beginning of James, might have contained Acts and the Catholic epistles. Into the sixth century we find that 08 contains Acts on its own (this manuscript will be discussed in detail in the next section), and there is another example of such a manuscript in the ninth (014). In the seventh century we have the first certain example of a manuscript containing Acts and the seven letters together. In the same century we have what may be a manuscript of all the epistles (0209), and in the ninth one which we may claim to be such with more certainty (018). The remaining three examples (020, 025, 049) contain the entire Apostolos, 025 with the addition of Revelation.

The evidence overall suggests a lack of fixed practice before the seventh century at the earliest. On the other hand, the order of the seven Catholic letters is very uniform, especially among Greek manuscripts. The stage at which the eight writings were first counted together is, so far as the manuscripts attest, the fourth century. The fact that both 01 and 03, the two great Bible codices, treat them as a unity (manifest by the fact that they disagree as to the order of the larger blocks) is our earliest example.

For P72 see 9.3.2. For 05 see Parker, *Codex Bezae*, 8f.; for the order of the Catholic letters, see 9.3.2.

9.2 THE ACTS OF THE APOSTLES

9.2.1 The genre of Acts and textual variation

Acts is unique among the New Testament writings in its subject matter and presentation. Its textual problems are also unique. While each of the Gospels has its own character and typical textual problems, they also have certain strong similarities. Acts, like Revelation, is the only writing of its kind, so it is no surprise to find that the textual history is quite different. What this textual history may be is best illustrated at the outset with an example. I take the wordings of the Apostolic Decree, as it is given the first time (Acts 15.19–20). The text upon the left is that found in 03 (Codex Vaticanus), while that of 05 (Codex Bezae) is on the right.

διὸ ἐγὼ κρείνω μὴ παρενοχλεῖν τοῖς ἀπὸ τῶν ἐθνῶν ἐπιστρέφουσιν ἐπὶ τὸν θεόν, ἀλλ᾽ ἐπιστεῖλαι αὐτοῖς τοῦ ἀπεχέσθαι τὸν θεόν, ἀλλ᾽ ἐπιστεῖλαι αὐτοῖς τοῦ ἀπεχέσθαι τῶν ἀλισγημάτων τῶν εἰδώλων καὶ τῆς πορνείας καὶ πνικτοῦ καὶ τοῦ αἵματος·

διὸ ἐγὼ κρείνω μὴ παρενοχλεῖν τοῖς ἀπὸ τῶν ἐθνῶν ἐπιστρέφουσιν ἐπὶ τὸν θεόν, ἀλλὰ ἐπιστεῖλαι αὐτοῖς τοῦ ἀπεχέσθαι τὸν θεόν, ἀλλ᾽ ἐπιστεῖλαι αὐτοῖς τοῦ ἀπεχέσθαι τῶν ἀλισγημάτων τῶν εἰδώλων καὶ τῆς πορνείας καὶ τοῦ αἵματος, καὶ ὅσα μὴ θέλουσιν ἑαυτοῖς γείνεσθαι ἑτέροις μὴ ποιεῖτε·

Text with accentuation and punctuation taken from J.H. Ropes, *The Text of Acts* (*Beginnings of Christianity*, vol. III), London, 1926, 144–5.

The texts are for the most parts identical. At the end, 05 omits καὶ πνικτοῦ and adds the negative version of the Golden Rule. There is some evidence that the text as found in 05 underwent later development: 1739 provides a similar reading and a marginal note. It too omits πνικτοῦ and reads the grammatically more sophisticated καὶ ἂν μὴ θέλωσιν αὐτοῖς γενέσθαι ἑτέροις μὴ ποιεῖν. This polish suggests a development of the version found in 05.

Throughout Acts, we find that Codex Bezae contains such readings, some of them additions, some alternative phrasings of the text as it is found in 03. But it is not alone in containing distinctive readings. The climax of the story of the Ethiopian eunuch (8.36–8, a passage no longer extant in Codex Bezae) is found in these forms in 03 and the other Graeco-Latin bilingual, 08 (Codex Laudianus):

Codex Vaticanus	Codex Laudianus
φησιν ὁ εὐνοῦχος· Ἰδοὺ ὕδωρ· τί κωλύει με βαπτιστῆναι;	φησιν ὁ εὐνοῦχος· Ἰδοὺ ὕδωρ· τί κωλύει με βαπτιστῆναι; εἶπεν δὲ αὐτῷ ὁ Φίλιππος ἐαν πιστεύεις ἐξ ὅλης τῆς καρδίας σου, σωθήσει. ἀποριθεὶς δὲ εἶπεν· πιστεύω εἰς τὸν χριστὸν τὸν υἱὸν τοῦ θεοῦ·
καὶ ἐκέλευσε στῆναι τὸ ἅρμα, καὶ κατέβησαν ἀμφότεροι εἰς τὸ ὕδωρ ὅ τε Φίλιππος καὶ ὁ εὐνοῦχος, καὶ ἐβάπτισεν αὐτόν.	καὶ ἐκέλευσε στῆναι τὸ ἅρμα, καὶ κατέβησαν ἀμφότεροι εἰς τὸ ὕδωρ ὅ τε Φίλιππος καὶ ὁ εὐνοῦχος, καὶ ἐβάπτισεν αὐτόν.

Text of 03 as above taken from Ropes, *The Text of Acts*; text of 08 taken from the Nestle–Aland apparatus.

This, with some inner variation, is a widespread reading found in a number of minuscules, including 1739. The precise text of 08 is also found in 1884, a sixteenth-century manuscript of Acts only which according to *Text und Textwert* agrees with 08 more than with any other extensive manuscript (in 53 out of 57 Teststellen). In all, *Text und Textwert* lists twenty-two versions of this addition, one attested in thirty manuscripts, the rest in between one and four. These are two significant and typical differences. The ways in which they may be explained will be discussed once the principal witnesses have been described.

9.2.2 *The Greek witnesses*

Among the Greek manuscripts, we have the constants 01, 02, 03 and 04. There are also several manuscripts to be described which contain the Gospels as well.

The first of these is P45, a third-century manuscript. It was dated by its editor, F.G. Kenyon, to the first half of the century. It contains parts of Matthew 20–1, 25–6; Mark 4–9, 11–12; Luke 6, 9–14; John 4, 5, 10, 11; Acts 4–17. This sounds extensive, but in Acts the leaves are not very well preserved, those containing Chapters 4–8 being typically about 6 cm across and 11 cm high, with seventeen lines or so of text and about as many letters on a line. The later leaves are a similar height but preserve more of the width of the page. Since the leaves are from the top of the page, the latest ones in particular preserving some of the top margin, two page numbers remain. F27v has the number 193, and the last page (F30r) is numbered 199, so that the manuscript would originally – assuming that it had nothing else after Acts – have consisted of 218 pages. The outside pages must have been blank, giving a total of 110 leaves (55 sheets each folded in half). The manuscript is one of the very few certain examples of a codex composed of single-sheet gatherings ('uniones'). This is proved by the occurrence of two conjoint gatherings in Luke. The script is aptly described by Kenyon as 'a small and very clear hand', 'square in formation', 'with a decided slope to the right'. He gave it a third-century date.

F.G. Kenyon, *Chester Beatty Biblical Papyri. Descriptions and Texts of Twelve Manuscripts on Papyrus of the Greek Bible*, vol. 11: *The Gospels and Acts. Text*, London, 1933, viii. For single-sheet gatherings, see Turner, *Typology*, 61.

Another significant papyrus, in spite of its late date (seventh century) is P74. Agreeing with 02 in eighty-one out of ninety-two Teststellen (88 per cent), with 03 in seventy-five (82 per cent) and with 01 in seventy-four (80 per cent), it is a major witness to the form of text found in these manuscripts.

Also to be noted is the Michigan Papyrus, P38, containing parts of Chapters 18 and 19 (18.27–19.6, 12–16). It is dated to about 300. It aroused interest upon its publication because it seemed to provide older evidence for the form of the text found in Codex Bezae.

Among the majuscules, 03 usually stands as the main representative of the alternative text to that represented by 05. This may be partly because it stands on the left-hand page of Ropes' edition, in which the two manuscripts are transcribed. To Ropes it is the best representative of what he calls the 'Old Uncial Text', along with 01, 02, 04, 81 and some other minuscules (p. ccl).

I turn now to 05, Codex Bezae. Having written in brief and at length on this manuscript in a number of places, I am reluctant even to offer the barest outline here. What follows summarises my own conclusions. The manuscript is bilingual, with Greek on the left page and a Latin version (5 in the Vetus Latina numbering) on the right, in irregular lines broadly following units of sense. It was copied about 400, by a scribe trained in Latin legal copying, possibly in the city of Berytus (modern Beirut). It is descended from other bilingual copies, being derived from a copy of the Gospels written by two scribes, in the order Matthew–Mark–John–Luke, itself possibly derived from a bilingual text in the order Matthew–Mark–Luke–John; Acts was copied from a second bilingual exemplar, the whole being brought into a uniform presentation by the scribe. A number of correctors were responsible for changes to the manuscript in the fifth to seventh centuries, and the manuscript had some leaves supplemented at Lyons in the ninth century (see 4.2.2).

Thus much for the manuscript. What about its text? By a comparison of the Greek and Latin columns, I concluded that the form of text of Acts found in the manuscript was due to evolution rather than to a single comprehensive revision. The evidence lies in differences between the columns, where the Latin often seems to be a witness to a form of Greek text which lies somewhere between the form in 03 and that in 05.

Parker, *Codex Bezae*. See also: 'Codex Bezae', *The Anchor Bible Dictionary*, New York, 1992, 1.1070–1; 'Codex Bezae', in P. Fox (ed.), *Cambridge University Library. The Great Collections*, Cambridge, 1998, 33–43; D.C. Parker and C.-B. Amphoux (eds.), *Codex Bezae. Studies from the Lunel Colloquium June 1994* (NTTS 22), Leiden, New York and Cologne, 1996; 'Codex Bezae: the Manuscript as Past, Present and Future', in McKendrick and O'Sullivan, 43–50.

The bibliography for Codex Bezae is greater than for any other New Testament manuscript, as a glance at the selection in Elliott's *Bibliography* will show. For discussion of the textual affiliations with other manuscripts (with which my monograph did not deal), see most recently *Text und Textwert* III/1 (ANTF 20), 709–19. For the influence of theological and religious views on the text, see 9.2.4. K.E. Panten, 'A History of Research on Codex Bezae', *Tyndale Bulletin* 47 (1996), 185–7 is a summary of 'A History of Research on Codex Bezae, with Special Reference to the Acts of the Apostles: Evaluation and Future Directions', unpublished PhD thesis, Murdoch University, Western Australia, 1995.

There is an English translation by J. M. Wilson, *The Acts of the Apostles Translated from the Codex Bezae with an Introduction on its Lucan Origin and Importance*, London, 1923 (reissued with corrections 1924), with longer readings in bold face. In addition to the transcription on the right-hand page of Ropes' edition of Acts, Clark's edition of the Greek text (very dated so far as his interpretations are concerned) also indicates additions in 05 and other manuscripts in bold type: A.C. Clark, *The Acts of the Apostles A Critical Edition with Introduction and Notes on Selected Passages*, Oxford, 1933.

A significant point I failed to develop in arguing that the manuscript may have been produced in Berytus (pp. 266–78) is in the connection with Romanos Melodus. Several passages in his Kontakia reflect knowledge of a form of Greek text only found also in Codex Bezae. Is this because Romanos was at one period of his life a deacon at the Church of the Resurrection in Berytus? See R. Maisano (ed.), *Cantici di Romano il Melodo*, 2 vols., Turin, 2002, 1.35.

08, Codex Laudianus (Vetus Latina number 50, letter e), is a second Graeco-Latin bilingual with an important text and an interesting history. Perhaps written in either Sardinia or Rome in about 600, it was used by Bede at Jarrow in Northumbria in the early eighth century in his commentary on Acts (*CPL* 1357), written soon after 709. This is a rare example of an ancient commentator's having used an identified extant manuscript. It was then taken to Würzburg later in the same century and was bought by William Laud, Archbishop of Canterbury in the early seventeenth century, who subsequently presented it to the Bodleian Library. The Latin text belongs to the European Old Latin type and is a rather pedantic rendering of the Greek. The layout consists of two columns, often of a single word, and it is unique among the ancient Graeco-Latin manuscripts in having the Latin on the left. The close agreement of the Greek column with 1884 has already been noted. No other manuscript has such a similar text, the next closest with an extensive text being 02, with an agreement of thirty-six out of sixty test passages (60 per cent).

0189 deserves mention for discussion of its date. It is in the *Liste* as II/III, as it is also in K. Aland, 'Das Neue Testament auf Papyrus', *Studien zur Überlieferung des Neuen Testaments und seines Textes* (ANTF 2), Berlin, 1967, 91–136, p. 92. Aland and Aland, *The Text of the New Testament*, give it as third/fourth, noting that it was formerly assigned to the fourth (p. 104 and plate 27). Turner, *Typology*, 159, reports the fourth-century date. In Parker, 'The Majuscule Manuscripts', 29, I present palaeographical evidence for a date in the early fourth century.

The appraisal of the minuscules has to be carried out in the light of *Text und Textwert*. Previous researches, based upon only some manuscripts, led to some dubious results. 614 was claimed as a supporter of 05. In *Text und Textwert* it is shown to be a Byzantine witness, with an agreement rate with 05 too low to appear in the Hauptliste, and crucially with very few Sonderlesarten (special readings) in common with 05 (only TS 42, SL 4 and TS 49, SL 4).

A. V. Valentine-Richards†, *The Text of Acts in Codex 614 (Tisch. 137) and its Allies*, Cambridge, 1934.

It was shown that 1739 is one of the most important witnesses in Paul. There it has close agreement with some majuscules, for example in Romans with 04 (86 per cent), 01 (81 per cent). In Acts, by contrast, its closest agreements are with two other minuscules, 1891 (89 per cent) and 945 (81 per cent), its closest agreement with a majuscule being with 02 (64 per cent). Since this is in a total of seventy-four test passages, the difference in the rates of agreement is truly significant. Nevertheless, as in Paul, 1739 remains a valuable witness for its marginal notes, of which there are fifteen (recorded in Lake and New, *Six Collations*, 194–6).

When we look for minuscules with a close rate of agreement with the majuscules, we find that there are not many. 81 is closest to 03 (74 per cent), the next highest being 1175 (59 per cent), and the two stand in a similar relationship to 01 (75 per cent and 62 per cent), 02 (75 per cent and 63 per cent) and 04 (71 per cent and 66 per cent). This evidence, so far as the minuscules are concerned, seems to bear out even more strongly than before the traditional picture of two sharply contrasted ancient texts with a later Byzantine text quite removed from either.

9.2.3 The versions

9.2.3.1 The Syriac versions

As with Paul, there are no manuscripts of an Old Syriac version, and the evidence consists of citations in early writers, which again have been gathered and analysed by Kerchensteiner. Even these are more meagre than in Paul, and his references are confined to the writings of Ephraem, the *Liber Graduum* (*PS* §28) and Aphraates (*PS* §13).

Writers about the Peshitta are not particularly forthcoming with regard to the origin and date of the version so far as Acts is concerned. What can be said is that the Gospels and other parts of the New Testament are not consistent in their translation styles, so that the Peshitta did not come into existence all at once. For an edition of the Peshitta we depend on Gwilliam and Pinkerton (see 8.5.1).

Turning to the Harklean, the marginalia are a major source of evidence for Ropes' Western Text. We lack any modern edition, and are dependent still upon the only one in existence, that of Joseph White. The readings are accessible to the reader who does not have Syriac in a Latin translation, with the critical symbols provided, in a separate apparatus in Ropes' edition. Only two manuscripts are known. White was wholly dependent upon an eleventh-century copy in Oxford (New College MS 333). The other is dated 1169–70 (Cambridge University Library, Add. 1700).

There are few traces of the Christian Palestinian Aramaic Version.

J. Kerchensteiner, 'Beobachtungen zum altsyrischen Actatext', *Biblica* 45 (1964), 63–74; Vööbus, *Early Versions*; White, *Actuum Apostolorum*.

9.2.3.2 *The Latin versions*

Two Old Latin manuscripts, 5 (the Latin of Codex Bezae, 05) and 50 (the Latin of Codex Laudianus, 08) have already been described.

We have evidence of similar Old Latin text-types to those found in Paul. Petzer lists the following:

African: **K** 55 (the Fleury palimpsest, see 7.4.1) is the sole manuscript attesting this, which was the text known to Cyprian

European: **I**, the more widely attested, supported by 50. There are subtypes **C** (strong African element), **A** (local text of Augustine) and **M** (Milanese). **D** ('more limited and homogeneous'), found in 51, Codex Gigas (see 1.8.9 and 7.4.1), very similar to that cited by Lucifer of Cagliari. Other important witnesses are 52 and 60. **B** (Codex Bezae)

The text of Codex Bezae he describes as basically European, being closer to **I** than to **D**, and possibly derived from an ancient form of it, since it shows some affiliation with one representative of the **K** text. Many of its readings are strange and probably the result of 'thorough and deliberate revision' (Petzer). It had no further influence upon the Latin tradition.

J.H. Petzer, 'Texts and Text Types in the Latin Version of Acts', in Gryson, *Philologia Sacra*, 259–84, p. 283, p. 276. This replaces two older works as the first place of reference for information on the Latin text of Acts: A. Jülicher, 'Kritische Analyse der lateinischen Übersetzung der Apostelgeschichte', *ZNW* 15 (1914), 163–88; B. Fischer, 'Das Neue Testament in lateinischer Sprache', 28–30, 64–7 = *Beiträge*, 194–5, 239–42. See also Petzer's 'A Quantitative Analysis of the Relationship among Latin Manuscripts in Acts 6', in J.C. Coetzee (ed.), *Koninkryk. Gees en Woord*, Pretoria, 1988, 98–112.

An edition of Acts for the Vetus Latina edition was begun by J.H. Petzer but none was published. The work has now been taken up by another editor.

The origins of the Vulgate text of Acts are far from clear, and authorities regularly fail to discuss the matter. The evidence suggests that the Vulgate text is a revision of the European text, being more influenced by **I** than by **D**. This revision included consultation of Greek manuscripts, these manuscripts being of the general character of 01, 02, 03 and 04 (Fischer, 'Das Neue Testament in lateinischer Sprache', 65 = *Beiträge* 239, citing H.J. White). The Vulgate tradition was grouped by White into three families.

9.2.3.3 *The Coptic versions*

The study of the Coptic versions down to 1972 is described by Mink: The Sahidic and Bohairic versions are independent translations from Greek. The Fayyumic is derived from the Bohairic. The most significant event since 1972 is the discovery of a manuscript in Middle Egyptian, containing Acts 1.1–15.2 (perhaps the first of a two-volume set). Known as the Glazier Codex, also by its Pierpont Morgan Library classmark Cop G^{67}, and dated to the fourth century, this manuscript has been seen as a new witness to the Western Text. Petersen argues that this translation, totally independent of the Sahidic, and possibly older, represents a form of text current in Egypt in the second and third centuries.

Study of the textual characteristics of the Sahidic tends to rather uncertain conclusions as to the relative proportions of 'Alexandrian' and 'Western' readings. Since these studies predate the *Text und Textwert* analysis of all Greek witnesses, they have to be treated with caution.

G. Mink, 'Die koptischen Versionen des Neuen Testaments. Die sprachlichen probleme bei ihre Bewertung für die griechischen Textgeschichte', in K. Aland, *Die alten Übersetzungen*, 160–299;

A. Joussen, *Die koptischen Versionen der Apostelgeschichte (Kritik und Wertung)* (Bonner biblische Beiträge 34), Bonn, 1969. Compare for example the differing assessments in the 1958 and 1975 editions of Kenyon, *Greek Bible* (pp. 234 and 140).

H.-M. Schenke (ed.), *Apostelgeschichte 1,1–15,3 im mittelägyptischen Dialekt des Koptischen (Codex Glazier)* (TU 137), Berlin, 1991 (with a German translation and eighteen plates). The manuscript took a long time to be published (it was purchased in 1961; a transcription begun by T.C. Petersen and completed by P. Beret exists only in typescript). Schenke's edition deals mainly with linguistic phenomena and has few textual notes. T.C. Petersen, 'An Early Coptic Manuscript of Acts: an Unrevised Version of the Ancient So-called Western Text', *Catholic Biblical Quarterly* 26 (1964), 225–41; E.J. Epp, 'Coptic Ms G67 and the Rôle of Codex Bezae as a Western Witness in Acts', *JBL* 85 (1966), 197–212, reprinted in *Collected Essays*, 15–36, with an additional note, 37–9. The manuscript is also of interest because it contains a miniature and has excellently preserved binding.

For the other dialects see again Horner, *Northern Dialect*, vol. IV, 1905; *Southern Dialect*, vol. VI, 1922.

9.2.4 *Interpreting the textual phenomena*

How are the textual phenomena of Acts to be interpreted? Generally speaking, there has been a polarisation of two contrasting forms of text. In Ropes' schema there were the 'Old Uncial', the 'Western' (a second-century revision), and the 'Antiochian' (his name for Westcott and Hort's Syrian text, i.e. what was to develop into the Byzantine text). This is a broadly Hortian view, with Hort's Neutral and Alexandrian texts reduced to a single entity, the Old Uncial. It is noteworthy that Westcott and Hort have little enough to say about the text of Acts in their Introduction. Even in defining the characteristics of the Western Text they make no reference to Acts, nor do they take any readings from it as examples (pp. 120–6). To repeat, it should not be assumed that an interpretation of the evidence which holds good for one part of the New Testament holds good for another, and the case of Acts shows why it must not.

To show how research has developed, I take P38 and its relationship to 05. It was obviously an exciting prospect when a papyrus dating from about 300 which seemed to have a similar text to 05 was published (this at a time when 05 itself was dated into the fifth century). According to Clark, their most striking agreement is at 18.27. The texts of P38, 05 and 03 are as follows (the text of P38 follows normal conventions by indicating uncertain letters with underdots and reconstructed text within square brackets):

P38
]σ̣τ̣ην αχαϊα πολυ συνε[βαλετο εν ταις εκκλη
σι]α̣ι̣[ς] ευτονως γαρ τοις ι̣ο̣υ[δαι]οις διακ̣[ατηλεγ]
χετο] δημοσια δια̣[λεγομεν]ο̣ς επι[δεικνυς
δια τ]ων γραφων χρ̅υ̅[ειναι] ι̅η̅ν̅

05
εν δε τη εφεσω επιδημουντες τινες κορινθιοι και ακουσαντες αυτου
παρεκαλουν διελθειν συν αυτοις εις την πατριδα αυτων. συνκατανευσαντος
δε αυτου οι εφεσιοι εγραψαν τοις εν κορινθω μαθηταις οπως αποδεξωνται τον
ανδρα· ος επιδημησας εις την αχαιαν πολυ συνεβαλλετο εν ταις εκκλησιαις·
ευτονως γαρ τοις ιουδαιοις διακατηλεγχετο δημοσια διαλεγομενος και
επιδικνυς δια των γραφων τον ι̅η̅ν̅ ειναι χ̅ρ̅ν̅
03
βουλομενου δε αυτου διελθειν εις την αχαιαν προτρεψαμενοι οι αδελφοι
εγραψαν τοις μαθηταις αποδεξασθαι αυτον· ος παραγενομενος συνεβαλετο
πολυ τοις πεπιστευκοσιν δια της χαριτος· ευτονως γαρ τοις ιουδαιοις
διακατηλεγχετο δημοσια επιδικνυς δια των γραφων ειναι τον χ̅ρ̅ν̅ ι̅η̅ν̅

Text of P38 taken from S. New, 'Note XXIII. The Michigan Papyrus Fragment 1571', in K. Lake
and H. J. Cadbury (eds.), *Additional Notes to the Commentary* (*Beginnings of Christianity* 5), London,
1933, 262–8. This is based upon afterthoughts by the first editor, H. A. Sanders. Their quality suggests
that a review is needed. A digital image is available at http://lib.umich.edu/pap/index.html. Text of
03 and 05 taken from Ropes, as above, but without accentuation (for easier comparison with the
papyrus).

The fact that both P38 and 05 omit προτρεψάμενοι οἱ ἀδελφοὶ
ἔγραψαν τοῖς μαθηταῖς ἀποδέξασθαι αὐτόν· ὃς παραγενόμενος is an
apparent argument in favour of their agreement. But P38 has its own
characteristics with χ̅ρ̅ν̅ [ειναι] ι̅η̅ν̅, which differs from both 03 and 05,
and a difference from 05 in the wording διαλεγόμενος καί, omitting the
conjunction. *Text und Textwert* includes three more places where P38 is
extant, and in each it has not merely a different reading from 05, but a
reading found in no other manuscript:

19.1–2 κ̣α̣ι̣ [ειπεν τοι]ς μαθηταις (05 and most other manuscripts have
καὶ εὑρών τινας μαθητὰς εἶπεν πρὸς αὐτούς) (TS 67)
19.3 ο δε παυλος προς αυ[του]ς (05 has εἶπεν δέ) (TS 68)
19.14 (TS 69) is more complicated. Both P38 and 05 have a longer form
of text not found elsewhere. The Teststellen analysis takes the form
in 05 to be a secondary form of that in P38, and there are several
differences between them, notably the reading [σκευ]ϊα [ζ ιου]δ̣αιου
τινος αρχιερεως in P38 against σκευα τινος ιερέως in 05 (the
reconstruction of P38 is difficult).

Enough evidence has been given to suggest that while there is a
measure of agreement between the two, it is no more than approximate.
It is noteworthy, by contrast, that the texts of P74 01 02 03 (04 is missing)
are far more consistent in these three passages. It seems possible that
the assumption based on previous evidence that there were two opposed

forms of the text led scholars to place all new texts in either one camp or the other. This view has dominated scholarship, not only in the study of the evidence, but also in theories of how the two forms of text came into being.

For the history of research, see W. A. Strange, *The Problem of the Text of Acts* (SNTSMS 71), Cambridge, 1992, 1–34. See also E. Grässer, 'Acta-Forschung seit 1960', *Theologische Rundschau* 41 (1976), 141–94, esp. pp. 175–81; Parker, *Codex Bezae*, 183–93. It is instructive to read Sir Frederic Kenyon's 1938 summary of the problem, 'The Western Text in the Gospels and Acts', *PBA* 24 (1938), 187–315. There is a recent collection of papers on different aspects of the text of Acts: T. Nicklas and M. Tilly (eds.), *The Book of Acts as Church History. Apostelgeschichte als Kirchengeschichte. Text, Textual Traditions and Ancient Interpretations. Text, Texttraditionen und antike Auslegungen* (Beihefte zur Zeitschrift für die neutestamentliche Wissenschaft 120), Berlin and New York, 2003.

The following three views have held sway:

1. The 'Old Uncial' text is Lucan, and the Western Text is a later creation.

This is the view of most critical scholarship. Thus, the editions of Lachmann, Tregelles, Tischendorf, Westcott and Hort and Nestle–Aland all present a text which prefers 01 and 03 to 05. It is the conclusion which Ropes uncompromisingly adopts in his edition. In this point of view, the Western Text is wholly derivative, and the debate concerns only the manner and circumstances under which it came into being.

Strange (*The Text of Acts*, 8f.) points to a slightly different approach in the volume of commentary on the text by Lake and Cadbury, noting that here there is some willingness to adopt Western readings when they seem superior: K. Lake and H. J. Cadbury (eds.), *English Translation and Commentary* (*Beginnings of Christianity* 4), London, 1933.

2. The Western Text is Lucan, and the 'Old Uncial' text is a later creation.

Although this opinion is not widely held, it has not lacked support since it was advanced by William Whiston (better known for his translation of Josephus) in the eighteenth century. I single out a few examples of arguments in support of this view.

A. C. Clark came to believe the longer text to be superior, not only in Acts, but in other textual traditions, on the grounds that 'A text is like a traveller who goes from one inn to another, losing an article of luggage at each halt.'

A. C. Clark, *The Descent of Manuscripts*, Oxford, 1918, 23 (quoting himself, from 'The Primitive Text of the Gospels and Acts, a Rejoinder' [to reviews by Sanday, Souter and Kenyon], *JTS* 16 (1915), 225–40, p. 233). For a summary of his views, see D. C. Parker, 'The Development of Textual Criticism since B. H. Streeter', *NTS* 24 (1977), 149–62, pp. 154f. Coming to the New Testament from classical texts, Clark first wrote *The Primitive Text of the Gospels and Acts* (Oxford, 1914). The significance of this work is the enthusiasm with which Streeter referred to it in *The Four Gospels* (pp. 131–5).

It is appropriate to compare here the views of Royse who, from an analysis of scribal habits in the papyri, argues that the rule *'lectio brevior potior'* (i.e. that the shorter reading is to be preferred to the longer reading) is deficient. That is to say, since we can observe that papyri and other manuscripts frequently omit text, the longer reading is likely to be original, the shorter one having arisen from accidental omission. Conclusions in favour of the shorter text at every place are, however, problematical. We may observe without surprise that a copyist will be more likely to commit errors of omission than addition, since less work is normally preferable to more, even if the scribe omits unawares. But one has to distinguish between the habits of individual manuscripts and the habits of textual histories. A glance at the margins of Codex Sinaiticus, where the frequent omissions of Scribe A have been repaired, will show that the users of a text did not often suffer significant omissions to remain for long. The Byzantine Text as a text tends to be inclusive of material from the tradition, yet Byzantine copyists also frequently omitted words and phrases. J. R. Royse, 'Scribal Habits in the Transmission of New Testament Texts', in W. D. O'Flaherty (ed.), *The Critical Study of Sacred Texts*, Berkeley, 1979, 143–50; 'Scribal Habits in Early NT Papyri', ThD dissertation, Graduate Theological Seminary, 1981. See also P. M. Head, 'Observations on Early Papyri of the Synoptic Gospels, especially on the "Scribal Habits"', *Biblica* 71 (1990), 240–7. The canon *'lectio brevior potior'* is in any case a rule to be applied in a certain type of circumstance, namely in a place where one suspects either an expansion which is intended to clarify the text, or a conflation of several older forms of text.

The analysis of P38 by Silva New (later Silva Lake) concludes that some 'Neutral' readings in this mostly Western witness indicate that the 'Neutral' text was created out of the Western. Again we see an attempt to fit new evidence into a framework derived from earlier research.

New, 'Note XXIII. The Michigan Papyrus Fragment 1571'.

A series of studies by Read-Heimerdinger, latterly in cooperation with J. Rius-Camps, analyse the text of 05 on the understanding that it is Lucan. They explicitly reject the view that the best text is made by selecting readings from Western witnesses, arguing that 'there has been a failure to notice the inner coherence of both language and contents throughout the text of Acts' in Codex Bezae (*The Message of Acts in Codex Bezae*, 1.9). Discourse analysis is used as a tool for describing this 'inner coherence'.

J. Read-Heimerdinger, *The Bezan Text of Acts. A Contribution of Discourse Analysis to Textual Criticism* (JSNTSS 236), Sheffield, 2002; J. Read-Heimerdinger and J. Rius-Camps, *The Message of Acts in Codex Bezae. A Comparison with the Alexandrian Tradition* (JSNTSS 257), London, 2004; vol. II, London, 2006; vol. III, London, 2007. These writings present internally consistent arguments, and some useful data (especially the beginning of *The Bezan Text of Acts*). What is lacking hitherto is any engagement with objections to their theories or with data which suggest an alternative conclusion. See, e.g., the comment on Parker, *Codex Bezae*: 'new contributions which are important but with which we do not always agree' (*The Message of Acts in Codex Bezae*, 1.6). If the case put in Parker, *Codex Bezae*, is right, then they are wrong, and the reader will want to be given some justification for accepting the one or the other.

3. Both are Lucan, the 'Old Uncial' text being an authorial revision.

The name of Friedrich Blass is most strongly associated with this opinion. In his view, the Western Text was a rough draft and the other the final and polished version.

Broadly the same view is taken by Boismard and Lamouille, who believe that some years separated the two editions. Their view of the subsequent textual history is that the two forms became fused into a form of the Alexandrian text which no longer survives, while the Western Text divided into two streams, of which the one to which Codex Bezae belongs is less authentic.

Most recently, Strange has argued that Luke never finished Acts, and that the two forms of the text represent two independent attempts to edit what he had written. 'At Luke's death the first volume of his work had been published, but . . . the second had not. This second volume, near completion but still in draft form, remained in obscurity until published relatively late in the second century, perhaps in the third quarter' (*The Text of Acts*, 182). The two texts of Acts that we know were produced by two editors, working independently. The 'non-Western' editor was cautious in his treatment of the narrative, and in his attitude to 'some issues which had become sensitive matters for the second century church' (p. 187).

F. Blass, *Acta Apostolorum sive Lucae ad Theophilum Liber Alter. Editio Philologica*, Göttingen, 1895; *Acta Apostolorum sive Lucae ad Theophilum Liber Alter. Secundum formam quae videtur romanam*, Leipzig, 1896. The former has a fuller introduction, more textual information and a commentary omitted from the 1896 edition. For a contemporary assessment, see the review by T. E. Page, *The Classical Review* 11 (1897), 317–20.

M.-É. Boismard and A. Lamouille, *Le texte occidental des Actes des Apôtres. Reconstitution et réhabilitation*, 2 vols., Paris, 1984. Second edition of the text only by M.-É. Boismard (Études bibliques NS 40), Paris, 2000. Boismard's theory of the two forms of the Western text and of 05 led him into a system of reconstructing the text which required a search for potential data in a wide range of sources. The data they present is interesting (the first edition has a second volume with critical apparatus and an index of stylistic characteristics), even if the eclectic longer text constructed from the data is not convincing.

É. Delebecque, *Les deux Actes des Apôtres* (Études bibliques NS 6), Paris, 1986 takes a similar view on the grounds that both texts conform to Lucan style.

If we turn to questions concerning the origin of the Western Text among those who consider it secondary, we find again the assumption that it came into being at one time. According to Zuntz, a rewritten text of Acts was already in existence and in use in Edessa as early as about AD 100. According to B. Aland, the text was made in the third century.

Zuntz, 'On the Western Text of the Acts', *Opuscula Selecta*, 189–215 (a paper read in 1939 and first published in these papers). See also 'An Analysis of the Report about the "Apostolic Council"', ibid., 216–49, also its first publication. B. Aland, 'Entstehung, Charakter und Herkunft des sog. westlichen Textes untersucht an der Apostelgeschichte', *ETL* 62 (1986), 5–65, esp. pp. 12–36.

All of these approaches are based upon the concept of two texts, whether one sees either or both as Lucan, whether one prefers the one or the other, and whether or not one regards Codex Bezae alone or a selection of readings as the alternative to the text found in 01, 03 and others. How strong is the evidence that there is such a situation? Supposing that the text of Codex Bezae could be shown to be the product of a process rather than a text produced at a single point in time (whether by Luke or a reviser is then no longer a possible question)? Is there not evidence even in what has been noted in this short survey to justify such a claim? My study of Codex Bezae produced evidence that its text of Acts is a product of stages of growth. The comparison of 05 and P38 suggests that there was no single revised form of the verses, but that both manuscripts testify to different stages in a process. The comments of Adams on the Sahidic illustrate the difficulties in insisting on alternative equally stable texts: 'although Alexandrian readings predominate, there is a strong Western element... On the other hand, of the major additions and variants characteristic of D and its allies it has very few'. Such a form of text, not 'Alexandrian', but not 'Western' either, might suggest a derivative of an earlier stage of the development of a more periphrastic text. If we return to Acts 18.27, two points might be noted: first that the revised text seems to bring the narrative into accordance with 1 Corinthians 16.12; second that the repetition of the verb, ἐπιδημοῦντες/ἐπιδημήσας, suggests that the existing text may have been exploited to produce the extra material.

Kenyon, *Greek Bible*, 1975, 140.

If we abandon the theory of two texts, what does the text of Acts look like? In the first place, there is the possibility that where the stages of revision have not changed it for ever, the text found in 05 may join the other ancient manuscripts in attesting primitive forms of the text. That is to say, the textual criticism of Acts is in essence not very different from any other kind of textual criticism, in that it involves the study of individual witnesses to remove error, followed by the comparison of different forms of text in order to recover the oldest possible form, for which all witnesses potentially provide evidence. This should include a recognition that the text found in 01, 03 and other manuscripts with a similar text is not immune from error. One might even point to 12.25 as a place where the witnesses may all be in error:

εἰς Ἰερουσαλήμ (01 03) apparently has them returning to the place where they already are;

ἐξ Ἰερουσαλήμ (P74 02) and ἀπό Ἰερουσαλήμ (05), are simple emendations (and ἀπό looks more convincing);

ἐξ Ἰερουσαλήμ εἰς Ἀντιοχείαν (1739) and ἀπὸ Ἰερουσαλὴμ εἰς Ἀντιοχείαν (08) are more complex emendations.

For a convoluted argument why the reading of 01 03 is preferable as they punctuate it, see Lake and Cadbury, *Translation and Commentary*, ad loc. Westcott and Hort proposed an emendation in word order to τὴν εἰς Ἰερουσαλὴμ διακονίαν πληρώσαντες (vol. 11, 'Notes on Select Readings', p. 94). If one adjusted the punctuation, not even that would be necessary.

It is now important to seek the causes of the form of text found in its most developed form in Codex Bezae. The task of tracing the development of a tradition which evolved and changed over many decades, if not several centuries, is a great deal harder than describing a single event. However, the best way of illustrating the possibility which lies behind this view is in the emphasis which has been placed since the pioneering work of E. J. Epp upon the way in which changes in the text follow changes in the beliefs and customs of Christians. A number of different emphases have been identified: anti-Judaic tendencies; a greater interest in the role of the Holy Spirit; a greater interest in one or more of the Apostles; a minimising of the significance of women in the life of early Christianity.

E. J. Epp, *The Theological Tendency of Codex Bezae Cantabrigiensis in Acts* (SNTSMS 3), Cambridge, 1966; M. Black, 'The Holy Spirit in the Western Text of Acts', in Epp and Fee, *Metzger Festschrift*, 159–70; C. M. Martini, 'La figura di Pietro secondo le varianti del codice D negli Atti degli Apostoli', in M. Laconi (ed.), *Settimana Biblica dei Professori di Sacra Scrittura in Italia*, Rome, 1966, 279–89. For a summary of later research, see in J. Delobel, 'Focus on the "Western" Text in Recent Studies', *ETL* 73 (1997), 401–10; 'The Text of Luke–Acts. A Confrontation of Recent Theories', in J. Verheyden (ed.), *The Unity of Luke–Acts* (BETL 142), Leuven, 1999, 83–107. Stepping outside Acts, similar research has looked elsewhere in the Codex for similar evidence. For bibliography, see Parker, *Codex Bezae*; Elliott, *Bibliography*. Recent studies are R. Maisano, 'Il prologo di Marco nel codice di Beza', in S. Graziani (ed.), *Studi sul vicino oriente antico dedicati alla memoria di Luigi Cagni* (Istituto universitario orientale, Dipartimento di studi asiatici series minor 61), Naples, 2000, 1745–73; A. G. Brock, 'Scribal Blunder or Textual Plunder? Codex Bezae, Textual-rhetorical Analysis, and the Diminished Role of Women', in C. Vander Stichele and T. Penner, *Her Master's Tools? Feminist and Postcolonial Engagements of Historical-critical Discourse* (Global Perspectives on Biblical Scholarship 9), Atlanta, 2005, 253–64.

If Acts was a book particularly susceptible to revision and expansion, that is more likely to be because of its literary character than for any other reason. The stories do grow in the telling, and according to Read-Heimerdinger there is more textual variation in the narrative than there is in dialogue and discourse (*The Bezan Text of Acts*, 17–19). If this is the case, then the rewritings and revisions will reflect the assumptions and customs of the reviser. We have no need to look for a theological mastermind, if what we have is a developing text, with changes made broadly in sympathy with Luke's writing out of a deep familiarity with the genre.

A remaining problem is the relationship between the Greek and the Latin forms of the text. Study of this question concentrates on Codex Bezae, since it contains both. Although discussion has often focused on the question whether one is dependent on the other, it is more helpful to follow the approach already outlined, which finds in the Latin a witness to a Greek text at a different stage of development. An example of a reading which illustrates this approach is found at 19.29. The variants are as follows:

ἐπλήσθη ἡ πόλις τῆς συγχύσεως 01* 02 03
ἐπλήσθη ἡ πόλις συγχύσεως 01ᶜ al
ἐπλήσθη ἡ πόλις ὅλη τῆς συγχύσεως 014 018 025 al cop ˢᵃ (Chester Beatty MS)
ἐπλήσθη ἡ πόλις ὅλη συγχύσεως 08 pler
συνεχύθη ὅλη ἡ πόλις αἰσχύνης 05*
συνεχύθη ὅλη ἡ πόλις cop ˢᵃ (BL Or 7594) Lvt gig syᴾ
ἐπλήσθη ὅλη ἡ πόλις τῆς συγχύσεως 05ᶠ Lvt d (et repleta est tota ciuitas confusionem)

Evidence derived from Tischendorf and Ropes. For Tischendorf's abbreviations, see 6.3.1. Corrector F of Codex Bezae is a hand datable to the second half of the fifth century.

There are three issues here:

the presence or absence of the article before συγχύσεως
the inclusion of ὅλη and its position
the substitutions for ἐπλήσθη and συγχύσεως (and its omission)

There is a simple explanation for the last. The Latin of Codex Bezae, *repleta est...confusionem*, reads more like a translation of συνεχύθη than of ἐπλήσθη...συγχύσεως. But the word used at the end of the phrase, *confusio*, had two meanings in Latin, specifically in Christian usage, from the second century onwards: the traditional meaning of mingling or disorder, and a second one, disgrace, shame. The Greek column's αἰσχύνης may be explained as a revision of the Greek out of a misunderstanding of the Latin, which seemed to have an extra word. The form of text in Codex Bezae is then a secondary form of συνεχύθη ὅλη ἡ πόλις, attested only in versional evidence, distinctive in placing ὅλη before ἡ πόλις and for substituting συνεχύθη for ἐπλήσθη. It may be a revision of the form of text ἐπλήσθη ἡ πόλις συγχύσεως under the influence of 2.6, συνῆλθεν τὸ πλῆθος καὶ συνεχύθη and 21.30–1, ἐκινήθη τε ἡ πόλις ὅλη...ὅλη συχύννεται (variant συγκέχυται) Ἰερουσαλήμ (compare also 1 Sam. 5.11 LXX, ἐγενήθη σύγχυσις ἐν ὅλῃ τῇ πόλει). The reading of 08 and most other manuscripts preserves a hint of the reading of 05 in including the adjective (unless the addition of ὅλη is an earlier and separate development from the substitution of συνεχύθη).

The recognition that both the form of text found in Codex Bezae and that from which it is derived are secondary does not exhaust the value of their study, since a further examination of this reading leads us to the form of text from which they are derived. One is left then with two oldest forms of text, differing in the presence or absence of the article before συγχύσεως. The choice between these two forms of text will then require a study of Lucan usage of the article as it is found in the manuscripts, leading finally to an initial text.

The expanded forms of text remain of interest for two reasons. They are undoubtedly the most important aspect of the history of the text of Acts, and are essential both for the study of the ways in which it developed and for the recovery of the oldest forms of text. They are no less important in another respect, namely the study of the ways in which Acts was read and used in early Christianity.

9.3 THE CATHOLIC EPISTLES

9.3.1 Introduction

With this section of the book, we deal with the collected form of some of the smallest writings in the New Testament, diverse in character and contents, but united textually in having a common history of transmission from quite an early stage. Because we have here for the first time full critical editions of the three major versions and the Greek text, we are better placed than anywhere else for the gathering of material. Unfortunately, this book is written too soon to make use of the companion studies being produced to accompany the *Editio critica maior*.

9.3.2 The Greek manuscripts

The oldest manuscripts have already been listed (9.1). Of these, the Codices Sinaiticus and Vaticanus remain the oldest complete copies. Both contain the epistles in the order found in all Greek manuscripts (James, the Petrines, the Johannines and Jude). In this arrangement, the longest is placed first, then the next longest with the other letter attributed to the same author after it, then the third longest and its two associated letters, and finally Jude. It also happens to place the letters of James, Peter and John in the order in which Paul mentions these three Apostles in Galatians 2.9 according to the majority of witnesses. James is quite well served with manuscripts older than 01 and 03 (P23, P20 and P100), but the most extensive older papyrus is P72, containing Jude and the two letters of Peter in their entirety. The latest and very thorough account of the manuscript (about which conflicting theories and even inconsistent information has circulated since its first publication) by Wasserman concludes that the three canonical texts were all copied by a single scribe. The manuscript may have been produced for private rather than public use. The character of notes in the margin of 1 Peter leads to the conclusion that the scribe was a Coptic speaker, possibly either from or working in southern Egypt. The text is rather prone to harmonisation, notably towards liturgical usage, but without harmonisation between the parallel passages of 2 Peter and Jude. There are also three places where it seems to show a 'theological tendency', emphasizing the divinity of Christ:

Jude 5b, θεὸς χριστός against the alternatives κύριος, ἰησοῦς and θεός

1 Peter 5.1, τῶν τοῦ θεοῦ παθημάτων against τῶν τοῦ Χριστοῦ παθημάτων

2 Peter 1.2, ἐν ἐπιγνώσει τοῦ θεοῦ ἰησοῦ τοῦ κυρίου ἡμῶν, without καί after θεοῦ

For Gal. 2.9, see the Nestle–Aland *apparatus*: P46 prefers Πέτρος to Κηφᾶς and the Graeco-Latin bilinguals place Πέτρος before Ἰάκωβος (out of a regard for the primacy of the Bishop of Rome?).

T. Wasserman, *The Epistle of Jude: Its Text and Transmission* (CBNTS 43), Lund, 2006, 30–50 (a revision of 'Papyrus 72 and the *Bodmer Miscellaneous Codex*', *NTS* 51 (2005), 137–54). See also K. Haines-Eitzen, *Guardians of Letters. Literacy, Power and the Transmitters of Early Christian Literature*, New York, 2000, 96–104; T. Nicklas and T. Wasserman, 'Theologische Linien im *Codex Bodmer Miscellani*? [*sic*]', Kraus and Nicklas, *New Testament Manuscripts*, 161–88. For the theological context of the readings, see Ehrman, *Orthodox Corruption*, 85f., 266f. It is rare to find a single manuscript consistently supporting a particular type of reading in Ehrman's categories.

For the papyri, see *NT auf Papyrus I*.

9.3.3 *The versions*

9.3.3.1 *The Latin versions*

Thiele's edition of the Old Latin in the Vetus Latina series is the foundation stone of modern research. The introduction devotes a section to each of the letters, defining the text-types and setting out the evidence. Again, we are largely dependent upon citations (wholly dependent for the African version known to Cyprian).

W. Thiele, *Epistulae Catholicae* (*Vetus Latina* 26/1), 1956–69; see also 'Probleme der Versio Latina in den Katholischen Briefen', in K. Aland, *Die alten Übersetzungen*, 93–119; *Wortschatzuntersuchungen zu den lateinischen Texten der Johannesbriefe* (GLB 2), 1958; *Die lateinischen Texte des 1. Petrusbriefes* (GLB 5), 1965.

The Oxford Vulgate edition has the letters in the familiar order, beginning with James, although other orders were known in the west with Peter placed first (for example, in the list of canonical books inserted in Codex Claromontanus in the sixth century, which also gives the number of lines in each writing). The Vulgate contains a preface to the collection as well as to each letter.

The origin of the Vulgate text of these letters is described in detail by Thiele, who finds throughout the collection that it is a revision made by a comparison with Greek manuscripts, the influence being seen in the word order and sentence construction and in the character of readings which agree with those of manuscripts such as 02 and 03 (e.g. pages 89*, 91*).

For the 'Catalogus Claromontanus', see Frede, *Altlateinische Paulus-Handschriften*, 25–6, and Metzger, *Canon of the New Testament* (310–11 for a summary of the text and 230 for further references).

9.3.3.2 *The Syriac versions*

There are, as has already been stated, only three Catholic letters in the Peshitta canon: James, 1 Peter and 1 John, the so-called major Catholic epistles. The other four were added to the Philoxenian and consequently to the Harklean edition. The edition in *Das Neue Testament in syrischer Überlieferung* contains only the major epistles, in the Peshitta and Harklean versions. Nine Peshitta and three Harklean manuscripts, along with six containing the evidence of the West Syrian Massora, are used.

There is no evidence for the Philoxenian text of the major epistles, but there is a version of the minor epistles which is generally agreed to be the Philoxenian (although the *Editio critica maior* notes that it might be a revision of the Harklean).

Aland and Juckel, *NT in syrischer Überlieferung 1*. J. Gwynn, (first title page) *Remnants of the Later Syriac Versions of the Bible in Two Parts, Part 1: New Testament . . .* (second title page) *The Four Minor Catholic Epistles in the Syriac of the Original Philoxenian Version made in the Sixth Century by Polycarpus the Chorepiscopus. 2 Peter: 2 and 3 John: Jude and the History of the Woman Taken in Adultery (St John VII.53–VIII.12) in two Recensions (Sixth and Seventh Centuries). A Revised Text*, London and Oxford, 1909 (repr. Amsterdam, 1973). Part 2 consists of Old Testament texts. The edition includes a retroversion into Greek. A new edition of the Philoxenian is in preparation in Münster. Clemons, *Index of Syriac Manuscripts*.

The Harklean version of the minor epistles has not been re-edited since the first edition by White, which used only one manuscript. The *Editio critica maior* cites the readings of White's manuscript and two others (with a third in 2 Peter).

White, *Actuum Apostolorum*. A new edition is in preparation in Münster.

To sum up: the major epistles (James, 1 Peter, 1 John) are available in the Peshitta and Harklean versions; the minor epistles (2 Peter, 2, 3 John, Jude) are available in the Philoxenian and Harklean versions.

9.3.3.3 *The Coptic versions*
For study of the Coptic of James and the letters of Peter we now have available the researches of F.-J. Schmitz. He lists seventy Sahidic manuscripts, two Akhmimic, three Fayyumic, one in Dialect V and one Bohairic. Among other useful tools, the work provides a synoptic transcription of the witnesses one above the other with an apparatus based on the *Editio critica maior*, and a table for each Coptic manuscript showing its proportion of agreements with all Greek witnesses cited in the *Editio critica maior*. These materials make it possible to place them accurately in the history of the text. Schmitz rejects the traditional view that the Coptic versions attest an 'Alexandrian' text, arguing that the situation with regard to the majority of witnesses is a great deal more complicated.

F.-J. Schmitz, *Das Verhältnis der Koptischen zur griechischen Überlieferung des Neuen Testaments. Dokumentation und Auswertung der gesamtmaterialen beider Traditionen zum Jakobusbrief und den beiden Petrusbriefen* (ANTF 33), Berlin and New York, 2003. For these three letters it replaces Horner, *Northern Dialect*, vol. IV. For the relationship of the Coptic witnesses to Greek forms of text, see Schmitz's excursus on the Crosby-Schøyen Codex (p. 595).

9.3.3.4 *Other versions*
The *Editio critica maior* includes four other versions in its apparatus. The Armenian is cited principally from an 1805 edition, with additional collations from 1994. There is a more useful edition of the Georgian, made in 1956, which classifies the witnesses into four redactions. The Slavonic is cited from a number of editions of individual manuscripts. Finally, the Ethiopic is available in an edition from 1993. Five manuscripts, dated between the fourteenth and the sixteenth centuries, contain an older form of text. The other seventeen cited (copied in the period 1500 to 1900) have been influenced by Arabic versions. This is a free translation which also shows a poor understanding of the Greek text.

J. Hofmann† and S. Uhlig (eds.), *Novum Testamentum Aethiopice: Die Katholischen Briefe* (Äthiopistische Forschungen 29), Stuttgart, 1993. For all other information see the General Introduction to the *ECM*, 15*f.

The editors of the *Editio critica maior* cite all these editions sparingly, on the grounds that 'their origins and history are not sufficiently understood, so that critical editions of these traditions are not yet available' (p. 15*).

9.3.4 *Commentaries*

The oldest are again either lost or not fully extant in Greek. Clement of Alexandria included the Catholic letters in his commentary on selected biblical passages called *Hypotyposeis* ('Outlines') (*CPG* 1.1380). Fragments survive in a Latin translation by Cassiodorus (*CPL* 903). Didymus the Blind wrote a short commentary on the seven letters (*CPG* II.2562), which survives in fragments from the *catenae* and in the sixth-century Latin version of Epiphanius Scholasticus (cited in the *Vetus Latina* as Ep-SC – see Gryson, *Répertoire général*).

The Greek *Clavis* lists five entries under *catenae* on the Catholic epistles: a *Commentarius primigenius* (*CPG* IV.C175) which forms the foundation of the *catena* of Andreas (*CPG* IV.C176), the commentaries of Pseudo-Oecumenius (*CPG* IV.C177) and Theophylact (*CPG* IV.C178), and the '*Catena arabica*'. A Latin commentary formerly attributed to Hilary of Arles is now considered to be an Irish production, dated to the period 690–708 (*CPL* 508).

K. Staab, 'Die griechischen Katenenkommentare zu den katholischen Briefen', *Biblica* 5 (1924), 296–353, and his two books on Pauline commentaries (see 8.6). Kannengiesser 1.362–7. *Catena* fragments from Chrysostom are collected from his other writings and not from a commentary. The same holds true for at least the majority of fragments from Cyril of Alexandria.

9.3.5 *The history of the text*

It is convenient to begin this section with the later history of the text, and Wachtel's researches on the Byzantine text. Not only does this work illuminate the study of the text of the Catholic letters, it also challenges the established view of the nature and thereby of the development of the Byzantine text as a whole.

K. Wachtel, *Der byzantinischen Text der Katholischen Briefe. Eine Untersuchung zur Entstehung der Koine der Neuen Testaments* (ANTF 24), Berlin and New York, 1995. For two more recent studies, see Wachtel, Spencer and Howe, 'The Greek Vorlage of the Syra Harclensis'; Wachtel, Spencer and Howe, 'Representing Multiple Pathways'.

The established view was that of Westcott and Hort, who claimed that the Syrian text (as they called it) was 'the result of a "recension" in the proper sense of the word, a work of attempted criticism, performed deliberately by editors and not merely by scribes', replacing the three existing forms of text (Western, Neutral and Alexandrian) by a single form which drew on all. This is a conclusion reached on the basis of the view that the Byzantine text has particular characteristics, namely 'to remove all stumbling-blocks out of the way of the ordinary reader' and to include 'instructive matter contained in all the existing texts'. 'Entirely blameless on either literary or religious grounds as regards vulgarised or unworthy diction, yet showing no marks of either critical or spiritual insight, it presents the New Testament in a form smooth and attractive, but appreciably impoverished in sense and force, more fitted for cursory perusal or recitation than for repeated or diligent study'.

Westcott and Hort, ii. 134, 135. The reader is again encouraged to study in detail what is written, since it explains so much subsequent work.

Thus Westcott and Hort. By contrast Wachtel, who it must be remembered had access to the ninety-eight test passages and thus to a sampling of the whole manuscript tradition, rejects the claim that the Byzantine text is the result of a recension. The Harklean Syriac is essential to his argument, since there is a group of minuscules (Family 2138) containing a form of text closely resembling that on which Thomas of Harkel's revision was based. This text is a stage in the development of the Byzantine text, containing nine Majority readings (from the test passages) not found in older Greek manuscripts but known from versions and citations, and six more for which Thomas' Vorlage is the oldest witness (194f).

For a retroversion of the Harklean, with the readings of Family 2138, see Aland and Juckel, *NT in syrischer Überlieferung I*, 271–86. The manuscripts of the family are 2138 (dated 1072), 1505, 1611 (tenth century, the oldest of the four) and 2495.

The older readings (found both here and elsewhere) demonstrate that the Byzantine text had begun to develop at an earlier stage. There are also later Byzantine readings, dating from the eighth and ninth centuries. Thus the Byzantine text of the tenth century onwards is not a 'recension' but the result of a long process of development. Wachtel uses another method to wind up the argument. The Byzantine text does not consistently contain a single kind of reading, as Westcott and Hort argued. He draws attention to 'untypical Majority Readings' to prove this.

The Byzantine text of the tenth century onwards is not totally homogeneous either. One should draw attention to the form of text known as K^r. The term comes from von Soden, and the Kappa is his siglum for the Koine or Byzantine text, the r standing for 'recension'. This is a very well-presented and controlled text, with an orthography in its best representatives which is actually the basis for that found in our editions. Such best representatives include 35, an eleventh-century manuscript of the entire New Testament.

Coming to the earlier stages in the history of the text, we begin with the observation that the making of the text of the *Editio critica maior* requires the drawing up of a stemma of *readings* at each point of variation in the Greek manuscripts selected for the edition (see 5.1.6). The table provided by Mink for the 'predominant textual flow', that is the most probable relationships between the manuscripts, in the Epistle of James is noteworthy for the key role played by a few witnesses in the transmission of the Byzantine text. P74, P100, 01, 03, 04, 025, 81, 307, 1175, 1243, 1739 and 1852 are all shown in an equal relationship to the Initial Text. Moving down the stemma, 424 (at one remove from 307) is the most probable ancestor of twelve witnesses, including 617, from which are descended the great majority of witnesses.

This is a rather surprising picture, one which is irreconcilable with the traditional view of text-types.

At first glance a number of the witnesses of the Catholic epistles ☛ (50) appear to be presented as standing in an equal relationship to the Initial Text. What in fact is recorded is that the study of the textual flow does not permit us to claim that any one of these can be shown to be before or after any other or, to put it differently, all they have in common is that A is their closest potential ancestor. Positively, we are left with a greater number of witnesses of this kind than we might have hoped to find. Negatively, we can see that there is a textual distance between the Initial Text and our witnesses which cannot be filled in with a stemma. That is to say, the twelve witnesses all standing at an equal distance from the Initial Text are only represented in this way because we do not have the data to put in the lines of descent which must intervene. This problem is heightened by the places where there is a textual problem which is particularly difficult to solve.

It was stated that the letters are predominantly transmitted in a single order. Is there any evidence about the transmission of any letter before, or independently of, the collection? The question is rather different from that which was raised about the Pauline corpus. There the issues concerned the ways in which the letters may have been edited to make a collection, and the possible role of Paul in the process. Such issues cannot arise here, because of the lack of a single author and of any compositional connection between the letters. The editors of the *Editio maior* show that there is not a single diagram of predominant textual flow which applies to the whole collection. Instead, different diagrams describe different parts of the collection. The introductions describe the different situations, with differing numbers of manuscripts closest to the Initial Text, and how they differ from James.

ECM, 4.1.2, *Die Petrusbriefe*, 21*–22* (German), 23*–24* (English); 4.1.3, *Der erste Johannesbriefe*, 25*–27* (German), 28*–30* (English); 4.1.4, *Der zweite und dritte Johannesbriefe, Der Judasbrief*, 31*–34* (German), 35*–38* (English).

9.3.6 Conjectural emendation

An important instance of a passage where this 'gap' beyond the witnesses with the Initial Text as their closest potential ancestor is 2 Peter 3.10. Here the editors read οὐχ εὑρηθήσεται. This is worth studying in detail, because it illustrates very well the theory behind the concept of the conjectural emendation. Here the Greek manuscripts contain the following different readings:

(b) εὑρηθήσεται
(c) εὑρηθήσονται
(d) εὑρηθήσεται λυόμενα
(e) ἀφανισθήσονται
(f) κατακαήσεται
(g) κατακαήσονται
(h) καήσεται

There is thus no Greek manuscript attesting the reading of the edition. There is, however, some versional evidence, namely the Coptic manuscript in Dialect V and manuscripts of the Philoxenian Syriac. That is to say, the versional text of these editions when retroverted into Greek would be οὐχ εὑρηθήσεται. Strictly speaking, this probably rules out οὐχ εὑρηθήσεται as a conjectural emendation (even if the versional readings are themselves conjectures), but the example still illustrates the theory, which is this: When no reading of the extant witnesses (1) explains the origin of the others and (2) makes sense, the editor should seek an explanation by suggesting a reading which fulfils these two conditions in as simple a way as possible. It is fairly easy to see why the readings (b) and (c) meet only the first criterion and readings (d)–(h) meet only the second criterion. οὐχ εὑρηθήσεται, however, meets both, while providing a simple change to the text. οὐχ, it is to be concluded, dropped out of the text at an early stage of the transmission, leaving the strange reading (b). Readings (d)–(g) represent attempts to improve the text – they are conjectural emendations by early readers, in fact.

Conjecture has often been condemned as unnecessary in so rich a textual tradition as that of the New Testament. While it has been used often enough by editors of classical texts, trying to restore poetic metre perhaps in the face of medieval misconceptions, the situation in New Testament editing has always been rather different. There are several reasons for this. The first is that many conjectures have been made which are more accurately literary rather than textual suggestions. That is to say, they have been made on the basis either of criterion (2) or something similar (often theological consistency within the New Testament). Such examples were not the result of the kind of stemmatological research which has led to the example discussed here, but are the consequence of a scholar's views with regard to the literary formation of a text. This confusion has been present since the sixteenth century, as Krans has shown. The second reason is that while the classical scholar has been able to emend on the basis of a knowledge of the single extant witness, or both of the extant witnesses, or even all of them, New Testament textual scholarship has been forced by weight of numbers to work with only a partial knowledge of the extant witnesses, so that criterion (1) could not be properly met. The very different situation which we now have as a result of the *Editio maior* resolves this difficulty. A third reason is that when a text is so frequently commented upon and exhaustively explained as is the New Testament, there will never be lacking an explanation for the meaning of every traditional wording, however improbable its sense may be.

J. L. H. Krans, *Beyond What Is Written. Erasmus and Bezae as Conjectural Critics of the New Testament* (NTTS 35), Leiden and New York, 2006; see also 'Theodorus Beza and New Testament Conjectural Emendation', in Weren and Koch, *Recent Developments*, 109–28. Two famous conjectures illustrate the problems involved: at Matt. 19.24, it is suggested that κάμιλος (a thick ship's rope) be substituted for κάμηλος. This is read by a few manuscripts (Nestle–Aland cites 579 1424 pc (i.e. *pauci*, a few)) and by the Armenian, and was mentioned by several ancient commentators. So is this a conjecture? The ancient suggestion may have led to its introduction into manuscripts; alternatively, the form in the manuscripts might be examples of a fairly common confusion in Byzantine copies, between *iota* and *eta*. One would have to study the manuscripts to decide whether this explanation is plausible or not. The second example is Jn 19.29, where the sixteenth-century scholar Camerarius suggested ὑσσῷ ('spear') for ὑσσώπῳ (some Old Latin manuscripts read *pertica* ('pole'), providing a situation analogous to 2 Pet. 3.10). These examples illustrate the difficulties.

Traditionally, the Nestle edition has included conjectures in the apparatus. Whether or not it has been right to do so has been a debate within the conjecture debate. Because many of the reported conjectures are not textual, but of the literary kind, their presence seems inappropriate, and it seems that the future editions will omit them. And yet it would seem appropriate to keep the genuine conjecture.

9.3.7 The Epistle of Jude

Separate mention must be made of Jude, because we now have available the edition by Wasserman, who has made an apparatus which contains *all* the readings in *all* the Greek witnesses, without patristic or versional evidence. Of course this is more practicable in such a short writing as Jude. The edition follows the *ECM* in both construction and format. It provides an opportunity for comparing Wasserman's conclusions with the *Editio maior*. How different is the apparatus when 560 rather than 140 continuous-text and lectionary manuscripts are included? The answer is as one would expect, that there are more variants as well as more witnesses for the same variants. As a complete picture of all witnesses in the original language to a single text, Wasserman's edition is a unique piece of work.

Two passages in the Catholic epistles have a relationship which raises problems similar to those found in studying the relationship between the Gospels. 2 Peter 2.1–18; 3.1–3 and Jude 4–13, 16–18 are so similar that it is necessary to posit a literary relationship. It is generally agreed that 2 Peter is dependent upon Jude. Just as the parallel narratives in the Gospels have influenced each other, so there is some harmonisation between these two passages. In fact Wasserman lists seven places where this occurs (pp. 99–102), noting that there are no instances in P72 or 03.

CHAPTER 10

The Gospels

10.1 INTRODUCTION

The Four Gospels, the Tetraevangelium, is *the* book of Christianity – not four books, but one codex. Such manuscripts comprise more than a half of all continuous-text Greek copies of New Testament writings. In every ancient language of Christianity, copies of the Gospels predominate among what survives. And in case this preoccupation is seen as an ancient phenomenon, be it noted that the Gospels in these ancient languages are traditionally far better served with editions and results of research than is any other part of the New Testament. Moreover, more editions of Gospel manuscripts have been published, in facsimile or in some other form. Finally, it should be observed that many statements made about the New Testament text in general are really statements about the Gospels which have been extrapolated to the rest. I am thinking particularly about the entire concept of text-types and textual groupings. The result is that, while the number of research questions on which nothing has been said is small, the selection of views on many matters which have been discussed is a challenge to the author of a book such as this.

I have already written an introduction to the text of the Gospels, and see no value for anyone in my repeating myself. What follows will therefore contain some cross-referencing to matters which I have discussed in detail there. Fortunately, the approach of the current work is sufficiently different for me to be able to avoid repetition of more than the most general matters.

Parker, *Living Text*.

The literary character of the Gospels again plays an important part in the way in which they were transmitted, and here there are two other important factors to be considered. The first is that the transmission together of four similar but different accounts had a strong effect upon the text of each Gospel. The belief that there was a single account of the Gospel, to which each written version bore witness, led to the phenomenon called harmonisation, where the text of a Gospel is altered to conform with that of one or more of the others (10.2). The second factor is that the Gospels are more complex texts than the other writings, even than Acts, in that they are the literary medium for the presentation of the teaching of Jesus. By contrast, the letters are all the work of the writer (we need not speak here of modern theories of the inclusion of older hymnic material, for example in Philippians 2, for that was not an ancient concern), and so is Revelation. Acts contains the speeches of the Apostles, and it has already been noted that there is evidence that these speeches underwent less modification than the narrative in the earlier transmission. By contrast, it turns out for the Gospels that sayings of Jesus are frequently places where textual variation is particularly pronounced. Textual criticism has therefore to take account, not only of the way in which the Gospels functioned and were received and transmitted, but also of the treatment of the sayings of Jesus within the Gospels.

10.2 THE FOURFOLD GOSPEL

The formation of the fourfold Gospel was an important stage in the development of Christian textual history. It is a matter which has attracted some attention, about which our theories may be in danger of outstripping our information. The role of the codex in the appearance of the four-Gospel book has been discussed in a number of places. We know from P45 that such books were in existence in the third century. We know from Irenaeus, writing in about 180, that the four Gospels were viewed as a set (the Gospel has four forms but a single spirit). How much earlier can we go? Justin Martyr refers a few times to the 'Gospels', but more commonly to the 'memoirs of the Apostles' (ἐν τοῖς ἀπομνημονεύμασιν, ἃ καλεῖται εὐαγγέλια, *Apologia* 66.3). Which of the Gospels Justin cites and in what form of text he knew them have long been matters of debate which do not need to be discussed. Our concern here is not with the origins and early use of individual Gospels, but with the point at which the Gospels came to be transmitted as a single unit rather than as four separate texts.

For Justin's *Apology* and the editions, see *CPG* 1.1073; T. K. Heckel, *Vom Evangelium des Markus zum viergestaltigen Evangelium* (WUNT 120), Tübingen, 1999. See also M. Hengel, 'The Titles of the Gospels and the Gospel of Mark', *Studies in the Gospel of Mark*, London, 1985, 64–84 (English translation of *Die Evangelienüberschriften* (Sitzungsberichte der Heidelberger Akademie der Wissenschaften, Philologisch-historische Klasse, 4), Heidelberg, 1984; *The Four Gospels and the One Gospel of Jesus Christ*, London, 2000; see also the self-designated summary of this book, 'The Four Gospels and the One Gospel of Jesus Christ', in Horton, *The Earliest Gospels*, 13–26.

The transmission of the Gospels as a unit is rather complicated by the papyrus evidence. A discussion of this problem by Head indicated that few if any of the Gospel papyri from Oxyrhynchus ever contained more than one Gospel. This might suggest that even in the third and fourth centuries the Gospels circulated as independent units. On the other hand, some papyri do contain more than one Gospel, and it must be conceded that papyri may also have circulated as collections in several, perhaps even four volumes. Most tellingly, the names of the books, where they occur in surviving fragments, are those of the collection. The ancient titles of κατὰ Μαθθαῖον, κατὰ Μάρκον, κατὰ Λουκᾶν, κατὰ Ἰωάννην are titles designed to distinguish the four Gospels from one another.

The dates at which these titles are first found in manuscripts has to take into account the fact that they were sometimes added in a different hand from that of the scribe. Information on super-scriptions, subscriptions and running titles on all Greek and Latin manuscripts copied before 500 is found in Parker, *Codex Bezae*, 10–22 (the only Gospel papyri to have been published since then are the Oxyrhynchus papyri in volumes 64–6, and none of them contains any fresh evidence in this respect). No papyrus has any indication of having had running titles, which first appear in the fourth-century parchment Bibles. The fact that a title was added in a different hand (as in P4 and P66) does not itself mean that it was added very much later, or even that it was not written by the scribe, since a skilled writer will have commanded several styles. One needs clear evidence that the hand is of a later type before ruling out either of these possibilities.

The oldest sure evidence of a contemporary name comes in the beginning of the third century in P75 of Luke and John, which contains the end of the first and beginning of the second book. The page begins with the last six lines of Luke. Then is written

ευαγ᾽γελιον
κατα
λουκαν

ευαγγελιον
κατα
ϊωαννην

The Gospel of John follows immediately.

The question with regard to the transmission of the Gospels as a unit is significant in two respects. In the first place, the understanding of har-monisation and transference of material for other reasons between the Gospels requires at least an awareness of the chronology by which the collection emerged. In the second place, it is very important to consider the implications of the difference between the singly transmitted and the collected Gospels for the editor.

A few words must be said separately about textual criticism and the Synoptic Problem. The fact that the Gospels of Matthew, Mark and Luke are more similar to each other than any one of them is to John has affected their text, in that harmonisation has had a greater effect on them than on John. The different character of John is fairly evident but, where it runs close to one or more of the others, harmonisation still occurs. The study of harmonisation, however, is not influenced by modern Synoptic Problem theory. It is based upon study of harmonising practices in the manuscripts and other witnesses. This leads to the observation that Mark is harmonised to Matthew much more than Matthew is to Mark, as is Luke to Matthew.

The critical study of the text has made modern Synoptic study possible, because it has restored the unharmonised texts of the Gospels. Before that, much of the distinctive character of each Gospel had been hidden by the general tendency from quite an early stage in the manuscript tradition to bring them into conformity with each other. Compare the Lord's Prayer in the Received Text of Matthew and Luke with Nestle–Aland, and the debt which Synoptic study owes to editors since Lachmann will become evident.

Unfortunately, much of modern debate on the Synoptic Problem seems to have become so enamoured of the critical text that it believes not only that it presents the text as it was written by Matthew, Mark and Luke but also that it contains Mark's text as it was known to Matthew and to Luke, and so on. In fact, unless we had grounds for arguing that Matthew and Luke had access to the same copy of Mark, one sure statement is that the version of Mark known to Matthew was not identical to that known to Luke. What we do not know is how much these copies differed from each other.

It is even more remarkable that attempts to reconstruct the supposed document 'Q' (the lost collection used by both Matthew and Luke postulated by those who argue that Matthew and Luke are independent) use text-critical terminology to describe their activities. However, since all they are doing is making selections from a twentieth-century printed text, which does not even presume to provide confidently the text of the four-Gospel collection, never mind that of the independent first-century texts, this use of language must be dismissed as illusory.

M.S. Goodacre has pointed to the dubious methodology used in reconstructing Q: 'The incautious reader might easily and mistakenly assume that the reconstruction of a "Critical Text of Q" is more than superficially akin to the reconstruction of a critical text of a document like the Gospel of

Matthew', *The Case against Q. Studies in Markan Priority and the Synoptic Problem*, Harrisburg, 2002, 9. See also 158–62 for a discussion of the use of conjectural emendation to change readings in conflict with a particular theory, and *The Synoptic Problem. A Way Through the Maze* (The Biblical Seminar 80), London, 2001, 99–102; J.K. Elliott, 'The Relevance of Textual Criticism to the Synoptic Problem', in D.L. Dungan (ed.), *The Interrelations of the Gospels* (BETL 95), Leuven, 1990, 348–59; 'Printed Editions of Greek Synopses and their Influence on the Synoptic Problem', in F. van Segbroeck *et al.* (eds.), *The Four Gospels 1992. Festschrift Frans Neirynck* (BETL 100), Leuven, 1992, 337–57; 'Resolving the Synoptic Problem Using the Text of Printed Greek Synopses', *Filologia Neotestamentaria* 6 (1993), 51–8.

Whether an editor's opinions with regard to the best 'solution' to the Synoptic Problem will influence text-critical decisions is an interesting question, one which can only be answered in relation to one's understanding of the editorial task as a whole.

10.3 ANCILLARY MATERIAL

10.3.1 The Eusebian Apparatus

The Eusebian Apparatus should be described first. This is a system providing a means for users to navigate their way between parallel passages in the Gospels. It has four elements, whose description may be followed from the Nestle–Aland edition (also described in the Introduction, 38*–39*, 79*). First is that every Gospel is divided into numbered paragraphs (the manuscripts are not wholly consistent), Matthew having 355, Mark up to 241 (depending on the ending in the manuscripts – see 10.10.3), Luke 342 and John 232. These are written in the margin against the beginning of the section. The second component is a list of ten tables at the beginning of the Gospels. The first table has four columns, one for each Gospel, listing the number in each of every paragraph with a parallel in all four Gospels. The following three tables list the parallels in three Gospels (the pairings shown are Matthew, Mark and Luke, Matthew, Luke and John, and Matthew, Mark and John). The next five tables list the parallels between two Gospels, and the remaining table gives the paragraphs found only in one of each of the four. Note that the entries are only in numerical order in the left-hand column, the order in the others being affected by the ways in which the Gospels vary the order of their shared materials. The third component, the one vital to the working of the whole system, is that the number of the table containing that paragraph number is written underneath every paragraph number in the margin of the text. Thus, seeing paragraph 64 in Mark with the number 1 beneath it, I know that this paragraph comes in all four Gospels. If I turn to table 1, I find that the parallel paragraphs in the other four are 147 in

Matthew, 93 in Luke and 49 in John. I can then look it up in each Gospel and compare the accounts. The fourth element is a short explanation of how they work, written by Eusebius to one Carpianus (text on pp. 84*–85* of Nestle–Aland). What we have is a kind of simple synopsis. It is still useful today if one is working with a manuscript and wishes to find a particular place in the text (see 2.2).

The Epistle to Carpianus expresses Eusebius' debt to Ammonius. It seems that Ammonius had divided the Gospels into paragraphs for the sake of the reader. Eusebius' contribution was the system of tables to link the paragraphs. Thus the paragraphs are properly called the Ammonian Sections, and the numbers themselves the Ammonian Section numbers, they and the table number together being the Eusebian Numbers. Sometimes the Ammonian Sections are found on their own in manuscripts. This is the case in Codex Bezae, in which they were added by a hand of the second half of the sixth century. The Eusebian Apparatus made its way into other languages, so that, for example, it became as much a fixture in Latin and Syriac manuscripts as it was from the fourth century in Greek ones.

10.3.2 *The Vatican paragraphs and other divisions*

Another system of paragraph division and numbering is found in Codex Vaticanus (03). These paragraphs are longer than the Ammonian Sections, there being 170 in Matthew, 62 in Mark, 152 in Luke and 50 in John. The same divisions are found in Codex Zacynthius (040), extant only in part of Luke.

Codex Alexandrinus has even longer divisions. These, which became the standard κεφάλαια (chapters) in later Greek manuscripts, are present in Nestle–Aland (in italic numbers, also in the inner margin). There are 68 in Matthew, 48 in Mark, 83 in Luke and 18 in John plus the unnumbered opening of each book. These became provided with names, such as περὶ τοῦ λεπροῦ or περὶ τῶν σαδδουκαίων. Later manuscripts have a list of the chapters for each book, giving the number and the chapter title.

For further details of the κεφάλαια and a full list, see von Soden, 1.402–75.

10.4 THE GREEK MANUSCRIPTS

The figures for Gospel manuscripts in 1989 were 2,361 manuscripts containing the Gospels, of which 2,152 contained only the Gospels, 198 of these being fragmentary (of the others, 59 contain the entire New

Testament and 150 the New Testament without Revelation). These figures are moving slowly upwards. In 1998 *Text und Textwert* included information on 1,997 manuscripts of the Synoptic Gospels, and in 2005 of 1,987 of John.

Aland and Aland, *The Text of the New Testament*, 83 (chart 4); *Text und Textwert IV. Die Synoptischen Evangelien. 1. Das Markusevangelium. Band 1,1* (ANTF 26), pp. 1*, 17* (the printed number 1984 is incorrect (and for 1754 two lines below, read 1756)); *V. Das Johannesevangelium. 1. Teststellenkollation der Kapitel 1–10, Band 1,1* (ANTF 35), pp. 1, 2.

As elsewhere, the number of manuscripts dating from the Byzantine era and written in minuscule is a high proportion.

There are a number of ways in which this section could be presented. In the end I have decided to detail the materials for each Gospel in turn, referring the reader to a previous section where appropriate. In this way the uneven quantity and quality of the materials for the different Gospels should become more apparent.

10.4.1 Matthew

The editors of *Text und Textwert* were able to access 1,812 manuscripts of Matthew. First, table 10.1 lists the manuscripts dated to the period before the end of the fourth century (entries in *Liste* order within a date sequence). Table 10.2 shows the most significant majuscule manuscripts after the end of the fourth century.

Transcriptions of all the early papyri and 0171 may be found in K.Ş. Min, *Die früheste Überlieferung des Matthäusevangeliums (bis zum 3./4. Jh.). Edition und Untersuchung* (ANTF 34), Berlin and New York, 2005. For P45 and 05, see 9.1 and 9.2.2; for 01 and 03, see 1.8.1. The date of 032 remains somewhat uncertain. The latest assessment very tentatively, but in my view persuasively, advocates caution with regard to the date of IV/V customarily given, suggesting instead a date in the middle of the sixth century: U. Schmid, 'Reassessing the Palaeography and Codicology of the Freer Gospel Manuscript', in L. W. Hurtado (ed.), *The Freer Biblical Manuscripts. Fresh Studies of an American Treasure Trove* (Text-Critical Studies 6), Atlanta, 2006, 227–49, p. 244. For this manuscript see also the articles in the same volume by J.-F. Racine, 'The Text of Matthew in the Freer Gospels: a Quantitative and Qualitative Appraisal', 123–46; J.B. Prior, 'The Use and Nonuse of *Nomina Sacra* in the Freer Gospel of Matthew', 47–66; D. Haugh, 'Was Codex Washingtonianus a Copy or a New Text?', 167–84 (suggests that the scribe copied rather than made the distinctive readings of the codex); J.R. Royse, 'The Corrections in the Freer Gospels Codex', 185–226.

It has been argued by Skeat that P4/64/67 is the oldest example of a four-Gospel codex, but the evidence is extremely slight: T.C. Skeat, 'The Oldest Manuscript of the Four Gospels?', *NTS* 43 (1997), 1–34, reprinted in *Collected Biblical Writings*, 158–92.

There are fragmentary manuscripts from the fifth century onwards, and the number of extensive manuscripts increases in the end of the majuscule period.

Table 10.1

Century	Manuscript	Extent
II	P104	8 verses (Ch. 21)
II/III	P4/64/67	parts of Matthew 3, 5, 26 and Luke
	P77	10 verses (Ch. 23)
	P103	5 verses (Chs. 13, 14)
III	P1	17 verses (Ch. 1)
	P45	parts of Matthew 20–1, 25–6, Mark, Luke, John and Acts
	P53	12 verses (Ch. 26) and Acts (12 verses from Chs. 9–10)
	P70	15 verses (Chs. 2, 24)
	P101	8 verses (Chs. 3, 4)
III/IV	P37	34 verses (Ch. 26)
	P102	4 verses (Ch. 4)
	0171	15 verses (Ch. 10) and Luke
IV	P35	8 verses (Ch. 25)
	P62	6 verses (Ch. 11)
	P71	4 verses (Ch. 19)
	P86	8 verses (Ch. 5)
	P110	6 verses (Ch. 10)
	01	all
	03	all
	058	8 verses (Ch. 18)
	0231	4 verses (Chs. 26–7)
	0242	26 verses (Chs. 8–9, 13)
IV end	P25	11 verses (Chs. 18, 19)

Table 10.2

Century	Manuscript	Extent
c. 400	05	most
V	02	lacks 1.1–25.6
	04	most
VI	032	all

Among the minuscules, two groups deserve particular reference. The first is Family 1 (see 4.3). There it was noted that 1582, the manuscript copied by Ephraim, the scribe also of 1739 (see 8.4), has been shown to be the most important witness to the text of the family.

Anderson, *Family 1 in Matthew*. The edition of Family 1 by Lake, *Codex 1*, needs correcting as indicated by Anderson, 98–100.

The significance of the marginalia, representing an ancient form of text and according to the tradition associated with it derived from the Caesarean text of Origen, makes the reconstructed archetypal text of Family 1 an important witness to the Gospels.

The second family is a less clearly knit group, Family 13 (also known as the Ferrar Group). A number of members of this group are written in a hand which shows them to have been copied in southern Italy in the eleventh and subsequent centuries. Minuscule 13 is the manuscript which gives this family its name. Geerlings lists twelve manuscripts which are family members in Matthew.

J. Geerlings, *Family 13 – the Ferrar Group. The Text According to Matthew* (SD 19), Salt Lake City, 1961. Of these, seven come out at the top of the list of manuscripts closest to 13 in *Text und Textwert* (IV.2.2,2, p. 163).

It is clear that although there are twenty-three manuscripts dated to the end of the fourth century, most, including all the papyrus fragments of the earliest centuries, are tiny scraps. 01 and 03 remain not only the oldest complete copies of this Gospel, but also the oldest copies to contain more than a tiny portion of the text.

A glance at the Hauptliste in *Text und Textwert* reveals that the minuscules with the highest proportion of agreement with 03 are Family 1 (1582 and 1), but even these agree closely only in 21 out of 53 and 21 out of 55 readings respectively, followed by 892, of the ninth century. These manuscripts agree as closely with 01 as with 03.

Of the 1,812 manuscripts for which data could be collected, 1,555 contain the Byzantine text, that is they agree with the majority reading in 90 per cent or more of the test passages. Only 202 manuscripts differ from it more than that, of which 22 (including 02) are so fragmentary that the information is too partial for it to be worth including them in the Hauptliste.

The two preceding paragraphs point us towards an interesting conclusion with regard to the text of Matthew: that it is comparatively stable in as much as the vast majority of manuscripts conform to a clearly defined Byzantine text. The oldest witness to this text is 04, which already in the fifth century differs from the majority in only 11 out of 52 test passages.

10.4.2 Mark

Again (and in the following two sections), all manuscripts down to about 400 and the most important from the following two centuries are listed (see tables 10.3, 10.4 and 10.5). For Family 1, we are solely dependent upon Lake, *Codex 1*.

Table 10.3

Century	Manuscript	Extent
III	P45	parts of Mark 4–9, 11–12 and Matthew, Luke, John, Acts
IV	P88	27 verses (Ch. 2)
	01	all
	03	all
	0188	7 verses (Ch. 11)
*c.*400	05	1.1–16.14
V	02	all
	04	most
VI	032	all

Whether this is by chance or reflects a low degree of interest in it, Mark is particularly poorly represented among the papyri and ancient majuscules, with the exception of P45.

Of the manuscripts examined in the Gospel of Mark in the *Text und Textwert* series, 1,566 agree with the Byzantine reading in 90–100 per cent of readings and 172 agree below 90 per cent.

10.4.3 Luke

Here we find at last a Gospel in which an early papyrus find is extensive enough to provide a detailed insight into the early text. P75 was purchased by the Bodmer Foundation and until recently was in the foundation's library in Geneva. In 2006 it was purchased by the Vatican Library. P75 still contains 36 complete or almost complete pages of Luke. Originally the entire manuscript was a single-quire codex made out of 144 pages (36 sheets), of which Luke took up the first 86 pages and a part of the eighty-seventh. C.M. Martini's *Il problema della recensionalità del codice B alla luce del papiro Bodmer XIV* belongs with Zuntz's *The Text of the Epistles* as one of the major studies of modern times. The New Testament textual critic should certainly learn enough Italian to be able to work through Martini's arguments. I here present a very brief summary, with an emphasis on those points to which I wish to draw attention.

Martini, *Codice B alla luce del papiro Bodmer XIV*. In antiquity the papyrus became part of the same collection as P66. See 1.1.2.1. See also J. Duplacy, 'P⁷⁵ *(Pap.Bodmer XIV–XV)* et les formes les plus anciennes du texte de Luc', in F. Neirynck (ed.), *L'Évangile de Luc. Problèmes littéraires et théologiques. Memorial Lucien Cerfaux (BETL* 32) 1973, 111–28, reprinted in Duplacy, *Études*, 151–68. The *editio princeps* has been updated with plates and transcriptions of further sections in M.-L. Lakmann, 'Papyrus Bodmer XIV–XV (P⁷⁵) Neue Fragmente', *Museum Helveticum* 64 (2007), 22–41.

Table 10.4

Century	Manuscript	Extent
II/III	P4/64/67	parts of Matthew and Luke 1–5
III	P7	3 verses (Ch. 4)
	P69	8 verses (Ch. 22)
	P45	parts of Chs. 6, 7, 9–14 and Matthew, Mark, John, Acts
	P75	parts of Luke 3–18, 22 and John 1–15
	P111	5 verses (Ch. 17)
IV	01	all
	03	all
	0171	17 verses (Ch. 22), and Matthew

After a description of each witness, he moves to an analysis of the differences between them (listed on pp. 153–65). This list is then reduced by the removal of those due to manifest errors in one or the other (also listed at the end; the list for 03 is much the shorter). Once these have been eliminated, he finds about 479 differences. Once differences in abbreviation have been removed, the total is about 361. He further reduces these to around 240. This contrasts dramatically with the 791 significant differences between 03 and 01 in Luke. If we consider that these two manuscripts, B ℵ, the 'Neutral text' of Westcott and Hort, were and continue to be regarded as very close, one may see how similar P75 and 03 are. Martini goes on to study the types of difference, concluding that most of them are slight and accidental ('di origine puramente casuale'), as would occur in every handwritten tradition (p. 60). He then goes on to enquire whether there are any common errors in P75 and 03 which demonstrate a direct genealogical relationship (i.e. that 03 is a direct copy pf P75), to which the answer is in the negative. The following section (chapter III) uses Colwell's Multiple Method, drawing also on Birdsall's study of P66 (see below), to relate what has been established with regard to the relationship between P75 and 03 to the rest of the tradition. Of the 94 readings selected, the two manuscripts are found to agree in 85 (p. 71). Particular attention is then paid to the characteristics of the distinctive shared readings of the two manuscripts. The conclusion of this section is that the two manuscripts are independent representatives of a form of text which 'must have preceded the date of origin of P75 by enough time to explain how B could be descended from a text which was substantially identical without being contaminated by the errors which appear separately in one or the other of these two documents' (p. 82). Martini goes on to study the character of the 'recension' (his inverted commas) of 03 and P75, looking in turn at the orthography (chapter IV), stylistic and doctrinal readings (chapter V) and the differences between the two manuscripts (chapter VI). In the final section of conclusions (pp. 149ff.) he states that the two manuscripts, uniquely similar among our ancient codices, are descendants of an archetype datable not later than the end of the second century (p. 149).

I have paid more attention to the way in which he studies the manuscripts, but it is important to record also Martini's views with regard to the text of this archetype, namely that stylistically it shows fewer signs of revision than other forms of text.

What features of his method deserve particular notice? First, the transparency of his arguments, in that all the data are provided in the ten lists with which the book closes. Second, the way in which the argument is built up by careful stages, involving study of the characteristics of manuscripts considered both individually and by comparison with others, and by the use of several different forms of analysis. Third, the way in which the use of criteria judging the quality of *readings* (do they reveal a particular scribal habit, do they appear to develop the text in a certain direction? or do the alternatives seem more likely to be secondary?) leads to a judgement about the quality of text found in a manuscript, and from that to the study of the history of the text as a whole.

The recovery of a manuscript so old and so similar to the famous Codex Vaticanus is probably the most significant in the history of papyrus finds. It has led to a greater understanding not only of the antecedents of the form of text found in 03, but also to firmer ground in the comparison of ancient witnesses, as well as to a confirmation of the methods of nineteenth-century scholarship.

It had often been stated that, compared with apparently more authentic Semitisms found in other witnesses, notably in Codex Bezae and other witnesses containing similar readings, Codex Vaticanus showed signs of 'Atticisation'. Martini set a question mark against this view, arguing that the P75/B text shows fewer signs of textual improvement. Martini uses the theory set out in Colwell, 'Method in Locating a Newly-discovered Manuscript'. On the other hand, it has been argued that 'there does seem to be a very strong possibility of a theological *Tendenz* in p[75]' and that 'the scribe of p[75] intentionally heightened the Christology of the Lucan resurrection narrative': M.C. Parsons, 'A Christological Tendency in P[75]', *JBL* 105 (1986), 463–79, pp. 475, 477.

The Multiple Method shows some affinity with the Münster Test Passage method, with the important difference that the latter is based upon a comparison of all witnesses in the selected passage. A comparison reveals that the data in *Text und Textwert* bear out Martini's conclusions. He found P75 and 03 in agreement in 171 out of 190 variants (90 per cent). In the test passages they agree in 31 out of 33 (93.9 per cent). The next closest in agreement to P75 are 070 (9 out of 11, 81.8 per cent, not included by Martini) and 01 (24 out of 32, 75 per cent).

No minuscule is very similar to 03 or P75. It is noticeable that here 1 and 1582 (i.e. Family 1) agree with 03 in only 14 out of 51 test readings.

The overall situation is very similar to that which we found in Matthew: out of 1,756 manuscripts, only 224 differ from the Byzantine text in more than 10 per cent or more of the test passages, of which 18 are too fragmentary to be worth including in the Hauptliste.

10.4.4. John

The remarkably high number of papyri of John has already been noted. Table 10.5 substantiates this. The great majority of these copies are from Oxyrhynchus, and we have no way of knowing whether its apparent popularity there was unusual or typical of other places as well. Among the copies are several with *hermeneiai* (see 1.3.2). John is also unique in being

Table 10.5

Century	Manuscript	Extent
II	P52	5 verses (Ch. 18)
	P90	12 verses (Chs. 18, 19)
II/III	P66	nearly all of 1–14, + fragments
III	P5	48 verses (Chs. 1, 16, 20)
	P22	17 verses (Chs. 15, 16)
	P28	11 verses (Ch. 6)
	P39	8 verses (Ch. 8)
	P45	parts of 4, 5, 10, 11 and Matthew, Mark, Luke and Acts
	P75	parts of Luke. 3–18, 22; John 1–15
	P95	7 verses (Ch. 5)
	P106	14 verses (Ch. 1)
	P107	3 verses (Ch. 17)
	P108	7 verses (Chs. 17, 18)
	P109	6 verses (Ch. 21)
IV	P6	24 verses (Chs. 10, 11)
	01	all
	03	all

preserved in two second-century manuscripts, the one (P52) being the oldest extant fragment, dated to the middle of the century. John is unique in a third way. Chapters 10 and 11 are the only place where three extensive papyri overlap: P45, P66 and P75 cover John 10.7–11.57 with lacunae (the fragments of P45 in Chapters 4 and 5 are very slight). All of the papyri down to P95 have been edited by the International Greek New Testament Project.

Elliott and Parker, *The Papyri*. The book contains fresh transcriptions of all the papyri except for P66 and P75, most based upon autopsy, a critical apparatus containing all variants from the Received Text in all the papyri, and plates, again of all except for P66 and P75, of which there are representative images. The fragmentary majuscules have been edited according to similar principles: Schmid, Elliott and Parker, *Majuscules*. There is also an electronic edition, containing transcriptions of all the majuscule manuscripts and an apparatus: U.B. Schmid with W.J. Elliott and D.C. Parker, 'An Electronic Version of the New Testament in Greek ... volume 11, The Majuscules', at www.iohannes.com.

A note of caution with regard to the dating of P52 has recently been offered: B. Nongbri, 'The Use and Abuse of P52: Papyrological Pitfalls in the Dating of the Fourth Gospel', *HTR* 98 (2005), 23–48. The papyri he offers as comparative evidence unknown to Roberts are a reminder that such a fixed date as is sometimes offered (e.g. 'first quarter of the second century') needs to be kept under review.

It is a really surprising omission that no one has applied Martini's technique to the study of P75 in John. That is an important piece of research waiting to be written. We do have several valuable studies of P66. Two years after Martini, G.D. Fee published a monograph which by the nature of the problem had to proceed very differently. Here there was no similar majuscule standing to P66 as 03 did to P75. Instead, the situation was a much more recognisable one from other papyri: a form of text which was not very easy to express in terms of the traditional reconstruction of the textual history. This was, however, the route which Fee took, reaching the conclusion that P66 is a 'basically Neutral text', especially in Chapters 1–5, with increasing tendencies towards Byzantine and Western readings thereafter (p. 35). Fee then turns to the textual characteristics of P66, reaching identical conclusions to those of Birdsall, that there is a mixture 'of original readings previously known and others here attested for the first time, with readings plainly secondary, solecisms of every kind and attempts at a mannered revision' ('Bodmer Papyrus', 18 (*Collected Papers* 71). Fee then turns his attention to one of the most interesting features of P66, the large number of corrections by the first hand (see 1.1.2.1 and plate 1), many of them showing knowledge of different readings, perhaps from a second exemplar. These corrections may again be described in the words of Birdsall just quoted.

C.L. Porter, 'Papyrus Bodmer XV (P75) and the Text of Codex Vaticanus', *JBL* 81 (1962), 363–76 sets out briefly the case that the two manuscripts have a very similar text in John, but the argument lacks detail. This is presumably to be found in 'A Textual Analysis of the Earliest Manuscripts of the Gospel of John', unpublished PhD thesis, Duke University, 1961. For P66, see Fee, *Papyrus Bodmer II (P66)*; J. N. Birdsall, 'The Bodmer Papyrus of the Gospel of John', The Tyndale New Testament Lecture, 1958, London, 1960, reprinted in Birdsall, *Collected Papers*, 57–72. The three main papyri (P45, P66 and P75) have been studied together by Colwell, 'Scribal Habits in Early Papyri: a Study in the Corruption of the Text', in J. P. Hyatt (ed.), *The Bible in Modern Scholarship*, Nashville, 1965, 370–89, reprinted as 'Method in Evaluating Scribal Habits: a Study of P^{45}, P^{66}, P^{75}' in Colwell, *Studies in Methodology*, 106–24. Since this covers the papyri wherever they are extant, extracting material pertinent to John is not particularly easy or helpful.

We saw with the *Text und Textwert* volumes of the Synoptic Gospels that the number of manuscripts not conforming in 90 per cent or more to the Majority Text form was rather slight. The situation in John is somewhat different (the volume currently available covers the first ten chapters only, with a higher number of test passages (153). Here, out of 1,763 manuscripts, there are 1,484 agreeing at 90 per cent or over, and 303 below. That is to say the homogeneity suggested by the figures for the other Gospels is less marked.

One of the most interesting features of the test passages analysis in John is the results for Family 1. Here again 1582 and 1 are closely related, agreeing in 150 out of 153 test passages. But the two also show a strong measure of agreement with 565, a purple manuscript of the ninth century, certainly never thought before to be a family member, even though it has long been known to be a significant manuscript. The Family itself has a far smaller number of agreements with 03 (which does not even come in the Hauptliste for 1582 or 1). The closest agreements of 1582 with extensive ancient manuscripts are with P75 (15 out of 36 non-Majority readings) and with 01 (13 out of 39).

10.5 THE VERSIONS

10.5.1 *The Syriac versions*

For the Gospels we have direct evidence of an Old Syriac version, namely a translation predating the Peshitta. It is known in two manuscripts, the Curetonian (called after its first editor William Cureton) and the Sinaitic (since it is in the library of St Catherine's Monastery, Mount Sinai). Cureton published his edition in 1848, three more leaves being found and published in 1872. The Sinaitic manuscript was first published in 1894. It is a difficult palimpsest, and there have been several revisions to this first printing. With regard to their date, both have been assigned to the fifth century, although the late fourth century has also been suggested for the

Sinaitic manuscript. Both contain many lacunae (less than half of the Curetonian's leaves are extant). Interest in them quickly centred on two features: similarities with the Old Latin and with the Greek of Codex Bezae. These similarities are best explained by the hypothesis that both the Old Syriac and the Old Latin are derived from a second- to third-century Greek base from which Codex Bezae is also descended. It would be a mistake to expect too close a similarity between these witnesses, and even between the two Syriac manuscripts, and it must also be remembered that this hypothesis was advanced before the discovery of Greek Gospel manuscripts predating the fourth-century codices with which these materials were being compared.

The quest for further evidence of Old Syriac readings has had an impact on our understanding of the Peshitta, notably through the work of Vööbus, who found non-standard Peshitta readings in Peshitta manuscripts. He argued that these were vestiges of the Old Syriac. Readings that are not Peshitta are not, however, necessarily Old Syriac. The main result of this episode is the recognition that the Peshitta manuscripts are not quite as consistent as had been supposed (notably from the edition of Pusey and Gwilliam), and that the connection between Rabbula of Edessa and the origins of the version is not straightforward. There is no shortage of Gospel manuscripts of the Peshitta. Eleven are described by Metzger, the oldest dating to the fifth century. Pusey and Gwilliam cited forty-two in their edition, along with several manuscripts of the Massora.

A. Vööbus, *Studies in the History of the Gospel Text in Syriac* (CSCO 128, Subsidia 3), Louvain, 1951; Pusey and Gwilliam, *Tetraeuangelium*.

The Harklean version is known to be extant in a number of manuscripts (there are also manuscripts of the 'Harklean Passiontide Harmony'). The first printed edition by White was supplemented by Bernstein in 1853. More recently, Juckel produced a new version of the text as part of Kiraz's comparative edition.

Three lectionary manuscripts (all dated precisely – 1030, 1104 and 1118) and a few fragments are known of the Christian Palestinian Aramaic version. The date of this version has been much debated. The fact that it seems to be cited by a seventh-century Arabic writer places it in the sixth at the latest. There is some evidence against a fourth-century date, and there the matter rests. Textually, it seems to represent an early form of the Byzantine text.

B. M. Metzger, 'A Comparison of the Palestinian Syriac Lectionary and the Greek Gospel Lectionary', in E. E. Ellis and M. Wilcox (eds.), *Neotestamentica et Semitica. Studies in Honour of*

Matthew Black, Edinburgh, 1969, 209–20, reprinted in Metzger, *New Testament Studies*, 114–26. For a text with passages from the New Testament, see M. Black, *A Christian Palestinian Syriac Horologion (Berlin MS. Or. Oct. 1019)* (TS 2. 1), Cambridge, 1954.

Particularly useful for most of these versions is Kiraz, *Comparative Edition of the Syriac Gospels* (an earlier edition was published in NTTS 21, Leiden, New York and Cologne, 1996).

P. E. Kahle, 'The Chester Beatty Manuscript of the Harklean Gospels', *Miscellanea Giovanni Mercati*, vol. VI: *Paleografia, Bibliografia, Varia* (Studi e Testi 126), Vatican City, 1946, 208–33; J. D. Thomas, 'The Gospel Colophon of the Harclean Syriac Version', *Theological Review of the Near East School of Theology* 3 (1980), 16–26.

Finally, the following concordances: G. Kiraz, *A Computer-Generated Concordance to the Syriac New Testament*, 6 vols., Leiden, 1993. J. Lund, *The Old Syriac Gospel of the Distinct Evangelists, a Key-Word-In-Context Concordance*, 3 vols., Piscataway, 2004.

10.5.2 The Latin versions

With the Latin versions also we are on firmer ground in some respects. In the first place, we have enough surviving Old Latin manuscripts to have from them alone a broad picture of the Old Latin text-types. In the second, we know the origin of the Vulgate text, that it was made by Jerome as a revision of an Old Latin version, with reference to Greek manuscripts, and we know that he did so in response to a commission by Pope Damasus, executing the work in 383–4. The dedicatory letter which he wrote to Damasus is included in editions of the Vulgate. At the same time, problems with identifying the Vulgate text remain. We know that Jerome carried out the work, but it is not so clear which manuscripts best represent what he produced. The oldest manuscript of the Vulgate (St Gall, Stiftsbibliothek 1395 and fragments elsewhere, siglum Σ), written in the first half of the fifth century, is disappointing textually, in spite of its great age.

The most recent study of the Old Latin Gospels is by Burton. In three main sections, it deals with the textual history, aspects of the translation and linguistic features. In his view, the manuscripts fall into two main classes, an older European group and a newer one (in which the Vulgate is included).

The history of the Gospels down to the tenth century has been outlined by the four volumes of Bonifatius Fischer, *Die lateinischen Evangelien bis zum 10. Jahrhundert*.

P. H. Burton, *The Old Latin Gospels. A Study of their Texts and Language* (Oxford Early Christian Studies), Oxford, 2000. B. Fischer, *Die lateinischen Evangelien bis zum 10. Jahrhundert*, vol. I: *Varianten zu Matthäus (GLB 13), 1988;* vol. II: *Varianten zu Markus* (GLB 15), 1989; vol. III: *Varianten zu Lukas* (GLB 17), 1990; vol. IV: *Varianten zu Johannes* (GLB 18), 1991.

Fischer took sixteen test sections, four from each Gospel. He collated approximately 450 manuscripts dated before the tenth century in these passages. Rather than simply treating them as text carriers, Fischer classified his manuscripts by origin, with the exception of the Old Latin copies, which are grouped together as X. The groups are indicated with an upper-case roman letter. Generally, the letters denoting the groups are a pointer to geographical location (e.g. E = England, A = Aachen). The manuscripts within a group are shown by lower-case roman letters. The full list of twenty-six groupings locates manuscripts either within a wider area (such as England or Brittany) or even in a city (usually true of Germany and France in the later period). The precision of many of these identifications of groups owes a great debt to the work of Lowe and Bischoff (see 1.4.2).

The test passages produced about 5,690 places of variation (p. 8*: pp. 1*–47* are identical in each volume), a formidable amount of data. The result is a picture rather like the Latin text of Revelation after the Vetus Latina edition. That is, the Vulgate itself can be seen as a number of particular, often local texts, rather than as an entity which was produced by Jerome and then preserved in a single form.

Turning back to the Old Latin, there are a few manuscripts of great antiquity. We have two representatives of the African text, Codex Bobiensis (1, k) and Codex Palatinus (2, e). The oldest Italian manuscript is Codex Vercellensis (3, a), written according to tradition by Eusebius, Bishop of Vercelli, in the early 360s, a date which Lowe considers possible, and the purple manuscript Codex Veronensis (4, b). Both are important representatives of the Italian text. Manuscripts of the Vulgate of special importance include again Codex Amiatinus.

Editions of the manuscripts of the Old Latin Gospels were made by Jülicher and subsequently revised by Aland and Matzkow. These are made from published transcriptions of the manuscripts and not from fresh inspection.

A. Jülicher (ed.), rev. W. Matzkow† and K. Aland, *Itala. Das Neue Testament in altlateinischer Überlieferung nach den Handschriften*, vol. 1: *Matthäusevangelium*, Berlin and New York, 1972; vol. 11: *Marcusevangelium*, Berlin, 1970; vol. 111: *Lucasevangelium*, 2te verb. Auflage, Berlin and New York, 1976; vol. 1V: *Johannesevangelium*, Berlin, 1963. Transcriptions of the Old Latin manuscripts of John with an apparatus are now available in the electronic edition prepared by the Verbum Project at the University of Birmingham (www.iohannes.com).

10.5.3 The Coptic versions

As one would expect, all the versions are most fully represented in the Gospels. Of particular significance among modern discoveries are the Gospel of Matthew in Middle Egyptian (the Scheide Codex). Equally exciting is the Codex Schøyen 2650, of the same Gospel in the same dialect. The claim by its editor that it represents an independent translation of an original Hebrew or Aramaic version of Matthew in rather a free rendering of the Greek is not supported by Baarda, who considers its significance to lie in the fact that it represents a Coptic version independent of all other Coptic versions.

Horner, *Northern Dialect*, vol. I: *The Gospels of S. Matthew and S. Mark*; vol. II. *The Gospel of S. Luke*; vol. III: *The Gospel of S. John; Southern Dialect*, vol. I: *The Gospels of S. Matthew and S. Mark edited from Ms. Huntington 17 in the Bodleian Library*; vol. II: *The Gospels of S. Luke and S. John edited from Ms. Huntington 17 in the Bodleian Library*. Scheide Codex: B. M. Metzger, 'An Early Coptic Manuscript of the Gospel according to Matthew', in Elliott, *Studies*, 301–12, reprinted in Metzger, *New Testament Studies*, 93–104; H.-M. Schenke (ed.), *Das Matthäus-Evangelium im mittelägyptischen Dialekt des koptischen (Codex Scheide)* (TU 127), 1981; Schøyen Codex: H.-M. Schenke, *Das Matthäus-Evangelium im mittelägyptische Dialekt des Koptischen (Codex Schøyen)* (Coptic Papyri 1), Oslo, 2001; T. Baarda, 'Mt. 17:1–9 in Codex Schøyen', *NovT* 46 (2004), 265–87. Full details of the manuscripts and editions are conveniently available in Metzger, *Early Versions*, chapter 2. Materials on single Gospels include H. Quecke, *Das Markusevangelium saïdisch. Text der Handschrift Palau Rib. Inv.-Nr. 182 mit den Varianten der Handschrift M 569* (Papyrologica Castroctaviana 4), Barcelona, 1972; H. Thompson, *The Gospel of St John according to the earliest Coptic Manuscript*, London, 1924; R. Kasser, *L'Évangile selon saint Jean et les versions coptes de la Bible* (Bibliothèque Théologique), Neuchâtel, 1966. A critical edition of the Gospel of John is currently in progress in the Forschungsabteilung Koptologie und Ägyptenkunde, University of Salzburg, as part of the IGNTP electronic and print editions of John.

10.5.4 Recent editions of other versions

The Slavonic version has received careful attention in recent years. An edition of John has been based upon eight witnesses selected from an analysis of all witnesses in John 18 (by coincidence the same block of text as has been used by the International Greek New Testament Project for profiling Greek witnesses). There is also a recent edition of John in Ethiopic.

A. Alexeev *et al.* (eds.), *Evangelium secundum Ioannem* (Novum Testamentum Palaeoslovenice 1), St Petersburg, 1998 (main title page in Russian); M.G. Wechsler (ed.), *Evangelium Iohannis Aethiopicum* (CSCO 617, Scriptores Aethiopici), Leuven, 2005.

10.6 COMMENTARIES

The *catenae* on the Gospels have been classified by several writers. The work of Reuss is particularly important.

For a survey, see Kannengiesser, 1.336–53. The standard edition of the *catenae* by J. A. Cramer, *Catenae graecorum patrum in Novum Testamentum*, vol. II, Oxford, 1844, is of course sadly out of date; J. Thomas, *Les collections anonymes de scolies grecques aux évangiles*, 2 vols., Rome, 1912; J. Reuss, *Matthäus-, Markus- u. Johannes-Katenen nach den handschriftlichen Quellen untersucht* (NTA 18/4–5),

Münster i. W., 1941; *Matthäus-Kommentare aus der griechischen Kirche aus Katenenhandschriften gesammelt und herausgegeben* (TU 61), Berlin, 1957; *Johannes-Kommentare aus der griechischen Kirche aus Katenenhandschriften gesammelt und herausgegeben* (TU 89), Berlin, 1966; *Lukas-Kommentare aus der griechischen Kirche aus Katenenhandschriften gesammelt und herausgegeben* (TU 130), Berlin, 1984. These three volumes provide editions of the quotations by author.

The oldest manuscript containing commentary material is a majuscule which has been most recently dated to around the year 700, Codex Zacynthius (Ξ, 040). A palimpsest, its lower text contains portions of a *catena* on Luke's Gospel drawn from writers who include Origen and Severus.

Parker and Birdsall, 'Codex Zacynthius'.

Cyril of Alexandria wrote commentaries on Matthew (*CPG* III.5206), Luke (*CPG* III.5207) and John (*CPG* III.5208) whose manuscripts are included in the *Liste*. The first survives only in *catenae*, the second in *catenae* and three homilies but the John commentary survives in full for Books 1–6 and 9–12 (for 7–8 we are again dependent on citations in the *catenae*). Von Soden (1.249) listed five manuscripts, which by reference to the *Liste* (1.404) translate into 849 850 1819 1820 2129. The biblical text and commentary are written as a single text block in two of these (850 and 1820), that is, the biblical text is written at the beginning of the section of the commentary which discusses it.

The fragments of the Matthew commentary are to be found in Reuss, *Matthäus-Kommentare*, 153–269; those of Luke in Migne, *PG* 77.1040–9; of John in P.E. Pusey, *Sacris Patris Nostrum Cyrilli archiepiscopi Alexandrini in D. Iohannis euangelium*, 3 vols., Oxford, 1872, 2nd edn, Brussels, 1965; Reuss, *Johannes-Kommentare*, 188–95. See also J. Reuss, 'Cyrill von Alexandrien und sein Kommentar zum Johannes-Evangelium', *Biblica* 25 (1944), 207–9; G.D. Fee, 'The Text of John in Origen and Cyril of Alexandria: a Contribution to Methodology in the Recovery and Analysis of Patristic Citations', *Biblica* 52 (1971), 357–94, reprinted in Epp and Fee, *Studies*, 301–34.

The fourth-century writer Titus of Bostra wrote a commentary on Luke which has survived as *catena* fragments (*CPG* III.3576).

J. Sickenberger, *Titus v. Bostra. Studien zur dessen Lukashomilien* (TU 21/1), Leipzig, 1901.

The commentary on Mark by the fifth-century presbyter Victor of Antioch is better described as a *catena* (*CPG* III.6533). It exists in two recensions. Reuss lists fifty-three manuscripts of the first and fifteen of the second (*Matthäus, Markus- u. Johannes-Katenen*, 118–41). There are also fragments on Luke (*CPG* III.6534).

Nicetas of Heraclea (see 8.6) was responsible for *catenae* which are called Type C by Reuss (Matthew = *CPG* IV.C113, Luke = *CPG* IV.C135, John = *CPG* IV.C144).

J. Sickenberger, *Die Lukaskatene des Niketas von Herakleia* (TU 22/4), Leipzig, 1902.

Theophylact's Commentaries on the Gospels were popular. Reuss lists sixty-seven manuscripts (all but four are included in the *Liste*; *Matthäus, Markus- u. Johannes-Katenen*, 221–37). The commentaries on Matthew and John make use of a collection of excerpts from Chrysostom made by an unknown sixth-century writer (the basic form of Reuss' Type A). Mark is a compilation based on the commentary by Victor of Antioch.

Euthymius Zigabenus' commentaries on the Gospels draw heavily on John Chrysostom throughout. They were edited by C.F. Matthaei (3 vols., Leipzig, 1792), and also printed in Migne, *PG* (vols. 128–31). Reuss lists the following manuscripts as containing them: 136 196 305 379 600 730 2583 (*Matthäus, Markus- u. Johannes-Katenen*, 238–43).

Peter of Laodicea's dates are only very approximately known (*c*. 7th–8th century is the usual view). Authorship of a *catena* is attributed to him in a few manuscripts. Heinrici supported the attribution, but subsequent writers have not.

G. Heinrici, *Des Petrus von Laodicea Erklärung des Matthäusevangeliums* (Beiträge zur Geschichte und Erklärung des Neuen Testaments 5), Leipzig, 1908; M. Rauer, *Der dem Petrus von Laodicea zugeschriebene Lukaskommentar* (NTA 8/2), 1920.

10.7 TATIAN'S DIATESSARON

W.L. Petersen, *Tatian's Diatessaron. Its Creation, Dissemination, Significance, and History in Scholarship* (Supplements to *VC* 25), Leiden, New York and Cologne, 1994; U. Schmid, *Unum ex Quattuor. Eine Geschichte der lateinischen Tatianüberlieferung* (GLB 37), Freiburg, Basel and Vienna, 2005; 'In Search of Tatian's Diatessaron in the West', *VC* 57 (2003), 176–99; see also 'Genealogy by Chance!'.

Tatian was a Syrian who came to Rome and was converted to Christianity at some time between 150 and 165, returning to the east after 172. At an unknown point he made his Diatessaron, a Gospel harmony in which the four narratives are woven into a single fabric (he may in fact have drawn also on a fifth source, but this is by no means clear). This was a very popular text in ancient times, especially in Syrian circles. In spite of this, no copy is known to survive. It is not known whether the Diatessaron was composed in Greek or in Syriac.

It has often been claimed that a Greek fragment of a Gospel harmony, found at Dura Europos on the Euphrates and dated by archaeological as well as palaeographical means to the middle of the second century, is the Diatessaron. Doubt has recently been cast on this by D.C. Parker, D.G.K. Taylor and M.S. Goodacre, 'The Dura-Europos Gospel Harmony', in Taylor, *Studies in the Early Text*, 192–228. After a detailed study of the manuscript, which is a fragment of a roll, including a fresh edition of the text, we concluded by comparison with other witnesses to the Diatessaron, that what evidence there was did not support the possibility that it might be Tatianic. Our views have since been challenged by J. Joosten, 'The Dura Parchment and the Diatessaron', *VC* 57 (2003), 159–75. For reasons which will become clear below, the topic needs to be revisited, since not all the witnesses which the two articles cite are still relevant. The Dura fragment has a Gregory–Aland number 0212 – wrongly, since a fragment of a harmony is not a fragment of a New Testament manuscript.

In the absence of any copies of the Diatessaron, we are wholly dependent upon a range of indirect witnesses. These are divided into two branches, one eastern and one western. The most valuable eastern evidence is provided by the Commentary on the Diatessaron by Ephraem (*c.* 306–73; the commentary was probably written after 363). An Armenian version published in 1836 was an important impetus to the growth of Diatessaronic study, which until then had not existed. The discovery and publication (in 1963) of a Syriac manuscript containing more than half of the work was a major step forward. Two Gospel harmonies in other languages are our other eastern witnesses, one in Persian and one in Arabic.

For Ephraem's commentary see *PS*, pp. 61–3; Petersen, *Tatian's Diatessaron*; for an example of its use in reconstructing the text, T. Baarda, '"The Flying Jesus". Luke 4:29–30 in the Syriac Diatessaron', *VC* 40 (1986), 313–41, reprinted in *Essays on the Diatessaron* (Contributions to Biblical Exegesis and Theology 11), Kampen, 1994, 59–85. For discussions of research on the Persian and Arabic versions see Petersen, *Tatian's Diatessaron* (especially pp. 259–63 and 133–8). T. Baarda, 'The Author of the Arabic Diatessaron', in T. Baarda *et al.* (eds.), *Miscellanea Neotestamentica*, vol. 1, Leiden, 1978, 61–103, reprinted in *Early Transmission of the Words of Jesus. Thomas, Tatian and the Text of the New Testament*, Amsterdam, 1983, 207–49.

Study of the way in which the Diatessaron is attested in the west has a more complicated history. In addition to an important ancient Latin source there is a rich medieval vernacular harmony tradition which has been extensively studied. Harmonies in two Italian dialects, Old High German, a variety of Dutch sources and Middle English have been edited, and readings found in them which have been said to attest the text of the Diatessaron. This kind of study went through a boom in the 1920s and 30s, many typical contributions of the time being published in the *Bulletin of the Bezan Club*, a privately circulating journal which ran intermittently between 1925 and 1937. A typical modern application of the approach is given in the article by Parker, Taylor and Goodacre. It seems on the face of it rather surprising that fourteenth- or fifteenth-century harmonies in Dutch could have very much to contribute to the study of a second-century text written in Greek or Syriac. Why they have been valued is explained by the textual history presupposed. The principal ancient western witness to the Diatessaron is the Latin Codex Fuldensis. The manuscript contains the Gospels as a continuous narrative based upon the Diatessaron. The structure of the text is more significant than the wording, since the original form of the translation has been altered to agree with the Vulgate. Comparison of the medieval vernacular harmonies showed readings which seemed to agree with eastern witnesses against Codex Fuldensis, encouraging the conclusion that there was another ancient Latin version of the Diatessaron now lost, which was the source of these readings shared between eastern and western vernacular witnesses.

What this theory overlooked was the existence throughout the Middle Ages of a vigorous Latin harmony tradition. A recent study of this tradition by Schmid has led to the conclusion that there is a more immediate and also more credible source for the non-Fuldensian readings in the vernacular versions, namely that they are translations from these Latin sources. The Latin tradition includes the Harmony by Clement of Llanthony (died *c.* 1190), and William of Nottingham's adaptation in the following century.

Schmid, *Unum ex Quattuor*, 'In Search of Tatian's Diatessaron in the West'. These researches seem to signal the end of an especially enjoyable form of research, in which the scholar was able to study a rich variety of texts in various languages, an activity affording many opportunities for various philological *tours de force*, out of which a number of elements, very disparate in every respect except for their genre, were shown to be closely related. It even gave the northern European the possibility that texts in earlier forms of their own tongues were valuable witnesses to a lost second-century text. For myself, my views have gone through a series of changes in which I cannot be alone. First as a student captivated by the way in which the annals of the Bezan Club seemed to offer a vista of a sort of text-critical theme park, after a few years I began to question the likelihood of such remote texts being related. When I returned to the topic after an interval of perhaps twenty years, the fact that scholars seemed to be using the western vernaculars to telling effect led me to change my mind again. However, Schmid's arguments have led me to a renewed and reinforced scepticism. Undoubtedly reason has prevailed, but one cannot suppress a sigh.

A footnote to the Diatessaron is the question whether Justin Martyr made a harmony before Tatian. According to one theory of the western tradition, a Latin version of this harmony predating Codex Fuldensis was a source, or the source, for the non-Fuldensian readings in the vernacular harmonies. While under certain circumstances it is reasonable to hypothesise a lost version of a lost text, Schmid's revision of the history of the medieval harmony tradition has taken away the need for this hypothesis also. This is not to deny the possibility that there were pre-Tatianic harmonies, only that we have any textual evidence for them, or need them to explain other phenomena.

This brief description of the Diatessaron has been offered because the Diatessaron is of significance in two ways. In the first place, it is of textual value. Where the text of the Diatessaron may be reconstructed, it provides indirect evidence for the text of the separated Gospels out of which Tatian wove his account. They are to be treated, in fact, in the same way as patristic citations: they tell us about the text in the codex or codices which he used. Secondly, the very creation of the Diatessaron provides an insight into the way in which second-century Christians thought about the Gospels. Where modern scholarship has been at pains to describe the distinctiveness of each of the four, ancient Christianity (embarrassed perhaps at the jibes by such as Celsus at the disparity between them) was at pains to emphasize the unity of the four. Two ways of doing so, Marcion's solution and the alternative of harmonising differences, will be discussed later (10.8 and 10.10.2). Tatian took the most painstaking and thorough route, altering the sequence of the phrases so that they precisely expressed the oneness of the Gospel. First, what do we know about the text of the Diatessaron? The answer is that while it is often tempting to ascribe known variants to the Diatessaron, the argument is often circumstantial. While many harmonising variants might be Tatianic, the power of harmonisation is such that the hypothesis will always be questionable.

An example of a possible Diatessaronic reading in a Greek Gospel manuscript is found at Matthew 17.26, the story of the temple tribute. Into the dialogue between Jesus and Simon Peter the following words are added in 713 (Birmingham, Mingana Collection, Peckover Gr. 7):☛ (51)

ἆραγε ἐλεύθεροι εἰσὶν οἱ υἱοί; ἔφη Σίμων· ναί. λέγει ὁ Ἰησοῦς.
δὸς οὖν καὶ σύ, ὡς ἀλλότριος αὐτῶν.

Similar wording is found in Ephraem's Commentary ('give thou also as one of the strangers') and in the Arabic Harmony. The theory is that this reading from the Diatessaron found its way back into the separate text of Matthew. Other famous readings which may also be from the Diatessaron include the detail at Jesus' baptism of a fire or light appearing (mentioned in various sources, including two Old Latin manuscripts at Matt. 3.15–16).

For Matt. 17.25, see J.R. Harris, 'The First Tatian Reading in the Greek New Testament', *Expositor*, 8th series, 23 (1922), 120–9, reprinted in A. Falcetta (ed.), *James Rendel Harris. New Testament Autographs and Other Essays* (New Testament Monographs 7), Sheffield, 2006, 185–91. For the fire at the baptism, see Petersen, *Tatian's Diatessaron*, 14–20.

As a witness older than our oldest manuscripts, the Diatessaron is potentially a source of information about readings in manuscripts known to Tatian. That is, it may be used like any other patristic testimony. But the special circumstances of our access to it requires caution in each instance.

10.8 MARCION'S GOSPEL

Marcion, working in Rome at a similar time to Tatian, produced a single Gospel by another means. It was seen that his theological views led to a distinctive collection of Paul's letters. His views with regard to the

Gospels also had a textual result. For Marcion, Christianity had been Judaicised, and in his eyes this meant that something had gone wrong. For him, the Gospel could only be a single Gospel, and he found it in a version of Luke emended by himself. This version is, like the Diatessaron, not known directly. It has to be reconstructed as one may from the way in which it is quoted by his opponents. The most valuable source is the long work which Tertullian wrote against Marcion, although text-critically it suffers from the fact that Marcion wrote in Greek and Tertullian is citing him in Latin. However, Tertullian not only quoted Marcion; he sometimes referred specifically to Tatian's form of text. Another, less satisfactory, source for the study of Marcion's text is Epiphanius of Salamis.

The text of Marcion was reconstructed in the famous work of A. von Harnack, *Marcion: Das Evangelium vom fremden Gott. Eine Monographie zur Geschichte der Grundlegung der katholischen Kirche*, Leipzig, 1921, 2nd edn, 1924; Schmid, *Marcion und sein Apostolos*, cites also an edition of 1923 (TU 44), and a reprint, Darmstadt, 1960, and several contemporary reviews. A useful place for finding information about Marcion's text is the IGNTP *Luke*, which provides the relevant citations from Tertullian and others after the main Greek patristic citations index.

What influence did Marcion have on the text of the New Testament? It is tempting to see him behind various shorter forms of text in Luke. However, because Marcion produced a shorter text, it does not follow that all shorter forms of text are Marcionite. One has therefore to be cautious, not least because the fact that there is a lack of positive evidence that a writer knew a passage is not compelling evidence that he did not know, or at least that he did not accept, it.

For a discussion of the problems of reconstructing Marcion's text, see U. Schmid, 'How Can We Access Second Century Gospel Texts? The Cases of Marcion and Tatian', in Amphoux and Elliott, *New Testament Text*, 139–50. There is an older assessment of the influence of Marcion's on other forms of the text in C. S. C. Williams, *Alterations to the Text of the Synoptic Gospels and Acts*, Oxford, 1951, 10–18.

10.9 EDITIONS

The older editions of Matthew and Mark, the first-fruits of the Critical Greek New Testament (precursor of the International Greek New Testament Project) by Legg are no longer useful. The Greek evidence is outdated, and the versional material had always to be used with caution. The two Lucan volumes of the International Greek New Testament Project contain much material, including a wide range of versional and patristic data and a large selection of Greek manuscripts, including all majuscules (for the principles of the work see 6.3.3). The subsequent volumes of this Project have already been mentioned. Another resource for Greek manuscripts is the four volumes of Swanson.

IGNTP *Luke*. Some additional evidence is given separately in A. J. B. Higgins, 'The Arabic Diatessaron in the New Oxford Edition of the Gospel According to St Luke in Greek', *JTS* 37 (1986), 415–19; Elliott and Parker, *Papyri*; Schmid, Elliott and Parker, *Majuscules*; Swanson, *Greek Manuscripts*; the Gospels are in four volumes, subtitled *Matthew, Mark*, etc., Sheffield and Pasadena, 1995.

10.10 TEXTUAL VARIATION

10.10.1 Studying textual variation in the Gospels

This is a topic which traditionally deals with some of the longest major units of variation: the different endings of Mark; the story of the woman in John 7.53–8.11; additional passages in different manuscripts such as the otherwise unreported saying of Jesus at Luke 6.4 in Codex Bezae, the bloody sweat in Luke 22. 43–4; the angel troubling the water in John 5.4, and so on; along with some of the more significant (or at least most frequently discussed) variants such as whether Jesus was angry or compassionate in Mark 1.41, or whether the text should read 'son' or 'God' in John 1.18. Some of these will be discussed below. But to introduce this topic, I have selected a very small variant which makes a large impact on the sense of a passage, where the significance of the readings is discussed by exegetes.

The Sermon on the Mount has at various times been seen as a blueprint for the Christian life, as a summary of all that is necessary for ethical behaviour, as Jesus' instructions to his disciples of a new way of life. And within it the so-called Antitheses have an important place. In the first of these, Jesus is recorded as taking the commandment 'Thou shalt not kill' and making the pronouncement 'But I say to you that every one who is angry with his brother shall be liable to judgment' (Matt. 5.22). This is the reading of twenty-eight Greek manuscripts, including the oldest witnesses of this part of Matthew, the rest representing every century down to the sixteenth. All of the other 1,449 legible manuscripts containing this verse include four more letters, the word εἰκῇ, 'without cause' (data from *Text und Textwert*, ad loc.). This was the form of the saying best known to readers and hearers of Matthew in Greek from the fifth century onwards. We may see this development in its insertion by a sixth-century corrector into Codex Sinaiticus. Only by Lachmann and in subsequent critical editions was it supplanted. It appears that an unconditional command not to hate was replaced by one containing a let-out clause, permitting anger with one's brother where there is cause, the cause being undefined and therefore leaving room for interpretation. The movement in the development of the Greek text was from the unconditional form of the saying to the conditional. John Chrysostom commented on the conditional reading and was able to justify his interpretation from Scripture, notably the words of Psalm 4.5 'Be angry and sin not', concluding that Jesus is condemning not anger but anger at the wrong time.

The movement in the Latin text was in the opposite direction, from the restricted to the absolute form. The Old Latin manuscripts include the qualification, reading *sine causa*. But Jerome's Vulgate omits it. The ninth-century Irish commentator Sedulius noted the variant, and created an argument to justify the absolute form. Like John Chrysostom's, it was based on passages of Scripture, namely the commands to turn the other cheek, to love one's enemies and to pray for one's persecutors, and the observation that 'human anger does not work the righteousness of God' (Jas. 1.20). He concludes that the command is unconditional and the words 'without cause' spurious.

John Chrysostom, *In Matthaeum Homiliae 1–90* (CPG 11.4424), Homily 16, cited from B. de Montfaucon (ed.), *Sancti Patris Nostri Chrysostomi Archiespiscopi Constantinopolitani Opera Omnia* etc., vol. VII, Paris, 1727, cols. 213–14; B. Löfstedt (ed.), *Sedulius Scotus. Kommentar zum Evangelium nach Matthäus 1,1–11,1* (GLB 14), 1989, 153f. Note that D. Bonhoeffer, not a name we associate with textual criticism, reading the unconditional form, offers the opinion that the addition of εἰκῇ is 'the first attempt to mitigate the harshness of this saying' (D. Bonhoeffer, *The Cost of Discipleship*, tr. R.H. Fuller, London, 1959, 116, n. 1). Was George Orwell thinking of this variant when writing *Animal Farm*? The commandment which had read 'No animal shall kill any other animal' later states 'No animal shall kill any other animal *without cause*' (*Animal Farm*, London, 1974 [1945], 23, 78).

The difference between the two is, when we set it against the different interpretations provided by two commentators, a striking instance of the way in which difference in interpretation could lead to alterations to the text.

The value of this simple variant (there are no other wordings besides these two) is that it highlights so well the way in which an apparently slight difference in wording – four letters only! – can provide a complete commentary on two different interpretations of Christian ethics. Where texts are as frequently and as devotedly studied as the Gospels have always been, one is almost tempted to say that there is no such thing as an insignificant variant.

This would be exaggeration, of course. But where there is variation in the sayings of Jesus, and in certain other passages, the issues at stake for many people go beyond the confines of textual criticism. They involve ways in which we understand the role of the written text and its interpretation both in antiquity and today, as well as basic ethical issues. It is perhaps a meeting of these concerns which has led to the growth in the search for variants motivated by debates in early Christianity.

Because of the ways in which the figure of Jesus and his teaching have often, even generally, been received in Christianity, and because of the inclusion of four Gospels in the New Testament canon, there are characteristic forms of textual variation which are either not found elsewhere in Christian writings or are not such important elements in other branches of text-critical research. It must be stressed again that what is written about the Gospels is by no means necessarily true of the other parts of the New Testament, and vice versa. The number of manuscripts, the extent of variation, the historical problems, and the far greater extent of critical study are a combination of circumstances that has produced particularly intense debate. In *The Living Text of the Gospels*, I offered an approach that emphasised the significance of the fact that there *is* such a degree of textual variation, arguing that early Christians changed the wording of the text (especially of sayings of Jesus) in order to bring out the meaning they found in it. In my opinion, too much emphasis had been placed upon the search for and emphasis upon a putative 'original text'. The argument was not about the rejection of stemmatology and the reconstruction of an earliest attainable text (I took the provisional view that the earliest text attained by such methods could not be shown to be older than late second century). It was a challenge to the claim that there is a single authoritative form of text, whether that form be taken to be 'authorial', 'original', or 'the final canonical form' (whatever that might be).

For a detailed discussion of the topic, see E. J. Epp, 'The Multivalence of the Term "Original Text" in New Testament Textual Criticism', *HTR* 92 (1999), 245–81, reprinted in *Collected Essays*, 551–92, with Added Notes (592–3). For another approach, J. Delobel, 'The Achilles' Heel of New Testament Textual Criticism', *Bijdragen, International Journal in Philosophy and Theology* 63 (2002), 3–21.

10.10.2 Harmonisation

This feature has been mentioned already. It is not wholly confined to the Gospels. But it is most marked in these books, especially in the Synoptists. It consists of alterations which vary between slight or sequential changes of wording to bring about a closer agreement to the addition of whole phrases or even longer blocks of text from another Gospel, and between changes found in a few or even in a single document and changes which have affected almost the whole tradition. An example of a single slight change is at Mark 2.9, where a few manuscripts add γάρ between τί and ἐστιν under the influence of Matthew 9.5. Examples of the addition of a sequence of changes are found in a passage I used in my earlier book, setting the different versions of Luke 6.1–11 in 03, 05 and 045 in parallel

columns, and then Luke 6.1–5 in 02 and 05 against the parallel passage
Mark 2.23–8 in 05. An example of the insertion of a longer block is found
in Matthew 27.35, where a number of manuscripts add the words from
John 19.24 citing a proof-text.

Parker, *Living Text*, 31–48.

The manuscript which contains the most harmonisations is Codex
Bezae, computed by H. J. Vogels to have 1,278. Of course, the precise
number depends upon the text from which Vogels considered it to have
been altered, and alternative explanations might be found for some of
them. Not all are unique to Codex Bezae (in fact it takes some time to
find an example that is). I select at random Mark 12.17, where the
wording of most manuscripts (τὰ Καίσαρος ἀπόδοτε Καίσαρι) is
replaced by 05 and a few other manuscripts with the better-known
Matthaean (and Lucan) form ἀπόδοτε τὰ Καίσαρος Καίσαρι (without
the οὖν found in most manuscripts of Matthew and Luke).

An example of a reading found in almost the whole tradition is the
Lucan version of the Lord's Prayer, whose non-harmonised form is found
in only a few manuscripts (P75 01 03 1582 and a few other minuscules).

H. J. Vogels, *Die Harmonistik im Evangelientext des Codex Cantabrigiensis. Ein Beitrag zur neutestamentlichen Textkritik* (TU 36/1a), Leipzig, 1910. See Parker, *Codex Bezae*, 189. For the Lord's Prayer,
see Parker, *Living Text*, chapter 4, esp. pp. 60–4.

A few brief canons describing their behaviour are the best way of saying
more about harmonisations.

(1) Matthew is the least harmonised of the Synoptists; Mark and Luke
are more generally harmonised to conform with Matthew. This is in
line with the ancient view that Matthew's was the oldest Gospel.

(2) Other possible causes must be considered before a variant is adjudged
a harmonisation. For example, Family 13 inserts Luke 22.43–4 at the
end of Matthew 26.39 (the verses are also written here in the margin
of 04 by a later hand). This looks like a harmonisation, and in a sense
it is. But it is probably due to the fact that these two verses stand as a
separate lection between two long readings in the Holy Week
sequence, Matthew 26.31–9 and 26.40–27.2. Rather than being a
harmonisation, it is more probable that this section became
associated with the Matthaean passage from the lectionary and thus
found its way into some continuous-text manuscripts.

(3) Harmonisation is not always clearly distinguished from other forms
of change. For example, the removal of an element of the distinctive

harshness of Marcan style will most easily be effected by the use of Matthew where this Gospel has already revised Mark's style.

(4) Harmonisation between Gospels is not the only kind. There is also a tendency for texts to show harmonisation within a Gospel, and particularly in the immediate context. Indeed, harmonisation to the context is one of the strongest forms of textual variation (it is generally easy to detect in a manuscript).

(5) Harmonisation is not consistent, and it does away with differences in what seems a very haphazard manner.

(6) Harmonisation may not necessarily be made in the direction of what the modern synopsis would present as a parallel but might be to a passage which today is considered to be one that is unrelated.

(7) Harmonisation in a particular manuscript may not bring about a form of text identical to that found in the parallel passage in the same manuscript. In fact, it is rather unlikely to do so, for two reasons. First, it is reasonable to suppose that harmonisation is likely to have been effected either by comparison with another codex, or from memory. Second, harmonisation is sufficiently common to have happened long enough before the production of a particular manuscript for one (or both) of its texts of the parallel passage containing the source harmonisation and the harmonised passage to have undergone further changes.

(8) Centuries of harmonisation produced forms of the Gospel texts which masked many of their differences. Why did harmonisation occur so frequently? It is hard not to see an analogy with the Diatessaron, in that both contain an underlying assumption that the four are truly one. One may suppose also the influence of the better-known text over the less familiar (generally, Matthew over Mark, and Matthaean material found in Luke). More recently, a hypothesis has been advanced with regard to the extensive harmonisation of some Lucan parables in Codex Bezae, that the harmonisings of Luke towards Matthew reflect a sophisticated exegetical concept, namely mimesis, in which the imitative form of a text reflects another Gospel in a subtle way.

Dela Cruz, 'Allegory, Mimesis and the Text'.

Extrapolating from the specific, dela Cruz's approach shows yet again how forms of variation which have traditionally been treated as almost mechanical, certainly not as pregnant with significance, are today explored in a quest for finding meaning and interpretation not only in the variant, but in the act of changing the text itself. The new approaches which have been mentioned in a number of places already in this book will provide a framework for its final section, in which different ways of interpreting textual variations are described.

10.10.3 The endings of Mark

Mark ends in various ways in different witnesses.

(1) The Short Ending (the Gospel ends with the last words of 16.8, ἐφοβοῦντο γάρ). Read by 01 03 304, the Sinaitic Syriac, a Sahidic manuscript, some Armenian manuscripts and manuscripts known to Eusebius and Jerome.
(2) The Intermediate Ending (a brief conclusion after 16.8). This on its own is found only in the African Old Latin manuscript Codex Bobiensis, which also has unique additional text after verse 3.
(3) The Long Ending (verses 9–20), found in all other witnesses, although some of them mark the passage as suspect in one way or another: either with obeloi or with asterisks, the ancient indications that a passage is spurious (see 6.1.1), or with a note indicating that the text is not present in all copies. This is the text of most witnesses.
(4) The Intermediate *and* the Long Endings, with or without notes about each. This is found in 044, a few other manuscripts, the Harklean margin and some Sahidic and Bohairic manuscripts.

The wordings of Endings 2, 3 and 4 all contain variants between the manuscripts attesting them. The most striking of these is the Freer Logion, an addition after Verse 14 which had been known from a comment in Jerome, now known in Greek in the Freer Gospels, 032.

The existence of these readings has been explained in various ways. First, the suggestion has been made that the end of Mark's work was lost in an early copy from which all known forms of the text are descended. Thus it is pure chance that it ends at 16.8, and the endings we do have are ancient attempts to make good this loss. In favour of this theory is the improbability of the choice of γάρ as the final word of a book. It is suggested that the endings of Matthew and Luke may contain elements of Mark's original ending, but of course we cannot know what they were.

The second explanation finds Mark's own intentional ending at 16.8 and argues that the additions to it are attempts in early Christianity to overcome a rather shocking omission, namely, resurrection narratives. Such texts as the Intermediate and the Long Endings may be read in several ways. Historical analysis is used by Kelhoffer to develop a picture

of the unknown second-century author of the Long Ending, 'an individual who stood at a critical transitional period in the history of early
Christian literature ... [O]ne can wonder whether the Gospel of Mark
would ultimately have been included in the NT canon without the
addition(s) of the Longer Ending.' Alternatively, recent critical theory
may be called into service in order to study the nature of the additions
and their contribution to the narrative. Gilfillan Upton uses speech act
theory, studying among other things oral language to understand aural
texts (that is, writings designed to be heard).

For the endings, see Parker, *The Living Text*, chapter 8; J. A. Kelhoffer, *Miracle and Mission. The
Authentication of Missionaries and their Message in the Longer Ending of Mark* (WUNT 112),
Tübingen, 2000, 479, 480. The book includes a history of research (which has been considerable,
since this passage has been important to defenders of the Received Text). B. Gilfillan Upton, *Hearing
Mark's Endings. Listening to Ancient Popular Texts through Speech Act Theory* (Biblical Interpretation
Series 79), Leiden and Boston, 2006. J. K. Elliott has argued that the first three verses of the Gospel
are not Marcan, suggesting that an early codex of the work lost its outer sheet: 'Mark 1.1–3 – A Later
Addition to the Gospel?', *NTS* 46 (2000), 584–8.

10.10.4 John 7.53–8.11

This is another long passage of dubious origin. The vast majority of
manuscripts include it after John 7.52. There are variants within it. In particular, Codex Bezae has a different form from the majority of manuscripts,
sufficiently different for Tischendorf to decide to print the two forms on
facing pages (05 on the left, the Received Text on the right, with a single
apparatus beneath). The passage is omitted by P66 P75 01 03 032 044 and 288
other witnesses. Other manuscripts include them but with asterisks or
obeloi. Family 1 places it at the end of the Gospel. Family 13 places it after
Luke 21.25 (a place where it sits quite neatly). Further details may be seen in
Nestle–Aland.

Study of this passage is well served: von Soden selected the passage for the analysis of manuscript
groupings (von Soden, 1.486–524). M. Robinson has collated all manuscripts not only in the passage
but in the verses on either side and is currently analysing the results. T. Wasserman has studied thirty-
four manuscripts to determine whether a possible relation was a sustainable theory: 'The Patmos
Family of New Testament MSS and its Allies in the Pericope of the Adulteress and Beyond', http://
rosetta.reltech.org/TC/vol07/Wasserman2002/Wasserman2002.html/.

The information given above is taken from *Text und Textwert* (test passage 100). See also Parker,
Living Text, chapter 6. For recent discussions, see J. W. Knust, 'Early Christian Re-writing and the
History of the *Pericope Adulterae*', *Journal of Early Christian Studies* 14 (2006), 485–536; J. G. Skiadareses,
Ὁ Ἀναμάρτητος καί ἡ Μοιχαλίδα. Ἰωάνν. 7,53–8,11 (Bibliotheca Biblica 19), Thessaloniki, 2007.

Given the nature of this passage and its position in John, it is almost
impossible to find mechanical theories to account for its omission. One
is therefore forced to look upon it as a place where intentional changes

were made. There are a number of approaches necessary to gain an understanding of the passage. Literary analysis, which tests the style and vocabulary, is important. It has been argued that there are features of both which are atypical of Johannine style, while there are also traits which may be more Lucan. It is also necessary to look for attestation which will provide information about the history of the pericope both within and outside John. This has made it possible to date the passage (or at least provide a *terminus ante quem*). Petersen has argued that it was already known to the author of the text known as the *Protevangelium Iacobi*, and therefore was in existence in the second half of the second century. The date at which it was introduced to John is a separate question.

W. L. Petersen, 'ΟΥΔΕ ΕΓΩ ΣΕ [ΚΑΤΑ]ΚΡΙΝΩ. John 8:11, the *Protevangelium Iacobi*, and the History of the *Pericope Adulterae*', in *Baarda Festschrift*, 191–222.

Another approach is the study of the passage as a narrative. Ehrman has concluded that it is composed of two originally separate stories, one an 'entrapment story in which Jesus freely pardons a sinful woman, known to Papias and the author of the Didascalia [Apostolorum]', the other 'the story of Jesus' intervention in an execution proceeding, preserved in the Gospel according to the Hebrews and retold by Didymus [the Blind]'. Like Petersen, Ehrman makes full use of patristic sources, thereby showing how important it is to gather all available evidence from ancient sources before trying to develop text-critical theories. Another form of the story, found in a tenth-century Armenian codex, seems more like a version of Ehrman's entrapment story.

B. D. Ehrman, 'Jesus and the Adulteress', *NTS* 34 (1988), 24–44, reprinted in Ehrman, *Studies*, 196–220, p. 220 of *Studies*; F. C. Conybeare, 'On the Last Twelve Verses of Mark', *Expositor*, fifth series (1895), 401–21, p. 406; see also F. C. Burkitt, *Two Lectures on the Gospels*, London and New York, 1901, 88.

It has sometimes been argued that the passage may have been excised on the grounds that it was offensive, and here again patristic testimony is cited: Ambrose of Milan, who notes that Jesus' failure to condemn the woman disturbed some people, and Augustine of Hippo, who said that some people removed the story from their manuscripts in case their wives decided that it gave them carte blanche.

For the citations, see Petersen, 'John 8:11', 198ff.

10.10.5 Marcan style and thoroughgoing eclecticism

The starting point for this section is an important series of studies written by C. H. Turner about eighty years ago. Turner set out in these studies to

refine the definition of the characteristics of Mark's style, and to comment
on the variants attesting changes to that style. These views were influential
in the thinking of G. D. Kilpatrick, and through him of J. K. Elliott.

Details of the various articles by Turner are given in the most convenient place to study them,
J. K. Elliott, *The Language and Style of the Gospel of Mark. An Edition of C. H. Turner's 'Notes on
Marcan Usage' together with Other Comparable Studies* (NovTSuppl 71), Leiden, New York and
Cologne, 1993. The 'other comparable studies' are eight pieces by G. D. Kilpatrick (some previously
unpublished), two by Elliott, and the section on Mark's style in J. H. Moulton, *Grammar of the Greek
New Testament*, vol. IV: *Style*, by N. Turner, Edinburgh, 1976. J. K. Elliott (ed.), *The Principles and
Practice of New Testament Textual Criticism. Collected Papers of G. D. Kilpatrick* (BETL 96), Leuven,
1990; J. K. Elliott, *Essays and Studies in New Testament Textual Criticism* (Estudios de Filologa
Neotestamentaria 3), Cordova, n.d.[1990].

Turner's studies contributed to the formation of Kilpatrick's views.
The theory that in some eyes Mark's rough style needed improving
provides a framework for understanding many of the changes in the
manuscripts. This was clear to Turner. Kilpatrick brought two more
distinctive observations to the table. The first was an understanding of the
place of the Atticising movement in this, the attempt in the second and
third centuries to restore the late Hellenistic Greek of the day by the Attic
standard. For example, on the question of whether ζήσω or ζήσομαι is
correct, we are referred immediately to the 'Antiatticista' (an eighteenth-
century name for a text which rebelled against the Atticisers): ζήσει·
Πλάτων Πολιτείας ἕκτω, οὐ ζήσεται (That is, ζήσει is found six times in
Plato's *Republic*, and ζήσεται not at all).

Kilpatrick's second observation was a distinctive view of the transmission
of the New Testament text, that all significant variants had already come
into existence by the end of the second century. This was not a new theory,
as it had already been offered by Vogels. The result is to set all the variants
in a period from which virtually no manuscripts survive, so that there is no
external evidence to be considered. The evidence of P66, notably the places
where the scribe substituted one reading for another, indicates that 'many
of the differences between what our scribe first wrote and his subsequent
corrections go back well into the second century'.

The result was a very distinctive approach, in which the strongest
element is the rejection of what is often called the 'cult of the best
manuscript'. Kilpatrick insists against this that, in determining the correct
reading in any one instance, we must accord precedence to the criteria by
which we first decided which manuscript was best.

Just as patristic citations played an important role in the studies of
John 7.53–8.11 which were described, so ancient grammarians play a
central role in Kilpatrick's studies. As a result, variants are set in the

context of the history of the Greek language, within the style of the individual writer, and thus of the development of early Christianity.

For ζήσω or ζήσομαι, see Kilpatrick, 'Atticism and the Text of the Greek New Testament', in J. Blinzler *et al.* (eds.), *Neutestamentliche Aufsätze (Festschrift für J. Schmid)*, Regensburg, 1963, 125–37, reprinted in Elliott, *Principles and Practice*, 15–32, p. 25. For Vogels' views, see his *Handbuch der Textkritik des neuen Testaments*, 2nd edn, 1955, 162. Kilpatrick cites a statement to the same effect by K. Aland, 'Der Schluss des Markusevangeliums', in M. Sabbe (ed.), *L'évangile selon Marc, tradition et rédaction*, Leuven, 1974, 435–70, pp. 451–2 (also a revised edition (BETL 34), Leuven, 1988) in 'Some Thoughts on Modern Textual Criticism and the Synoptic Gospels', *NovT* 19 (1977), 275–92, reprinted in *Principles and Practice*, 80–97, p. 81. For P66, see 'The Transmission of the New Testament and its Reliability', *Proceedings of the 945th Ordinary General Meeting of the Victoria Institute* (1957), 92–101 and *Bible Translator* 9 (1958), 127–36, reprinted in *Principles and Practice*, 3–14, p. 5. For a more detailed assessment of the collected papers, see the review by D. C. Parker in *JTS* 43 (1992), 210–14.

It is undeniable that in many ways Kilpatrick followed the kinds of principle which would be taken for granted by scholars editing classical texts, that he walked in the footsteps of Porson and Housman and the like. It is undeniable too that when we compare his work with that of scholars such as Josef Schmid and Gunther Zuntz, we may see the same strain of philology. Where Kilpatrick differs is in the insistence on first principles to the exclusion of the reconstruction of textual history on the basis of a pattern of variant readings, with a rejection of the value of stemmatics.

The approach of J. K. Elliott is very similar to that of Kilpatrick. There is the same insistence on the first principles, the same concentration on variants of a grammatical and lexicographical nature. At the same time Elliott has dealt with a wider range of types of variant, and has shown a much greater interest in manuscripts (as his *Bibliography* attests).

Among discussions of thoroughgoing eclecticism, see E. J. Epp, 'The Eclectic Method in New Testament Textual Criticism: Solution or Symptom?', *Society of Biblical Literature Seminar Papers* (1975) 2.47–82, reprinted in Epp and Fee, *Studies*, 141–73 and in Epp, *Collected Essays*, 125–72, with added notes, 172–3; J. H. Petzer, 'Eclecticism and the Text of the New Testament', in P. J. Hartin and J. H. Petzer (eds.), *Text and Interpretation. New Approaches in the Criticism of the New Testament* (NTTS 15), Leiden, New York, Copenhagen and Cologne, 1991, 47–62.

A somewhat similar approach to the variants of Mark's Gospel is taken in a work by Greeven, completed by Güting. It is a study of the textual decisions taken in Greeven's *Synopsis* (A. Huck (ed.), *Synopse der drei ersten Evangelien mit Beigabe der johanneischen Parallelstellen / Synopsis of the First Three Gospels with the Addition of the Johannine Parallels*, 13th edn, rev. H. Greeven, Tübingen, 1981). For each variant there are three sections: a statement of the forms of text, an analysis of the textual tradition with an indication of the decisions made by other editors, and finally some comments on the views of other scholars. The work functions therefore as a textual commentary on Mark's Gospel. Its decisions show sympathy with many of Kilpatrick's views, but the methodology pays more attention to manuscript value, especially to the significance of the geographical spread of readings. H. Greeven, *Textkritik des Markusevangeliums*, ed. E. Güting (Theologie. Forschung und Wissenschaft 11), Münster, 2005.

10.11 CONCLUSION

The previous sections have offered an outline of the materials available for the study of the text of the Gospels, and of a few of the ways in which they have been used. In concluding, the main problems of research and some comments on the immediate future will be described.

One way of illustrating the difficulties of understanding what happened to the Gospel text up to the end of the second century is to take an extreme solution to the problem. Such a solution often casts light on a problem and on other solutions, even if it is unsatisfactory itself. The views outlined here are those of C.-B. Amphoux. To state the theory very briefly: until the time of Polycarp, around 135, there were no Gospels, only a mass of inchoate traditions. It is to the era of Polycarp that we owe the making of a four-Gospel collection, the whole being in the order Matthew–John–Luke–Mark, the Long Ending of Mark serving as a conclusion to the four. This oldest version of the text is now known to us from Codex Bezae and manuscripts attesting similar forms of text. The so-called Alexandrian text is a recension produced in Rome later in the century.

C.-B. Amphoux: 'Schéma d'histoire du texte grec du Nouveau Testament', *New Testament Textual Research Update* 3/3 (1995), 41–6; D. C. Parker, 'Professor Amphoux's History of the New Testament Text: a Response', *New Testament Textual Research Update* 4/3 (1996), 41–5; C. B. Amphoux, 'A propos de l'histoire du texte grec de Nouveau Testament. Réponse à David C. Parker', *New Testament Textual Research Update* 6 (1998), 1–8. See also C.-B. Amphoux, *La Parole qui devint évangile. L'évangile – ses rédacteurs – son auteur*, Paris, 1993.

Another approach which stresses the limitations of our evidence for reconstructing the earliest forms of text is by W. L. Petersen (d. 2006). His last observations concerned the text forms known to the Apostolic Fathers (Petersen, 'Textual Traditions Examined').

I describe this theory because it neatly encapsulates some real problems, even though its answers are based on very little evidence. The key issues in Gospel research which it highlights are

(1) The degree to which the separate Gospels were changed by the creation of the four-Gospel collection.
(2) The difficulty of establishing that any form of text is older than the second century.
(3) The possibility that whatever the forms of text were like in the year 100, they were very different from the late second-century forms still available to us.
(4) The degree to which literary questions predating the known textual history (for example, possible earlier forms of the Gospel of John) should be considered in the study of the history of the text.

Can one come up with a better hypothesis? A detailed answer to this will have to await the detailed studies which will accompany the editions of the Gospels in the *Editio critica maior*. Such work is at its earliest stages so far as the Gospel of John is concerned. Whether the editors will find techniques and evidence for improving our picture of the second-century or even of the first-century text remains to be seen.

Final thoughts

As I come to the end of this book, I offer some reflections.

In the first place, I am struck by how little we know (certainly how little I know) about almost everything I have written about. Given the tiny number of manuscripts to have survived from antiquity, our theories can be no more than provisional attempts to understand these fragments of the textual tradition. This is not to denigrate either the quality of past and present research, or to say that nothing can be said about anything. But time and again, whether collecting information on manuscripts or on versions or on the forms of the text known to us, I have come upon the edge of voids which I could not cross. Some may be due to gaps in my knowledge. Others I believe to be at least currently impassable. Writing this has therefore been an exercise in humility.

Secondly, the study of the documents of the New Testament writings and their texts is flourishing. In the variety of ways of studying the manuscripts and the texts and in the vitality of various projects conceived and being executed on the largest scale, there are more grounds for optimism than for gloom. There are many recent studies which offer fresh insights.

That said, there remain a number of rather important matters which need study sooner rather than later, and I set out some of them here, in the hope that either potential research students or older scholars will be minded to take them up.

(1) The gaps in our knowledge of some of the versions remain glaring. Important for the study of the history of the reception of the New Testament and of the cultures in which they arose if not necessarily for the understanding of the ancient text, they are deserving of attention which they have hardly received, and which would provide research opportunities for many people.

(2) There are important commentaries and other writings significant in their citations of the New Testament which require critical editions.

(3) There remain many Greek manuscripts whose study would explain some part of the history of the text or cast light on the use of the New Testament at a place and a period in history.

(4) There are many particular puzzles which merit studies for their better understanding. For example, what might not be said about the various colophons, many of which have been discussed, reporting that the manuscript's text is Origen's, produced by Pamphilus and Eusebius in prison? Is it credible that it could be true of them all? Is this a genre of colophon, or what is it?

(5) Finally, there are textual theories, text-editing principles, and the new disciplines of electronic editing to be learned and developed.

There are certainly more people than ever before looking for topics for doctoral work in the New Testament. While some areas of New Testament scholarship appear intolerably crowded, there is room enough in these fields, and the opportunity for acquiring some good disciplines, as well as of making a lasting contribution.

Textual criticism has come to greater notice recently as a result of studies which have emphasised its wider significance and dealt with more approachable matters. It is worth saying that it remains the case that there are no short cuts to producing such research. It remains as much the case as ever that there is much solid groundwork to be done before this stage can be reached. There may be emerging a tendency to find a theological reason for variants without the necessary research on manuscripts, scribal tendencies and other such matters. And so we end as we began:

The first step towards obtaining a sure foundation is a consistent application of the principle that KNOWLEDGE OF DOCUMENTS SHOULD PRECEDE FINAL JUDGEMENT UPON READINGS.

The lasting contribution is another thing I have noted. Works written a century and more ago remain invaluable tools in the field, making textual criticism a discipline with a strong sense of its continuing debt to scholars of the past. It is remarkable that textual scholarship, far more than other branches of biblical criticism, remains in touch with scholarship of the nineteenth and even of the eighteenth century and at the same time is changing quickly. The current generation is experiencing one of the most momentous periods in the transmission of biblical texts and of much in textual scholarship. It will be equally exciting to see what happens in the next few years.

Glossary

abs (superscript after a manuscript number). Indicates that the manuscript is confidently believed to be a copy of the manuscript carrying the same number without any addition (e.g. 205^{abs} is a copy of 205). From the German 'Abschrift', copy.

apparatus A *critical apparatus* (often given its Latin name *apparatus criticus*) refers to the section usually at the bottom of the page (or after a block of text – in either case below the text) which contains the variant readings and statements of manuscripts supporting each one. The word *apparatus* is good English, with a plural *apparatuses*, but it is also good Latin. A Latin noun of this class has a plural form which is spelt the same, but with a long instead of a short u, so one will find the plural *apparatus* or *apparatus critici*. Like other Latin nouns of this class, it tended to become confused with another class also ending in *–us*, but with a plural in *–i*. So one may occasionally find the plural form *apparati critici*. Whether one chooses English or Latin, the correct plural form is unambiguous so long as the adjective is supplied.

catena A collection of quotations from early Christian writers linked together to form a commentary on a biblical writing.

citation A quotation of a passage from the New Testament in an early Christian writer.

Clavis In the present context, a manual listing all the works of the Church Fathers to have been written in a particular language, including brief details and information on the available editions.

codex A document made by folding sheets of material in half and combining them in one of a number of possible ways to make what is recognised as a book today.

collation A list of differences between a manuscript and a base text. Sometimes a number of separate collations are combined into one. Such a collation is the base of an apparatus.

continuous-text manuscript This term distinguishes manuscripts which are not lectionaries, that is they contain the text or texts in full and in an accepted order.

ductus The way in which a particular scribe has written, referring not so much to the shape of the letters as to the way the pen is handled and the letters are put together.

family of manuscripts At least two but generally more manuscripts which may be shown to be related to each other and derived from a common archetype, it being possible to illustrate this relationship by means of a stemma.

folio The name for one side of a leaf. The two sides are called the recto and the verso. These terms are used in two ways:

(1) In a parchment or paper manuscript the right hand page is called the recto, so it is often indicated with the numeral followed by *r*. The left-hand page is the verso and thus called *v*. The possible ways of numbering leaf 50 of a manuscript are

    recto   50r   50a   50
    verso   50v   50b   50v or 50b

    Abbreviated as fol., F, f. Plural folios abbreviated as foll., Ff, ff.

(2) In a papyrus manuscript, the recto is the side in which the horizontal fibres are uppermost, the verso the side in which the vertical fibres are uppermost. These are often indicated as

    recto   50→
    verso   50↑

    Note that older works may use the terminology now applied to parchment and paper manuscripts also to papyri.

gathering A set of sheets bound together at the centre as one of the units making up a codex (in the case of a single-quire codex, the only unit). The most common number of sheets is four, called a quaternion. The word quire is synonymous with gathering.

Gregory's Rule The general custom in production of parchment manuscripts of folding the sheets so that an opening contains two hair sides (which are darker) or two flesh sides. It was described by C. R. Gregory, *Canon and Text of the New Testament*, Edinburgh, 1907, 323–5. (To be precise, Gregory's Rule applies to the observation that Greek manuscripts contained quires of four sheets and ensured that the outermost side was flesh; but it is also used in this more general way.)

group of manuscripts At least two but generally more manuscripts which show clear signs of being closely related, but whose stemma cannot be reconstructed.

incipit (1) The standardised phrase introducing a lection intended to indicate the context (for example, 'Jesus said').

(2) The opening half-dozen or so words of a writing used in identifying it.

itacism Strictly speaking, a spelling variation involving the letter iota, it is also used more generally for any kind of spelling variation where vowels or diphthongs are exchanged.

K A siglum used by von Soden for the Byzantine text (K = Κοινή). Generally used with an added identifier, such as K^r for the most controlled form, or K^x for all manuscripts not classified.

lacuna A loss of text, usually caused by the material on which a manuscript was written having been lost. Sometimes it is due to the disappearance of ink. Plural 'lacunae'.

lectionary A manuscript containing the text of church lections rather than the full text of a writing, the readings being in their lectional sequence.

lemma The passage of Scripture about to be discussed quoted at the beginning of a section in a commentary.

majuscule A Greek script written with each character written separately, the letter shapes generally conforming to the upper case equivalent in modern printed and written Greek. Sometimes in the past called uncial.

minuscule A compact Greek script developed in the ninth century, which combined certain letters in sequence and increasingly used ligatures and symbols representing commonly occurring sequences such as nominal and verbal endings. Also used of Latin manuscripts showing the same general characteristics.

negative apparatus A critical apparatus in which only differences from the base text are cited, silence being taken to be agreement with the base.

opening The two pages of a codex when it is opened flat, with verso on the left and recto on the right.

opisthograph A roll which has been written on the outside. Usually only the inside carried writing. Such use of the outside usually constitutes the reuse of the roll once the text on the better side is no longer required.

palimpsest A manuscript which has been rewritten. The first writing (the underwriting) has been scraped off (Greek πάλιν (= 'again') and ψάω (= 'scrape')) and a second (the overwriting) replaces it. Some manuscripts are overwritten twice; sometimes a new manuscript is made from the scraped leaves of more than one older manuscript.

papyrus   A writing material made from a reed of this name, and hence a manuscript written on this material.

paratextual   Textual material in a manuscript which is not a part of the text(s) which the manuscript transmits, such as running titles, page, quire or paragraph numbers.

patristic citation   See **citation**.

positive apparatus   An apparatus in which differences from the base text and agreements with it are both given.

quaternion   See **gathering**.

quire   See **gathering**.

Received Text   Most accurately applied to any printing of the text of the Greek New Testament as it was published by the Elzevir Brothers in 1633. It is also used generically of all such texts, including its precursors, namely the editions of Erasmus, Stephanus and Beza. Often referred to in its Latin form as the Textus Receptus.

recto   See **folio**.

scholia   (1) Comments or notes in the margin of a manuscript. (2) Excerpts from commentaries, placed in the margin of a copy of the text.

siglum   (Latin) The number, letter or abbreviation used to indicate a witness in an apparatus. Plural sigla.

singular reading   A reading found in only one manuscript.

stemma   A 'family tree' of manuscripts, showing how a family of known manuscripts is related, and what missing links (lost manuscripts) there are between them.

subscription   A statement added at the end of a copy of a text, indicating what it is. Sometimes followed immediately by a statement of the next book.

sub-singular reading   A reading found in only two manuscripts.

surrogate   A reproduction of a manuscript in photographic form (printed, microform, or digital image). A version available on the Internet may be from any of these three sources.

tradent   'A person or community that passes on the tradition of the Scriptural text' (dela Cruz's definition – see 4.1). Used here to describe the role of a manuscript as a carrier of the text.

transcription A word-for-word and letter-by-letter copy of a manuscript, usually preserving its page layout. It may be in either paper or electronic format.

uncial A term denoting a type of Latin script, broadly analogous to Greek majuscule.

verso See **folio**.

Index of manuscripts

This index generally excludes manuscripts enumerated in lists and those cited in support of readings.

1 Of Greek manuscripts by Gregory–Aland

P4 *see* P64

P12 19

P13 19, 257

P18 19, 240

P20 301

P22 19

P23 301

P24 240

P38 288, 293−4, 296

P45 287−8, 312, 320, 325

P46 250, 252 4, 257, 263, 272, 281

P47 231, 234, 235, 240, 242

P52 324

P64 (+P4, P67) 34, 313, 317

P66 21−3, 23, 24−5, 71, 141−2, 153, 163, 313, 320, 321, 324, 325, 344

P72 42, 286, 301−2

P74 24, 288, 294, 307

P75 44, 153, 313, 320−3, 324−5

P98 234

P99 41

P100 301, 307

P115 232, 234−5, 240, 242

01 (Codex Sinaiticus) 4, 23−5, 36, 37, 38, 42, 48, 71−2, 74, 104, 129, 144, 146, 155, 163, 197, 201−2, 218, 229, 235, 240, 242, 254−5, 256, 257, 263, 267, 269, 286, 287, 288, 290, 292, 294, 295, 301, 307, 319, 321, 325

02 (Codex Alexandrinus) 36, 71, 72, 74, 81, 163, 195, 201−2, 228, 229, 235, 240, 242, 257, 263, 267, 287, 288, 290, 292, 294, 303, 316, 319

03 (Codex Vaticanus) 4, 36, 71, 72−3, 74, 195, 201−2, 234, 254−5, 256, 257, 263, 267, 269, 281, 286−7, 288, 289, 290, 292, 294, 295, 301, 303, 307, 316, 319, 321−3, 324−5, 338−9

04 (Codex Ephraemi Rescriptus) 71, 73−4, 146, 195, 228, 229, 235, 240, 242, 257, 263, 287, 288, 290, 292, 294, 307, 319, 339

05 (Codex Bezae) 36, 37, 70, 136−7, 144, 146, 157, 164, 195, 201−2, 286−7, 288−9, 290, 291−2, 293−4, 295, 296, 326, 338−9, 340, 346

06 (Codex Claromontanus) 37, 256, 259−60, 265, 272, 281

06 [abs 1] 260, 265

06 [abs 2] 260, 265

07 26

08 (Codex Laudianus) 70, 285, 287, 289−90, 291

010 (Codex Sangermanensis) 260, 265, 281

012 (Codex Augiensis) 260, 265, 272, 281

014 285

015 (Codex Coislianus) 258, 270

016 259

018 285

020 285

022 43−4, 146, 194

025 235, 239, 240, 285, 307

028 146

032 146, 163, 201−2, 317, 341

037 146

038 144, 201−2

040 316, 330

045 146, 192, 338−9

046 235

048 263, 285

049 285

054 146

057 146

070 68, 323

091 146

0109 53, 146

Index of biblical citations

Index of names and subjects

Writers are only included where their views are described.